OLD

Being Plain Sta

the Weig.... Matters

of Christianity

by
J. C. Ryle

If the trumpet does not sound a clear call,
who will get ready for battle?
I Cor. 14:8

BENEDICTION CLASSICS

ISBN: 978-1-78943-063-9.

PREFACE.

——◆——

THE volume now in the reader's hands consists of a series
of papers, systematically arranged, on the leading truths
of Christianity which are "necessary to salvation."

Few, probably, will deny that there are some things in
religion about which we may think other people hold very
erroneous views, and are, notwithstanding, in no danger of
being finally lost. About baptism and the Lord's Supper,
—about the Christian ministry,—about forms of prayer and
modes of worship,—about the union of Church and State,
—about all these things it is commonly admitted that
people may differ widely, and yet be finally saved. No
doubt there are always bigots and extreme partisans, who
are ready to excommunicate every one who cannot pronounce their Shibboleth on the above-named points. But,
speaking generally, to shut out of heaven all who disagree with us about these things, is to take up a position
which most thoughtful Christians condemn as unscriptural,
narrow, and uncharitable.

On the other hand, there are certain great truths of which some knowledge, by common consent, appears essential to salvation. Such truths are the immortality of the soul,—the sinfulness of human nature,—the work of Christ for us as our Redeemer,—the work of the Holy Ghost in us,—forgiveness,—justification,—conversion,—faith,—repentance,—the marks of a right heart,—Christ's invitations,—Christ's intercession,—and the like. If truths like these are not absolutely necessary to salvation, it is difficult to understand how any truths whatever can be called necessary. If people may be saved without knowing anything about these truths, it appears to me that we may throw away our Bibles altogether, and proclaim that the Christian religion is of no use. From such a miserable conclusion I hope most people will shrink back with horror.

To open out and explain these great necessary truths,—to confirm them by Scripture,—to enforce them by home appeals to the conscience of all who read this volume,—this is the simple object of the series of papers which is now offered to the public.*

---

* To this statement, I frankly admit, the first and two last papers in the volume form an exception. Inspiration, Election, and Perseverance are undoubtedly points about which good men in every age have disagreed, and will disagree perhaps while the world stands. The immense importance of inspiration in this day, and the extraordinary neglect into which election and perseverance have fallen, notwithstanding the Seven-teenth Article, are my reasons for inserting the three papers.

PREFACE.

The name which I have selected will prepare the reader to expect no new doctrines in this volume. It is simple, unadulterated, old-fashioned Evangelical theology. It contains nothing but the "Old Paths" in which the Apostolic Christians, the Reformers, the best English Churchmen for the last three hundred years, and the best Evangelical Christians of the present day, have persistently walked. From these "paths" I see no reason to depart. They are often sneered at and ridiculed, as old-fashioned, effete, worn out, and powerless in the Nineteenth Century. Be it so. "None of these things move me." I have yet to learn that there is any system of religious teaching, by whatever name it may be called, High, or Broad, or Romish, or Neologian, which produces one quarter of the effect on human nature that is produced by the old, despised system of doctrine which is commonly called Evangelical. I willingly admit the zeal, earnestness, and devotedness of many religious teachers who are not Evangelical. But I firmly maintain that the way of the school to which I belong is the "more excellent way." The longer I live the more I am convinced that the world needs no new Gospel, as some profess to think. I am thoroughly persuaded that the world needs nothing but a bold, full, unflinching teaching of the "old paths." The heart of man is the same in every age. The spiritual medicine which it requires is always the same. The same

Gospel which was preached by Latimer, and Hooper, and Bradford,— by Hall, Davenant, Usher, Reynolds, and Hopkins,—by Manton, Brooks, Watson, Charnock, Owen, and Gurnall,—by Romaine, Venn, Grimshaw, Hervey, and Cecil,—this is the gospel which alone will do real good in the present day. The leading doctrines of that gospel are the substance of the papers which compose this volume. They are the doctrines, I firmly believe, of the Bible and the Thirty-nine Articles of the Church of England. They are doctrines which, I find, wear well, and in the faith of them I hope to live and die.

I repeat most emphatically that I am not ashamed of what are commonly called "Evangelical principles." Fiercely and bitterly as those principles are assailed on all sides,—loudly and scornfully as some proclaim that they have done their work and are useless in this day,—I see no evidence whatever that they are defective or decayed, and I see no reason for giving them up. No doubt other schools of thought produce great *outward* effects on man-kind, gather large congregations, attain great popularity, and by means of music, ornaments, gestures, postures,and a generally histrionic ceremonial, make a great show of religion. I see it all, and I am not surprised. It is exactly what a study of human nature by the light of the Bible would lead me to expect. But for real *inward* effects on hearts, and outward effects on lives, I see no teaching so powerful as thorough, genuine Evangelical teaching. Just in proportion as the preachers of other schools borrow Evangelical weapons and Evangelical phraseology I see them obtaining influence. No doubt the good that is done in the world is little, and evil abounds. But I am certain that the teaching which does most good is that of the despised Evangelical school. It is not merely true and good up to a certain point, and then defective and needing additions, as some tell us; it is true and good all round, and needs no addition at all. If those who hold Evangelical views were only more faithful to their own principles, and more bold, and uncompromising, and decided, both in their preaching and their lives, they would soon find, whatever infidels and Romanists may please to say, that they hold the only lever which can shake the world.

The readers of the many tracts which God has allowed me to send forth for thirty years, must not expect much that they have not seen before, in " Old Paths." Experience has taught me, at last, that the peculiar tastes of all classes of society must be consulted, if good is to be done by the press. I am convinced that there are thousands of people in England who are willing to read a *volume*, but will never look at anything in the form of a *tract*. It is for them that I now send forth " Old Paths."

Those who read through this book continuously, and

without a pause, will, doubtless, observe a certain degree of sameness and similarity in some of the papers. The same thoughts are occasionally repeated, though in a different dress. To account for this, I will ask them to remember that most of the papers were originally written separately, and at long intervals of time, in some cases of as much as twenty years. On calm reflection, I have thought it better to republish them, pretty much as they originally appeared. Few readers of a religious book like this read it all through at once; and the great majority, I suspect, find it enough to read quietly only one or two chapters at a time.

I now send forth the volume with a deep sense of its many defects; but with an earnest prayer that it may do some good.

J. C. LIVERPOOL.

CONTENTS.

OLD PATHS.

~~~~~~

I.

INSPIRATION.

"All Scripture is given by inspiration of God."—2 Tim. iii. 16.

How was the Bible written?—"Whence is it? From heaven, or of men?"—Had the writers of the Bible any special or peculiar help in doing their work?—Is there anything in the Bible which makes it unlike all other books, and therefore demands our respectful attention?—These are questions of vast importance. They are questions to which I wish to offer an answer in this paper. To speak plainly, the subject I propose to examine is that deep one, the inspiration of Scripture. I believe the Bible to have been written by inspiration of God, and I want others to be of the same belief.

The subject is *always important.* I place it purposely in the very forefront of the papers which compose this volume. I ask a hearing for the doctrines which I am about to handle, because they are drawn from a book which is the "Word of God." Inspiration, in short, is the very keel and foundation of Christianity. If Christians have no Divine book to turn to as the warrant of their doctrine and practice, they have no solid ground for present peace or hope, and no right to claim the attention of mankind. They are building on a quicksand, and their faith is vain. We ought to be able to say boldly, "We are what we are, and we do what we do, because we have here a book which we believe to be the Word of God."

The subject is one of *peculiar importance* in the present day. Infidelity and scepticism abound everywhere. In one form or another they are to be found in every rank and class of society. Thousands of Englishmen are not ashamed to say that they regard the Bible as an old obsolete Jewish book, which has no special claim on our faith and obedience, and that it contains many inaccuracies and defects. Myriads who will not go so far as this are wavering and shaken in their belief, and show plainly by their lives that they are not quite sure the Bible is true. In a day like this the true Christian should be able to set his foot down firmly, and to render a reason of his confidence in God's Word. He should be able by sound arguments to meet and silence the gainsayer, if he cannot convince him. He should be able to show good cause why he thinks the Bible is "from heaven, and not of men."

The subject without doubt is a *very difficult one.* It cannot be followed up without entering on ground which is dark and mysterious to mortal man. It involves the discussion of things which are miraculous, and supernatural, and above reason, and cannot be fully explained. But difficulties must not turn us away from any subject in religion. There is not a science in the world about which questions may not be asked which no one can answer. It is poor philosophy to say we will believe nothing unless we can understand everything! We must not give up the subject of inspiration in despair because it contains things "hard to be understood." There still remains a vast amount of ground which is plain to every common understanding. I invite my readers to occupy this ground with me to-day, and to hear what I have got to say on the Divine authority of God's Word.

In considering the subject before us, there are two things which I propose to do:—

I. In the first place, I shall try to show the general truth, *that the Bible is given by inspiration of God.*

II. In the second place, I shall try to show *the extent to which the Bible is inspired.*

I trust that all who read this paper will take up the subject in a serious and reverent spirit. This question of inspiration is no light one. It involves tremendously grave consequences. If the Bible is not the Word of God and inspired, the whole of Christendom for 1800 years has been under an immense delusion;—half the human race has been cheated and deceived, and churches are monuments of folly.—If the Bible is the Word of God and inspired, all who refuse to believe it are in fearful danger; —they are living on the brink of eternal misery. No man, in his sober senses, can fail to see that the whole subject demands most serious attention.

I. In the first place, I propose to show the general truth,—*that the Bible is given by inspiration of God.*

In saying this, I mean to assert that the Bible is utterly unlike all other books that were ever written, because its writers were specially inspired, or enabled by God, for the work which they did. I say that the Book comes to us with a claim which no other book possesses. It is stamped with Divine authority. In this respect it stands entirely alone. Sermons, and tracts, and theological writings of all kinds, may be sound and edifying, but they are only the handiwork of uninspired man. The Bible alone is the Book of God.

Now I shall not waste time in proving that the Scriptures are genuine and authentic, that they were really written by the very men who profess to have written them, and that they contain the very things which they wrote.

I shall not touch what are commonly called external
evidences. I shall bring forward the book itself, and put
it in the witness box. I shall try to show that nothing
can possibly account for the Bible being what it is, and
doing what it has done, except the theory that it is the
Word of God. I lay it down broadly, as a position which
cannot be turned, that the Bible itself, fairly examined, is
the best witness of its own inspiration. I shall content
myself with stating some plain facts about the Bible,
which can neither be denied nor explained away. And
the ground I shall take up is this,—that these facts ought
to satisfy every reasonable inquirer that the Bible is of
God, and not of man. They are simple facts, which
require no knowledge of Hebrew, or Greek, or Latin, in
order to be understood; yet they are facts which prove to
my own mind conclusively that the Bible is superhuman,
or not of man.

(a) It is a fact, that there is an *extraordinary fulness
and richness in the contents of the Bible.* It throws more
light on a vast number of most important subjects than
all the other books in the world put together. It boldly
handles matters which are beyond the reach of man, when
left to himself. It treats of things which are mysterious
and invisible,—the soul, the world to come, and eternity,—
depths which man has no line to fathom. All who have
tried to write of these things, without Bible light, have
done little but show their own ignorance. They grope
like the blind; they speculate; they guess; they generally
make the darkness more visible, and land us in a region
of uncertainty and doubt. How dim were the views of
Socrates, Plato, Cicero, and Seneca! A well-taught
Sunday scholar, in this day, knows more spiritual truth
than all these sages put together.

The Bible alone gives a reasonable account of the
beginning and end of the globe on which we live. It
starts from the birthday of sun, moon, stars, and earth in

their present order, and shows us creation in its cradle.
It foretells the dissolution of all things, when the earth
and all its works shall be burned up, and shows us creation
in its grave. It tells us the story of the world's youth;
and it tells us the story of its old age. It gives us a
picture of its first days; and it gives us a picture of its
last. How vast and important is this knowledge! Can
this be the handiwork of uninspired man? Let us try to
answer that question.

The Bible alone gives a *true and faithful account of
man.* It does not flatter him as novels and romances do;
it does not conceal his faults and exaggerate his goodness;
it paints him just as he is. It describes him as a fallen
creature, of his own nature inclined to evil,—a creature
needing not only a pardon, but a new heart, to make him
fit for heaven. It shows him to be a corrupt being under
every circumstance, when left to himself,—corrupt after
the loss of paradise,—corrupt after the flood,—corrupt
when fenced in by divine laws and commandments,—
corrupt when the Son of God came down and visited him
in the flesh,—corrupt in the face of warnings, promises,
miracles, judgments, mercies. In one word, it shows man
to be by nature always a sinner. How important is this
knowledge! Can this be the work of uninspired minds?
Let us try to answer that question.

The Bible alone gives us *true views of God.* By nature
man knows nothing clearly or fully about Him. All his
conceptions of Him are low, grovelling, and debased.
What could be more degraded than the gods of the
Canaanites and Egyptians,—of Babylon, of Greece, and of
Rome? What can be more vile than the gods of the
Hindoos and other heathen in our own time?—By the
Bible we know that *God hates sin.* The destruction of
the old world by the flood; the burning of Sodom and
Gomorrah; the drowning of Pharoah and the Egyptians
in the Red Sea; the cutting off the nations of Canaan;

the overthrow of Jerusalem and the Temple; the scattering of the Jews;—all these are unmistakable witnesses.—By the Bible we know that *God loves sinners.* His gracious promise in the day of Adam's fall; His longsuffering in the time of Noah; His deliverance of Israel out of the land of Egypt; His gift of the law at Mount Sinai; His bringing the tribes into the promised land; His forbearance in the days of the Judges and Kings; His repeated warnings by the mouth of His prophets; His restoration of Israel after the Babylonian captivity; His sending His Son into the world, in due time, to be crucified; His commanding the Gospel to be preached to the Gentiles;— all these are speaking facts.—By the Bible we learn that *God knows all things.* We see Him foretelling things hundreds and thousands of years before they take place, and as He foretells so it comes to pass. He foretold that the family of Ham should be a servant of servants,—that Tyre should become a rock for drying nets,—that Nineveh should become a desolation,—that Babylon should be made a desert—that Egypt should be the basest of kingdoms,— that Edom should be forsaken and uninhabited,—and that the Jews should not be reckoned among the nations. All these things were utterly unlikely and improbable. Yet all have been fulfilled. Once more I say, how vast and important is all this knowledge! Can this Book be the work of uninspired man? Let us try to answer that question.

The Bible alone teaches us that *God has made a full, perfect, and complete provision for the salvation of fallen man.* It tells of an atonement made for the sin of the world, by the sacrifice and death of God's own Son upon the cross. It tells us that by His death for sinners, as their Substitute, He obtained eternal redemption for all that believe on Him. The claims of God's broken law have now been satisfied. Christ has suffered for sin, the just for the unjust. God can now be just, and yet the justifier of the ungodly. It tells us that there is now a complete remedy for the guilt of sin,—even the precious blood of Christ; and peace, and rest of conscience for all who believe on Christ. "Whosoever believeth on Him shall not perish, but have eternal life." It tells us that there is a complete remedy for the power of sin,—even the almighty grace of the Spirit of Christ. It shows us the Holy Ghost quickening believers, and making them new creatures. It promises a new heart and a new nature to all who will hear Christ's voice, and follow Him. Once more I say, how important is this knowledge! What should we know of all this comfortable truth without the Bible? Can this Book be the composition of uninspired men? Let us try to answer that question.

The Bible alone *explains the state of things that we see in the world around us.* There are many things on earth which a natural man cannot explain. The amazing inequality of conditions,—the poverty and distress,—the oppression and persecution,—the shakings and tumults,—the failures of statesmen and legislators,—the constant existence of uncured evils and abuses,—all these things are often puzzling to him. He sees, but does not understand. But the Bible makes it all clear. The Bible can tell him that the whole world lieth in wickedness,—that the prince of the world, the devil, is everywhere,—and that it is vain to look for perfection in the present order of things. The Bible will tell him that neither laws nor education can ever change men's hearts,—and that just as no man will ever make a machine work well, unless he allows for friction,—so also no man will do much good in the world, unless he always remembers that human nature is fallen, and that the world he works in is full of sin. The Bible will tell him that there is "a good time" certainly coming,—and coming perhaps sooner than people expect it,—a time of perfect knowledge, perfect justice, perfect happiness, and perfect peace. But the Bible will tell him this time shall not be brought in by any power but that of Christ coming to earth again. And for that second coming of Christ, the Bible will tell him to prepare. Once more, I say, how important is all this knowledge!

All these are things which men could find nowhere except in the Scriptures. We have probably not the least idea how little we should know about these things if we had not the Bible. We hardly know the value of the air we breathe, and the sun which shines on us, because we have never known what it is to be without them. We do not value the truths on which I have been just now dwelling, because we do not realize the darkness of men to whom these truths have not been revealed. Surely no tongue can fully tell the value of the treasures this one volume contains. Set down that fact in your mind, and do not forget it. The extraordinary contents of the Bible are a great fact which can only be explained by admitting its inspiration. Mark well what I say. It is a simple broad fact, that in the matter of *contents*, the Bible stands entirely alone, and no other book is fit to be named in the same day with it. He that dares to say the Bible is not inspired, let him give a reasonable account of this fact, if he can.

(*b*) It is another fact that there is an *extraordinary unity and harmony in the contents of the Bible,* which is entirely above man. We all know how difficult it is to get a story told by any three persons, not living together, in which there are not some contradictions and discrepancies. If the story is a long one, and involves a large quantity of particulars, unity seems almost impossible among the common run of men. But it is not so with the Bible. Here is a long book written by not less than thirty different persons. The writers were men of every rank and class in society. One was a lawgiver. One was a warlike king. One was a peaceful king. One was a herdsman. One had been brought up as a publican,—

another as a physician,—another as a learned Pharisee,—two as fishermen,—several as priests. They lived at different intervals over a space of 1500 years; and the greater part of them never saw each other face to face. And yet there is a perfect harmony among all these writers? They all write as if they were under one dictation. The style and hand-writing may vary, but the mind that runs through their work is always one and the same. They all tell the same story. They all give one account of man,—one account of God,—one account of the way of salvation,—one account of the human heart. You see truth unfolding under their hands, as you go through the volume of their writings,—but you never detect any real contradiction, or contrariety of view.

Let us set down this fact in our minds, and ponder it well. Tell us not that this unity might be the result of chance. No one can ever believe that but a very credulous person. There is only one satisfactory account to be given of the fact before us.—The Bible is not of man, but of God.

(c) It is another fact that there is *an extraordinary wisdom, sublimity and majesty in the style of the Bible,* which is above man. Strange and unlikely as it was, the writers of Scripture have produced a book which even at this day is utterly unrivalled. With all our boasted attainments in science and art and learning, we can produce nothing that can be compared with the Bible. Even at this very hour, in 1877, the book stands entirely alone. There is a strain and a style and a tone of thought about it, which separate it from all other writings. There are no weak points, and motes, and flaws, and blemishes. There is no mixture of infirmity and feebleness, such as you will find in the works of even the best Christians. "Holy, holy, holy," seems written on every page. To talk of comparing the Bible with other "sacred books" so-called, such as the Koran, the Shasters, or the book of

Mormon, is positively absurd. You might as well compare the sun with a rushlight,—or Skiddaw with a mole hill,— or St. Paul's with an Irish hovel,—or the Portland vase with a garden pot,—or the Koh-i-noor diamond with a bit of glass. * God seems to have allowed the existence of these pretended revelations, in order to prove the immeasurable superiority of His own Word. To talk of the inspiration of the Bible, as only differing *in degree* from that of such writings as the works of Homer, Plato, Shakspeare, Dante, and Milton, is simply a piece of blasphemous folly. Every honest and unprejudiced reader must see that there is a gulf between the Bible and any other book, which no man can fathom. You feel, on turning from the Scriptures to other works, that you have got into a new atmosphere. You feel like one who has exchanged gold for base metal, and heaven for earth. And how can this mighty difference be accounted for ? The men who wrote the Bible had no special advantages. They lived in a remote corner of the civilized earth. They had, most of them, little leisure, few books, and no learning,—such as learning is reckoned in this world. Yet the book they compose is one which is unrivalled ! There is but one way of accounting for this fact.—*They wrote under the direct inspiration of God.*

(*d*) It is another fact that there is an *extraordinary accuracy in the facts and statements of the Bible, which*

---

* Carlyle's estimate of the Koran is given, in "Hero-worship," in the following words. "It is a wearisome, confused jumble, crude, recondite, abounding in endless iterations, long-windedness, entanglement, insupportable stupidity. In short nothing but a sense of duty could carry any European through the Koran, with its unreadable masses of lumber."

John Owen says, "There are no other writings in the world, beside the Bible, that ever pretended unto a divine original, but they are not only from their matter, but from the manner of their writing, and the plain footsteps of human artifice and weakness therein, sufficient for their own conviction, and do openly discover their own vain pretensions." (*The Reason of Faith.* Works, vol iv., p. 34, Johnston's Edition.)

is above man. Here is a book which has been finished and before the world for nearly 1800 years. These 1800 years have been the busiest and most changeful period the world has ever seen. During this period the greatest discoveries have been made in science, the greatest alterations in the ways and customs of society, the greatest improvements in the habits and usages of life. Hundreds of things might be named which satisfied and pleased our forefathers, which we have laid aside long ago as obsolete, useless, and old-fashioned. The laws, the books, the houses, the furniture, the clothes, the arms, the machinery, the carriages of each succeeding century, have been a continual improvement on those of the century that went before. There is hardly a thing in which faults and weak points have not been discovered. There is scarcely an institution which has not gone through a process of sifting, purifying, refining, simplifying, reforming, amending, and changing. But all this time men have never discovered a weak point or a defect in the Bible. Infidels have assailed it in vain. There it stands,—perfect, and fresh, and complete, as it did eighteen centuries ago. The march of intellect never overtakes it. The wisdom of wise men never gets beyond it. The science of philosophers never proves it wrong. The discoveries of travellers never convict it of mistakes. —Are the distant islands of the Pacific laid open ? Nothing is found that in the slightest degree contradicts the Bible account of man's heart.—Are the ruins of Nineveh and Egypt ransacked and explored ? Nothing is found that overturns one jot or tittle of the Bible's historical statements.—How shall we account for this fact ? Who could have thought it possible that so large a book, handling such a vast variety of subjects, should at the end of 1800 years, be found so free from erroneous statements ? There is only one account to be given of the fact.—The Bible was *written by inspiration of God.*

(e) It is another fact that there is in the Bible an

extraordinary *suitableness to the spiritual wants of all mankind.* It exactly meets the heart of man in every rank or class, in every country and climate, in every age and period of life. It is the only book in existence which is never out of place and out of date. Other books after a time become obsolete and old-fashioned: the Bible never does. Other books suit one country or people, and not another: the Bible suits all. It is the book of the poor and unlearned no less than of the rich and the philosopher. It feeds the mind of the labourer in his cottage, and it satisfies the gigantic intellects of Newton, Chalmers, Brewster, and Faraday. Lord Macaulay, and John Bright, and the writers of brilliant articles in the *Times*, are all under obligations to the same volume. It is equally valued by the converted New Zealander in the southern hemisphere, and the Red River Indian in the cold north of America, and the Hindoo under the tropical sun.

It is the only book, moreover, which seems always fresh and evergreen and new. For eighteen centuries it has been studied and prayed over by millions of private Christians, and expounded and explained and preached to us by thousands of ministers. Fathers, and Schoolmen, and Reformers, and Puritans, and modern divines, have incessantly dug down into the mine of Scripture, and yet have never exhausted it. It is a well never dry, and a field which is never barren. It meets the hearts and minds and consciences of Christians in the nineteenth century as fully as it did those of Greeks and Romans when it was first completed. It suits the " Dairyman's daughter " as well as Persis, or Tryphena, or Tryphosa,—and the English Peer as well as the converted African at Sierra Leone. It is still the first book which fits the child's mind when he begins to learn religion, and the last to which the old man clings as he leaves the world.* In short, it suits all ages,

---

* "I have always been strongly in favour of secular education in the sense of education without theology. But I must confess I have been

ranks, climates, minds, conditions. It is the one book which suits the world.

Now how shall we account for this singular fact? What satisfactory explanation can we give? There is only one account and explanation.—The Bible was *written by Divine inspiration.* It is the book of the world, because He inspired it who formed the world,—who made all nations of one blood,—and knows man's common nature. It is the book for every heart, because He dictated it who alone knows all hearts, and what all hearts require. *It is the book of God.*

(*f*) Last, but not least, it is a great fact that the Bible *has had a most extraordinary effect on the condition of those nations* in which it has been known, taught, and read.

I invite any honest-minded reader to look at a map of the world, and see what a story that map tells. Which are the countries on the face of the globe at this moment where there is the greatest amount of idolatry, or cruelty, or tyranny, or impurity, or misgovernment, or disregard of

---

no less seriously perplexed to know by what practical measures the religious feeling, which is the essential basis of conduct, could be kept up in the present chaotic state of opinion on these matters *without the use of the Bible.*"

" Consider the great historical fact that for three centuries this Book has been woven into the life of all that is best and noblest in English history ;—that it has become the national epic of Britain, and is as familiar to noble and simple from John o' Groat's Home to the Land's End, as Danté and Tasso once were to the Italians ;—that it is written in the best and purest English, and abounds in exquisite beauties of mere literary form ;—and finally, that it forbids the veriest hind who never left his village to be ignorant of other countries and other civilizations, and of a great past, stretching back to the furthest limits of the oldest nations in the world. By the study of what other book could children be so much humanized and made to feel that each figure in that vast historical procession fills, like themselves, but a momentary space in the interval between two eternities, and earns the blessings or the curses of all time, according to its effort to do good and hate evil, even as they also are earning their payment for their work ?"—*Professor Huxley on School Boards (Huxley's Critiques and Essays,* p 51.)

life and liberty and truth? Precisely those countries where the Bible is not known.—Which are the Christian countries, so-called, where the greatest quantity of ignorance, superstition, and corruption, is to be found at this very moment? The countries in which the Bible is a forbidden or neglected book,—such countries as Spain and the South American States.—Which are the countries where liberty, and public and private morality have attained the highest pitch? The countries where the Bible is free to all, like England, Scotland, Germany, and the United States. Yes! when you know how a nation deals with the Bible, you may generally know what a nation is.

But this is not all. Let us look nearer home. Which are the cities on earth where the fewest soldiers and police are required to keep order? London, Manchester, Liverpool, New York, Philadelphia,—cities where Bibles abound. —Which are the countries in Europe where there are the fewest murders and illegitimate births? The Protestant countries, where the Bible is freely read.—Which are the Churches and religious bodies on earth which are producing the greatest results by spreading light and dispelling darkness? Those which make much of the Bible, and teach and preach it as God's Word. The Romanist, the Neologian, the Socinian, the deist, the sceptic, or the friends of mere secular teaching, have never yet shown us one Sierra Leone, one New Zealand, one Tinnevelly, as the fruit of their principles. We only can do that who honour the Bible and reverence it as as God's Word. Let this fact also be remembered. He that denies the Divine inspiration of the Bible, let him explain this fact if he can.*

* "The Bible is the fountain of all true patriotism and loyalty in States;—it is the source of all true wisdom, sound policy, and equity in Senates, Council-chambers, and Courts of Justice;—it is the spring of all true discipline and obedience, and of all valour and chivalry, in armies and fleets, in the battlefield and on the wide sea;—it is the

I place these six facts about the Bible before my readers, and I ask them to consider them well. Take them all six together, treat them fairly, and look at them honestly. Upon any other principle than that of divine inspiration, those six facts appear to me inexplicable and unaccountable. Here is a book written by a succession of Jews, in a little corner of the world, which positively stands alone. Not only were its writers isolated and cut off in a peculiar manner from other nations, but they belonged to a people who have never produced any other book of note except the Bible! There is not the slightest proof that, unassisted and left to themselves, they were capable of writing anything remarkable, like the Greeks and Romans. Yet these men have given the world a volume which for depth, unity, sublimity, accuracy, suitableness to the wants of man, and power of influencing its readers, is perfectly unrivalled. How can this be explained? How can it be accounted for? To my mind there is only one answer. The writers of the Bible were divinely helped and qualified for the work which they did. The book which they have given to us was *written by inspiration of God*.[*]

For my own part, I believe that in dealing with sceptics, and unbelievers, and enemies of the Bible, Christians are too apt to stand only on the defensive. They are too often content with answering this or that little objection,

---

origin of all probity and integrity in commerce and in trade, in marts and in shops, in banks and exchanges, in the public resorts of men and the secret silence of the heart;—it is the pure, unsullied fountain of all love and peace, happiness, quietness and joy, in families and households. —Wherever it is duly obeyed it makes the desert of the world to rejoice and blossom as the rose."—*Wordsworth on Inspiration*, p. 113.

[*] "The little ark of Jewish literature still floats above the surges of time, while mere fragments of the wrecked archives of the huge oriental empires, as well as of the lesser kingdoms that surrounded Judæa, are now and then cast on our distant shores."—*Rogers on the Superhuman Origin of the Bible*, p. 311.

or discussing this or that little difficulty, which is picked out of Scripture and thrown in their teeth. I believe we ought to act on the aggressive far more than we do, and to press home on the adversaries of inspiration the enormous difficulties of their own position. We have a right to ask them how they can possibly explain the origin and nature of the Bible, if they will not allow that it is of Divine authority? We have a right to say,—"Here is a book which not only courts inquiry but demands investigation. We challenge you to tell us how that 'Book was written."—How can they account for this Book standing so entirely alone, and for nothing having ever been written equal to it, like it, near it, or fit to be compared with it for a minute? I defy them to give any rational reply on their own principles. On our principles we can. To tell us that man's unassisted mind could have written the Bible is simply ridiculous. It is worse than ridiculous: it is the height of credulity. In short, the difficulties of unbelief are far greater than the difficulties of faith. No doubt there are things "hard to be understood" if we accept the Scriptures as God's Word. But, after all, they are nothing compared to the hard things which rise up in our way, and demand solution if we once deny inspiration. There is no alternative. Men must either believe things which are grossly improbable, or else they must accept the great general truth that *the Bible is the inspired Word of God.*

II. The second thing which I propose to consider is *the extent to which the Bible is inspired.* Assuming, as a general truth, that the Bible is given by Divine inspiration, I wish to examine how far and to what degree its writers received Divine help. In short, what is it exactly that we mean when we talk of the Scriptures as "the Word of God"?

This is, no doubt, a difficult question, and one about

which the best Christians are not entirely of one mind.
The plain truth is that inspiration is *a miracle;* and, like
all miracles, there is much about it which we cannot fully
understand.—We must not confound it with intellectual
power, such as great poets and authors possess. To talk
of Shakespeare and Milton and Byron being inspired, like
Moses and St. Paul, is to my mind almost profane.—Nor
must we confound it with the gifts and graces bestowed
on the early Christians in the primitive Church. All the
Apostles were enabled to preach and work miracles, but
not all were inspired to write.--We must rather regard it
as a special supernatural gift, bestowed on about thirty
people out of mankind, in order to qualify them for the
special business of writing the Scriptures; and we must
be content to allow that, like everything miraculous, we
cannot entirely explain it, though we can believe it. A
miracle would not be a miracle, if it could be explained.
That miracles are possible, I do not stop to prove here. I
never trouble myself on that subject until those who deny
miracles have fairly grappled with the great fact that
Christ rose again from the dead. I firmly believe that
miracles are possible, and have been wrought; and among
great miracles I place the fact that men were inspired by
God to write the Bible. Inspiration, therefore, being a
miracle, I frankly allow that there are difficulties about it
which at present I cannot fully solve.

The exact manner in which the minds of the inspired
writers of Scripture worked when they wrote, I do not
pretend to explain. Very likely they could not have explained it themselves. I do not admit for a moment
that they were mere machines holding pens, and, like
type-setters in a printing-office, did not understand what
they were doing. I abhor the "mechanical" theory of
inspiration. I dislike the idea that men like Moses and
St. Paul were no better than organ pipes, employed by the
Holy Ghost, or ignorant secretaries or amanuenses who

wrote by dictation what they did not understand. I
admit nothing of the kind. I believe that in some marvellous manner the Holy Ghost made use of the reason,
the memory, the intellect, the style of thought, and the
peculiar mental temperament of each writer of the Scriptures. But how and in what manner this was done I can
no more explain than I can the union of two natures, God
and man, in the person of our blessed Lord Jesus Christ.
I only know that there is both a Divine and a human
element in the Bible, and that while the men who wrote
it were really and truly men, the book that they wrote
and handed down to us is really and truly the Word of
God. I know the *result*, but I do not understand the
process. The result is, that the Bible is the written Word
of God; but I can no more explain the process than I can
explain how the water became wine at Cana, or how five
loaves fed five thousand men, or how a word raised Lazarus
from the dead. I do not pretend to explain miracles,
and I do not pretend to explain fully the miraculous
gift of inspiration. The position I take up is that, while
the Bible-writers were not "machines," as some sneeringly
say, they only wrote what God taught them to write.
The Holy Ghost put into their minds thoughts and
ideas, and then guided their pens in writing them. When
you read the Bible you are not reading the unaided,
self-taught composition of erring men like ourselves, but
thoughts and words which were suggested by the eternal
God. The men who were employed to indite the Scripture spake not of themselves. They "spake as they were
moved by the Holy Ghost." (2 Peter i. 21.) He that
holds a Bible in his hand should know that he holds "not
the word of man but of God." (1 Thess. ii. 13.)

Concerning the precise extent to which the Bible is
inspired, I freely admit that Christians differ widely.
Some of the views put forth on the subject appear to me
erroneous in the extreme. I shall not shrink from giving

my own opinion and stating my reasons for maintaining it. In matters like these I dare not call any man master. Painful as it is to disagree with able and gifted men on religious questions, I dare not take up views of inspiration which my head and heart tell me are unsound, however high and honoured the names of those who maintain them. I believe in my conscience that low and defective views of the subject are doing immense damage to the cause of Christ in these last days.

Some hold that some of the books of Scripture are not inspired at all, and have no more authority or claim to our reverence than the writings of any ordinary man.— Others who do not go so far as this, and allow that all the books in the Bible are inspired, maintain that inspiration was only partial, and that there are portions in almost every book which are uninspired.—Others hold that inspiration means nothing more than general superintendence and direction, and that, while the Bible writers were miraculously preserved from making mistakes in great things and matters necessary to salvation, in things indifferent they were left to their own unassisted faculties, like any other writers.—Some hold that all the ideas in the Bible were given by inspiration, but not the words and language in which they are clothed,—though how to separate ideas from words it is rather hard to understand ! —Some, finally, allow the thorough inspiration of all the Bible, and yet maintain that it was possible for the writers to make occasional mistakes in their statements, and that such mistakes do exist at this day.

From all these views I totally and entirely dissent. They all appear to me more or less defective, below the truth, dangerous in their tendency, and open to grave and insuperable objections. The view which I maintain is that every book, and chapter, and verse, and syllable of the Bible was originally given by inspiration of God. I hold that not only the substance of the Bible, but its language,

—not only the ideas of the Bible, but its words,—not only
certain parts of the Bible, but every chapter of the book,
—that all and each are of Divine authority. I hold that
the Scripture not only *contains* the Word of God, but *is*
the Word of God. I believe the narratives and statements
of Genesis, and the catalogues in Chronicles, were just as
truly written by inspiration as the Acts of the Apostles.
I believe Ezra's account of the nine-and-twenty knives,
and St. Paul's message about the cloak and parchments,
were as much written under Divine direction as the 20th
of Exodus, the 17th of John, or the 8th of Romans. I
do not say, be it remembered, that all these parts of the
Bible are of equal importance to our souls. Nothing of
the kind ! But I do say they were all equally given by
inspiration.*

In making this statement I ask the reader not to misunderstand my meaning. I do not forget that the Old
Testament was written in Hebrew and the New Testament
in Greek. The inspiration of every word, for which I
contend, is the inspiration of every original Hebrew and
Greek word, as the Bible writers first wrote it down. I
stand up for nothing more and nothing less than this. I
lay no claim to the inspiration of every word in the various
versions and translations of God's Word. So far as those
translations and versions are faithfully and correctly done,
so far they are of equal authority with the original Hebrew
and Greek. We have reason to thank God that many of
the translations are, in the main, faithful and accurate.
At any rate our own English Bible, if not perfect, is so far
correct, that in reading it we have a right to believe that

---

* "We affirm that the Bible is the Word of God, and that it is not
marred with human infirmities. We do not imagine, with some, that
the Bible is like a threshing-floor, on which wheat and chaff lie mingled
together, and that it is left for the reader to winnow and sift the wheat
from the chaff by the fan and sieve of his own mind."— *Wordsworth on
"Inspiration."* (P. 11.)

we are reading in our own tongue not the word **of** man, but of God.

Now the view for which I contend,—that every word of the Bible is inspired,—is not accepted by many good Christians, and is bitterly opposed in many quarters. I shall therefore mention a few reasons why it appears to me the only safe and tenable view which can be adopted, and the only one which is free from innumerable objections. If I err in maintaining it I have the comfort, at any rate, of erring in good company. I only take up the same ground which almost all the Fathers occupied; which Bishop Jewell, and Hooker, and Owen, took up long ago; and which Chalmers, Robert Haldane, Gaussen, Bishop Wordsworth, M'Caul, Burgon, and Archdeacon Lee of the Irish Church, have ably defended in modern days. I know, however, that men's minds are variously constituted. Arguments and reasons which appear weighty to some are of no weight with others. I shall content myself with setting down in order the reasons which satisfy me.

(a) For one thing, I cannot see *how the Bible can be a perfect rule of faith and practice* if it is not fully inspired, and if it contains any flaws and imperfections. If the Bible is anything at all it is the statute-book of God's kingdom,—the code of laws and regulations by which the subjects of that kingdom are to live,—the register-deed of the terms on which they have peace now and shall have glory hereafter. Now, why are we to suppose that such a book will be loosely and imperfectly drawn up, any more than legal deeds are drawn up on earth? Every lawyer can tell us that in legal deeds and statutes every word is of importance, and that property, life, or death may often turn on a single word. Think of the confusion that would ensue if wills, and settlements, and conveyances, and partnership-deeds, and leases, and agreements, and acts of parliament were not carefully drawn up and carefully interpreted, and every word allowed its due weight. Where would be the use of such documents if particular words went for nothing, and every one had a right to add, or take away, or alter, or deny the validity of words, or erase words at his own discretion? At this rate we might as well lay aside our legal documents altogether. Surely we have a right to expect that in the book which contains our title-deeds for eternity every word will be inspired, and nothing imperfect admitted. If God's statute-book is not inspired, and every word is not of Divine authority, God's subjects are left in a pitiable state. I see much in this.

(b) For another thing, if the Bible is not fully inspired and contains imperfections, I cannot understand *the language which is frequently used about it* in its own pages. Such expressions as "The oracles of God;"—"He saith;"—"God saith"—"the Holy Ghost spake by Esaias the prophet;"—"the Holy Ghost saith, "To-day if ye will hear His voice,"—would appear to me inexplicable and extravagant if applied to a book containing occasional blemishes, defects, and mistakes. (Acts vii. 38; Rom. iii. 2; Heb. v. 12; 1 Peter iv. 11; Ephes. iv. 8; Heb. i. 8; Acts xxviii. 25; Heb. iii. 7; x. 15; Rom. ix. 25.) Once grant that every word of Scripture is inspired, and I see an admirable propriety in the language. I cannot understand "the Holy Ghost," making a mistake, or an "oracle" containing anything defective! If any man replies that the Holy Ghost did not *always* speak by Isaiah, I will ask him who is to decide when He did and when He did not? I see much in this.

(c) For another thing, the theory that the Bible was not given by inspiration of God, appears to me utterly *at variance with several quotations from the Old Testament* which I find in the New. I allude to those quotations in which the whole force of the passage turns on one single word, and once even on the use of the singular instead of the plural number. Take, for instance, such quotations as

"The Lord said unto my Lord." (Matt. xxii. 44.—"I said, Ye are gods." (John x. 34.)—"To Abraham and his seed were the promises made. He saith not, And to seeds, as of many; but as of one, And to thy seed, which is Christ." (Gal. iii. 16.)—"He is not ashamed to call them brethren, saying, I will declare Thy name unto my brethren." (Heb. ii. 11, 12.)—In every one these cases the whole point of the quotation lies in a single word.* But if this is so, it is hard to see on what principle we can deny the inspiration of all the words of Scripture. At any rate, those who deny verbal inspiration will find it difficult to show us which words are inspired and which are not. Who is to draw the line, and where is it to be drawn? I see much in this.

(*d*) For another thing, if the words of Scripture are not all inspired, *the value of the Bible as a weapon in controversy is greatly damaged*, if not entirely taken away. Who does not know that in arguing with Jews, Arians, or Socinians, the whole point of the texts we quote against them often lies in a single word? What are we to reply if an adversary asserts that the special word of some text, on which we ground an argument, is a mistake of the writer, and therefore of no authority? To my mind it appears that the objection would be fatal. It is useless to quote texts if we once admit that not all the words of which they are composed were given by inspiration. Unless there is some certain standard to appeal to we may as well hold our tongues. Argument is labour in vain if our mouths are to be stopped by the retort, "That text is not inspired." I see much in this.

(*e*) For another thing, to give up verbal inspiration appears to me to *destroy the usefulness of the Bible as an instrument of public preaching and instruction.* Where

---

* It would be easy to multiply texts in proof of this point. I will only name the following: Heb. ii. 8; iii. 7—19; iv. 2—11; xii. 27.

is the use of choosing a text and making it the subject of
a pulpit address, if we do not believe that every word of
the text is inspired ?   Once let our hearers get hold of the
idea that the writers of the Bible could make mistakes in
the particular words they used, and they will care little for
any reproofs, or exhortations, or remarks which are based
on words.—" How do you know," they might ask us, " that
this word, about which you made such ado yesterday, was
given by the Holy Ghost ?   How do you know that St.
Paul, or St. Peter, or St. John did not make a mistake,
and use the wrong word ?   That they could make mistakes
about words you yourself allow."—I know not what others
may think.   For myself, I could give no answer.   I see
much in this.

(*f*)   Last, but not least, the denial of verbal inspiration
appears to me to *destroy a great part of the usefulness of
the Bible as a source of comfort and instruction in private reading.*   Where is the true Christian student of the
Bible who does not know that words, particular words,
afford a large portion of the benefit which he derives from
his daily reading ?   How much the value of many a
cherished text depends on some single phrase, or the
number of a substantive, or the tense of a verb ?   Alas !
there would be an end of all this if we once concede that
each word is not inspired ; and that, for anything we know,
some much loved favourite substantive, or verb, or pronoun,
or adverb, or adjective, was an Apostle's mistake, and the
word of man, not of God !   What others might think I
know not.   For myself, I should be tempted to lay aside
my Bible in despair, and become of all men most miserable.
I see much in this.

Now, I freely grant that many excellent Christians think
that the view I maintain is open to serious objections.
That the Bible, generally speaking, is given by inspiration,
they firmly maintain.   But they shrink from maintaining
that inspiration extends to every word of Scripture.   I

a.m sorry to differ from these worthy people. But I cannot see the weight and force of their objections. Fairly and honestly examined, they fail to carry conviction to my mind.

(a) Some object that there are occasional statements in the Bible which *contradicct the facts of history.* Are these all verbally inspired ?—My answer is that it is far more easy to assert this than to prove it. There is nothing of which we have so few trustworthy remains as very ancient history, and if ancient uninspired history and Bible history seem to disagree, it is generally safer and wiser to believe that Bible history is right and other history wrong. At any rate, it is a singular fact that all recent researches in Assyria, Babylon, Palestine, and Egypt, show an extraordinary tendency to confirm the perfect accuracy of the Word of God. The lamented Mr. Smith's discoveries at Babylon are a remarkable example of what I mean. There are buried evidences which God seems to keep in reserve for these last days. If Bible history and other histories cannot be made to agree at present, it is safest to wait.

(b) Some object that there are occasional statements in the Bible which *contradict the facts of natural science.* Are these all inspired ?—My answer is again, that it is far more easy to assert this than to prove it. The Bible was not written to teach a system of geology, botany, or astronomy, or a history of birds, insects, and animals, and on matters touching these subjects it wisely uses popular language, such as common people can understand. No one thinks of saying that the Astronomer Royal contradicts science because he speaks of the sun's "rising and setting." If the Bible said anywhere that the earth was a flat surface,—or that it was a fixed globe round which the sun revolved,—or that it never existed in any state before Adam and Eve,—there might be something in the objection. But it never does so. It speaks of scientific subjects as they appear. But it never flatly contradicts science.[*]

(c) Some object that there are occasional statements in the Bible which are *monstrous, absurd, and incredible.* Are they really obliged to believe that Eve was tempted by the devil in the form of a serpent,—that Noah was saved in an ark,—that the Israelites crossed the Red Sea between two walls of water,—that Balaam's ass spoke,—and that Jonah actually went into the whale's belly ? Are all these statements inspired ?—My answer is that Christ's apostles speak of these things as historical facts, and were more likely to know the truth about them than we are. After all, do we believe in miracles or not ? Do we believe that Christ Himself rose from the dead ? Let us stick to that one grand miracle first, and disprove it if we can. If we do believe it, it is foolish to object to things because they are miraculous.

(d) Some object that there are things mentioned occasionally in the Bible which are so *trifling* that they are unworthy to be called inspired. They point to St. Paul's writing about his cloak, and books, and parchments, and ask if we really think that the Apostle wrote about such little matters by inspiration of God ?—I answer that the least things affecting any of God's children are not too small for the notice of Him who "numbers the hairs of our heads." There are excellent and edifying lessons to be learned from the cloak and the parchments, as Robert Haldane has shown most convincingly, in his work on the Evidences

---

[*] "The language of Scripture is necessarily adapted to the common state of man's intellectual development, in which he is not supposed to be possessed of science. Hence the phrases used by Scripture are precisely those which science soon teaches man to consider inaccurate. Yet they are not on that account the less fitted for their purpose, for if any terms had been used adapted to a more advanced state of knowledge, they must have been unintelligible to those to whom the Scripture was first addressed."— *Whewell's Philosophy of Inductive Science.* Vol. i., p. 686.

of Divine Revelation. After all, man knows very little what is great and what is small in God's sight. The history of Nimrod "the mighty hunter" is dispatched in three verses of Genesis, and the history of a Syrian dwelling in tents, called Abraham, fills up no less than fourteen chapters. The microscope applied to the book of nature, can show us God's hand in the least lichen that grows on the top of Scawfell as well as in the cedar of Lebanon. The veriest trifles, as they seem to us in the Book of Scripture, may turn out to be most striking confirmations of its truth. Paley has shown this admirably in his "Horæ Paulinæ," and Professor Blunt in his "Undesigned Coincidences."

(e) Some object that there are grave discrepancies in some of the *Bible histories*, especially in the four Gospels, which *cannot be made to harmonize and agree.* Are the words, they ask, all inspired in these cases ? Have the writers made no mistakes ?—I answer that the number of these discrepancies is grossly exaggerated, and that in many cases they are only apparent, and disappear under the touch of common sense. Even in the hardest of them we should remember, in common fairness, that circumstances are very likely kept back from us which entirely reconcile everything, if we only knew them. Very often in these days when two honest, veracious men give a separate account of some long story, their accounts do not quite tally, because one dwells on one part and the other on another. All well-informed students of history know that the precise day when Charles I. erected his standard at Nottingham, in the Parliamentary war, has not been settled to this hour.

(f) Some object that *Job's friends*, in their long speeches, *said many weak and foolish things.* Were all their words inspired ?—An objection like this arises from an illogical and confused idea of what inspiration means. The book of Job contains an historical account of a wonderful part

of the old patriarch's history, and a report both of his
speeches and of those of his friends.   But we are nowhere
told that either Job or Eliphaz and his companions spoke
all that they spoke by the Holy Ghost.   The writer of the
book of Job was thoroughly inspired to record all they said.
But whether they spoke rightly or wrongly is to be decided
by the general teaching of Scripture.   No one would say
that St. Peter was inspired when he said, " I know not the
Man," in the High Priest's palace.   But the writer of the
Gospel was inspired when he wrote it down for our learning.
In the Acts of the Apostles the letter of Claudius Lysias
was certainly not written by inspiration, and Gamaliel,
and the town clerk of Ephesus and Tertullus were not
inspired when they made their speeches.   But it is
equally certain that St. Luke was inspired to write them
down and record them in his book.

(g) Some object that St. Paul, *in the 7th chapter of the
1st epistle to the Corinthians,* when giving certain advice
to the Corinthian Church, says at one time, " Not I, but
the Lord," and at another, " I, not the Lord."   And they
ask, Does not this show that in part of his advice he was
not inspired ?—I answer, Not at all.   A careful study of the
chapter will show that when the Apostle says " Not I, but
the Lord," he lays down some principles on which the
Lord had spoken already ; and when he says " I, not the
Lord," he gives advice on some point about which there
had been no revelation hitherto.   But there is not the
slightest proof that he is not writing all the way through
under direct inspiration of God.

(h) Some object that there are many *various readings*
of the words of Scripture, and that we cannot, therefore,
feel sure that we have the original inspired Word of God.
I answer that the various readings, when fairly examined,
will prove to be absurdly exaggerated in number and importance.   Dr. Kennicott, Bengel, and others have proved
this long ago.   No doubt we may have lost a few of the

original words. We have no right to expect infallibility in transcribers and copyists, before the invention of printing. But there is not a single doctrine in Scripture which would be affected or altered if all the various readings were allowed, and all the disputed or doubtful words were omitted. Considering how many hands the Bible passed through before printing was invented, and who the transcribers were, it is marvellous that the various readings are so few! The fact that about the immense majority of all the words in the old Hebrew and Greek Scriptures there is no doubt at all, is little short of a miracle, and demands much thanksgiving to God. One thing is very certain. There is no ancient book which has been handed down to us with so good a text and so few various readings as the Bible.

(i) Finally, some object that occasional parts of the Bible are taken out, copied, and *extracted from the writings of uninspired men,* such as historical chronicles, and pedigrees, and lists of names. Are all these to be regarded as inspired ?—I reply that there seems no reason why the Holy Ghost should not direct the Bible writers to use materials made ready to their hands, as well as facts which they had seen themselves, and by so directing them, invested such words as they used with Divine authority. When St. Paul quoted lines from heathen poets he did not mean us to regard them as inspired. But he was taught by God to clothe his ideas in the words which they had used, and by so doing he very likely obtained a favourable reading from many. And when we read such quotations, or read lists of names taken from Jewish chronicles and registers, we need not doubt that Bible writers were taught to use such materials by inspiration of God.

I leave the objections to verbal inspiration at this point, and will detain my readers no longer with them. I will not pretend to deny that the subject has its difficulties, which will probably never be completely solved. I cannot perhaps clear up such difficulties as the mention of

"Jeremy the prophet" in Matthew xxvii., or reconcile the
third and sixth hour in St. John's and St. Mark's account
of the crucifixion, or explain Stephen's account of Jacob's
burial in the seventh chapter of Acts, to my own entire
satisfaction. But I have no doubt *these difficulties can
be explained,* and perhaps will be some day. These things
do not move me. I expect difficulties in such a deep and
miraculous matter as inspiration, which I have not eyes to
see through. I am content to wait. It was a wise saying
of Faraday, that "there are many questions about which
it is the highest philosophy to keep our minds in a state of
judicious suspense." It should be a settled rule with us
never to give up a great principle, when we have got hold
of it, on account of difficulties. Time often makes things
clear which at first look dark. The view of inspiration
which presents to my own mind the fewest difficulties, is
that in which all the words of Scripture, as well as the
thoughts, are regarded as inspired. **Here I** take my
stand.

Remember what I have just said. Never give up a
great principle in theology on account of difficulties. Wait
patiently, and the difficulties may all melt away. Let
that be an axiom in your mind. Suffer me to mention an
illustration of what I mean. Persons who are conversant
with astronomy know that before the discovery of the planet
Neptune there were difficulties which greatly troubled the
most scientific astronomers, respecting certain aberrations
of the planet Uranus. These aberrations puzzled the
minds of astronomers; and some of them suggested that
they might possibly prove the whole Newtonian system
to be untrue. But just at that time a well-known French
astronomer, named Leverrier, read before the Academy of
Science at Paris a paper, in which he laid down this great
axiom,—that it did not become a scientific man to give up
a principle because of difficulties which apparently could
not be explained. He said in effect, "We cannot explain

the aberrations of Uranus now; but we may be sure that the Newtonian system will be proved to be right, sooner or later. Something may be discovered one day which will prove that these aberrations may be accounted for, and yet the Newtonian system remain true and unshaken." A few years after, the anxious eyes of astronomers discovered the last great planet, Neptune. This planet was shown to be the true cause of all the aberrations of Uranus; and what the French astronomer had laid down as a principle in science was proved to be wise and true. The application of the anecdote is obvious. Let us beware of giving up any first principle in theology. Let us not give up the great principle of plenary verbal inspiration because of apparent difficulties. The day may come when they will all be solved. In the meantime we may rest assured that the difficulties which beset any other theory of inspiration are tenfold greater than any which beset our own.

Let me now conclude this paper with a few words of plain application. Let us lay aside all deep discussion of hard things about the manner of inspiration. Let us take it for granted that, in some way or other, whether we can explain it or not, we hold the Bible to be the Word of God. Let us start from this point. Let my readers give me a hearing, while I say a few things which appear to me to deserve their attention.

1. Is the Bible the Word of God? Then *mind that you do not neglect it.* Read it: read it! Begin to read it this very day. What greater insult to God can a man be guilty of than to refuse to read the letter God sends him from heaven? Oh, be sure, if you will not read your Bible, you are in fearful danger of losing your soul!

You are in danger, because *God will reckon with you for your neglect of the Bible in the day of judgment.* You will have to give account of your use of time, strength, and money; and you will also have to give account of your use of the Word. You will not stand at that bar on the same level, in point of responsibility, with the dweller in central Africa, who never heard of the Bible. Oh, no! To whom much is given, of them much will be required. Of all men's buried talents, none will weigh them down so heavily as a neglected Bible. As you deal with the Bible, so God will deal with your soul. Will you not repent, and turn over a new leaf in life, and read your Bible ?

You are in danger, because *there is no degree of error in religion into which you may not fall*. You are at the mercy of the first clever Jesuit, Mormonite, Socinian, Turk, or Jew, who may happen to meet you. A land of unwalled villages is not more defenceless against an enemy than a man who neglects his Bible. You may go on tumbling from one step of delusion to another, till at length you are landed in the pit of hell. I say once more, Will you not repent and read your Bible ?

You are in danger, because *there is not a single reasonable excuse you can allege for neglecting the Bible*. You have no time to read it forsooth ! But you can make time for eating, drinking, sleeping, getting money and spending money, and perhaps for newspaper reading and smoking. You might easily make time to read the Word. Alas, it is not want of time, but waste of time that ruins souls !—You find it too troublesome to read, forsooth ! You had better say at once it is too much trouble to go to heaven, and you are content to go to hell. Truly these excuses are like the rubbish round the walls of Jerusalem in Nehemiah's days. They would all soon disappear if, like the Jews, you had " a mind to work." I say for the last time, Will you not repent and read your Bible ?

Believe me, believe me, the *Bible* itself is the best witness of its own inspiration. The men who quibble and make difficulties about inspiration are too often the very men who never read the Scriptures at all. The darkness and hardness and obscurity they profess to complain of are far more often in their own hearts than in the book. Oh, be persuaded! Take it up and begin to read.

2. Is the Bible the Word of God? Then be sure you always *read it with deep reverence.* Say to your soul, whenever you open the Bible, "O my soul, thou art going to read a message from God." The sentences of judges, and the speeches of kings, are received with awe and respect. How much more reverence is due to the words of the Judge of judges and King of kings! Avoid, as you would cursing and swearing, that irreverent habit of mind into which some modern divines have unhappily fallen, in speaking about the Bible. They handle the contents of the holy book as carelessly and disrespectfully as if the writers were such men as themselves. They make one think of a child composing a book to expose the fancied ignorance of his own father,—or of a pardoned murderer criticising the handwriting and style of his own reprieve. Enter rather into the spirit of Moses on Mount Horeb:—"Put thy shoes from off thy feet; the place whereon thou standest is holy ground."

3. Is the Bible the Word of God? Then be sure you never read it without *fervent prayer for the help and teaching of the Holy Spirit.* Here is the rock on which many make shipwreck. They do not ask for wisdom and instruction, and so they find the Bible dark, and carry nothing away from it. You should pray for the Spirit to guide you into all truth. You should beg the Lord Jesus Christ to "open your understanding," as He did that of His disciples. The Lord God, by whose inspiration the book was written, keeps the keys of the book, and alone can enable you to understand it profitably. Nine times over in one Psalm does David cry, "Teach me." Five times over, in the same Psalm, does he say, "Give me understanding." Well says John Owen, Dean of Christ Church, Oxford, "There is a sacred light in the Word: but there is a covering and veil on the eyes of men, so that they,

cannot behold it aright. Now, the removal of this veil is the peculiar work of the Holy Spirit." Humble prayer will throw more light on your Bible than Poole, or Henry, or Scott, or Burkitt, or Bengel, or Alford, or Wordsworth, or Barnes, or Ellicott, or Lightfoot, or any commentary that ever was written.

The Bible is a large book or a small one, a dark or a bright one, according to the spirit in which men read it. Intellect alone will do nothing with it. Wranglers and first-class men will not understand it unless their hearts are right as well as their heads. The highest critical and grammatical knowledge will find it a sealed book without the teaching of the Holy Ghost. Its contents are often "hid to the wise and prudent and revealed to babes." Remember this, and say always, when you open your Bible, "O God, for Christ's sake, give me the teaching of the Spirit."

4. Finally, is the Bible the Word of God? Then let us all resolve *from this day forward to prize the Bible more*. Let us not fear being idolaters of this blessed book. Men may easily make an idol of the Church, of ministers, of sacraments, or of intellect. Men cannot make an idol of the Word. Let us regard all who would damage the authority of the Bible, or impugn its credit, as spiritual robbers. We are travelling through a wilderness: they rob us of our only guide. We are voyaging over a stormy sea: they rob us of our only compass. We are toiling over a weary road: they pluck our staff out of our hands. And what do these spiritual robbers give us in place of the Bible? What do they offer as a safer guide and better provision for our souls? Nothing! absolutely nothing! Big swelling words! Empty promises of new light! High sounding jargon; but nothing substantial and real! They would fain take from us the bread of life, and they do not give us in its place so much as a stone. Let us turn a deaf ear to them. Let us firmly grasp and prize the Bible more and more, the more it is assaulted.

Let us hear the conclusion of the whole matter. God has given us the Bible to be a light to guide us to everlasting life. Let us not neglect this precious gift. Let us read it diligently, walk in its light, and we shall be saved.

The following quotations about inspiration, from the works of four eminent British theologians, I venture to think deserve attentive perusal. They are valuable in themselves on account of the arguments which they contain. They also supply abundant proof that the high view of verbal inspiration which I advocate in this paper is no modern invention, but an " old path," in which many of God's ablest children have walked, and found it a good way.

1. Bishop Jewell, author of the "Apology," was unquestionably one of the most learned of the English Reformers. Let us hear what he says:—

"St. Paul, speaking of the Word of God, saith, 'the whole Scripture is given by inspiration of God, and is profitable.' Many think the Apostle's speech is hardly true of the whole Scripture,—that all and every part of the Scripture is profitable. Much is spoken of genealogies and pedigrees, of lepers, of sacrificing goats and oxen, etc. These seem to have little profit in them: to be idle and vain. If they show vain in thine eyes, yet hath not the Lord set them down in vain. The words of the Lord are pure words, as the silver tried in a furnace of earth refined seven times. There is no sentence, no clause, no word, no syllable, no letter, but it is written for thy instruction: there is not one jot but it is sealed and signed with the blood of the Lamb. Our imaginations are idle, our thoughts are vain: there is no idleness, no vanity, in the Word of God. Those oxen and goats which were sacrificed teach thee to kill the uncleanness and filthiness of thine heart: they teach thee that thou art guilty of death, when thy life must be redeemed by the death of some beast: they lead thee to believe the forgiveness of sins by a more perfect sacrifice, since it was not possible that the blood of bulls or of goats should take away sins. That leprosy teacheth thee the uncleanness and leprosy of thy soul. These genealogies and pedigrees lead us to the birth of our Saviour Christ, so that the whole Word of God is pure and holy. No word, no letter, no syllable, nor point or prick thereof, but is written and preserved for thy sake."— *Jewell on the Holy Scriptures.*

2. Richard Hooker, author of the "Ecclesiastical Polity," is justly respected by all schools of thought in the Church of England as "the judicious Hooker." Let us hear what he says :—

"Touching the manner how men, by the Spirit of Prophecy in Holy Scripture, have spoken and written of things to come, we must understand, that as the knowledge of that they spake, so likewise *the utterance of that they knew*, came not by those usual and ordinary means whereby we are brought to understand the mysteries of our salvation, and are wont to instruct others in the same. For whatsoever we know, we have it by the hands and ministry of men, who led us along like children from a letter to a syllable, from a syllable to a word, from a word to a line, from a line to a sentence, from a sentence to a side, and so turn over. But God Himself was their instructor. He Himself taught them, partly by dreams and visions in the night, partly by revelations in the day, taking them aside from amongst their brethren, and talking with them as a man would talk with his neighbours in the way. Thus they became acquainted even with the secret and hidden counsels of God ; they saw things which themselves were not able to utter, they beheld that whereat men and angels are astonished, they understood in the beginning what should come to pass in the last days. God, who lightened thus the eyes of their understanding, giving them knowledge by unusual and extraordinary means, *did also miraculously Himself frame and fashion their words and writings*, insomuch that a greater difference there seemeth not to be between the manner of their knowledge, than there is between the manner of their speech and ours. 'We have received,' saith the Apostle, 'not the spirit of the world, but the Spirit which is of God, that we might know the things that are given to us of God : which things also we speak, not in words which man's wisdom teacheth, but which the Holy Ghost doth teach.' This is that which the Prophets mean by those books written full within and without ; which books were so often delivered them to eat, not because God fed them with ink and paper, but to teach us, that so often as He employed them in this heavenly work, *they neither spake nor wrote any word of their own, but uttered syllable by syllable as the Spirit put it in their mouths*, no otherwise than the harp or the lute doth give a sound according to the direction of his hands that holdeth it and striketh it with skill."—*Hooker's Works.* Vol. iii., pp. 537, 540.

3. John Owen, Dean of Christ Church, Oxford, was the most learned and argumentative of the Puritans. Let us hear what he says :—

"Holy men of God spake as they were moved by the Holy Ghost. When the word was thus brought to them it was not left to their own understandings, wisdom, minds, memories, to order, dispose, and give it out ; but they were borne, actuated, carried out by the Holy Ghost, to speak, deliver, and write all that, and nothing but that,—to very tittles,—that was so brought unto them. They invented not words themselves, suited to the things they had learned, but only expressed the word that they received. Though their mind and understanding were used in the choice of words (whence arise all the differences in their manner of expression), yet they were so guided that their words were not their own, but immediately supplied unto them. Not only the doctrine they taught was the word of truth,—truth itself,—but the words whereby they taught it were words of truth from God Himself. Thus, allowing the contribution of proper instruments for the reception and representation of words which answer to the mind and tongue of the Prophets in the coming of the voice of God to them,—every apex of the written Word is equally divine, and as immediately from God as the voice wherewith, or whereby, He spake to us in the Prophets ; and is therefore accompanied with the same authority in itself and to us." —*Owen on the Divine Original of the Scripture.* Vol. xvi., p. 305.

4. Dr. Chalmers was probably the most intellectual and deep-thinking theologian that intellectual Scotland has ever produced. Let us hear what he says :—

(a) "The subject-matter of the Bible had to pass through the minds of the selected Prophets and Apostles, and to issue thence in language ere it comes forth in the shape of Scripture upon the world. Now it is here that we meet the advocates of a *partial* or mitigated inspiration, and would make common cause *against one and all of them.* There is not one theory short, by however so little, of a thorough and perfect inspiration,—there is not one of them but is chargeable with the consequence, that the subject-matter of revelation suffers and is deteriorated in the closing footsteps of its progress; and just before it settles into that ultimate position, where it stands forth to guide and illuminate the world. It existed purely in heaven. It descended purely from heaven to earth. It was deposited purely by the great Agent of revelation in the minds of the Apostles. But then we are told that when but a little way from the final landing place, then, instead of being carried forward purely to the situation where alone the great purpose of the whole movement was to be fulfilled, then was it abandoned to itself, and then were human infirmities permitted to mingle with it, and to mar its lustre. Strange, that just when entering on the functions of an authoritative guide and leader to mankind, that then, and not till then, the soil and the feebleness of humanity should be suffered to gather around it. Strange, that, with the inspiration of thoughts, it should make pure ingress into the minds of the Apostles; but wanting the inspiration of words should not make pure egress to that world in whose behalf alone, and for whose admonition alone, this great movement originated in heaven, and terminated in earth. Strange, more especially strange, in the face of the declaration that not unto themselves but unto us they ministered these things,—strange, nevertheless, that this revelation should come in purely to themselves, but to us should come forth impurely, with somewhat, it would appear, with somewhat the taint and the obscuration of human frailty attached to it.—It matters not at what point in the progress of this celestial truth to our world the obscuration has been cast upon it. It comes to us a dim and desecrated thing at last; and man instead of holding converse with God's unspotted testimony, has an imperfect, a mutilated Bible put into his hands."

(b) "Such being our views, it is the unavoidable consequence of them that we should hold the Bible, for all the purposes of a revelation, to be perfect in its language, as well as perfect in its doctrine. And for this conclusion it is not necessary that we should arbitrate between the theories of superintendence and suggestion. The superintendence that would barely intercept the progress of error, we altogether discard,— conceiving, that, if this term be applicable to the process of inspiration at all, it must be that efficient superintendence which not only secures that, negatively, there shall be nothing wrong,—but which also secures that, affirmatively, there should at all times have emanated from the sacred penmen, the fittest topics, and these couched in the fittest and most appropriate expression. Whether this has been effected partly by superintendence and partly by suggestion, or wholly by suggestion, we care not. We have no inclination and no taste for these distinctions. Our cause is independent of them; nor can we fully participate in the fears of those alarmists who think that our cause is materially injured by them. The important question with us is not the *process* of the manufacture, but the *qualities* of the resulting commodity. The former we hold not to be a relevant, and we are not sure that it is a legitimate inquiry. It is on the latter we take our stand; and the superabundant testimonies of Scripture on the worth and the perfection and the absolute authority of the Word—these form the strong-holds of an argument that goes to establish all which the most rigid advocates for a *total and infallible inspiration* ought to desire. Our concern is with the work, and not with the workmanship; nor need we intrude into the mysteries of the hidden operation, if only assured by the explicit testimonies of Scripture that the product of that operation, is, both in substance and expression, a perfect directory of faith and practice. We believe that, in the composition of that record, men not only thought as they were inspired, but spake as they were moved by the Holy Ghost. But our argument for the absolute perfection of Holy Writ is invulnerably beyond the reach even of those who have attempted to trace with geographical precision the line which separates the miraculous from the natural; and tell us when it was that Apostles wrote the words which the Spirit prompted them, and when it was that they wrote the words which the Spirit permitted them. To the result, in our humble apprehension, it positively matters not. Did they speak the words that the Spirit prompted,—these words were therefore the best. Did they speak the words which the Spirit permitted,—it was because these words were the best. *The optimism of the Bible is alike secured in both these ways;*

and the sanction of the Spirit extended, both in respect of sentiments and of sayings, *to every clause* of it. In either way, they effectively are the words of the Spirit; and God through the Bible is not presenting truths through the medium of others' language. He in effect has made it His own language ; and God, through the Bible, is speaking to us."

(c) "It is the part of Christians to rise like a wall of fire around the integrity and inspiration of Scripture ; and to hold them as intact and inviolable as if a rampart were thrown around them whose foundations are on earth and whose battlements are in heaven. It is this tampering with limits that destroys and defaces everything ; and therefore it is precisely when the limit is broken that the alarm should be sounded. If the battle-cry is to be lifted at all, it should be lifted at the outset ; and so on the first mingling, by however so slight an infusion, of things human with things divine, all the friends of the Bible should join heart and hand against so foul and fearful a desecration."—*Chalmers' Christian Evidences*, Vol. ii., pp. 371, 372, 375, 376, 396.

II

OUR SOULS!

"For what shall it profit a man, if he shall gain the whole world, and lose his own soul?—MARK VIII. 36.

THE saying of our Lord Jesus Christ, which stands at the head of this page, ought to ring in our ears like a trumpet-blast. It concerns our highest and best interests. It concerns OUR SOULS.

What a solemn question these words of Scripture contain! What a mighty sum of profit and loss they propound to us for calculation! Where is the accountant who could reckon it up? Where is the clever arithmetician who would not be baffled by that sum?—"What shall it profit a man, if he shall gain the whole world, and lose his own soul?"

I wish to offer a few plain remarks, to enforce and illustrate the question which the Lord Jesus asks in the passage before us. I invite the serious attention of all who read this volume. May all who take it up feel more deeply than they ever yet felt the value of an immortal soul! It is the first step toward heaven to find out the true worth of our souls.

I. The FIRST remark I have to make is this. EVERY ONE OF US HAS AN UNDYING SOUL.

I am not ashamed to begin my paper with these words. I dare say that they sound strange and foolish to some readers. I dare say that some will exclaim, "Who knoweth not such things as these? Who ever thinks of doubting that we have souls?" But I cannot forget that the world is just now fixing its attention on material things to a most extravagant extent. We live in an age of progress,—an age of steam-engines and machinery, of locomotion and invention. We live in an age when the multitude are increasingly absorbed in earthly things,—in railways, and docks, and mines, and commerce, and trade, and banks, and shops, and cotton, and corn, and iron, and gold. We live in an age when there is a false glare on the things of time, and a great mist over the things of eternity. In an age like this it is the bounden duty of the ministers of Christ to fall back upon first principles. Necessity is laid upon us. Woe is unto us, if we do not press home on men our Lord's question about the soul! Woe is unto us, if we do not cry aloud, "The world is not all. The life that we now live in the flesh is not the only life. There is a life to come. We have souls."

Let us stablish it in our minds as a great fact, that we all carry within our bosoms something that will never die. This body of ours, which takes up so much of our thoughts and time, to warm it, dress it, feed it, and make it comfortable,—this body alone is not all the man. It is but the lodging of a noble tenant, and that tenant is the immortal soul! The death which each of us has one day to die does not make an end of the man. All is not over when the last breath is drawn, and the doctor's last visit has been paid,—when the coffin is screwed down, and the funeral preparations are made,—when "ashes to ashes and dust to dust" has been pronounced over the grave,—when our place in the world is filled up, and the gap made by our absence from society is no longer noticed. No: all is not over then! The spirit of man still lives on. Every one has within him an undying soul.

I do not stop to prove this. It would be a mere waste of time. There is a conscience in all mankind which is worth a thousand metaphysical arguments. There is a voice within, which speaks out loudly at times, and will be heard,—a voice which tells us, whether we like it or not, that we have, every one of us, an undying soul. What though we cannot see our souls? Are there not millions of things in existence which we cannot see with the naked eye? Who that has looked through the telescope or microscope can doubt that this is the case?— What though we cannot see our souls? We can *feel* them. When we are alone, on the bed of sickness, and the world is shut out,—when we watch by the death-bed of a friend, —when we see those whom we love lowered into the grave, —at times like these, who does not know the feelings which come across men's minds? Who does not know that in hours like these something rises in the heart, telling us that there is a life to come, and that all, from the highest to the lowest, have undying souls?

You may go all over the world, and take the evidence of every age and time. You will never receive but one answer on this subject. You will find some nations buried in degrading superstition, and mad after idols. You will find others sunk in the darkest ignorance, and utterly unacquainted with the true God. But you will not find a nation or people amongst whom there is not some consciousness that there is a life to come. The deserted temples of Egypt, Greece, and Rome, the Druidical remains of our own native land, the splendid pagodas of Hindostan, the Fetish worship of Africa, the funeral ceremonies of the New Zealand chiefs, the conjurers' tents among the North American tribes,—all, all speak with the same voice, and tell the same story. Far down in the human heart, beneath the rubbish heaped up by the Fall, there is an inscription which nothing can efface, telling us that this world is not all, and that every one of us has an undying soul.

I do not stop to prove that men have souls, but I do ask every reader of this paper to keep it ever before his mind. Perhaps your lot is cast in the midst of some busy city. You see around you an endless struggle about temporal things. Hurry, bustle, and business hem you in on every side. I can well believe you are sometimes tempted to think that this world is everything, and the body all that is worth caring for. But resist the temptation, and cast it behind you. Say to yourself every morning when you rise, and every night when you lie down, " The fashion of this world passeth away. The life that I now live is not all. There is something beside business, and money, and pleasure, and commerce, and trade. There is a life to come. We have all immortal souls."

I do not stop to prove the point, but I do ask every reader to realize the dignity and responsibility of having a soul. Yes: realize the fact, that in your soul you have the greatest talent which God has committed to your charge. Know that in your soul you have a pearl above all price, compared to which all earthly possessions are trifles light as air. The horse that wins the Derby or the St. Leger, attracts the attention of thousands : painters paint it, and engravers engrave it, and vast sums of money turn on its achievements. Yet the weakest infant in a working man's family, is far more important in God's sight than that horse. The spirit of the beast goeth downwards ; but that infant has an immortal soul.—The pictures at our great exhibitions are visited by admiring crowds : people gaze on them with wonder, and talk with rapture of the " immortal works " of Rubens, Titian, and other great masters. But there is no immortality about these things. The earth, and all its works shall be burned up. The little babe that cries in a garret, and knows nothing of fine art, shall outlive all those pictures, for it has a soul which shall never die.—There shall be a time when the Pyramids and the Parthenon shall alike crumble to nothing,—when Windsor Castle and Westminster Abbey shall be cast down and pass away,—when the sun shall cease to shine, and the moon no more give her light. But the soul of the humblest labourer is of far more enduring stuff. It shall survive the crash of an expiring universe, and live on to all eternity. Realize, I say once more, the responsibility and dignity of having a never-dying soul. You may be poor in this world; but you have a soul. You may be sickly and weak in body; but you have a soul. You may not be a king, or a queen, or a duke, or an earl; yet you have a soul. The soul is the part of us which God chiefly regards. The soul is "the man."

> "The guinea's worth is in the gold,
> And not the stamp upon it."

The soul which is in man is the most important thing about him.

I do not stop to prove that men have souls, but I do ask all men to live as if they believed it. Live as if you really believed that we were not sent into the world merely to spin cotton, and grow corn, and hoard up gold, but to "glorify God and to enjoy Him for ever." Read your Bible, and become acquainted with its contents. Seek the Lord in prayer, and pour out your heart before Him. Go to a place of worship regularly, and hear the Gospel preached. Keep the Sabbath holy, and give God His day. And if any ask you the reason why: if wife, or child, or companion say, "What are you about?"—answer them boldly, like a man, and say, "I do these things because I have a soul."

II. The SECOND remark I have to make is this. ANY ONE MAY LOSE HIS OWN SOUL.

This is a sorrowful portion of my subject. But it is one which I dare not, cannot pass by. I have no sympathy with those who prophesy nothing but peace, and keep back from men the awful fact, that they may lose their souls. I am one of those old-fashioned ministers who believe the *whole* Bible,—and everything that it contains. I can find no Scriptural foundation for that smooth-spoken theology, which pleases so many in these days, and according to which every body will get to heaven at last. I believe that there is a real devil. I believe that there is a real hell. I believe that it is not charity to keep back from men that they may be lost. Charity! shall I call it? If you saw a brother drinking poison, would you hold your peace?—Charity! shall I call it? If you saw a blind man tottering towards a precipice, would you not cry out "Stop"? Away with such false notions of charity! Let us not slander that blessed grace, by using its name in a false sense. It is the highest charity to bring the whole truth before men. It is real charity to warn them plainly when they are in danger. It is charity to impress upon them, that they may lose their own souls for ever in hell.

Man has about him a wonderful power for evil. Weak as we are in all that is good, we have a mighty power to do ourselves harm. You cannot save that soul of your's, my brother: remember that! You cannot make your own peace with God. You cannot wipe away a single sin. You cannot blot out one of the black records which stand in the book of God against you. You cannot change your own heart. But there is one thing you can do,—you can lose your own soul.

But this is not all. Not only can we all lose our own souls, but we are all in imminent peril of doing it. Born in sin, and children of wrath, we have no natural desire to have our souls saved. Weak, corrupt, inclined to sin, we "call good evil, and evil good." Dark and blind, and dead in trespasses, we have no eyes to see the pit which

yawns beneath our feet, and no sense of our guilt and
danger. And yet our souls are all this time in awful
peril! If any one were to sail for America in a leaky ship,
without compass, without water, without provisions, who
does not see that there would be little chance of his
crossing the Atlantic in safety? If you were to place the
Koh-i-noor diamond in the hands of a little child, and bid
him carry it from Tower Hill to Bristol, who does not
perceive the doubtfulness of that diamond arriving safely
at the end of the journey? Yet these are but faint
images of the immense peril in which we stand by nature
of losing our souls.

But some one may ask, *How can a man lose his soul?*
There are many answers to that question. Just as there
are many diseases which assault and hurt the body, so
there are many evils which assault and injure the soul.
Yet however numerous the ways in which a man may lose
his own soul, they may be classed under three general
heads. Let me show briefly what they are.

For one thing, you may *murder* your soul by running
into open sin, and serving lusts and pleasures. Adultery
and fornication, drunkenness and revelling, basphemy
and sabbath-breaking, dishonesty and lying, are all so
many short-cuts to perdition. "Let no man deceive
you with vain words, for because of these things cometh
the wrath of God upon the children of disobedience."
(Ephes. v. 6.)

For another thing, you may *poison* your own soul by
taking up some false religion. You may drug it with
traditions of man's invention, and a round of ceremonies
and observances which never came down from heaven.
You may lull it to sleep with opiates which stupify the
conscience, but do not heal the heart. Strychnine and
arsenic will do their work quite as effectually as the pistol
or sword, though with less noise. Let no man deceive
you. "Beware of false prophets." When men commit their

souls to blind leaders, both must fall into the ditch. A false religion is quite as ruinous as no religion at all.

For another thing, you may *starve* your soul to death by trifling and indecision. You may idle through life with a name upon the baptismal register, but not inscribed in the Lamb's Book of Life,—with a form of godliness, but without the power. You may trifle on year after year, taking no interest in that which is good, content to sneer at the inconsistencies of professors, and flattering yourself because you are no bigot, or party man, or professor, it will be "all right" with your soul at last. "Let no man deceive you with vain words." Indecision is just as ruinous to the soul as a false religion or no religion at all. The stream of life can never stand still. Whether you are sleeping or waking, you are floating down that stream. You are coming nearer and nearer to the rapids. You will soon pass over the falls, and, if you die without a decided faith, be cast away to all eternity.

Such then are the three chief ways in which you can lose your soul. Does any one who is reading this paper know which of these ways he is taking? Search and look whether I have touched your own case. Find out whether or not you are losing your soul.

But does it *take much trouble* to ruin a soul? Oh, no! It is a down-hill journey. There is nothing required at your hands. There is no need of exertion. You have only to sit still, and do as others do in the circle in which God's providence has placed you,—to swim with the tide, to float down the stream, to go with the crowd,—and by and by the time of mercy will be past for evermore! "Wide is the gate that leadeth to destruction."

But *are there many*, you will ask, who are losing their souls? Yes, indeed there are! Look not at the inscriptions and epitaphs on tombstones if you would find the true answer to that question! As Dr. Watts says, they are

"Taught to flatter and to lie."

All men are thought respectable and "good sort of people"
as soon as they are dead. But look at the Word of God,
and mark well what it says. The Lord Jesus Christ
declares, "Strait is the gate and narrow is the way which
leadeth unto life, and few there be that find it:—broad is
the way that leadeth to destruction, and many there be
that go in thereat." (Matt. vii. 13, 14.)

But who is *responsible* for the loss of our souls? No
one but ourselves. Our blood will be upon our own heads.
The blame will lie at our own door. We shall have
nothing to plead at the last day, when we stand before
the great white throne and the books are opened. When
the King comes in to see His guests, and says, "Friend,
how camest thou in, not having a wedding garment?" we
shall be speechless. We shall have no excuse to plead
for the loss of our souls.

But *where does the soul go to when lost?* There is only
one solemn answer to that question. There is but one
place to which it can go, and that is hell. There is no
such thing as annihilation. The lost soul goes to that
place where the worm dies not, and the fire is not quenched,
—where there is blackness and darkness, wretchedness
and despair for ever. It goes to hell,—the only place for
which it is meet,—since it is not meet for heaven. "The
wicked shall be turned into hell, with all the nations that
forget God." "The end of those things is death!" (Rom.
vi. 21.)

Let me say plainly that we ministers are full of fears about
many who profess and call themselves Christians. We
fear lest they should lose at last their precious souls. We
fear lest that arch-impostor, Satan, should cheat them out
of salvation, and lead them captive at his will. We fear
lest they should wake up in eternity, and find themselves
lost for evermore! We fear, because we see so many living
in sinful habits, so many resting in forms and ceremonies
which God never commanded, so many trifling with all

religion whatsoever, so many, in short, ruining their own souls. We see these things, and are afraid.

It is just because I feel that souls are in danger that I write this paper, and invite men to read it. If I thought there was no such place as hell I would not write as I do. If I thought that as a matter of course all people would go to heaven at last, I would hold my peace and leave them alone. But I dare not do so. I see danger ahead, and I would fain warn every man to flee from the wrath to come. I see peril of shipwreck, and I would light a beacon and entreat every man to seek the harbour of safety. Do not despise my warning. Examine your own heart : find out whether you are in a way to be lost or saved. Search and see how matters stand between yourself and God : do not commit the enormous folly of losing your own soul. We live in an age of great temptation. The devil is going about and is very busy. The night is far spent. The time is short. Do not lose your own soul.

III. The THIRD remark which I desire to make is this. THE LOSS OF ANY MAN'S SOUL IS THE HEAVIEST LOSS WHICH HE CAN SUFFER.

I feel unable to set forth this point as I ought. No living man can show the full extent of the loss of the soul. No one can paint that loss in its true colours. No : we shall never understand it till we have passed through the valley of the shadow of death, and wake up in another world ! Never till then shall we know the value of an immortal soul.

I might say that *nothing can make up* for the loss of the soul in the life which now is. You may have all the riches of the world,—all the gold of Australia and of California, all the honours which your country can bestow upon you. You may be the owner of half a county. You may be one whom kings delight to honour, and nations gaze upon with admiration. But all this time, if you are

losing your soul, you are a poor man in the sight of God.
Your honours are but for a few years. Your riches must
be left at last. "Naked came we into the world, and
naked must we go out." No light heart, no cheerful
conscience, will you have in life, unless your soul is saved.
Of all your money or broad acres, you will carry nothing
with you when you die. A few feet of earth will suffice
to cover that body of yours when life is over. And then,
if your soul be lost, you will find yourself a pauper to all
eternity. Verily it shall profit a man nothing to gain the
whole world if he lose his own soul.

I might say that when the soul is lost *it is a loss that
cannot be retrieved.* Once lost, it is lost for evermore.
The loss of property may be retrieved in this world. The
loss of health and character are not always irreparable.
But no man who has once drawn his last breath can ever
retrieve his lost soul. Scripture reveals to us no purgatory
beyond the grave. Scripture teaches us that, once lost,
we are lost for ever. Verily a man will find that there is
nothing he can give to buy back and redeem his soul.

But I feel deeply that arguments like these fall far
below the level of the subject. The time is not yet come
when we shall fully realize what a soul is worth. We
must look far forward. We must place ourselves in
imagination in a different position from that which we now
occupy, before we shall form a right estimate of the thing
we are considering. The blind man cannot understand
beautiful scenery. The deaf man cannot appreciate fine
music. The living man cannot fully realize the amazing
importance of a world to come.

Does any reader of this paper wish to have some faint
idea of the value of a soul? Then go and measure it
by the opinions of *dying people.* The solemnity of the
closing scene strips off the tinsel and pretence of things,
and makes men see them as they really are. What would
men do then for their souls? I have seen something of

this, as a Christian minister. Seldom, very seldom, have I found people careless, thoughtless, and indifferent about the world to come, in the hour of death. The man who can tell good stories, and sing good songs to merry companions, turns very grave when he begins to feel that life is leaving his body. The boasting infidel at such a season has often cast aside his infidelity. Men like Paine and Voltaire have often shown that their vaunted philosophy breaks down when the grave is in sight. Tell me not what a man thinks about the soul when he is in the fulness of health; tell me rather what he thinks when the world is sinking beneath him, and death, judgment, and eternity loom in sight. The great realities of our being will then demand attention, and must be considered. The value of the soul in the light of time is one thing, but seen in the light of eternity it is quite another. Never does living man know the value of the soul so well as when he is dying, and can keep the world no longer.

Does any one wish to have a still clearer idea of the soul's value? Then go and measure it by the opinions of the *dead*. Read in the sixteenth chapter of St. Luke the parable of the rich man and Lazarus. When the rich man awoke in hell and in torments, what did he say to Abraham? "Send Lazarus to my father's house:—For I have five brethren,—that he may testify to them,—lest they also come to this place of torment." That rich man probably thought little or nothing of the souls of others while he lived upon the earth. Once dead and in the place of torment, he sees things in their true colours. Then he thinks of his brethren, and begins to care for their salvation. Then he cries, "Send Lazarus to my father's house. I have five brethren. Let him testify unto them." If that wonderful parable did nothing else, it would teach us what men think when they awake in the next world. It lifts a corner of the veil which hangs over the world to come, and gives us a glimpse of what dead men think of the value of the soul.

Does any one wish to have the clearest idea that can be given of the soul's value ? Then go and measure it by the *price* which was paid for it 1800 years ago. What an enormous and countless price it was which was paid ! No gold, no silver, no diamonds were found sufficient to provide redemption : no angel in heaven was able to bring a ransom. Nothing but the blood of Christ,—nothing but the death of the eternal Son of God upon the cross, was found sufficient to buy for the soul deliverance from hell. Go to Calvary in spirit, and consider what took place there, when the Lord Jesus died. See the blessed Saviour suffering on the cross. Mark what happens there when He dies. See how there was darkness for three hours over the face of the earth. The earth quakes. The rocks are rent. The graves are opened. Listen to His dying words : "My God, my God, why hast thou forsaken Me ?" Then see in all that marvellous transaction something which may give you an idea of the value of the soul. In that awful scene we witness payment of the only price which was found sufficient to redeem men's souls.

We shall all understand the value of the soul one day, if we do not understand it now. God grant that no one who reads this paper may understand it too late.—A lunatic asylum is a pitiable sight. It wrings the heart to see in that gloomy building some man, who had once a princely fortune, but has squandered it, and brought himself to hopeless insanity by drunkenness.—A shipwreck is a pitiable sight. It makes one melancholy to see some gallant vessel, which once "walked the water like a thing of life," stranded on a rocky shore, with a drowned crew and a scattered cargo lying round her on the beach. But of all sights that can affect the eye and grieve the heart, I know none so pitiable as the sight of a man ruining his own soul. No wonder that Jesus wept when He drew nigh unto Jerusalem for the last time. It is written, that "He beheld the city and wept over it!" (Luke xix. 41.) *He* knew the value of souls, if the Scribes and Pharisees did not. We may learn from those tears of His,—if from nothing else,—the value of man's soul, and the amount of loss which he will sustain if that soul is cast away.

I charge every reader of this paper, while it is called to-day, to open his eyes to the worth of his soul. Rise to a sense of the awfulness of losing a soul. Strive to know the real preciousness of that mighty treasure committed to your charge. The value of all things will change greatly one day. The hour cometh when bank-notes shall be worth no more than waste paper, and gold and diamonds shall be as the dust of the streets,—when the palace of the peer and the cottage of the peasant shall both alike fall to the ground,—when stocks and funds shall be all unsaleable, and grace and faith and good hope be no longer underrated and despised. In that hour you will find out, in a way you never found out before, the value of the immortal soul. Soul-loss will then be seen to be the greatest of losses, and soul-gain the greatest of gains. Seek to know the value of the soul now. Do not be like the Egyptian Queen, who, in foolish ostentation, took a pearl of great value, dissolved it in acid, and then drank it off. Do not, like her, cast away the "pearl of great price," which God has committed to your charge. Once lost, no loss can compare with the loss of the soul.

IV. The FOURTH and last remark I have to make is this. ANY MAN'S SOUL MAY BE SAVED.

I bless God that the Gospel of Christ enables me to proclaim these glad tidings, and to proclaim them freely and unconditionally to every one who reads these pages. I bless God, that after all the solemn things I have been saying, I can wind up with a message of peace. I could not bear the awful responsibility of telling men that every one has a soul,—that any one may lose his soul,—that the loss of the soul is a loss for which nothing can make up,—if I could not also proclaim that any man's soul may be saved.

I think it possible that this proclamation may sound startling to some readers of this paper. I remember the time when it would have sounded startling to me. But I am persuaded that it is neither more nor less than the voice of the everlasting Gospel, and I am not ashamed to make it known to all who have an ear to hear. I say boldly, that there is salvation in the Gospel for the chief of sinners. I say confidently, that any one and every one may have his soul saved!

I know that we are all sinners by nature,—fallen, guilty, corrupt, covered with sin. I know that the God with whom we have to do is a most holy Being, of purer eyes than to behold iniquity, and One who cannot look upon that which is evil. I know also that the world in which our lot is cast, is a hard world for religion. It is a world full of cares and troubles, of unbelief and impurity, of opposition and hatred to God. It is a world in which religion is like an exotic,—a world which has an atmosphere that makes religion wither away. But, notwithstanding all this, hard as this world is, holy as God is, sinful as we are by nature,—I say, that any one and every one may be saved. Any man or woman may be saved from the guilt, the power, the consequences of sin, and be found at length at the right hand of God in everlasting glory.

I fancy I hear some reader exclaim, "How can these things be?" No wonder that you ask that question. This is the great knot which heathen philosophers could never untie. This is the problem which all the sages of Greece and of Rome could not solve. This is the question which nothing can answer but the Gospel of the Lord Jesus Christ. That answer of the Gospel I now desire to place before you.

I proclaim then, with all confidence, that any one's soul may be saved, (1) *because Christ has once died.* Jesus Christ, the Son of God, has died upon the cross to make atonement for men's sins. "Christ has once suffered for sins, the just for the unjust, that he might bring us to God." (1 Pet. iii. 18.) Christ has borne our sins in His own body on the tree, and allowed the curse we all deserved to fall on His head. Christ by His death has made satisfaction to the holy law of God which we have broken. That death was no common death: it was no mere example of self-denial; it was no mere death of a martyr, such as were the deaths of a Ridley, a Latimer, or a Cranmer. The death of Christ was a sacrifice and propitiation for the sin of the whole world. It was the vicarious death of an Almighty Substitute, Surety, and Representative of the sons of men. It paid our enormous debt to God. It opened up the way to heaven to all believers. It provided a fountain for all sin and uncleanness. It enabled God to be just, and yet to be the justifier of the ungodly. It purchased reconciliation with Him. It procured perfect peace with God for all who come to Him by Jesus. The prison-doors were set open when Jesus died. Liberty was proclaimed to all who feel the bondage of sin, and desire to be free.

For whom, do you suppose, was all that suffering undergone, which Jesus endured at Calvary? Why was the holy Son of God dealt with as a malefactor, reckoned a transgressor, and condemned to so cruel a death? For whom were those hands and feet nailed to the cross? For whom was that side pierced with the spear? For whom did that precious blood flow so freely down? Wherefore was all this done? It was done for you! It was done for the sinful,—for the ungodly! It was done freely, voluntarily,—not by compulsion,—out of love to sinners, and to make atonement for sin. Surely, then, as Christ died for the ungodly, I have a right to proclaim that any one may be saved.

Furthermore, I proclaim with all confidence, that any one may be saved, (2) *because Christ still lives.* That same Jesus who once died for sinners, still lives at tho right hand of God, to carry on the work of salvation which He came down from heaven to perform. He lives to receive all who come unto God by Him, and to give them power to become the sons of God. He lives to hear the confession of every heavy-laden conscience, and to grant, as an almighty High Priest, perfect absolution. He lives to pour down the Spirit of adoption on all who believe in Him, and to enable them to cry, Abba, Father! He lives to be the one Mediator between God and man, the unwearied Intercessor, the kind Shepherd, the elder Brother, the prevailing Advocate, the never-failing Priest and Friend of all who come to God by Him. He lives to be wisdom, righteousness, sanctification, and redemption to all His people,—to keep them in life, to support them in death, and to bring them finally to eternal glory.

For whom, do you suppose, is Jesus sitting at God's right hand? It is for the sons of men. High in heaven, and surrounded by unspeakable glory, He still cares for that mighty work which He undertook when He was born in the manger of Bethlehem. He is not one whit altered. He is always in one mind. He is the same that He was when He walked the shores of the sea of Galilee. He is the same that He was when He pardoned Saul the Pharisee, and sent him forth to preach the faith he had once destroyed. He is the same that He was when He received Mary Magdalene,—called Matthew the publican, —brought Zacchæus down from the tree, and made them examples of what His grace could do. And He is not changed. He is the same yesterday, and to-day, and for ever. Surely I have a right to say that any one may be saved, since Jesus lives.

Once more I proclaim, with all confidence, that any one may be saved, (3) *because the promises of Christ's gospel are full, free, and unconditional.* "Come unto Me," says the Saviour, "all ye that labour and are heavy laden, and I will give you rest."—"He that believeth on the Son shall not perish, but have eternal life."—"He that believeth on Him is not condemned."—"Him that cometh unto Me I will in no wise cast out."—"Every one which seeth the Son, and believeth on Him may have everlasting life."—"He that believeth on Me hath everlasting life." —"If any man thirst, let him come unto Me and drink." "Whosoever will, let him take of the water of life freely." (Matt. xi. 28; John iii. 15, 18; vi. 37, 40, 47; vii. 37; Rev. xxii. 17.)

For whom, do you suppose, were these words spoken? Were they meant for the Jews only? No: for the Gentiles also!—Were they meant for people in old times only? No: for people in every age!—Were they meant for Palestine and Syria only? No: for the whole world, —for every name and nation and people and tongue!— Were they meant for the rich only? No: for the poor as well as for the rich!—Were they meant for the very moral and correct only? No: they were meant for all,—for the chief of sinners,—for the vilest of offenders,—for all who will receive them! Surely when I call to mind these promises, I have a right to say that any one and every one may be saved. Any one who reads these words, and is not saved, can never blame the Gospel. If you are lost, it is not because you could not be saved. If you are lost, it is not because there was no pardon for sinners, no Mediator, no High Priest, no fountain open for sin and for uncleanness, no open door. It is because you would have your own way, because you would cleave to your sins, because you would not come to Christ, that in Christ you might have life.

I make no secret of my object in sending forth this

volume. My heart's desire and prayer to God for you is, that your soul may be saved. This is the grand object for which every faithful minister is ordained. This is the end for which we preach, and speak, and write. We want souls to be saved. They know not what they say, who charge us with worldly motives, and tell us we only wish to advance our order, and promote priest-craft. We know nothing of such feelings. May God forgive those who lay these things to our charge! We labour for higher objects. We want souls to be saved! We love the Church of England: we feel deep affection for her Prayer-book, her Articles, her Homilies, her Forms for the Worship of God. But one thing we feel even more deeply,—we want souls to be saved. We desire to pluck some brands from the burning. We desire to be the honoured instruments in the hand of God of leading some souls to a knowledge of Jesus Christ our Lord.

And now I will conclude this paper by three words of affectionate application, which I heartily pray God to bless to the spiritual good of many souls. I know not into whose hands these pages may fall. I draw my bow at a venture. I can only pray God that He may send an arrow home to some consciences, and that many who read this volume may lay it down smiting upon their breasts and saying, "What must I do to be saved?"

(1) My first word of application shall be a word of *affectionate warning.* That word of warning is short and simple,—Do not neglect your own soul.

I have little doubt that this volume will fall into the hands of some who are often tried with anxiety about the things of this life. You are "careful and troubled about many things." You seem to live in a constant whirl of business, hurry, and trouble. You see around you thousands who care for nothing but what they shall eat, and what they shall drink, and what they shall put on. You are often sorely tempted to think it is no use to try to have any religion. I say to you, in God's name, Resist the temptation. It comes from the devil. I say to you, Never forget the one thing needful! Never forget your immortal soul!

You may tell me, perhaps, that the times are hard. They may be hard; but it is my duty to remind you that time is short, and will be soon changed for eternity. You may tell me that you must live; but it is my duty to remind you that you must also die, and be ready to meet your God. What should we think of a man who in time of famine fed his dog and starved his child? Should we not say that he was a heartless and unnatural father? Well: take heed that you do not do something like this yourself. Do not forget your soul in your anxiety for your body. Do not, in your concern about the life that now is, forget that which is to come. Do not neglect your soul!

Whatever **you** may have been in time past, I beseech you for time to come to live as one who feels that he has an immortal soul! Lay down this book with a holy determination, by God's help, to "cease to do evil, and learn to do well." Do not be ashamed, from this time forward, to care about your soul's interests. Do not be ashamed to read your Bible, to pray, to keep the Sabbath holy, and to hear the Gospel preached. Of sin and ungodliness you may well be ashamed. You never need be ashamed of caring for your soul. Let others laugh if they will: they will not laugh at you one day. Take it patiently. Bear it quietly. Tell them you have made up your mind, and do not mean to alter. Tell them that you have learned one thing, if nothing else, and that is that you have a precious soul. And tell them you have resolved that, come what will, you will no longer neglect that soul.

(2) My second word of application shall be *an affec-*

tionate invitation to all who desire their souls to be saved. I invite every reader of this paper who feels the value of his soul, and desires salvation, to come to Christ without delay, and be saved. I invite him to come to Christ by faith, and commit his soul to Him, that he may be delivered from the guilt, the power, and the consequences of sin.

My tongue is not able to tell, and my mind is too weak to explain, the whole extent of God's love towards sinners, and of Christ's willingness to receive and save souls. You are not straitened in Christ, but in yourself. You mistake greatly if you doubt Christ's readiness to save. I know there are no obstacles between that soul of yours and eternal life, except your own will. "There is joy in the presence of the angels of God over one sinner that repenteth." (Luke xv. 10.) You may have heard something of the wonders of the choruses at the Crystal Palace concerts. But what is all that burst of harmony in the "Hallelujah Chorus," to the outburst of joy which is heard in heaven when a soul turns from darkness to light? What is it all but a mere whisper, compared to the "joy of angels" over one sinner taught to see the folly of sin, and to seek Christ? Oh, come and add to that joy without delay!

If you love life, I beseech you to lay hold on Christ at once, that your soul may be saved. Why not do it to-day? Why not this day join yourself to the Lord Jesus in an everlasting covenant which cannot be broken? Why not resolve, before to-morrow's sun dawns, to turn from the service of sin, and turn to Christ? Why not go to Christ this very day, and cast your soul on Him, with all its sins and all its unbelief, with all its doubts and all its fears?—Are you poor? Seek treasure in heaven and be rich.—Are you old? Hasten, hasten to be ready for your end, and prepare to meet your God.—Are you young? Begin well, and seek in Christ a never-failing friend, who will never forsake you.—Are you in trouble, careful about this life? Seek Him who alone can help you and bear your burdens: seek Him who will never disappoint you. When others turn their backs upon you, then will Jesus Christ the Lord take you up.—Are you a sinner, a great sinner, a sinner of the worst description? It shall all be remembered no more if you only come to Christ: His blood shall cleanse all sin away. Though your sins be as scarlet, they shall be made white as snow.

Go then, and cry to the Lord Jesus Christ. Think of the value of your soul, and think of the one way of salvation. Call on the Lord in earnest prayer. Do as the penitent thief did: pour out your heart before Him: cry, " Lord remember me, even me." Tell him you come to Him, because you have heard that He "receives sinners,' and because you are a sinner and want to be saved. Tell Him the whole story of your past life. Tell Him, if you will, that you have been an unbeliever, a profligate, a Sabbath-breaker, a godless, reckless, ill-tempered man. He will not despise you. He will not cast you out. He will not turn His back upon you. He never breaks the bruised reed, or quenches the smoking flax. No man ever came to Him and was cast out. Oh, come to Christ, and your soul shall live!

(3) My last word of application shall be an *affectionate exhortation* to every reader of this paper who has found out the value of his soul, and believed in Jesus Christ. That exhortation shall be short and simple. I beseech you to cleave to the Lord with all your heart, and to press towards the mark for the prize of your high calling.

I can well conceive that you find your way very narrow. There are few with you and many against you. Your lot in life may seem hard, and your position may be difficult. But still cleave to the Lord, and He will never forsake you. Cleave to the Lord in the midst of persecution. Cleave to the Lord, though men laugh at you and mock you, and try to make you ashamed. Cleave to the Lord, though the cross be heavy and the fight be hard. He was not ashamed of you upon the Cross of Calvary: then do not be ashamed of Him upon earth, lest He should be ashamed of you before His Father who is in heaven. Cleave to the Lord, and He will never forsake you. In this world there are plenty of disappointments,—disappointments in properties, and families, and houses, and lands, and situations. But no man ever yet was disappointed in Christ. No man ever failed to find Christ all that the Bible says He is, and a thousand times better than he had been told before.

Look forward, look onward and forward to the end! Your best things are yet to come. Time is short. The end is drawing near. The latter days of the world are upon us. Fight the good fight. Labour on. Work on. Strive on. Pray on. Read on. Labour hard for your own soul's prosperity. Labour hard for the prosperity of the souls of others. Strive to bring a few more with you to heaven, and by all means to save some. Do something, by God's help, to make heaven more full and hell more empty. Speak to that young man by your side, and to that old person who lives near to your house. Speak to that neighbour who never goes to a place of worship. Speak to that relative who never reads the Bible in private, and makes a jest of serious religion. Entreat them all to think about their souls. Beg them to go and hear something on Sundays which will be for their good unto everlasting life. Try to persuade them to live, not like the beasts which perish, but like men who desire to be saved. Great is your reward in heaven, if you try to do good to souls. Great is the reward of all who confess Christ before the sons of men. The honours of this world will soon be at an end for ever. The rewards which our gracious Queen bestows are only enjoyed for a few short years. The "Victoria Cross" will not be long worn by those brave soldiers who won it so gallantly and deserve it so richly. The place that knows them now shall soon know them no more: a few more years and they will be gathered to their fathers. But the crown which Christ gives never fades. Seek that crown, my believing reader. Labour for that crown. It will make amends for all that you have to pass through in this troublous world. The rewards of Christ's soldiers are for evermore. Their home is eternal. Their glory never comes to an end.

III

FEW SAVED!

"Are there few that be saved?"—LUKE xiii. 23.

I TAKE it for granted that every reader of this paper calls himself a Christian. You would not like to be reckoned a deist, or an infidel. You profess to believe the Bible to be true. The birth of Christ the Saviour,—the death of Christ the Saviour,—the salvation provided by Christ the Saviour,—all these are facts which you have probably never doubted. But, after all, will Christianity like this profit you anything at last? Will it do your soul any good when you die? In one word,—*Shall you be saved?*

It may be you are now young, healthy and strong. Perhaps you never had a day's illness in your life, and scarcely know what it is to feel weakness and pain. You scheme and plan for future years, and feel as if death was far away, and out of sight. Yet, remember, death sometimes cuts off young people in the flower of their days. The strong and healthy of the family do not always live the longest. Your sun may go down before your life has reached its mid-day. Yet a little while, and you may be lying in a narrow, silent home, and the daisies may be growing over your grave. And then, consider,—*Shall you be saved?*

It may be you are rich and prosperous in this world.

You have money, and all that money can command. You have "honour, love, obedience, troops of friends." But, remember, "riches are not for ever." You cannot keep them longer than a few years. "It is appointed unto men once to die, and after this the judgment." (Prov. xxvii. 24; Heb. ix. 27.) And then, consider,—*Shall you be saved?*

It may be you are poor and needy. You have scarcely enough to provide food and raiment for yourself and family. You are often distressed for want of comforts, which you have no power to get. Like Lazarus, you seem to have "evil things" only, and not good. But, nevertheless, you take comfort in the thought that there will be an end of all this. There is a world to come, where poverty and want shall be unknown. Yet, consider a moment,—*Shall you be saved?*

It may be you have a weak and sickly body. You hardly know what it is to be free from pain. You have so long parted company with health, that you have almost forgotten what it is like. You have often said in the morning, "Would God it were evening,"—and in the evening, "Would God it were morning." There are days when you are tempted by very weariness to cry out with Jonah, "It is better for me to die than to live." (Jonah iv. 3.) But, remember, death is not all. There is something else beyond the grave. And then, consider,—*Shall you be saved?*

If it was an easy thing to be saved, I would not write as I do in this volume. But is it so? Let us see.

If the common opinion of the world as to the number of the saved was correct, I would not trouble men with searching and hard questions. But is it so? Let us see.

If God had never spoken plainly in the Bible about the number of the saved, I might well be silent. But is it so? Let us see.

If experience and facts left it doubtful whether many or few would be saved, I might hold my peace. But is it so? Let us see.

There are four points which I propose to examine in considering the subject before us.

I.   Let me explain *what it is to be saved.*

II.   Let me point out *the mistakes which are common in the world about the number of the saved.*

III.   Let me show *what the Bible says about the number of the saved.*

IV.   Let me bring forward *some plain facts as to the number of the saved.*

A calm examination of these four points, in a day of wide-spread carelessness about vital religion, will be found of vast importance to our souls.

I.   *First of all let me explain what it is to be saved.*

This is a matter that must be cleared up.   Till we know this, we shall make no progress.   By being " saved " I may mean one thing, and you may mean another.   Let me show you what the Bible says it is to be " saved," and then there will be no misunderstanding.

To be saved, is not merely to profess and call ourselves Christians.   We may have all the outward parts of Christianity, and yet be lost after all.   We may be baptized into Christ's Church,—go to Christ's table,— have Christian knowledge,—be reckoned Christian men and women—and yet be dead souls all our lives,—and at last, in the judgment day, be found on Christ's left hand, among the goats.   No: this is not salvation!   Salvation is something far higher and deeper than this.   Now what is it?

(*a*) To be saved, is to be delivered in this present life from the *guilt of sin*, by faith in Jesus Christ, the Saviour.   It is to be pardoned, justified, and freed from every charge of sin, by faith in Christ's blood and mediation.   Whosoever with his heart believes on the

Lord Jesus Christ, is a saved soul. He shall not perish. He shall have eternal life. This is the first part of salvation, and the root of all the rest. But this is not all.

(b) To be saved, is to be delivered in this present life from *the power of sin,* by being born again, and sanctified by Christ's spirit. It is to be freed from the hateful dominion of sin, the world, and the devil, by having a new nature put in us by the Holy Ghost. Whosoever is thus renewed in the spirit of his mind, and converted, is a saved soul. He shall not perish. He shall enter into the glorious kingdom of God. This is the second part of salvation. But this is not all.

(c) To be saved, is to be delivered in the day of judgment, from all *the awful consequences of sin.* It is to be declared blameless, spotless, faultless, and complete in Christ, while others are found guilty, and condemned for ever. It is to hear those comfortable words,—"Come, ye blessed!" while others are hearing those fearful words,— "Depart, ye cursed!" (Matt. xxv. 34, 41.) It is to be owned and confessed by Christ, as one of His dear children and servants, while others are disowned and cast off for ever. It is to be pronounced free from the portion of the wicked,—the worm that never dies,—the fire that is not quenched,— the weeping, wailing, and gnashing of teeth, that never ends. It is to receive the reward prepared for the righteous, in the day of Christ's second coming;—the glorious body,—the kingdom that is incorruptible,—the crown that fadeth not away,—and the joy that is for evermore. This is *complete salvation.* This is the "redemption" for which true Christians are bid to look and long. (Luke xxi. 28.) This is the heritage of all men and women who believe and are born again. By faith they are saved already. In the eye of God their final salvation is an absolutely certain thing. Their names are in the book of life. Their mansions in heaven are even now prepared But still there is a fulness of redemption and salvation which they do not attain to while they are in the body. They are saved from the guilt and power of sin;—but not from the necessity of watching and praying against it. They are saved from the fear and love of the world;—but not from the necessity of daily fighting with it. They are saved from the service of the devil;—but they are not saved from being vexed by his temptations. But when Christ comes the salvation of believers shall be complete. They possess it already in the bud. They shall see it then in the flower.

Such is salvation. It is to be saved from the guilt, power, and consequences of sin. It is to believe and be sanctified now, and to be delivered from the wrath of God in the last day. He that has the first part in the life that now is, shall undoubtedly have the second part in the life to come. Both parts of it hang together. What God has joined together, let no man dare to put asunder. Let none dream he shall ever be saved at last, if he is not born again first. Let none doubt, if he is born again here, that he shall assuredly be saved hereafter.

Let it never be forgotten that the chief object of a minister of the Gospel is to set forward *the salvation of souls*. I lay it down as a certain fact that he is no true minister who does not feel this. Talk not of a man's orders! All may have been done correctly, and according to rule. He may wear a black coat, and be called a " reverend " man. But if the saving of souls is not the grand interest—the ruling passion—the absorbing thought of his heart,—he is no true minister of the Gospel: he is a hireling, and not a shepherd. Congregations may have called him,—but he is not called by the Holy Ghost. Bishops may have ordained him,—but not Christ.

For what purpose do men suppose that ministers are sent forth ? Is it merely to wear a surplice,—and read the services,—and preach a certain number of sermons ? Is it merely to administer the sacraments, and officiate at weddings and funerals ? Is it merely to get a comfortable living, and be in a respectable profession ? No, indeed ! we are sent forth for other ends than these. We are sent to turn men from darkness to light, and from the power of Satan unto God. We are sent to persuade men to flee from the wrath to come. We are sent to draw men from the service of the world to the service of God,—to awaken the sleeping,—to arouse the careless,—and "by all means to save some." (1 Cor. ix. 22.)

Think not that all is done when we have set up regular services, and persuaded people to attend them. Think not that all is done, when full congregations are gathered, and the Lord's table is crowded, and the parish school is filled. We want to see manifest work of the Spirit among people,—an evident sense of sin,—a lively faith in Christ, —a decided change of heart,—a distinct separation from the world,—a holy walk with God. In one word, *we want to see souls saved*; and we are fools and impostors,—blind leaders of the blind,—if we rest satisfied with anything less.

After all the grand object of having a religion is *to be saved*. This is the great question that we have to settle with our consciences. The matter for our consideration is not whether we go to church or chapel,—whether we go through certain forms and ceremonies,—whether we observe certain days, and perform a certain number of religious duties. The matter is whether, after all, we shall be "*saved*." Without this all our religious doings are weariness and labour in vain.

Never, never let us be content with anything short of a *saving* religion. Surely to be satisfied with a religion which neither gives peace in life, nor hope in death, nor glory in the world to come, is childish folly.

II. Let me, in the second place, *point out the mistakes which are common in the world about the number of the saved.*

I need not go far for evidence on this subject. I will speak of things which every man may see with his own eyes, and hear with his own ears.

I will try to show that there is a wide-spread delusion abroad about this matter, and that this very delusion is one of the greatest dangers to which our souls are exposed.

(a) What then do men generally think about the spiritual state of others *while they are alive?* What do they think of the souls of their relations, and friends, and neighbours, and acquaintances? Let us just see how that question can be answered.

They know that all around them are going to die, and to be judged. They know that they have souls to be lost or saved. And what, to all appearance, do they consider their end is likely to be?

Do they think those around them are in danger of hell? There is nothing whatever to show they think so. They eat and drink together; they laugh, and talk, and walk, and work together. They seldom or never speak to one another of God and eternity,—of heaven and of hell. I ask any one, who knows the world, as in the sight of God, is it not so?

Will they allow that anybody is wicked or ungodly? Never, hardly, whatever may be his way of life. He may be a breaker of the Sabbath; he may be a neglecter of the Bible; he may be utterly without evidence of true religion. No matter! His friends will often tell you, that he may not make so much profession as some, but that he has a "good heart" at the bottom, and is not a wicked man. I ask any one, who knows the world, as in God's sight, is it not so?

And what does all this prove? It proves that men flatter themselves there is no great difficulty in getting to heaven. It proves plainly that men are of opinion that most persons will be saved.

(*b*) But what do men generally think about the spiritual state of others *after they are dead?* Let us just see how this question can be answered.

Men allow, if they are not infidels, that all who die have gone to a place of happiness, or of misery. And to which of these two places do they seem to think the greater part of persons go, when they leave this world?

I say, without fear of contradiction, that there is an unhappily common fashion of speaking well of the condition of all who have departed this life. It matters little, apparently, how a man has behaved while he lived. He may have given no signs of repentance, or faith in Christ; he may have been ignorant of the plan of salvation set forth in the Gospel; he may have shown no evidence whatever of conversion or sanctification; he may have lived and died like a creature without a soul. And yet, as soon as this man is dead, people will dare to say that he is "probably happier than ever he was in his life." They will tell you complacently, they "hope he is gone to a better world." They will shake their heads gravely, and say they "hope he is in heaven." They will follow him to the grave without fear and trembling, and speak of his death afterwards as "a blessed change for him." They may have disliked him, and thought him a bad man while he was alive; but the moment he is dead they turn round in their opinions and say they trust he is gone to heaven! I have no wish to hurt any one's feelings. I only ask any one, who knows the world,—Is it not true?

And what does it all prove? It just supplies one more awful proof that men are determined to believe it is an easy business to get to heaven. Men will have it that most persons are saved.

(*c*) But again, what do men generally *think of ministers* who preach fully the doctrines of the New Testament? Let us see how this question can be answered.

Send a clergyman into a parish who shall "declare all the

counsel of God," and "keep back nothing that is profitable."
Let him be one who shall clearly proclaim justification
by faith,—regeneration by the Spirit,—and holiness of
life. Let him be one who shall draw the line distinctly
between the converted and the unconverted, and give both
to sinners and to saints their portion. Let him frequently
produce out of the New Testament a plain, unanswerable description of the true Christian's character. Let
him show that no man who does not possess that character
can have any reasonable hope of being saved. Let him
constantly press that description on the consciences of
his hearers, and urge upon them repeatedly that every
soul who dies without that character will be lost. Let
him do this, ably and affectionately, and after all, what
will the result be ?

The result will be, that while some few repent and are
saved, the great majority of his hearers will not receive
and believe his doctrine. They may not oppose him
publicly. They may even esteem him, and respect him as
an earnest, sincere, kind-hearted man, who means well. But
they will go no further. He may show them the express
words of Christ and His Apostles ; he may quote text upon
text, and passage upon passage : it will be to no purpose.
The great majority of his hearers will think him "too
strict," and "too close," and "too particular." They will
say among themselves, that the world is not so bad as the
minister seems to think,—and that people cannot be so
good as the minister wants them to be,—and that after
all, they hope they shall be all right at the last ! I appeal
to any minister of the Gospel, who has been any length
of time in the ministry, whether I am not stating the
truth. Are not these things so ?

And what does it prove ? It just makes one more
proof that men generally are resolved to think that
salvation is not a very hard business, and that after all
most people will be saved.

Now what solid reason can men show us for these common opinions? Upon what Scripture do they build this notion, that salvation is an easy business, and that most people will be saved? What revelation of God can they show us, to satisfy us that these opinions are sound and true?

They have none,—literally none at all. They have not a text of Scripture which, fairly interpreted, supports their views. They have not a reason which will bear examination. They speak smooth things about one another's spiritual state, just because they do not like to allow there is danger. They build up one another into an easy, self-satisfied state of soul, in order to soothe their consciences and make things pleasant. They cry "Peace, peace," over one another's graves, because they want it to be so, and would fain persuade themselves that so it is. Surely against such hollow, foundationless opinons as these, a minister of the Gospel may well protest.

The plain truth is that the world's opinion is worth nothing in matters of religion. About the price of an ox, or a horse, or a farm, or the value of labour,—about wages and work,—about money, cotton, coals, iron and corn, —about arts, and sciences, and manufactures,—about railways, and commerce, and trade, and politics,—about all such things the men of the world may give a correct opinion. But we must beware, if we love life, of being guided by man's judgment in the things that concern salvation. "The natural man receiveth not the things of the Spirit of God, for they are foolishness unto him." (1 Cor. ii. 14.)

Let us remember, above all, that it never will do to think as others do, if we want to get to heaven. No doubt it is easy work to "go with the crowd" in religious matters. It will save us much trouble to swim with the stream and tide. We shall be spared much ridicule: we shall be freed from much unpleasantness. But let us remember, once for all, that the world's mistakes about salvation are many and dangerous. Unless we are on our guard against them we shall never be saved.

III. Let me show, in the third place, *what the Bible says about the number of the saved.*

There is only one standard of truth and error to which we ought to appeal. That standard is the Holy Scripture. Whatsoever is there written we must receive and believe: whatsoever cannot be proved by Scripture we ought to refuse.

Can any reader of this paper subscribe to this? If he cannot, there is little chance of his being moved by any words of mine. If he can, let him give me his attention for a few moments, and I will tell him some solemn things.

Let us look, then, for one thing, at one single text of Scripture, and examine it well. We shall find it in Matthew vii. 13, 14:—"Enter ye in at the strait gate: for wide is the gate, and broad is the way that leadeth to destruction, and many there be which go in thereat: because strait is the gate, and narrow is the way which leadeth unto life, and *few there be that find it.*" Now these are the words of our Lord Jesus Christ. They are the words of Him who was very God, and whose words shall never pass away. They are the words of Him who knew what was in man,—who knew things to come, and things past,—who knew that He should judge all men at the last day. And what do those words mean? Are they words which no man can understand without a knowledge of Hebrew or Greek? No: they are not! Are they a dark, unfulfilled prophecy, like the visions in Revelation, or the description of Ezekiel's temple? No: they are not! Are they a deep mysterious saying, which no human intellect can fathom? No: they are not! The words are clear, plain, and unmistakable. Ask any labouring man who can read, and he will tell you so. There is only one meaning which can be attached to them. Their meaning is, that many people will be lost, and few will be found saved.

Let us look, in the next place, at the whole history of mankind as respects religion, as we have it given in the Bible. Let us go through the whole four thousand years, over which the history of the Bible reaches. Let us find, if we can, one single period of time at which godly people were many, and ungodly people were few.

How was it in the *days of Noah?* The earth we are told expressly was "filled with violence." The imagination of man's heart was only " evil continually." (Gen. vi. 5, 12.) " All flesh had corrupted his way." The loss of paradise was forgotten. The warnings of God, by Noah's mouth, were despised. And at length, when the flood came on the world and drowned every living thing, there were but eight people who had faith enough to flee for refuge to the ark! And were there many saved in those days? Let any honest reader of the Bible give an answer to that question. There can be no doubt what the answer must be.

How was it in the *days of Abraham, and Isaac, and Lot?* It is evident that in the matter of religion they stood very much alone. The family from which they were taken was a family of idolaters. The nations among whom they lived were sunk in gross darkness and sin. When Sodom and Gomorrah were burned there were not five righteous people to be found in the four cities of the plain. When Abraham and Isaac desired to find wives for their sons, there was not a woman in the land where they sojourned to whom they could wish to see them married. And were there many saved in those days? Let any honest reader of the Bible give an answer to that question. There can be no doubt what the answer must be.

How was it with Israel in the *days of the Judges?* No

one can read the book of Judges, and not be struck with
the sad examples of man's corruption which it affords.
Time after time we are told of the people forsaking God,
and following idols. In spite of the plainest warnings,
they joined affinity with the Canaanites, and learned their
works. Time after time we read of their being oppressed
by foreign kings, because of their sins, and then miraculously delivered. Time after time we read of the deliverance being forgotten, and of the people returning to their
former sins, like the sow that is washed to her wallowing
in the mire. And were there many saved in those days?
Let any honest reader of the Bible give an answer to that
question. There can be no doubt what the answer
must be.

How was it with Israel in the *days of the Kings?*
From Saul, the first king, down to Zedekiah, the last king,
their history is a melancholy account of backsliding, and
declension, and idolatry,—with a few bright exceptional
periods. Even under the best kings there seems to have
been a vast amount of unbelief and ungodliness, which only
lay hid for a season, and burst out at the first favourable
opportunity. Over and over again we find that under the
most zealous kings " the high places were not taken away."
Mark how even David speaks of the state of things around
him: " Help, Lord, for the godly man ceaseth ; for the
faithful fail from among the children of men." (Psalm xii.
1.) Mark how Isaiah describes the condition of Judah
and Jerusalem : " The whole head is sick, and the whole
heart faint. From the sole of the foot, even unto the
crown of the head, there is no soundness in it."—" Except the Lord of Hosts had left unto us a very small
remnant, we should have been as Sodom, and should have
been like unto Gomorrah." (Isaiah i. 5—9.) Mark how
Jeremiah describes his time : " Run ye to and fro through
the streets of Jerusalem, and see now, and know, and seek
in the broad places thereof, if ye can find a man, if there

be any that executeth judgment, that seeketh the truth, and I will pardon it." (Jer. v. 1.) Mark how Ezekiel speaks of the men of his times: "The word of the Lord came unto me, saying, Son of man, the house of Israel is to me become dross: all they are brass, and iron, and tin and lead in the midst of the furnace: they are even the dross of silver." (Ezek. xxii. 17, 18.) Mark what he says in the sixteenth and twenty-third chapters of his prophecy about the kingdoms of Judah and Israel. And were there many saved in those days? Let any honest reader of the Bible give an answer to that question. There can be no doubt what the answer must be.

How was it with the Jews *when our Lord Jesus Christ was on earth?* The words of Saint John are the best account of their spiritual state: "He came unto His own, and His own received Him not." (John i. 11.) He lived as no one born of woman had ever lived before,—a blameless, harmless, holy life. "He went about doing good." (Acts x. 38.) He preached as no one ever preached before. Even the officers of his enemies confessed, "Never man spake like this man." (John vii. 46.) He did miracles to confirm His ministry, which, at first sight, we might have fancied would have convinced the most hardened. But, notwithstanding all this, the vast majority of the Jews refused to believe Him. Follow our Lord in all His travels over Palestine, and you will always find the same story. Follow Him into the city, and follow Him into the wilderness; follow Him to Capernaum and Nazareth, and follow Him to Jerusalem; follow Him among Scribes and Pharisees, and follow Him among Sadducees and Herodians: everywhere you will arrive at the same result. They were amazed;—they were silenced;—they were astonished;—they wondered;—but very few became disciples! The immense proportion of the nation would have none of His doctrine, and crowned all their wickedness by putting Him to death. And were there

many saved in those days ? Let any honest reader of the
Bible give an answer to that question. There can be no
doubt what the answer must be.

How was it with the world in the *days of the Apostles?*
If ever there was a period when true religion flourished
it was then. Never did the Holy Ghost call into the fold
of Christ so many souls in the same space of time.
Never were there so many conversions under the preaching
of the Gospel as when Paul and his fellow-labourers were
the preachers. But still, it is plain from the Acts of the
Apostles, that true Christianity was "everywhere spoken
against." (Acts xxviii. 22.) It is evident that in every city,
even in Jerusalem itself, true Christians were a small
minority. We read of perils of all kinds which the
Apostles had to go through,—not only perils from without,
but perils from within,—not only perils from the heathen,
but perils from false brethren. We hardly read of a
single city visited by Paul where he was not in danger
from open violence and persecution. We see plainly, by
some of his epistles, that the professing Churches were
mixed bodies, in which there were many rotten members.
We find him telling the Philippians a painful part of his
experience,—" Many walk, of whom I tell you, even weeping, that they are the enemies of the cross of Christ;
whose end is destruction, whose god is their belly, and
whose glory is their shame, who mind earthly things."
(Philip. iii. 18, 19.) And were there many saved in those
days ? Let any honest reader of the Bible give an answer
to this question. There can be no doubt what that answer
must be.

I ask any honest-minded unprejudiced reader of the
volume to weigh well the lessons of the Bible which I
have just brought forward. Surely they are weighty and
solemn, and deserve serious attention.

Let no one think to evade their force by saying that
the Bible only tells the story of the Jews. Think not to

comfort yourself by saying that "perhaps the Jews were more wicked than other nations, and many people were probably saved among other nations, though few were saved among the Jews." You forget that this argument tells against you. You forget that the Jews had light and privileges which the Gentiles had not, and with all their sins and faults, were probably the holiest and most moral nation upon earth. As to the moral state of people among the Assyrians, and Egyptians, and Greeks, and Romans, it is fearful to think what it must have been. But this we may be sure of,—that if many were ungodly among the Jews, the number was far greater among the Gentiles. If few were saved in the green tree, alas, how much fewer must have been saved in the dry!

The sum of the whole matter is this: the Bible and the men of the world speak very differently about the number of the saved. According to the Bible, few will be saved: according to the men of the world, many.— According to the men of the world few are going to hell: according to the Bible few are going to heaven.—According to the men of the world salvation is an easy business: according to the Bible the way is narrow and the gate is strait.—According to the men of the world few will be found at last seeking admission into heaven when too late: according to the Bible many will be in that sad condition, and will cry in vain, "Lord, Lord, open to us." Yet the Bible was never wrong yet. The most unlikely and improbable prophecies about Tyre, Egypt, Babylon, and Nineveh, have all come true to the letter. And as in other matters, so it will be about the number of the saved. The Bible will prove quite right and the men of the world quite wrong.

IV. *Let me show, in the last place, some plain facts about the number of the saved.*

I ask particular attention to this part of the subject.

I know well that people flatter themselves that the world
is far better and wiser than it was 1800 years ago. We
have churches, and schools, and books. We have civili-
zation, and liberty, and good laws. We have a far higher
standard of morality in society than that which once
prevailed. We have the power of obtaining comforts and
enjoyments which our forefathers knew nothing of. Steam,
and gas, and electricity, and chemistry, have effected
wonders for us. All this is perfectly true. I see it, and
I am thankful. But all this does not diminish the importance of the question ;—*Are there few or many of us
likely to be saved ?*

I am thoroughly satisfied that the importance of this
question is painfully overlooked. I am persuaded that the
views of most people about the quantity of unbelief and
sin in the world, are utterly inadequate and incorrect.
I am convinced that very few people, whether ministers or
private Christians, at all realize how few there are in a way
to be saved. I want to draw attention to the subject,
and I will therefore bring forward a few plain facts about
it.

But where shall I go for these facts ? I might easily
turn to the millions of heathen, who in various parts of
the world are worshipping they know not what. But I
shall not do so.—I might easily turn to the millions of
Mahometans who honour the Koran more than the Bible,
and the false prophet of Mecca more than Christ. But I
shall not do so.—I might easily turn to the millions of
Roman Catholics who are making the Word of God of
none effect by their traditions. But I shall not do so.
I shall look nearer home. I shall draw my facts from the
land in which I live, and then ask every honest reader
whether it be not strictly true that *few are saved.*

I invite any intelligent reader of these pages to imagine
himself in any parish in Protestant England or Scotland
at this day. Choose which you please, a town parish,

or a country parish,—a great parish or a small. Let us
take our New Testaments in our hands. Let us sift
the Christianity of the inhabitants of this parish, family
by family, and man by man. Let us put on one side
any one who does not possess the New Testament
evidence of being a true Christian. Let us deal honestly
and fairly in the investigation, and not allow any one
to be a true Christian who does not come up to the
New Testament standard of faith and practice. Let
us count every man a saved soul in whom we see something of Christ,—some evidence of true repentance,—
some evidence of saving faith in Jesus,—some evidence
of real evangelical holiness. Let us reject every man in
whom, on the most charitable construction, we cannot
see these evidences, as one "weighed in the balances, and
found wanting." Let us apply this sifting process to any
parish in this land, and see what the result would be.

(a) Let us set aside, first of all, those persons in a parish
who are *living in any kind of open sin.* By these I
mean such as fornicators, and adulterers, and liars, and
thieves, and drunkards, and cheats, and revilers, and
extortioners. About these I think there can be no difference
of opinion. The Bible says plainly, that "they which do
such things, shall not inherit the kingdom of God." (Gal.
v. 21.) Now will these persons be saved? The answer is
clear to my own mind: In their present condition they
will not.

(b) Let us set aside, in the next place, those persons who
are *Sabbath-breakers.* I mean by this expression, those who
seldom or never go to a place of worship, though they have
the power,—those who do not give the Sabbath to God,
but to themselves,—those who think of nothing but doing
their own ways, and finding their own pleasure upon
Sundays. They show plainly that they are not meet for
heaven! The inhabitants of heaven would be company
they could not like. The employments of heaven would

be a weariness to them, and not a joy. Now will these
persons be saved? The answer is clear to my mind: In
their present condition they will not.

(c) Let us set aside, in the next place, all those persons
who are *careless and thoughtless Christians.* I mean by
this expression, those who attend many of the outward
ordinances of religion, but show no signs of taking any real
interest in its doctrines and substance. They care little
whether the minister preaches the Gospel or not. They care
little whether they hear a good sermon or not. They would
care little if all the Bibles in the world were burned. They
would care little if an Act of Parliament were passed for-
bidding any one to pray. In short, religion is not the " one
thing needful" with them. Their treasure is on earth.
They are just like Gallio, to whom it mattered little
whether people were Jews or Christians: he "cared for
none of these things." (Acts xviii. 17.) Now will these
persons be saved? The answer is clear to my own mind:
In their present condition they will not.

(d) Let us set aside, in the next place, all those who are
formalists and self-righteous. I mean by this expression,
those who value themselves on their own regularity in the
use of the forms of Christianity, and depend either directly
or indirectly on their own doings for their acceptance with
God. I mean all who rest their souls on any work but
the work of Christ, or any righteousness but the righteousness of Christ. Of such the Apostle Paul has expressly
testified, "By the deeds of the law shall no flesh living be
justified."—"Other foundation can no man lay than that
is laid, which is Jesus Christ." (Rom. iii. 20; 1 Cor. iii. 11.)
And dare we say, in the face of such texts, that such as
these will be saved? The answer is plain to my own
mind: In their present condition they will not.

(e) Let us set aside, in the next place, all those who *know
the Gospel with their heads, but do not obey it with their
hearts.* These are those unhappy persons who have eyes

to see the way of life, but have not will or courage to walk
in it. They approve sound doctrine. They will not listen
to preaching which does not contain it. But the fear of man,
or the cares of the world, or the love of money, or the
dread of offending relations, perpetually holds them back.
They will not come out boldly, and take up the cross, and
confess Christ before men. Of these also the Bible speaks
expressly: "Faith, if it hath not works, is dead, being alone."
—"To him that knoweth to do good, and doeth it not, to
him it is sin."—"If any man is ashamed of Me and of
my words, of him will the Son of man be ashamed when
He shall come in His own glory, and in His Father's, and
of the holy angels." (James ii. 17; iv. 17; Luke ix. 26.)
Shall we say that such as these will be saved? The
answer is clear to my own mind: In their present condition
they will not.

(ƒ) Let us set aside, in the last place, all those who are
hypocritical professors. I mean by that expression, all
those whose religion consists in talk and high profession,
and in nothing besides. These are they of whom the
prophet Ezekiel speaks, saying, " With their mouth they
show much love, but their heart goeth after their covetousness."—"They profess that they know God, but in works
they deny Him."—They " have a form of godliness, but
they have not the power " of it. (Ezek. xxxiii. 31; Titus
i. 16; 2 Tim. iii. 5.) They are saints at church, and saints
to talk to in public. But they are not saints in private, and
in their own homes; and worst of all, they are not saints in
heart. There can be no dispute about such persons. Shall
we say that they will be saved? There can only be one
answer: In their present condition they will not.

And now, after setting aside these classes which I have
described, I ask any sensible thinking reader to tell me
how many persons in any parish in England will there be
left behind? How many, after sifting a parish thoroughly
and honestly,—how many men and women will remain

who are in a way to be saved ?   How many true penitents,
—how many real believers in Christ,—how many truly holy
people will there be found ?   I put it to the conscience of
every reader of this volume to give an honest answer, as
in the sight of God.   I ask you whether, after sifting a
parish with the Bible in the fashion described, you can
come to any conclusion but this,—that few persons,—sadly
few persons, are in a way to be saved ?

It is a painful conclusion to arrive at, but I know not
how it can be avoided.   It is a fearful and tremendous
thought, that there should be so many churchmen in
England, and so many dissenters, so many seat-holders, and
so many pew-renters, so many hearers, and so many communicants,—and yet, after all, so few in a way to be saved !
But the only question is, Is it not true ?—It is vain to shut
our eyes against facts.   It is useless to pretend not to see
what is going on around us.   The statements of the Bible
and the facts of the world we live in will lead us to the
same conclusion : *Many are being lost, and few being
saved !*

(*a*) I know well that many do not believe what I am
saying, because they *think there is an immense quantity of
death-bed repentance.*   They flatter themselves that multitudes who do not live religious lives will yet die religious
deaths.   They take comfort in the thought that vast
numbers of persons turn to God in their last illness and
are saved at the eleventh hour.   I will only remind such
persons that all the experience of ministers is utterly
against the theory.   People generally die just as they have
lived.   True repentance is never too late :—but repentance
deferred to the last hours of life is seldom true.   A man's
life is the surest evidence of his spiritual state, and if lives
are to be witnesses, then few are likely to be saved.

(*b*) I know well that many do not believe what I am
saying, because *they fancy it contradicts the mercy of God.*
They dwell on the love to sinners which the Gospel reveals.

They point to the offers of pardon and forgiveness which abound in the Bible. They ask us if we maintain, in the face of all this, that only few people will be saved. I answer, I will go as far as any one in exalting God's mercy in Christ, but I cannot shut my eyes against the fact that this mercy profits no man so long as it is wilfully refused. I see nothing wanting, on God's part, for man's salvation. I see room in heaven for the chief of sinners. I see willingness in Christ to receive the most ungodly. I see power in the Holy Ghost to renew the most ungodly. But I see, on the other hand, desperate unbelief in man: he will not believe what God tells him in the Bible. I see desperate pride in man: he will not bow his heart to receive the Gospel as a little child. I see desperate sloth in man: he will not take the trouble to arise and call upon God. I see desperate worldliness in man: he will not loose his hold on the poor perishable things of time, and consider eternity. In short, I see the words of our Lord continually verified: "Ye will not come unto Me, that ye might have life" (John v. 40), and therefore I am driven to the sorrowful conclusion that few are likely to be saved.

(c) I know well that many will not believe what I am saying, because *they refuse to observe the evil there is in the world.* They live in the midst of a little circle of good people: they know little of anything that goes on in the world outside that circle. They tell us the world is a world which is rapidly improving and going on to perfection. They count up on their fingers the number of good ministers whom they have heard and seen in the last year. They call our attention to the number of religious societies, and religious meetings, to the money which is subscribed, to the Bibles and tracts which are being constantly distributed. They ask us if we really dare to say, in the face of all this, that few are in the way to be saved. In reply, I will only remind these amiable

people, that there are other people in the world besides
their own little circle, and other men and women besides
the chosen few whom they know in their own congregation.
I entreat them to open their eyes, and see things as they
really are. I assure them there are things going on in
this country of ours of which they are at present in happy
ignorance. I ask them to sift any parish or congregation
in England, with the Bible, before they condemn me
hastily. I tell them, if they will do this honestly, they
will soon find that I am not far wrong, when I say that
few are likely to be saved.

(d) I know well that many will not believe me, because *they
think such a doctrine very narrow-minded and exclusive.*
I utterly deny the charge. I disclaim any sympathy with
those Christians who condemn everybody outside their
own communion, and appear to shut the door of heaven
against everybody who does not see everything with their
eyes. Whether Roman Catholics, or Episcopalians, or Free
Churchmen, or Baptists, or Plymouth Brethren, whosoever
does anything of this kind, I reckon him an exclusive
man. I have no desire to shut up the kingdom of heaven
against any one. All I say is, that none will enter that
kingdom, except converted, believing, and holy souls; and
all I take on myself to assert is, that both the Bible and
facts combine to prove that such persons are few.

(e) I know well that many will not believe what I am
saying, because they *think it a gloomy, uncharitable
doctrine.* It is easy to make vague, general assertions of
this kind. It is not so easy to show that any doctrine
deserves to be called "gloomy and uncharitable" which is
scriptural and true. There is a spurious charity, I am
afraid, which dislikes all strong statements in religion,—
a charity which would have no one interfered with,—
a charity which would have everyone let alone in his sins,
—a charity which, without evidence, takes for granted
that everybody is in a way to be saved,—a charity which

never doubts that all people are going to heaven, and seems to deny the existence of such a place as hell. But such charity is not the charity of the New Testament, and does not deserve the name. Give me the charity which tries everything by the test of the Bible, and believes nothing and hopes nothing that is not sanctioned by the Word. Give me the charity which St. Paul describes to the Corinthians (1 Cor. xiii. 1, etc.): the charity which is not blind, and deaf, and stupid, but has eyes to see and senses to discern between him that feareth God and him that feareth Him not. Such charity will rejoice in nothing but "the truth," and will confess with sorrow that I tell nothing but the truth when I say that few are likely to be saved.

(*f*) I know well that many will not believe me, because they *think it presumptuous to have any opinion at all about the number of the saved.* But will these people dare to tell us that the Bible has not spoken plainly as to the character of saved souls? And will they dare to say that there is any standard of truth except the Bible? Surely there can be no presumption in asserting that which is agreeable to the Bible. I tell them plainly that the charge of presumption does not lie at my door. I say that he is the truly presumptuous man who, when the Bible has said a thing clearly and unmistakably, refuses to receive it.

(*g*) I know, finally, that many will not believe me, because *they think my statement extravagant, and unwarrantable.* They regard it as a piece of fanaticism, unworthy of the attention of a rational man. They look on ministers who make such assertions, as weak minded persons, and wanting in common sense. I can bear such imputations unmoved. I only ask those who make them to show me some plain proof that they are right and I am wrong. Let them show me, if they can, that anybody is likely to get to heaven whose heart is not renewed, who is not a

believer in Jesus Christ, who is not a spiritually-minded
and holy man.   Let them show me, if they can, that people
of this description are many, compared with those who
are not.   Let them, in one word, point to any place on
EARTH where the great majority of the people are not
ungodly, and the truly godly are not a little flock.   Let
them do this, and I will grant they have done right to
disbelieve what I have said.   Till they do this, I must
maintain the sorrowful conclusion, that few persons are
likely to be saved.

And now it only remains to make some practical application of the subject of this paper.   I have set forth as
plainly as I can the character of saved people.—I have
shown the painful delusions of the world as to the number
of the saved.—I have brought forward the evidence of the
Bible on the subject.—I have drawn from the world
around us plain facts in confirmation of the statements I
have made.—May the Lord grant that all these solemn
truths may not have been exhibited in vain!

I am quite aware that I have said many things in this
paper which are likely to give offence.   I know it.   It
must be so.   The point which it handles is far too
serious and heart-searching to be otherwise than offensive to some.   But I have long had a deep conviction
that the subject has been painfully neglected, and that
few things are so little realized as the comparative
numbers of the lost and saved.   All that I have written,
I have written because I firmly believe it to be God's truth.
All that I have said, I have said, not as an enemy but
as a lover of souls.   You do not count him an enemy who
gives you a bitter medicine to save your life.   You do not
count him an enemy who shakes you roughly from your
sleep when your house is on fire.   Surely you will not
count me an enemy because I tell you strong truths for
the benefit of your soul.   I appeal, as a friend, to every

man or woman into whose hands this volume has come. Bear with me, for a few moments, while I say a few last words to impress the whole subject on your conscience.

(a) Are there few saved? Then, *shall you be one of the few?* Oh, that you would see that salvation is the one thing needful! Health, and riches, and titles, are not needful things. A man may gain heaven without them. But what shall the man do who dies not saved! Oh, that you would see that you must have salvation now, in this present life, and lay hold upon it for your own soul! Oh, that you would see that "saved" or "not saved" is the grand question in religion! High Church or Low Church, Churchman or Dissenter, all these are trifling questions in comparison. What a man needs in order to get to heaven is an actual personal interest in Christ's salvation. Surely, if you are not saved, it will be better at last never to have been born.

(b) Are there few saved? Then, *if you are not one of the few already, strive to be one without delay.* I know not who and what you are, but I say boldly, Come to Christ and you shall be saved. The gate that leads to life may be strait, but it was wide enough to admit Manasseh, and Saul of Tarsus, and why not you? The way that leads to life may be narrow, but it is marked by the footsteps of thousands of sinners like yourself. All have found it a good way. All have persevered, and got safe home at last. Jesus Christ invites you. The promises of the Gospel encourage you. Oh, strive to enter in without delay!

(c) Are there few saved? Then, *if you are doubtful whether you are one of the few, make sure work at once, and be doubtful no more.* Leave no stone unturned in order to ascertain your own spiritual state. Be not content with vague hopes and trusts. Rest not on warm feelings and temporary desires after God. Give diligence to make your calling and election sure. Oh, give me leave to say, that if you are content to live on uncertain about salvation, you live the maddest life in the world! The fires of hell are before you, and you are uncertain whether your soul is insured. This world below must soon be left, and you are uncertain whether you have a mansion prepared to receive you in the world above. The judgment will soon be set, and you are uncertain whether you have an Advocate to plead your cause. Eternity will soon begin, and you are uncertain whether you are prepared to meet God. Oh, sit down this day, and study the subject of salvation! Give God no rest till uncertainty has disappeared, and you have got hold of a reasonable hope that you are saved.

(d) Are there few that be saved? Then, *if you are one, be thankful.* Chosen and called of God, while thousands around you are sunk in unbelief,—seeing the kingdom of God, while multitudes around you are utterly blind,—delivered from this present evil world, while crowds are overcome by its love and fear—taught to know sin, and God, and Christ, while numbers, to all appearance as good as you, live in ignorance and darkness, —Oh, you have reason every day to bless and praise God! Whence came this sense of sin, which you now experience? Whence came this love of Christ,—this desire after holiness,—this hungering after righteousness, —this delight in the Word? Has not free grace done it, while many a companion of your youth still knows nothing about it, or has been cut off in his sins? You ought indeed to bless God! Surely Whitefield might well say, that one anthem among the saints in heaven will be "Why me, Lord? Why didst Thou choose me?"

(e) Are there few that be saved? Then, *if you are one, do not wonder that you often find yourself standing alone.* I dare believe you are sometimes almost brought to a standstill, by the corruption and wickedness that you see in the world around you. You see false doctrine abounding. You see unbelief and ungodliness of every description. You are sometimes tempted to say, " Can I really be in the right in my religion? Can it really be that all these people are in the wrong ? " Beware of giving way to thoughts like these. Remember, you are only having practical proof of the truth of your Master's sayings. Think not that His purposes are being defeated. Think not that His work is not going forward in the world. He is still taking out a people to His praise. He is still raising up witnesses to Himself, here and there, all over the world. The saved will yet be found to be a " multitude that no man can number," when all are gathered together at last. (Rev. vii. 9.) The earth will yet be filled with the knowledge of the Lord. All nations shall serve Him : all kings shall yet delight to do Him honour. But the night is not yet spent. The day of the Lord's power is yet to come. In the mean time all is going on as He foretold 1800 years ago. Many are being lost and few saved.

(f) Are there few saved ? Then, *if you are one, do not be afraid of having too much religion.* Settle it down in your mind that you will aim at the highest degree of holiness, and spiritual-mindedness, and consecration to God,—that you will not be content with any low degree of sanctification. Resolve that, by the grace of God, you will make Christianity beautiful in the eyes of the world. Remember that the children of the world have but few patterns of true religion before them. Endeavour, as far as in you lies, to make those few patterns recommend the service of your Master. Oh, that every true Christian would recollect that he is set as a lighthouse in the midst of a dark world, and would labour so to live that every part of him may reflect light, and no side be dim !

(g) Are there few saved ? Then, *if you are one, use every opportunity of trying to do good to souls.* Settle it down in your mind that the vast majority of

people around you are in awful danger of being lost for
ever. Work every engine for bringing the Gospel to bear
upon them. Help every Christian machinery for plucking
brands from the burning. Give liberally to every Society
which has for its object to spread the everlasting Gospel.
Throw all your influence heartily and unreservedly into
the cause of doing good to souls. Live like one who
thoroughly believes that time is short and eternity near,—
the devil strong and sin abounding,—the darkness very
great and the light very small,—the ungodly very many
and the godly very few,—the things of the world mere
transitory shadows, and heaven and hell the great substantial realities. Alas, indeed, for the lives that many
believers live! How cold are many, and how frozen,—
how slow to do decided things in religion, and how afraid
of going *too far*,—how backward to attempt anything new,
—how ready to discourage a good movement,—how in-
genious in discovering reasons why it is best to sit still,—
how unwilling ever to allow that "the time" for active exertion is come,—how wise in finding fault,—how shiftless in
devising plans to meet growing evils! Truly a man might
sometimes fancy, when he looks at the ways of many who
are counted believers, that all the world was going to
heaven, and hell was nothing but a lie.

Let us all beware of this state of mind! Whether
we like to believe it or not, hell is filling fast,—Christ is
daily holding out His hand to a disobedient people,—many
many are in the way to destruction,—few, few are in the
way to life. Many, many are likely to be lost. Few, few
are likely to be saved.

Once more I ask every reader, as I asked at the
beginning of this paper,—*Shall you be saved?* If you are
not saved already, my heart's desire and prayer to God is,
that you may seek salvation without delay. If you are
saved, my desire is that you may live like a saved soul,—
and like one who knows that saved souls are few.

IV

OUR HOPE!

"Good hope through grace."—2 Thess. ii. 16.

"I HOPE," is a very common expression. Everybody can say, "I hope." About no subject is the expression used so commonly as it is about religion. Nothing is more frequent than to hear men turn off some home-thrust at conscience by this convenient form of words, "I hope." —"I hope it will be all right at last."—"I hope I shall be a better man some day."—"I hope we shall all get to heaven."—But why do they hope? On what is their hope built? Too often they cannot tell you! Too often it is a mere excuse for avoiding a disagreeable subject. "Hoping," they live on. "Hoping," they grow old. "Hoping," they die at last,—and find too often that they are lost for ever in hell.

I ask the serious attention of all who read this paper. The subject is one of the deepest importance: "We are saved by hope." (Rom. viii. 24.) Let us, then, make sure that our hope is sound.—Have we a hope that our sins are pardoned, our hearts renewed, and our souls at peace with God? Then let us see to it that our hope is "good," and "lively," and one "that maketh not ashamed." (2 Thess. ii. 16; 1 Pet. i. 3; Rom. v. 5.) Let us consider our ways. Let us not shrink from honest, searching inquiry into the condition of our souls. If our hope is good examination will do it no harm. If our hope is bad, it is high time to know it, and to seek a better.

There are five marks of a really "good hope." I desire to place them before my readers in order. Let us ask ourselves what we know of them. Let us prove our own state by them. Happy is he who can say of each of these marks,—"I know it by experience. This is my hope about my soul."

I. In the first place, a good hope is *a hope that a man can explain.* What saith the Scripture? "Be ready always to give an answer to every man that asketh you a reason of the hope that is in you." (1 Pet. iii. 15.)

If our hope is sound we must be able to give some account of it. We must be able to show why, and wherefore, and on what grounds, and for what reason we expect to go to heaven when we die. Now can we do this?

Let no one misunderstand my meaning. I do not say that deep learning and great *knowledge* are absolutely needful to salvation. A man may know twenty languages, and have the whole body of divinity at his fingers' ends, and yet be lost; a man may be unable to read, and have a very weak understanding, and yet be saved. But I do say that a man must know *what* his hope is, and be able to tell us its nature. I cannot believe that a man has got possession of a thing if he knows nothing about it.

Once more, let no one misunderstand my meaning. I do not say that a power of *talking* well is necessary to salvation. There may be many fine words on a man's lips, and not a whit of grace in his heart; there may be few and stammering words, and yet deep feeling within, planted there by the Holy Ghost. There are some who cannot speak many words for Christ, and yet would die for Him. But for all this, I do say that the man who has a good hope ought to be able to tell us why. If he can tell us no more than this, that "he feels himself a

sinner, and has no hope but in Christ," it is something.
But if he can tell us nothing at all, I must suspect that
he has got no real hope.

I am aware that the opinion just expressed displeases
many. Thousands can see no necessity for that clear
knowledge which I believe to be essential to a saving
hope. So long as a man goes to church on Sunday, and
has his children baptized, they think we ought to be
content. "Knowledge," they tell us, "may be very well
for clergymen and professors of theology; but it is too
much to require it of common men."

My answer to all such people is short and simple. Where
in the whole New Testament shall we find that men were
called Christians, unless they knew something of Christianity? Will any one try to persuade me that a Corinthian
Christian, or a Colossian, or Thessalonian, or Philippian, or
Ephesian, could not have told us what was his hope about
his soul? Let those believe it who will: I, for one, cannot. I believe that in requiring a man to know the ground
of his hope I am only setting up the standard of the New
Testament. Ignorance may suit a Roman Catholic well
enough. He belongs to what he considers to be the true
Church! He does as his priest tells him! He asks no
more!—But ignorance ought never to be the characteristic
of a Protestant Christian. He ought to know what he
believes, and if he does not know he is in a bad way.

I ask every reader of this paper to search his heart,
and see how the matter stands with his soul. Can you
tell us nothing more than this, that "you hope to be
saved"? Can you give no explanation of the grounds of
your confidence? Can you show us nothing more satisfactory than your own vague expectation? If this be the
case you are in imminent peril of being lost for ever.
Like Ignorance, in Pilgrim's Progress, you may get to your
journey's end, and be ferried by Vainhope over the river,
without much trouble. But, like Ignorance, you may find

to your sorrow that there is no admission for you into the celestial city. None enter in there but those who " know what as well as whom they have believed." *

I lay down this principle as a starting point, and I ask my readers to consider it well. I admit most fully that there are different degrees of grace among true Christians. I do not forget that there are many in the family of God whose faith is very weak, and whose hope is very small. But I believe confidently, that the standard of require-ment I have set up is not a whit too high. I believe that the man who has a "good hope" will always be able to give some account of it.

II. In the second place, a good hope is a *hope that is drawn from Scripture*. What says David ? " I hope

---

* " Now, while I was gazing upon all these things, I turned my head to look back, and saw Ignorance coming up to the river side : but he soon got over, and that without half the difficulty which the other two men met with. For it happened that there was then in that place one Vain-hope, a ferry-man, that with his boat helped him over ; so he, as the other I saw, did ascend the hill to come up to the gate, only he came alone ; neither did any man meet him with the least encouragement. When he was come up to the gate, he looked up to the writing that was above, and then began to knock, supposing that entrance should have been quickly administered to him. But he was asked by the man that looked over the top of the gate, 'Whence come you ? And what would you have ?' He answered, 'I have ate and drank in the presence of the King, and He has taught in our streets.' Then they asked him for his certificate, that they might go in and show it to the King. So he fumbled in his bosom for one, and found none. Then said they, ' Have you none ?' But the man answered never a word.

" So they told the King ; but He would not come down to see him, but commanded the two shining ones that conducted Christian and Hopeful to the City, to take Ignorance and bind him hand and foot, and have him away. Then they took him up, and carried him through the air to the door that I saw in the side of the hill, and put him in there. Then I saw that there was a way to hell, even from the gate of heaven, as well as from the city of destruction."—*Bunyan's Pilgrim's Progress.*

in Thy word."—" Remember the word unto Thy servant, upon which Thou hast caused me to hope." What says St. Paul? "Whatsoever things were written aforetime, were written for our learning, that we through patience and comfort of the Scriptures might have hope." (Psalm cxix. 81, 49. Rom. xv. 4.)

If our hope is sound we ought to be able to turn to some text, or fact, or doctrine of God's Word, as the source of it. Our confidence must arise from something which God has caused to be written in the Bible for our learning, and which our heart has received and believed.

It is not enough to have *good feelings* about the state of our souls. We may flatter ourselves that all is right, and that we are going to heaven when we die, and yet have nothing to show for our expectations but mere fancy and imagination. "The heart is deceitful above all things."—" He that trusteth in his own heart is a fool." (Jer. xvii. 9. Prov. xxviii, 26.)—I have frequently heard dying people say that "they felt quite happy and ready to go." I have heard them say that "they felt as if they craved nothing in this world." And all this time I have remarked that they were profoundly ignorant of Scripture, and seemed unable to lay firm hold on a single truth of the Gospel! I never can feel comfort about such people. I am persuaded that there is something wrong in their condition. Good feelings without some warrant of Scripture do not make up a good hope.

It is not enough to have the *good opinion of others* about the state of our souls. We may be told by others on our death beds, to "keep up our spirits," and "not to be afraid." We may be reminded that we have "lived good lives,—or had a good heart,—or done nobody any harm,—or not been so bad as many;" and all this time our friends may not bring forward a word of Scripture, and may be feeding us on poison. Such friends are miserable comforters. However well meaning, they are downright enemies to our souls. The good opinion of others, without the warrant of God's Word, will never make up a good hope.

If a man would know the soundness of his own hope, let him search and look within his heart for some text or doctrine, or fact out of God's book. There will always be some one or more on which your soul hangs, if you are a true child of God. The dying thief in London, who was visited by a City Missionary, and found utterly ignorant of Christianity, laid hold on one single fact in a chapter of St. Luke's Gospel which was read to him, and found comfort in it. That fact was the story of the penitent thief. "Sir," he said, when visited the second time, "are there any more thieves in that book from which you read yesterday?"—The dying Hindoo who was found by a missionary on a roadside, had grasped one single text in the First Epistle of St. John, and found in it peace. That text was the precious saying, "The blood of Jesus Christ His Son, cleanseth us from all sin." (1 John i. 7.)—This is the experience of all true Christians. Unlearned, humble, poor, as many of them are, they have got hold of something in the Bible, and this causes them to hope. The hope which "maketh not ashamed" is never separate from God's Word.

Men wonder sometimes that ministers press them so strongly to read the Bible. They marvel that we say so much about the importance of preaching, and urge them so often to hear sermons. Let them cease to wonder, and marvel no more. Our object is to make you acquainted with God's Word. We want you to have a good hope, and we know that a good hope must be drawn from the Scriptures. Without reading or hearing you must live and die in ignorance. Hence we cry, "Search the Scriptures" "Hear, and your soul shall live." (John v. 39. Isa. lv. 3.)

I warn every one to beware of a hope not drawn from

Scripture. It is a false hope, and many will find out this to their cost. That glorious and perfect book, the Bible, however men despise it, is the only fountain out of which man's soul can derive peace. Many sneer at the 'old book while living, who find their need of it when dying. The Queen in her palace and the pauper in the workhouse, the philosopher in his study and the child in the cottage,— each and all must be content to seek living water from the Bible, if they are to have any hope at all. Honour your Bible,—read your Bible,—stick to your Bible. There is not on earth a scrap of solid hope for the other side of the grave which is not drawn out of the Word.*

III. In the third place, a good hope is *a hope that rests entirely on Jesus Christ.* What says St. Paul to Timothy ? He says that Jesus Christ " is our hope." What says he to the Colossians ? He speaks of " Christ in you the hope of glory." (1 Tim. i. ; 1 Coloss. i. 27.)

The man who has a good hope founds all his expectations of pardon and salvation on the mediation and redeeming work of Jesus the Son of God. He knows his own sinfulness ; he feels that he is guilty, wicked, and lost by nature : but he sees forgiveness and peace with God offered freely to him through faith in Christ. He accepts the offer : he casts himself with all his sins on Jesus, and rests on Him. Jesus and His atonement on

---

* " The hope of eternal life is a hope of the greatest blessing that can be conceived. It is a hope bottomed only on the pure Word of God. When you examine your hearts you find some hope of being saved, and that in the day of the Lord you shall stand with peace and confidence before your Judge. Why so ? Wherefore do you hope for this ? Is it not because God hath said it ? Is it not because the God that cannot lie hath spoken it ? If you expect to be saved upon any other ground but because God hath said it, ye must change your mind ere you be saved ; for ye are off the rock, ye are off the sure foundation that all God's Israel must rest upon."—*Traill.*

the cross,—Jesus and His righteousness,—Jesus and His finished work,—Jesus and His all-prevailing intercession, —Jesus, and Jesus only, is the foundation of the confidence of his soul.

Let us beware of supposing that any hope is good which is not founded on Christ. All other hopes are built on sand. They may look well in the summer time of health and prosperity, but they will fail in the day of sickness and the hour of death. "Other foundation can no man lay than that is laid, which is Jesus Christ." (1 Cor. iii. 11.)

Church-membership is no foundation of hope. We may belong to the best of Churches, and yet never belong to Christ. We may fill our pew regularly every Sunday, and hear the sermons of orthodox, ordained clergymen, and yet never hear the voice of Jesus, or follow Him. If we have nothing better than Church-membership to rest upon we are in a poor plight: we have nothing solid beneath our feet.

Reception of the sacraments is no foundation of hope. We may be washed in the waters of baptism, and yet know nothing of the water of life. We may go to the Lord's table every Sunday of our lives, and yet never eat Christ's body and drink Christ's blood by faith. Miserable indeed is our condition if we can say nothing more than this! We possess nothing but the outside of Christianity : we are leaning on a reed.

Christ Himself is the only true foundation of a good hope. He is the rock,—His work is perfect. He is the stone,—the sure stone,—the tried corner-stone. He is able to bear all the weight that we can lay upon Him. He only that buildeth and "believeth on Him shall not be confounded." (Deut. xxxii. 4; Isa. xxviii. 16; 1 Peter ii. 6.)

This is the point on which all true saints of God in every age have been entirely agreed. Differing on other matters, they have always been of one mind upon this. Unable to see alike about Church-government, and discipline, and liturgies, they have ever seen alike about the foundation of hope. Not one of them has ever left the world trusting in his own righteousness. Christ has been all their confidence: they have hoped in Him, and not been ashamed.*

Would any one like to know what kind of death-beds a minister of the Gospel finds comfort in attending? Would you know what closing scenes are cheering to us, and leave favourable impressions on our minds? We like to see dying people *making much of Christ.* So long as they can only talk of "the Almighty," and "Providence," and "God," and "mercy," we must stand in doubt. Dying in this state, they give no satisfactory sign. Give us the men and women who feel their sins deeply, and cling to Jesus,—who think much of His dying love,—who like to hear of His atoning blood,—who return again and again to the story of His cross. These are the death-beds which leave good evidence behind them. For my part I had rather hear the name of Jesus come heartily from a dying relative's lips, than see him die without a word about Christ, and then be told by an angel that he was saved." †

---

* "Consider how it is with the most holy and eminent saints when dying. Did you ever see or hear any boasting of their own works and performances? They may, and do own to the praise of His grace, what they have been made to be, what they have been helped to do or suffer for Christ's sake. But when they draw near to the awful tribunal, what else is in their eye and heart, but only free grace, ransoming blood, and a well-ordered covenant in Christ the surety? They cannot bear to have any make mention to them of their holiness, their own grace, and attainments.

"He is a wise and happy man that can anchor his soul on that rock on which he can ride out the storm of death. Why should men contend for that in their life that they know they must renounce at their death? or neglect that truth now, that they must betake themselves unto then? It is a great test of the truth of the doctrine about the way of salvation when it is generally approved by sensible dying men."— *Traill.*

† The dying words of Mr. Ash, the Puritan, are well-deserving of notice. He said, "When I consider my best duties, I sink, I die, I

IV. In the fourth place, a good hope is *a hope that is felt inwardly in the heart.* What says St. Paul? He speaks of "hope that maketh not ashamed, because the love of God is shed abroad in our hearts." He speaks of "rejoicing in hope." (Rom. v. 5; xii. 12.)

The man who has a good hope is conscious of it. He feels within him something that another man does not: he is conscious of possessing a well-grounded expectation of good things to come. This consciousness may vary exceedingly in different persons. In one it may be strong and well-defined; in another it may be feeble and indistinct.—It may vary exceedingly in different stages of the same person's experience. At one time he may be full of "joy and peace in believing;" at another he may be depressed and cast down. But in all persons who have a "good hope," in a greater or less degree, this consciousness does exist.

I am aware that this truth is one which has been fearfully abused and perverted. It has been brought into great disrepute by the fanaticism, enthusiasm, and extravagance of some professing Christians. Mere animal excitement has been mistaken for the work of the Holy Ghost. The over-wrought feelings of weak and nervous people have been prematurely and rashly supposed to be the result of grace. Men and women have been hastily

despair. But when I think of Christ, I have enough. He is all and in all."

The words of Mr. Cecil shortly before his death are very remarkable. He said, "I know myself to be a wretched, worthless sinner, having nothing in myself but poverty and sin. I know Jesus Christ to be a glorious and almighty Saviour. I see the full efficacy of His atonement and grace; and I cast myself entirely on Him, and wait at His footstool." A short time before his decease he requested one of his family to write down for him the following sentence in a book : " 'None but Christ, none but Christ,' said Lambert, dying at a stake : the same in dying circumstances, with his whole heart, says Richard Cecil."

pronounced "converted," who have soon gone back to the world, and proved utterly "unconverted" and dead in sins. And then has come in the devil. Contempt has been poured on religious feelings of every description : their very existence has been denied and scouted; and the result is that the very name of "feelings" in religion is in many quarters dreaded and disliked.

But the abuse and perversion of a truth must never be allowed to rob us of the use of it. When all has been said that can be said against fanaticism and enthusiasm, it is still undeniable that religious feelings are plainly spoken of and described in Scripture. The Word of God tells us that the true Christian has "peace," and "rest," and "joy," and "confidence." It tells us of some who have the "witness of the Spirit,"—of some who "fear no evil,"—of some who enjoy "assurance,"—of some who "know whom they have believed,"—of some who "are persuaded that they shall never be separated from the love of God in Christ." These are the feelings for which I contend : this is that sober, inward experience in which I see nothing extravagant, enthusiastic, or fanatical. Of such feelings I say boldly, no man need be ashamed. I go further, and say that no man has a "good hope" who does not know *something*, however faintly, of these feelings in his own heart. I go further still, and say that to hold any other doctrine is to cast dishonour on the whole work of the Holy Ghost.

Will any one tell us that God ever intended a true Christian to have no inward consciousness of his own Christianity ? Will any one say that the Bible teaches that people can pass from death to life, be pardoned, renewed, and sanctified, and yet feel nothing of this mighty change within ? Let those think it who will : I can hold no such doctrine. I would as soon believe that Lazarus did not know that he was raised from the grave, or Bartimeus that he was restored to sight,

as believe that a man cannot *feel* within him the Spirit
of God.

Can a weary man lie down in bed and not feel rested ?
Can the parched traveller in an African desert drink water
and not feel refreshed ?   Can the starved sailor, in Arctic
regions, draw near to the fire and not feel warmed ?   Can
the half-naked, hungry, homeless wanderer in our streets
be clothed, fed, and housed, and not feel comforted ?   Can
the fainting sick man receive the healing cordial, and
not feel revived ?   I cannot believe it.   I believe that in
each case something will be felt.—Just so I cannot believe
that a man can be a true Christian if he does not feel
something within.   A new birth, a pardon of sins, a conscience sprinkled with Christ's blood, an indwelling of the
Holy Ghost, are no such small matters as men seem to
suppose.   He that knows anything of them will feel them :
there will be a real, distinct witness in his inward man.

Let us beware of a hope that is not felt, and a Christianity that is destitute of any inward experience.   They
are idols of the present day, and idols before which
thousands are bowing down.   Thousands are trying to
persuade themselves that people may be born again, and
have the Spirit, and yet not be sensible of it,—or that
people may be members of Christ, and receive benefit
from Him, who have neither faith nor love towards His
name.   These are the favourite doctrines of modern days!
These be the gods which have taken the place of Diana
and Mercury, and "the image which fell down from Jupiter!"
These be the last new deities invented by poor, weak,
idolatrous man !   From all such idols let us keep ourselves
with jealous care.   Golden as their heads may be, their
feet are no better than clay.   They cannot stand : they
must, sooner or later, break down.   Miserable indeed are
the prospects of those who worship them !   Their hope is
not the hope of the Bible : it is the hope of a dead corpse.
Where Christ and the Spirit are their presence will be *felt !*

Can any one in his senses suppose that the apostle Paul would have been content with Christians who knew nothing of inward feelings? Can we fancy that mighty man of God sanctioning a religion which a person might have, and yet experience nothing within? Can we picture to ourselves a member of one of the Churches he founded, who was utterly unacquainted with peace, or joy, or confidence towards God, and was yet approved by the great apostle of the Gentiles as a true believer! Away with the idea! It will not bear reflection for a moment. The testimony of Scripture is plain and explicit. Talk as men will about enthusiasm and excitement, there are such things as *feelings* in religion. The Christian who knows nothing of them is not yet converted, and has everything to learn. The cold marble of a Grecian statue may well be unimpassioned. The dried mummy from Egypt may well look stiff and still. The stuffed beast in a museum may well be motionless and cold. They are all lifeless things. But where there is life there will always be some feeling. The "good hope" is a hope that can be felt.

V. In the last place, a good hope is *a hope that is manifested outwardly in the life.* Once more, what saith the Scripture? "Every one that hath this hope in Him purifieth himself, even as He is pure." (1 John iii. 3.)

The man that has a good hope will show it in all his ways. It will influence his life, his character, and his daily conduct; it will make him strive to be a holy, godly, conscientious, spiritual man. He will feel under a constant obligation to serve and please Him from whom his hope comes. He will say to himself, "What shall I render to the Lord for all His benefits to me?" He will feel, "I am bought with a price: let me glorify God with body and spirit, which are His."—"Let me show forth the praises of Him who hath called me out of darkness into His marvellous light." Let me prove that I am Christ's friend, "by keeping His commandments." (Psalm cxvi. 12; 1 Cor vi. 20; 1 Peter ii. 9; John xv. 14.)

This is a point which has been of infinite importance in every age of the Church. It is a truth which is always assailed by Satan, and needs guarding with jealous care. Let us grasp it firmly, and make it a settled principle in our religion. If there is light in a house it will shine through the windows: if there is any real hope in a man's soul it will be seen in his ways. Show me your hope in your life and daily behaviour. Where is it? Wherein does it appear? If you cannot show it, you may be sure it is nothing better than a delusion and a snare.

The times demand a very distinct testimony from all ministers on this subject. The truth on this point requires very plain speaking. Let us settle it in our minds deeply, and beware of letting it go. Let no man deceive us with vain words. "He that doeth righteousness is righteous." " He that saith he abideth in Him, ought himself also so to walk, even as He walked." (1 John ii. 6; iii. 7.) The hope that does not make a man honest, honourable, truthful, sober, diligent, unselfish, loving, meek, kind, and faithful in all the relations of life, is not from above. It is only "the talk of the lips which tendeth to penury." " He that boasteth himself of a false gift, is like clouds and wind without rain." (Prov. xiv. 23; xxv. 14.)

(a) There are some in the present day who flatter themselves they have a good hope because they possess *religious knowledge*. They are acquainted with the letter of their Bibles; they can argue and dispute about points of doctrine: they can quote texts by the score, in defence of their own theological opinions. They are perfect Benjamites in controversy:—they can " sling stones at an hair-breadth, and not miss." (Judges xx. 16.) And yet they have no fruits of the Spirit, no charity, no meekness, no gentleness, no humility, nothing of the mind that was

in Christ. And have these people a hope? Let those
believe it who will, I dare not say so. I hold with St.
Paul, "Though a man speak with the tongues of men
and angels, and have not charity, he is become as sounding
brass, or a tinkling cymbal. And though a man has the
gift of prophecy, and understands all mysteries, and all
knowledge, and has not charity, he is nothing." Yes:
hope without charity is no hope at all. (1 Cor. xiii. 1—3.)

(b) There are some again who presume to think they have
a good hope because of *God's everlasting election.* They
boldly persuade themselves that they were once called and
chosen of God to salvation. They take it for granted that
there was once a real work of the Spirit on their hearts, and
that all therefore must be well. They look down upon
others, who are afraid of professing as much as they do.
They seem to think, "We are the people of God, we are
the temple of the Lord, we are the favoured servants of
the Most High,—we are they that shall reign in heaven,
and none beside." And yet these very people can lie, and
cheat, and swindle, and be dishonourable! Some of them
can even get drunk in private, and secretly commit sins
of which it is a shame to speak! And have they a good
hope? God forbid that I should say so! The election
which is not "unto sanctification" is not of God, but of
the devil. The hope that does not make a man holy is no
hope at all.

(c) There are some in this day who fancy they have a good
hope because they *like hearing the Gospel.* They are fond
of hearing good sermons. They will go miles to listen to
some favourite preacher, and will even weep and be much
affected by his words. To see them in church one would
think, "Surely these are the disciples of Christ, surely
these are excellent Christians!"—And yet these very
people can plunge into every folly and gaiety of the world.
Night after night they can go with their whole heart to
the opera, the theatre, or the ball. They are to be seen

on the race-course. They are forward in every worldly revel. Their voice on Sunday is the voice of Jacob, but their hands on week days are the hands of Esau.—And have these people a good hope ? I dare not say so. "The friendship of the world is enmity with God;" the hope that does not prevent conformity to the world, is no hope at all. "Whatsoever is born of God overcometh the world." (James iv. 4 ; 1 John v. 4.)

Let us beware of any hope that does not exercise a sanctifying influence over our hearts, lives, tastes, conduct, and conversation. It is a hope that never came down from above. It is mere base metal, and counterfeit coin. It lacks the mint-stamp of the Holy Ghost, and will never pass current in heaven. The man that has a real hope, no doubt, may be overtaken in a fault; He may stumble occasionally in his practice, and be drawn aside from the right path for a while. But the man that can allow him-self in any wilful and *habitual* breach of God's law is rotten at the heart. He may talk of his hope as much as he pleases, but he has none in reality. His religion is a joy to the devil, a stumbling block to the world, a sorrow to true Christians, and an offence to God. Oh, that men would consider these things ! Oh, that many would use some such prayer as this, "From antinomianism and hypocrisy, good Lord, deliver me ! "

I have now done what I proposed to do. I have shown the five leading marks of a sound good hope.—(1) It is a hope that a man can explain. (2) It is a hope that is drawn from Scripture. (3) It is a hope that is founded on Christ. (4) It is a hope that is felt within the heart. (5) It is a hope that is manifested outwardly in the life.—Such, I firmly believe is the hope of all true Christians, of every name, and Church, and denomination, and people, and tongue. Such is the hope that we must have, if we mean to go to heaven. Such is the hope without which, I firmly believe, no man can be saved. Such is "the good hope through grace."

Suffer me now to apply the whole subject to the conscience of every reader in a practical way. What shall it profit us to know truths unless we use them ? What shall it avail us to see the real nature of a good hope unless the matter be brought home to our own souls ? This is what I now propose to do, if God permit, in the remainder of this paper. May the spirit of God apply my words to the heart of every reader of these pages with mighty power ! Man may speak, and preach, and write, but God alone can convert.

(1) My first word of application shall be *a question.* I offer it to all who read this paper, and I entreat each reader to give it an answer. That question is, " What is your own hope about your soul ? "

I do not ask this out of idle curiosity. I ask it as an ambassador for Christ, and a friend to your best interests. I ask it in order to stir up self-inquiry, and promote your spiritual welfare. I ask, " What is your hope about your soul ? "

I do not want to know whether you go to church or chapel : there will be no account of these differences in heaven. I do not want to know whether you approve of the Gospel, and think it very right and proper that people should have their religion, and say their prayers ; all this is beside the mark : it is not the point. The point I want you to look at is this, " What is your hope about your soul ? "

It matters nothing what your relations think. It matters nothing what other persons in the parish or town approve. The account of God will not be taken by towns, or by parishes, or by families : each must stand forth separately and answer for himself. " Every one of us shall give account of himself to God." (Rom. xiv. 12.) And what is the

defence you mean to set up ? What is to be your plea ?
" What is your hope about your soul ? "

Time is short, and is passing quickly away : yet a few
years, and we shall be all dead and gone. The trees perhaps are cut down out of which our coffins will be made :
the winding-sheets perhaps are woven which will surround
our bodies ; the spades perhaps are made that will dig our
graves. Eternity draws near. There ought to be no
trifling. " What, what is your hope about your soul ? "

Another world will soon begin. Trade, politics, money,
lands, cottages, palaces, eating, drinking, dressing, reading,
hunting, shooting, drawing, working, dancing, feasting, will
soon be at an end for ever. There will remain nothing
but a heaven for some, and a hell for others. " What, what
is your hope about your soul ? "

I have asked my question. And now I ask every
reader as in the sight of God, *What is your reply ?*

Many would say, I believe, if they spoke the truth, " I
don't know anything about it. I suppose I am not what
I ought to be. I dare say I ought to have more religion
than I have. I trust I shall have more some day. But as
to any hope at present, I really don't know."

I can quite believe that this is the state of many. I
have seen enough of the spiritual ignorance of men to fill
me with deep sorrow. I am convinced that there is no
error, or heresy, or "*ism*," which is ruining so many souls
as the heresy of ignorance. I am convinced that there are
myriads of people in England who do not even know the
A B C of Christianity, and are nothing better than
baptized heathen. I have heard of a man, in his last
days, whose only hope was, " that he had always kept his
Church, and voted for the Blues." I have heard of
a woman, who was asked on her death-bed where she hoped
to go, and said, " She hoped she should go with the crowd."
I have little doubt that there are thousands of people in
this country who are much in the same condition, knowing

nothing whatever about their state before God. If this be the condition of any reader of this paper, I can only say, May God convert you! May God awaken you! May God open your eyes before it is too late! *

Look at that man who goes to the Bank of England on a dividend day, and asks to be paid a large sum of money. Is his name down among the list of people to be paid? No!—Has he any title or right to claim payment? No: he has none!—He only knows that other people are receiving money, and that he would like to receive some too. You know well that you would call the man "out of his mind:" you would say he was nothing better than a madman. But stop! Take care what you are saying! You are the real madman, if you mean to claim heaven at last, when you have no title, no warrant, no ground of hope to show. Once more, I say, May God open your eyes!

But many, I believe, would reply to my question that "they have hope." They would say, "I am not as bad as some, at any rate. I am no heathen. I am no infidel. I have some hope about my soul."

---

* "When we deal with the carnal, secure, careless sinners (and they are a vast multitude), and ask them a reason of that hope of heaven they pretend to, is not this their common answer: "I live inoffensively; I keep God's law as well as I can; whenever I fail, I repent, and beg God's mercy for Christ's sake: my heart is sincere, though my knowledge and attainments be short of others." If we go on further to inquire what acquaintance they have with Jesus Christ? what application their souls have made to Him? what workings of faith on Him? what use they have made of His righteousness for justification and of His Spirit for sanctification? what they know of living by faith on Jesus Christ? we are barbarians to them. And in this sad state thousands in England live, and die, and perish eternally. Yet so thick is the darkness of the age, that many of them live here and go hence with the reputation of good Christians; and some of them may have their funeral sermon and praise preached by an ignorant flattering minister; though it may be the poor creatures did never, in the whole course of their lives, nor at their deaths, employ Jesus Christ so much for any entry to heaven, purchased by His blood and accessible by faith in Him, as a poor Turk doth Mahomet for a room in his beastly paradise!"—*Traill.*

If this be your case, I beseech you to consider calmly what your hope really is. I entreat you not to be content with saying, like a parrot, "I hope,—I hope,—I hope;" but to examine seriously into the nature of your confidence, and to make sure that it is well-founded.—Is it a hope you can explain ?—Is it scriptural ?—Is it built on Christ ?—Is it felt in your heart ?—Is it sanctifying to your life ?—All is not gold that glitters. I have warned you already that there is a false hope as well as a true : I offer the warning again. I beseech you to take heed that you be not deceived. Beware of mistakes.

There are ships lying quietly in Liverpool and London docks, about to sail for every part of the globe. They all look equally trustworthy, so long as they are in harbour; they have all equally good names, and are equally well-rigged and painted : but they are not all equally well-found and equally safe. Once let them put to sea, and meet with rough weather, and the difference between the sound and unsound ships will soon appear.—Many a ship which looked well in dock has proved not sea-worthy when she got into deep water, and has gone down at last with all hands on board ! Just so it is with many a false hope. It has failed completely, when most wanted : it has broken down at last, and ruined its possessor's soul. You will soon have to put to sea. I say again, beware of mistakes.

I leave my question here. I earnestly pray that God may apply it to the hearts of all who read this paper. I am sure it is much needed. I believe there never was a time when there was so much counterfeit religion current, and so many "false hopes" passing off for true. There never was a time when there was so much high profession, and so little spiritual practice, so much loud talk about preachers, and parties, and Churches, and so little close walking with God, and real work of the Spirit. There is no lack of blossoms in Christendom, but there is a melancholy scarcity of ripe fruit. There is an abundance of controversial theology, but a dearth of practical holiness. There are myriads who have a name to live, but few whose hearts are really given to Jesus Christ,—few whose affections are really set on things above. There will be some awful failures yet in many quarters : there will be still more awful disclosures at the last day. There are many hopes now-a-days, which are utterly destitute of foundation. I say, for the last time, Beware of mistakes.

(2) My second word of application shall be *a request*. I make it to all readers of this paper who feel they have no hope and desire to have it. It is a short simple request. I entreat them to seek " a good hope " while it can be found.

A good hope is within the reach of any man, if he is only willing to seek it. It is called emphatically in Scripture, a " good hope through grace." It is freely offered, even as it was freely purchased : it may be freely obtained, " without money and without price." Our past lives do not make it impossible to obtain it, however bad they may have been ; our present weaknesses and infirmities do not shut us out, however great they may be. The same grace which provided mankind with a hope, makes a free, full, and unlimited invitation :—" Whosoever will, let him take the water of life freely ;"—" Ask, and it shall be given you ; seek, and ye shall find." (Rev. xxii. 17 ; Matt. vii. 7.)

The Lord Jesus Christ is able and willing to give " a good hope " to all who really want it. He is sealed and appointed by God the Father to give the bread of life to all that hunger, and the water of life to all that thirst. " It pleased the Father that in Him should all fulness dwell." (Coloss. i. 19.) In Him there is pardon and peace with God, bought by the precious blood which He shed upon the cross. In Him there is joy and peace for any believer, and a solid, well-grounded expectation of good things to come. In Him there is rest for the weary, refuge for the fearful, a cleansing fountain for the unclean, medicine for the sick, healing for the broken-hearted, and hope for the lost. Whosoever feels labouring and heavy-laden with sin, whosoever feels anxious and distressed about his soul, whosoever feels afraid of death and unfit to die,—whosoever he is, *let him go to Christ and trust in Him.* This is the thing to be done: this is the way to follow. Whosoever wants "hope," let him go to Christ.

If any reader of this paper really wants to enjoy a good hope, let him seek it from the Lord Jesus Christ. There is every encouragement to do so. The Thessalonians in old time were, like the Ephesians, dead in trespasses and sins, having no hope, and without God in the world; but when St. Paul preached Jesus to them, they arose from their miserable state and became new men. God gave them a "good hope through grace." The door through which Manasseh and Magdalene entered, is still open: the fountain in which Zacchæus and Matthew were washed, is still unsealed. Seek hope from Christ, and you shall find it.

Seek it *honestly, and with no secret reserve.* The ruin of many is that they are not fair and straightforward. They say that they "try as much as they can," and that they really "want to be saved," and that they really "look to Christ;" and yet in the chamber of their own heart there lies some darling sin, to which they privately cling, and are resolved not to give it up. They are like Augustine, who said, "Lord convert me: but not now." Seek honestly, if you wish to find a good hope.

Seek it in *humble prayer.* Pour out your heart before the Lord Jesus, and tell Him all the wants of your soul. Do as you would have done had you lived in Galilee eighteen hundred years ago, and had a leprosy: go direct to Christ, and lay before Him your cares. Tell Him that you are a poor, sinful creature, but that you have heard He is a gracious Saviour, and that you come to Him for "hope" for your soul. Tell Him that you have nothing to say for yourself,—no excuse to make, nothing of your own to plead,—but that you have heard that He "receives sinners," and as such you come to Him. (Luke xv. 2.)

Seek it at once *without delay.* Halt no more between two opinions: do not linger another day. Cast away the remnants of pride which are still keeping you back: draw nigh to Jesus as a heavy-laden sinner, and "lay hold upon the hope set before you." (Heb. vi. 18.) This is the point to which all must come at last if they mean to be saved. Sooner or later they must knock at the door of grace and ask to be admitted. Why not do it at once ?—Why stand still looking at the bread of life ? Why not come forward and eat it?—Why remain outside the city of refuge? Why not enter in and be safe ?—Why not seek hope at once, and never rest till you find it ? Never did soul seek honestly in the way I have marked out, and fail to find ! *

---

* The words of Traill on this point of coming to Christ by faith, deserve many thoughts. They throw light on a subject which is constantly misunderstood.—He says, "When we come to deal with a poor, awakened sinner, who seeth his lost estate, and that he is condemned by the law of God, we find the same principles (pride and ignorance) working in him. We see him sick and wounded : we tell him where his help lies, in Jesus Christ ; and what his proper work is, to apply to Him by faith. What is his answer : 'Alas,' says the man, 'I have been, and I am so vile a sinner, my heart is so bad, and so full of plagues and corruptions, that I cannot think of believing on Christ. But if I had but repentance, and some holiness in heart and life, and such and such gracious qualifications, I would then believe." This his answer is as full of nonsense, ignorance and pride, as words can contain or express. It implies : (1) 'If I were pretty well recovered, I would employ the Physician, Christ ; (2) There is some hope to work out these good things by myself, without Christ ; (3) When I come to Christ with a price in my hand I shall be welcome ; (4) I can come to Christ when I will.' So ignorant are people naturally of faith in Jesus Christ ; and no words, or warnings, or plainest instructions can beat into men's heads and hearts that the first coming to Christ by faith, and believing on Him, is not a believing we shall be saved by Him, but a believing on Him, that we may be saved by Him."—*Traill's Works.*

(3) My last word of application shall be *counsel*. I offer it to all who have really obtained " good hope through grace." I offer it to all who are really leaning on Christ, walking in the narrow way, and led by the Spirit of God. I ask them to accept advice from one who hopes that he is "their brother and companion in the kingdom and patience of Jesus Christ." (Rev. i. 9.) I believe the advice to be sound and good.

(*a*) If you have a good hope *be zealous and watchful over it*. Beware that Satan does not steal it away for a season, as he did from David and Peter. Beware that you do not lose sight of it by giving way to inconsistencies, and by conformity to the world. Examine it often, and make sure that it is not becoming dim : keep it bright by daily carefulness over your temper, thoughts, and words; keep it healthy by hearty, fervent, and continual prayer. The hope of the Christian is a very delicate plant. It is an exotic from above : it is not a plant of natural growth. It is easily chilled and nipped by the cold frosts of this world. Unless watered and tended carefully, it will soon dwindle away to a mere nothing, and scarcely be felt or seen. None find out this so painfully as dying believers who have not walked very closely with God. They find that they have sown thorns in their dying pillows, and brought clouds between themselves and the sun.

(*b*) For another thing, if you have a good hope, *keep it always ready*. Have it at your right hand, prepared for immediate use : look at it often, and take care that it is in good order. Trials often break in upon us suddenly, like an armed man. Sicknesses and injuries to our mortal frame sometimes lay us low on our beds without any warning. Happy is he who keeps his lamp well trimmed, and lives in the daily sense of communion with Christ !

Did you ever see a fire-engine in some old country house ? Did you ever remark how often it lies for months in a dark shed, untouched, unexamined, and uncleaned? The valves are out of order; the leather hose is full of holes; the pumps are rusty and stiff. A house might be almost burnt to the ground before it could lift a pailful of water. In its present state it is a well-nigh useless machine.

Did you ever see a ship in ordinary, in Portsmouth harbour? The hull may perhaps be good and sound; the keel and topsides, and timbers and beams, and decks may be all that you could desire. But she is not rigged, or stored, or armed, or fit for service. It would take weeks and months to make her ready for sea. In her present state she could do little for her country's defence.

The hope of many a believer is like that fire-engine, and that ship. It exists,—it lives,—it is real,—it is true, it is sound,—it is good: it came down from heaven: it was implanted by the Holy Ghost. But, alas, *it is not ready for use!* Its possessor will find that out, by his own want of joy and sensible comfort, when he comes to his death-bed. Beware that your hope be not a hope of this kind. If you have a hope keep it ready for use, and within reach of your hand.

(c) For another thing, if you have a good hope, seek and pray that it may *grow more and more strong* every year. Do not be content with a "day of small things;" covet the best gifts: desire to enjoy full assurance. Strive to attain to Paul's standard, and to be able to say, "I know whom I have believed,"—"I am persuaded that neither death nor life shall separate me from the love of God which is in Jesus Christ." (2 Tim. i. 12; Rom. viii. 38.)

Believe me, this part of my counsel is one that deserves close attention. Believe me, the things before us all will try our hope of what sort it is. Sickness and death are solemn things. They strip off all the tinsel and paint from a man's religion; they discover the weak places in our Christianity; they strain our hopes to the very uttermost, and often make us well nigh despair. Old Christian,

in Pilgrim's Progress, had a sore trial at his latter end in
crossing the cold river before he entered the celestial city.
Faithful and true as he was, he still cried out, "All thy
billows go over me," and had a hard struggle to keep his
footing. May we all lay this to heart ? May we seek to
know and feel that we are one with Christ and Christ in
us! He that has hope does well; but he that has assurance does better. Blessed indeed are they who "abound
in hope through the power of the Holy Ghost." (Rom.
xv. 13.)

(*d*) Finally, if you have a good hope, *be thankful*,
for it, and give God daily praise. Who has made you to
differ ? Why have you been taught to feel your sins, and
nothingness, while others are ignorant and self-righteous ?
Why have you been taught to look to Jesus, while others
are looking to their own goodness, or resting on some
mere form of religion ? Why are you longing and striving
to be holy, while others are caring for nothing but this
world ? Why are these things so ? There is but one
answer,—Grace, grace, free grace, has done it all. For that
grace praise God. For that grace be thankful.

Go on, then, to your journey's end, "rejoicing in hope of
the glory of God." (Rom. v. 2.) Go on, rejoicing in the
thought that though you are a poor sinner Jesus is a most
gracious Saviour, and that though you have trials here for
a little season, heaven shall soon make amends for all.

Go on, wearing hope as a helmet in all the battles of
life,—a hope of pardon, a hope of perseverance, a hope of
acquittal in the judgment day, a hope of final glory. Put
on the breast-plate of righteousness : take the shield of
faith ; have your loins girt about with truth : wield valiantly
the sword of the Spirit. But never forget—as ever you
would be a happy Christian—never forget to put on the
"helmet of hope." (1 Thess. v. 8.)

Go on, in spite of an ill-natured world, and be not
moved by its laughter or its persecution, its slanders or its

sneers. Comfort your heart with the thought that the time is short, the good things yet to come, the night far spent, the "morning without clouds" at hand. (2 Sam. xxiii. 4.) When the wicked man dies his expectation perishes; but your expectation shall not deceive you,— your reward is sure.

Go on, and be not cast down because you are troubled by doubts and fears. You are yet in the body: this world is not your rest. The devil hates you because you have escaped from him, and he will do all he can to rob you of peace. The very fact that you have fears is an evidence that you feel you have something to lose. The true Christian may ever be discerned by his warfare quite as much as by his peace, and by his fears quite as much as by his hopes. The ships at anchor at Spithead may swing to and fro with the tide, and pitch heavily in a south-eastern gale; but so long as their anchors hold the ground they ride safely, and have no cause to fear. The hope of the true Christian is the "anchor of his soul, sure and steadfast." (Heb. vi. 19.) His heart may be tossed to and fro sometimes, but he is safe in Christ. The waves may swell, and lift him up and down, but he will not be wrecked.

Go on, and "hope to the end for the grace that is to be brought to you at the revelation of Jesus Christ." (1 Pet. i. 13.) Yet a little time, and faith shall be changed to sight, and hope to certainty: you shall see even as you have been seen, and know even as you have been known. A few more tossings to and fro on the waves of this troublesome world, —a few more battles and conflicts with our spiritual enemy, —a few more years of tears and partings, of working and suffering, of crosses and cares, of disappointments and vexations,—and then, then we shall be at home. The harbour lights are already in view: the haven of rest is not far off. *There* we shall find all that we have hoped for, and find that it was a million times better than our hopes. *There* we shall find all the saints,—and no sin, no cares of this world, no money, no sickness, no death, no devil. *There*, above all, we shall find Jesus, and be ever with the Lord! (1 Thess. iv. 17.) Let us hope on. It is worth while to carry the cross and follow Christ. Let the world laugh and mock, if it will; it is worth while to have "a good hope through grace," and be a thorough decided Christian. I say again,—Let us hope on.

"ALIVE OR DEAD?"

"You hath he quickened who were dead."—EPHES. ii. 1.

THE question which forms the title of this paper deserves a thousand thoughts. I invite every reader of this volume to look at it carefully, and ponder it well. Search your own heart, and do not lay down this book without solemn self-inquiry.—Are you among the living, or among the dead?

Listen to me while I try to help you to an answer. Give me your attention, while I unfold this matter, and show you what God has said about it in the Scriptures. If I say hard things, it is not because I do not love you. I write as I do, because I desire your salvation. He is your best friend who tells you the most truth.

I. First then, *let me tell you what we all are by nature.—We are spiritually* DEAD !

"Dead" is a strong word, but it is not my own coining and invention. I did not choose it. The Holy Ghost taught St. Paul to write it down about the Ephesians: "You hath he quickened who were *dead.*" (Eph. ii. 1.). The Lord Jesus Christ made use of it in the parable of the prodigal son: "This my son was *dead* and is alive again." (Luke xv. 24, 32.). You will read it also in the first Epistle to Timothy: "She that liveth in pleasure is *dead* while she liveth." (1 Tim. v. 6,). Shall a mortal man be wise above that which is written? Must I not take heed to speak that which I find in the Bible, and neither less nor more?

"Dead" is an awful idea, and one that man is most unwilling to receive. He does not like to allow the whole extent of his soul's disease: he shuts his eyes to the real amount of his danger. Many an one will allow us to say, that naturally most people "are not quite what they ought to be: they are thoughtless,—they are unsteady,—they are gay,—they are wild,—they are not serious enough." But dead? Oh, no! We must not mention it. It is going too far to say that. The idea is a stone of stumbling, and a rock of offence."*

But what we like in religion is of very little consequence. The only question is, What is written? What saith the Lord? God's thoughts are not man's thoughts, and God's words are not man's words. God says of every living person who is not a real, thorough, genuine, decided Christian,—be he high or low, rich or poor, old or young,—*He is spiritually dead.*

In this, as in every thing else, God's words are right. Nothing could be said more correct, nothing more accurate, nothing more faithful, nothing more true. Stay a little, and let me reason this out with you. Come and see.

What should you have said, if you had seen Joseph weeping over his father Jacob?—"He fell upon his face, and wept upon him, and kissed him." (Gen. l. 1.). But there was no reply to his affection. All about that aged countenance was unmoved, silent, and still. Doubtless you would have guessed the reason.—Jacob was dead.

---

* "This is the reason we are no better, because our disease is not perfectly known : this is the reason we are no better, because we know not how bad we are." — *Archbishop Usher's Sermons, preached at Oxford*, 1650.

What would you have said, if you had heard the Levite speaking to his wife, when he found her lying before the door in Gibeah ? " Up," he said, " and let us be going. But none answered." (Judges xix. 28.) His words were thrown away. There she lay, motionless, stiff, and cold. You know the cause.—She was dead.

What should you have thought, if you had seen the Amalekite stripping Saul of his royal ornaments in Mount Gilboa ? He " took from him the crown that was upon his head, and the bracelet that was on his arm." (2 Sam. i. 10.) There was no resistance. Not a muscle moved in that proud face : not a finger was raised to prevent him. And why ?—Saul was dead.

What should you have thought, if you had met the widow's son in the gate of Nain, lying on a bier, wrapped about with grave-clothes, followed by his weeping mother, carried slowly towards the tomb ? (Luke vii. 12.) Doubtless it would have been all clear to you. It would have needed no explanation.—The young man was dead.

Now I say this is just the condition of every man by nature in the matter of his soul. I say this is just the state of the vast majority of people around us in spiritual things. God calls to them continually,—by mercies, by afflictions, by ministers, by His word :—but they do not hear His voice. The Lord Jesus Christ mourns over them, pleads with them, sends them gracious invitations knocks at the door of their hearts :—but they do not regard it. The crown and glory of their being, that precious jewel, their immortal soul, is being seized, plundered, and taken away :—and they are utterly unconcerned. The devil is carrying them away, day after day, along the broad road that leads. to destruction :—and they allow him to make them his captives without a struggle. And this is going on everywhere,—all around us,—among all classes,—throughout the length and breadth of the land. You know it in your own conscience while

you read this paper: you must be aware of it. You
cannot deny it. And what then, I ask, can be said more
perfectly true than that which God says:—we are all by
nature spiritually *dead?*

Yes! when a man's heart is cold and unconcerned about
religion,—when his hands are never employed in doing
God's work,—when his feet are not familiar with God's
ways,—when his tongue is seldom or never used in prayer
and praise,—when his ears are deaf to the voice of Christ
in the Gospel,—when his eyes are blind to the beauty of
the kingdom of heaven,—when his mind is full of the
world, and has no room for spiritual things,—when these
marks are to be found in a man, the word of the Bible is the
right word to use about him,—and that word is, "Dead."

We may not like this perhaps. We may shut our eyes
both to facts in the world, and texts in the Word. But
God's truth must be spoken, and to keep it back does
positive harm. Truth must be spoken, however condemn-
ing it may be. So long as a man does not serve God with
body, soul, and spirit, he is not really alive. So long as he
puts the first things last and the last first, buries his talent
like an unprofitable servant, and brings the Lord no
revenue of honour, so long in God's sight he is dead. He
is not filling the place in creation for which he was intended; he is not using his powers and faculties as God
meant them to be used. The poet's words are strictly
true,—

> "He only lives who lives to God,
> And all are dead beside."

This is the true explanation of sin not felt,—and
sermons not believed,—and good advice not followed,—
and the Gospel not embraced,—and the world not forsaken,
—and the cross not taken up,—and self-will not mortified,
—and evil habits not laid aside,—and the Bible seldom
read,—and the knee never bent in prayer. Why is all
this on every side. The answer is simple: *Men are dead.*

This is the true account of that host of excuses, which so many make " with one consent." Some have no learning, and some have no time. Some are oppressed with business, and the care of money, and some with poverty. Some have difficulties in their own families, and some in their own health. Some have peculiar obstacles in their calling, which others, we are told, cannot understand ; and others have peculiar drawbacks at home, and they wait to have them removed. But God has a shorter word in the Bible, which describes all these people at once. He says, *They are dead.* If spiritual life began in these people's hearts, their excuses would soon vanish away.

This is the true explanation of many things which wring a faithful minister's heart. Many around him never attend a place of worship at all. Many attend so irregularly, that it is clear they think it of no importance. Many attend once on a Sunday who might just as easily attend twice. Many never come to the Lord's table,—and never appear at a week-day means of grace of any kind. And why is all this ? Often, far too often, there can be only one reply about these people : *They are dead.*

See now how all professing Christians should examine themselves and try their own state. It is not in church-yards alone where the dead are to be found ; there are only too many inside our churches, and close to our pulpits,—too many on the benches, and too many in the pews. The land is like the valley in Ezekiel's vision,— " full of bones, very many, and very dry." (Ezek. xxxvii. 2.) There are dead souls in all our parishes, and dead souls in all our streets. There is hardly a family in which all live to God ; there is hardly a house in which there is not some one dead. Oh, let us all search and look at home ! Let us prove our own selves. Are we *alive or dead ?*

See, too, how sad is the condition of all who have gone through no spiritual change, whose hearts are still the same as in the day they were born. There is a mountain of division between them and heaven. They have yet to "pass from death to life." (1 John iii. 14.) Oh, that they did but see and know their danger! Alas, it is one fearful mark of spiritual death, that, like natural death, it is not felt! We lay our beloved ones tenderly and gently in their narrow beds, but they feel nothing of what we do. "The dead," says the wise man, "know not anything." (Eccl. ix. 5.) And this is just the case with *dead souls*.

See, too, what reason ministers have to be anxious about their congregations. We feel that time is short, and life uncertain. We know that death spiritual is the high road that leads to death eternal. We fear lest any of our hearers should die in their sins, unprepared, unrenewed, impenitent, unchanged. Oh, marvel not if we often speak strongly and plead with you warmly! We dare not give you flattering titles, amuse you with trifles, say smooth things, and cry "Peace, peace," when life and death are at stake, and nothing less. The plague is among you. We feel that we stand between the living and the dead. We must and will "use great plainness of speech." "If the trumpet give an uncertain sound, who shall prepare himself for the battle?" (2 Cor. iii. 12; 1 Cor. xiv. 8.)

II. Let me tell you, in the second place, *what every man needs who would be saved.—He must be quickened and made spiritually alive.*

Life is the mightiest of all possessions. From death to life is the mightiest of all changes. And no change short of this will ever avail to fit man's soul for heaven.

Yes! it is not a little mending and alteration,—a little cleansing and purifying,—a little painting and patching,— a little whitewashing and varnishing,—a little turning over a new leaf and putting on a new out-side that is wanted. It is the bringing in of something altogether new,—the planting within us of a new nature,—a new being—a new principle,—a new mind; this alone, and nothing less than this, will ever meet the necessities of man's soul. We need not merely a new skin, but a new heart.*

To hew a block of marble from the quarry, and carve it into a noble statue,—to break up a waste wilderness, and turn it into a garden of flowers,—to melt a lump of iron-stone, and forge it into watch-springs,—all these are mighty changes. Yet they all come short of the change which every child of Adam requires, for they are merely the same thing in a new form, and the same substance in a new shape. But man requires the grafting in of that which he had not before. He needs a change as great as a resurrection from the dead: he must become a new creature. "Old things must pass away, and all things must become new." He must be "born again, born from above, born of God." The natural birth is not a whit more necessary to the life of the body, than is the spiritual birth to the life of the soul. (2 Cor. v. 17. John iii. 3.)

I know well this is a hard saying. I know the children of this world dislike to hear they must be born again. It pricks their consciences: it makes them feel they are further off from heaven than they are willing to allow. It seems like a narrow door which they have not yet stooped to enter, and they would fain make the door wider, or climb in some other way. But I dare not give place by subjection in this matter. I will not foster a delusion, and tell people they only need repent a little, and stir up a gift they have within them, in order to become real Christians. I dare not use any other language than that of the Bible; and I say, in the words which are written for our learning, "We all need to be born again: we are all naturally dead, and must be made alive."

If we had seen Manasseh, King of Judah, at one time

---

* "It is not a little reforming will save the man, no, nor all the morality in the world, nor all the common graces of God's Spirit, nor the outward change of the life; they will not do, unless we are quickened, and have a new life wrought in us."—*Usher's Sermons.*

filling Jerusalem with idols, and murdering his children in honour of false gods, at another purifying the temple, putting down idolatry, and living a godly life;—if we had seen Zacchæus the publican of Jericho, at one time cheating, plundering, and covetous, at another following Christ, and giving half his goods to the poor;—if we had seen the servants of Nero's household, at one time conforming to their master's profligate ways, at another of one heart and mind with the Apostle Paul,—if we had seen the ancient father Augustine, at one time living in fornication, at another walking closely with God;—if we had seen our own Reformer Latimer, at one time preaching earnestly against the truth as it is in Jesus, at another spending and being spent even to death in Christ's cause;—if we had seen the New Zealanders, or Tinnevelly Hindoos, at one time blood-thirsty, immoral, or sunk in abominable superstitions, at another holy, pure, and believing Christians;—if we had seen these wonderful changes, or any of them, I ask any sensible Christian what we should have said? Should we have been content to call them nothing more than amendments and alterations? Should we have been satisfied with saying that Augustine had "reformed his ways," and that Latimer had "turned over a new leaf"? Verily if we said no more than this, the very stones would cry out. I say in all these cases there was nothing less than a new birth, a resurrection of human nature, a quickening of the dead. These are the right words to use. All other language is weak, poor, beggarly, unscriptural, and short of the truth.

Now I will not shrink from saying plainly, we all need the same kind of change, if we are to be saved. The difference between us and any of those I have just named is far less than it appears. Take off the outward crust, and you will find the same nature beneath, in us and them,—an evil nature, requiring a complete change. The face of the earth is very different in different climates, but the heart of the earth, I believe, is everywhere the same. Go where you will, from one end to the other, you would always find the granite, or other primitive rocks, beneath your feet, if you only bored down deep enough. And it is just the same with men's hearts. Their customs and their colours, their ways and their laws, may all be utterly unlike; but the inner man is always the same.—Their hearts are all alike at the bottom,—all stony, all hard, all ungodly, all needing to be thoroughly renewed. The Englishman and the New Zealander stand on the same level in this matter. Both are naturally dead, and both need to be made alive. Both are children of the same father Adam who fell by sin, and both need to be " born again," and made children of God.

Whatever part of the globe we live in, our *eyes* need to be opened : naturally we never see our sinfulness, guilt, and danger. Whatever nation we belong to our *understandings* need to be enlightened : * naturally we know little or nothing of the plan of salvation;—like the Babel-builders, we think to get to heaven our own way. Whatever church we may belong to, our *wills* need to be bent in the right direction :—naturally we should never choose the things which are for our peace; we should never come to Christ. Whatever be our rank in life, our *affections* need to be turned to things above :—naturally we only set them on things below, earthly, sensual, short-lived, and vain. Pride must give place to humility,—self-righteousness to self-abasement,—carelessness to seriousness,—worldliness to holiness,—unbelief to faith. Satan's dominion must be put down within us, and the kingdom

---

* "Man's understanding is so darkened that he can see nothing of God in God, nothing of holiness in holiness, nothing of good in good, nothing of evil in evil, nor anything of sinfulness in sin. Nay, it is so darkened that he fancies himself to see good in evil, and evil in good, happiness in sin, and misery in holiness."—*Bishop Beveridge, on the Articles.*

of God set up. Self must be crucified, and Christ must reign. Till these things come to pass, we are dead as stones. When these things begin to take place, and not till then, we are *alive*.

I dare say this sounds like foolishness to some. But many a living man could stand up this day and testify that it is true. Many an one could tell us that he knows it all by experience, and that he does indeed feel himself a new man. He loves the things that once he hated, and hates the things that once he loved. He has new habits, new companions, new ways, new tastes, new feelings, new opinions, new sorrows, new joys, new anxieties, new pleasures, new hopes, and new fears. * In short, the whole bias and current of his being is changed. Ask his nearest relations and friends, and they would bear witness to it. Whether they liked it or not, they would be obliged to confess he was no longer the same.

Many an one could tell you that once he did not think himself such a very great transgressor. At any rate he fancied he was no worse than others. Now he would say with the apostle Paul, he feels himself the " chief of sinners." † (1 Tim. i. 15.)

---

* " How wonderfully doth the new born soul differ from his former self. He liveth a new life, he walketh in a new way, he steereth his course by a new compass, and towards a new coast. His principle is new, his pattern is new, his practices are new, his projects are new, all is new. He ravels out all he had wove before, and employeth himself wholly about another work."—*George Swinnocke.* 1660.

† " I cannot pray, but I sin : I cannot hear or preach a sermon, but I sin : I cannot give an alms, or receive the sacrament, but I sin : nay, I cannot so much as confess my sins, but my confessions are still aggravations of them. My repentance needs to be repented of, my tears want washing, and the very washing of my tears needs still to be washed over again with the blood of my Redeemer."—*Bishop Beveridge.*

" Woe is me, that man should think there is anything in me ! He is my witness, before whom I am as crystal, that the secret house-devils, that bear me too often company, that the corruption which I find within, make me go with low sails."—*Rutherford's Letters.* 1637.

Once he did not consider he had a bad heart. He might have his faults, and be led away by bad company and temptations, but he had a good heart at the bottom. Now he would tell you, he knows no heart so bad as his own. He finds it "deceitful above all things, and desperately wicked." (Jer. xvii. 6.)

Once he did not suppose it was a very hard matter to get to heaven. He thought he had only to repent, and say a few prayers, and do what he could, and Christ would make up what was wanting. Now he believes the way is narrow, and few find it. He is convinced he could never have made his own peace with God. He is persuaded that nothing but the blood of Christ could wash away his sins. His only hope is to be "justified by faith without the deeds of the law." (Rom. iii. 28.)

Once he could see no beauty and excellence in the Lord Jesus Christ. He could not understand some ministers speaking so much about Him. Now he would tell you He is the pearl above all price, the chiefest among ten thousand,—his Redeemer, his Advocate, his Priest, his King, his Physician, his Shepherd, his Friend, his All.

Once he thought lightly about sin. He could not see the necessity of being so particular about it. He could not think a man's words, and thoughts, and actions, were of such importance, and required such watchfulness. Now he would tell you sin is the abominable thing which he hates, the sorrow and burden of his life. He longs to be more holy. He can enter thoroughly into Whitefield's desire,—" I want to go where I shall neither sin myself, nor see others sin any more."

Once he found no pleasure in means of grace. The

"I am sick of all I do, and stand astonished that the Redeemer still continues to make use of and bless me. Surely I am more foolish than any man: no one receives so much and does so little."— *Whitefield's Letters.*

Bible was neglected. His prayers, if he had any, were a mere form. Sunday was a tiresome day. Sermons were a weariness, and often sent him to sleep. Now all is altered. These things are the food, the comfort, the delight of his soul.

Once he disliked earnest-minded Christians. He shunned them as melancholy, low-spirited, weak people. Now they are the excellent of the earth, of whom he cannot see too much. He is never so happy as he is in their company. He feels if all men and women were saints, it would be heaven upon earth.

Once he cared only for this world, its pleasures, its business, its occupations, its rewards. Now he looks upon it as an empty, unsatisfying place,—an inn,—a lodging,—a training-school for the life to come. His treasure is in heaven. His home is beyond the grave.

I ask once more, what is all this but new life? Such a change as I have described is no vision and fancy. It is a real actual thing, which not a few in this world have known or felt. It is not a picture of my own imagining. It is a true thing which some of us could find at this moment hard by our own doors. But wherever such a change does take place, there you see the thing of which I am now speaking,—you see the *dead made alive*, a new creature, a soul born again.

I would to God that changes such as this were more common! I would to God there were not such multitudes, of whom we must say even weeping, they know nothing about the matter at all. But, common or not, one thing I say plainly,—this is the kind of change we all need. I do not hold that all must have exactly the same experience. I allow most fully that the change is different, in degree, extent, and intensity, in different persons. Grace may be weak, and yet true;—life may be feeble, and yet real. But I do confidently affirm we must all go through something of this kind, if ever we mean to be saved. Till this sort of change has taken place, there is no life in us at all. We may be living Churchmen, but we are dead Christians.*

Take it home, every man or woman that reads this paper, take it home to your own conscience, and look at it well. Some time or other, between the cradle and the grave, all who would be saved must be made alive. The words which good old Berridge had graven on his tombstone are faithful and true: "Reader! art thou born again? Remember! no salvation without a new birth."

See now what an amazing gulf there is between the Christian in name and form, and the Christian in deed and truth. It is not the difference of one being a little better, and the other a little worse than his neighbour;— it is the difference between a state of life and a state of death. The meanest blade of grass that grows upon a Highland mountain is a more noble object than the fairest wax flower that was ever formed; for it has that which no science of man can impart, it has *life*. The most splendid marble statue in Greece or Italy is nothing by the side of the poor sickly child that crawls over the cottage floor; for with all its beauty it is *dead*. And the weakest member of the family of Christ is far higher and more precious in God's eyes than the most gifted man of the world. The one lives unto God, and shall live for ever;—the other, with all his intellect, is still dead in sins.

Oh, you that have passed from death to life, you have reason indeed to be thankful! Remember what you once were by nature,—dead. Think what you are now by

---

* If we be still our old selves, no changelings at all, the same man that we came into the world, without defalcation of our corruptions, without addition of grace and sanctification, surely we must seek us another Father, we are not yet the sons of God."—*Bishop Hall.* 1652.

"If thou hast anything less than regeneration, believe me, thou canst never see heaven. There is no hope of heaven till then,—till thou art born again."—*Archbishop Usher's Sermons.*

grace,—alive. Look at the dry bones thrown up from the graves. Such were ye; and who has made you to differ? Go and fall low before the footstool of your God. Bless Him for His grace, His free distinguishing grace. Say to Him often, " Who am I, Lord, that thou hast brought me hitherto? Why me? why hast thou been merciful unto me ?"

III. Let me tell you, in the third place, *in what way alone this quickening can be brought about,—by what means a dead soul can be made spritually alive.*

Surely, if I did not tell you this, it would be cruelty to write what I have written. Surely, it would be leading you into a dreary wilderness, and then leaving you without bread and water.—It would be like marching you down to the Red Sea, and then bidding you walk over.—It would be commanding you to make brick like Pharaoh, and yet refusing to provide you with straw.—It would be like tying your hands and feet, and then desiring you to war a good warfare, and "so run as to obtain the prize." I will not do so. I will not leave you, till I have pointed out the wicket-gate towards which you must run. By God's help, I will set before you the full provision there is made for dead souls. Listen to me a little longer, and I will once more show you what is written in the Scripture of truth.

One thing is very clear;—we cannot work this mighty change ourselves. It is not in us. We have no strength or power to do it. We may change our sins, but we cannot change our hearts. We may take up a new way, but not a new nature. We may make considerable reforms and alterations. We may lay aside many outward bad habits, and begin to do many outward duties. But we cannot create a new principle within us. We cannot bring something out of nothing. The Ethiopian cannot change his skin, nor the leopard his spots. No more can we put life into our own souls.* (Jerem. xiii. 23.)

Another thing is equally clear; no man can do it for us. Ministers may preach to us, and pray with us,—receive us at the font in baptism, admit us at the Lord's Table, and give us the bread and wine;—but they cannot bestow spiritual life. They may bring in regularity in the place of disorder, and outward decency in the place of open sin, But they cannot go below the surface. They cannot reach our hearts. Paul may plant and Apollos water, but God alone can give the increase. (1 Cor. iii. 6.)

Who then can make a dead soul alive ? No one can do it but God. He only who breathed into Adam's nostrils the breath of life, can ever make a dead sinner a living Christian. He only who formed the world out of nothing in the day of creation, can make man a new creature. He only who said, " Let there be light, and there was light," can cause spiritual light to shine into man's heart. He only who formed man out of the dust and gave life to his body can ever give life to his soul. His is the special office to do it by His Spirit, and His also is the power.†
(Gen. i. 2, 3.)

---

* "There is not one good duty which the natural man can do. If it should be said to him, Think but one good thought, and for it thou shalt go to heaven, he could not think it. Till God raise him from the sink of sin, as he did Lazarus from the grave, he cannot do anything that is well pleasing to God. He may do the works of a moral man, but to do the works of a man quickened and enlightened, it is beyond his power."—*Usher's Sermons.*

" Nature can no more cast out nature, than Satan can cast out Satan."
—*Thomas Watson.* 1653.

"Nature cannot raise itself to this, any more than a man can give natural being to himself."—*Archbishop Leighton.*

† "To create or bring something out of nothing, is beyond the power of the strongest creature. It is above the strength of all men and angels to create the least blade of grass ; God challengeth this as His prerogative royal. (Isaiah xl. 26.) Augustine said truly, To convert the little world man, is more than to create the great world."—*George Swinnocke.* 1660.

The glorious Gospel contains provision for our spiritual, as well as our eternal life. The Lord Jesus is a complete Saviour. That mighty living Head has no dead members. His people are not only justified and pardoned, but quickened together with Him, and made partakers of His resurrection. To Him the Spirit joins the sinner, and raises him by that union from death to life. In Him the sinner lives after he has believed. The spring of all his vitality is the union between Christ and his soul, which the Spirit begins and keeps up. Christ is the appointed fountain of all spiritual life, and the Holy Ghost the appointed agent who conveys that life to our souls.*

Come to the Lord Jesus Christ, if you would have life. He will not cast you out. He has gifts, even for the rebellious. The moment the dead man touched the body of Elisha, he revived and stood upon his feet. (2 Kings xiii. 21.)—The moment you touch the Lord Jesus with the hand of faith, you are alive unto God, as well as forgiven all trespasses. Come, and your soul shall live.

I never despair of any one becoming a decided Christian, whatever he may have been in days gone by. I know how great the change is from death to life. I know the mountains of division that seem to stand between some of us and heaven. I know the hardness, the prejudices, the desperate sinfulness of the natural heart. But I remember that God the Father made this beautiful and well-ordered world out of nothing. I remember the voice of the Lord Jesus could reach Lazarus when four days dead, and recall him even from the grave. I remember the amazing victories the Spirit of God has won in every nation under heaven. I remember all this, and feel that I never need

---

* "Then do we begin to live, when we begin to have union with Christ the Fountain of Life, by His Spirit communicated to us: from this time we are to reckon our life."—*Flavel.*

"Christ is an universal principle of all life."—*Sibbs.* 1635.

despair. Yes! those among us who now seem most utterly dead in sins, may yet be raised to a new being, and walk before God in newness of life.

Why should it not be so? The Holy Spirit is a merciful and loving Spirit. He turns away from no man because of his vileness. He passes by no one because his sins are black and scarlet.

There was nothing in the Corinthians that He should come down and quicken them. Paul reports of them that they were "fornicators, idolaters, adulterers, effeminate, thieves, covetous, drunkards, revilers, extortioners." "Such," he says, "were some of you." Yet even them the Spirit made alive. "Ye are washed," he writes, "ye are sanctified, ye are justified, in the name of the Lord Jesus, and by the spirit of our God." (1 Cor. vi. 9, 10, 11.)

There was nothing in the Colossians, that He should visit their hearts. Paul tells us that "they walked in fornication, uncleanness, inordinate affection, evil concupiscence, and covetousness, which is idolatry." Yet them also the Spirit quickened. He made them "put off the old man with his deeds, and put on the new man which is renewed in knowledge after the image of Him that created him." (Coloss. iii. 5—10.)

There was nothing in Mary Magdalene that the Spirit should make her soul alive. Once she had been "possessed with seven devils." There was once a time, if report be true, when she was a woman proverbial for vileness and iniquity. Yet even her the Spirit made a new creature, separated her from her sins, brought her to Christ, made her "last at the cross, and first at the tomb."

Never, never will the Spirit turn away from a soul because of its corruption. He never has done so;—He never will. It is His glory that He has purified the minds of the most impure, and made them temples for His own abode. He may yet take the worst of us, and make him a vessel of grace.

Why indeed should it not be so? The Spirit is an Almighty Spirit. He can change the stony heart into a heart of flesh. He can break up and destroy the strongest bad habits, like tow in the fire. He can make the most difficult things seem easy, and the mightiest objections melt away like snow in spring. He can cut the bars of brass, and throw the gates of prejudice wide open. He can fill up every valley, and make every rough place smooth. He has done it often, and He can do it again.*

The Spirit can take a Jew,—the bitterest enemy of Christianity,—the fiercest persecutor of true believers,— the strongest stickler for Pharisaical notions,—the most prejudiced opposer of Gospel doctrine,—and turn that man into an earnest preacher of the very faith he once destroyed. He has done it already.—He did it with the Apostle Paul.

The Spirit can take a Roman Catholic monk, brought up in the midst of Romish superstition,—trained from his infancy to believe false doctrine, and obey the Pope,— steeped to the eyes in error,—and make that man the clearest upholder of justification by faith the world ever saw. He has done so already.—He did it with Martin Luther.

The Spirit can take an English tinker, without learning, patronage, or money,—a man at one time notorious for nothing so much as blasphemy and swearing,—and make that man write a religious book, which shall stand unrivalled and unequalled, in its way, by any book since the time of the Apostles. He has done so already.—He did it with John Bunyan, the author of "Pilgrim's Progress."

The Spirit can take a sailor drenched in worldliness and sin,—a profligate captain of a slave ship,—and make that

---

* "Such is the power of the Holy Ghost to regenerate men, and as it were to bring them forth anew, so that they shall be nothing like the men they were before."—*Homily for Whit-Sunday.*

man a most successful minister of the Gospel,—a writer of letters, which are a store-house of experimental religion,—and of hymns which are known and sung wherever English is spoken. He has done it already.—He did it with John Newton.

All this the Spirit has done, and much more, of which I cannot speak particularly. And the arm of the Spirit is not shortened. His power is not decayed. He is like the Lord Jesus,—" the same yesterday, to-day, and for ever." (Heb. xiii. 8.) He is still doing wonders, and will do to the very end.

Once more then, I say, I never despair of any man's soul being made alive. I should if it depended on man himself. Some seem so hardened, I should have no hope. I should despair if it depended on the work of ministers. Alas, the very best of us are poor, weak creatures! But I cannot despair when I remember that God the Spirit is the agent who conveys life to the soul,—for I know and am persuaded that with Him nothing is impossible.

I should not be surprised to hear, even in this life, that the hardest man in the list of my acquaintances has become softened, and the proudest has taken his place at the feet of Jesus as a weaned child.

I shall not be surprised to meet many on the right hand, in the day of judgment, whom I shall leave, when I die, travelling in the broad way. I shall not start, and say, " What! you here!" I shall only remind them, " Was not this my word, when I was yet among you,—Nothing is impossible with Him that quickeneth the dead."

Does any one of us desire to help the Church of Christ? Then let him pray for a great outpouring of the Spirit. He alone can give edge to sermons, and point to advice, and power to rebukes, and can cast down the high walls of sinful hearts. It is not better preaching, and finer writing that is wanted in this day, but more of the presence of the Holy Ghost.

Does any one feel the slightest drawing towards God,—the smallest concern about his immortal soul? Then flee to that open fountain of living waters, the Lord Jesus Christ, and you shall receive the Holy Ghost. (John vii. 39.) Begin at once to pray for the Holy Spirit. Think not that you are shut up and cut off from hope. The Holy Ghost is promised to "them that ask Him." (Luke xi. 13.) His very name is the Spirit of promise and the Spirit of life. Give Him no rest till He comes down and makes you a new heart. Cry mightily unto the Lord,—say unto Him, "Bless me, even me also,—quicken me, and make me alive."

And now let me wind up all I have said with a few words of special application. I have shown what I believe to be the truth as it is in Jesus. Let me try, by God's blessing, to bring it home to the hearts and consciences of all into whose hands this volume may fall.

1. First, let me put this question to every soul who reads this paper: "Are you dead, or are you alive?"

Suffer me, as an ambassador for Christ, to press the inquiry on every conscience. There are only two ways to walk in, the narrow and the broad;—two companies in the day of judgment, those on the right hand, and those on the left;—two classes of people in the professing Church of Christ, and to one of them you must belong. Where are you? What are you? Are you among the living, or among the dead?

I speak to you yourself, and to none else,—not to your neighbour, but to you,—not to Africans or New Zealanders, but to you. I do not ask whether you are an angel, or whether you have the mind of David or Paul,—but I do ask whether you have a well-founded hope that you are a new creature in Christ Jesus,—I do ask whether you have reason to believe you have put off the old man and put on the new,—whether you are conscious of ever having gone through a real spiritual change of heart,—whether, in one word, you are dead or alive.*

(a) Think not to put me off by saying, "you were admitted into the Church by baptism, you received grace and the Spirit in that sacrament,—you are alive." It shall not avail you. Paul himself says of the baptized widow who lives in pleasure, " She is *dead* while she liveth." (1 Tim. v. 6.) The Lord Jesus Christ Himself tells the chief officer of the Church in Sardis, "Thou hast a name that thou livest, and art *dead*." (Rev. iii. 1.). The life you talk of is nothing if it cannot be seen. Show it to me, if I am to believe its existence. Grace is light, and light will always be discerned. Grace is salt, and salt will always be tasted. An indwelling of the Spirit which does not show itself by outward fruits, and a grace which men's eyes cannot discover, are both to be viewed with the utmost suspicion. Believe me, if you have no other proof of spiritual life but your baptism, you are yet a dead soul.

(b) Think not to tell me " It is a question that cannot be decided, and you call it presumptuous to give an opinion in such a matter." This is a vain refuge, and a false humility. Spiritual life is no such dim and doubtful thing as you seem to fancy. There are marks and evidences by which its presence may be discerned by those who know

---

* " All hangs upon this hinge. If this be not done, ye are undone—undone eternally. All your profession, civility, privileges, gifts, duties, are cyphers, and signify nothing, unless regeneration be the figure put before them."—*Swinnocke.* 1660.

" Believe me, whatsoever thou art, thou shalt never be saved for being a lord or a knight, a gentleman or a rich man, a learned man or a well-spoken, eloquent man ; nor yet for being a Calvinist, or a Lutheran, an Arminian, an Anabaptist, a Presbyterian, an Independent, or a Protestant, formally and merely as such ; much less for being a Papist, or of any such grossly deluded sect :—but as a regenerate Christian it is that thou must be saved,—or thou canst have no hope."—*Richard Baxter.* 1659.

the Bible. "We know," says John, "that we have passed from death unto life." (1 John iii. 14.) The exact time and season of that passage may often be hidden from a man. The fact and reality of it will seldom be entirely an uncertain thing. It was a true and beautiful saying of a Scotch girl, to Whitefield, when asked if her heart was changed: "Something was changed, she knew,—it might be the world, it might be her own heart,—but there was a great change somewhere, she was quite sure, for every thing seemed different to what it once did." Oh, cease to evade the inquiry! "Anoint your eyes with eye-salve that you may see." (Rev. iii. 18.) Are you dead or alive?

(*c*) Think not to reply, "You do not know;—you allow it is a matter of importance;—you hope to know some time before you die;—you mean to give your mind to it when you have a convenient season;—but at present you do not know."

You do not know! Yet heaven or hell is wrapped up in this question. An eternity of happiness or misery hinges upon your answer. You do not leave your worldly affairs so unsettled. You do not manage your earthly business so loosely. You look far forward. You provide against every possible contingency. You insure life and property. Oh, why not deal in the same way with your immortal soul?

You do not know! Yet all around you is uncertainty. You are a poor frail worm,—your body fearfully and wonderfully made,—your health liable to be put out of order in a thousand ways. The next time the daisies bloom, it may be over your grave. All before you is dark. You know not what a day might bring forth, much less a year. Oh! why not bring your soul's business to a point without delay?

Let every reader of this paper begin the great business of self-examination. Rest not till you know the length and breadth of your own state in God's sight. Backwardness in this matter is an evil sign. It springs from an uneasy conscience. It shows that a man thinks ill of his own case. He feels, like a dishonest tradesman, that his accounts will not bear inquiry. He dreads the light.

In spiritual things, as in everything else, it is the highest wisdom to make sure work. Take nothing for granted. Do not measure your condition by that of others. Bring everything to the measure of God's Word. A mistake about your soul is a mistake for eternity. "Surely," says Leighton, "they that are not born again, shall one day wish they had never been born."

Sit down this day and think. Commune with your own heart and be still. Go to your own room and consider. Enter into your own closet, or at any rate contrive to be alone with God. Look the question fairly, fully, honestly in the face. How does it touch you? Are you among the living or among the dead? *

2. In the second place, let me speak in all affection to those who are *dead*.

What shall I say to you? What can I say? What words of mine are likely to have any effect on your hearts?

This I will say,—I mourn over your souls. I do most unfeignedly mourn. You may be thoughtless and unconcerned. You may care little for what I am saying. You may scarcely run your eye over this paper, and after reading it you may despise it and return to the world; but you cannot prevent my feeling for you, however little you may feel for yourselves.

Do I mourn when I see a young man sapping the foundation of his bodily health by indulging his lusts and passions, sowing bitterness for himself in his old age? Much more then will I mourn over your souls.

---

* "If your state be good, searching into it will give you the comfort of it. If your state be bad, searching into it cannot make it worse; nay, it is the only way to make it better: for conversion begins with conviction."—*Bishop Hopkins.* 1680.

Do I mourn when I see men squandering away their inheritance, and wasting their property on trifles and follies ? Much more then will I mourn over your souls.

Do I mourn when I hear of one drinking slow poisons, because they are pleasant, as the Chinese take opium, —putting the clock of his life on, as if it did not go fast enough,—inch by inch digging his own grave ? Much more then will I mourn over your souls.

I mourn to think of golden opportunities thrown away, —of Christ rejected,—of the blood of atonement trampled under foot,—of the Spirit resisted,—the Bible neglected, —heaven despised, and the world put in the place of God.

I mourn to think of the present happiness you are missing,—the peace and consolation you are thrusting from you,—the misery you are laying up in store for your-selves,—and the bitter waking up which is yet to come.

Yes! I must mourn. I cannot help it. Others may think it enough to mourn over dead bodies. For my part, I think there is far more cause to mourn over dead souls. The children of this world find fault with us sometimes for being so serious and grave. Truly, when I look at the world, I marvel we can ever smile at all.

To every one who is dead in sins I say this day, Why will you die ? Are the wages of sin so sweet and good, that you cannot give them up ? Is the world so satisfying that you cannot forsake it ? Is the service of Satan so pleasant that you and he are never to be parted ? Is heaven so poor a thing that it is not worth seeking ? Is your soul of so little consequence, that it is not worth a struggle to have it saved ? Oh, turn ! turn before it be too late ! God is not willing that you should perish. "As I live," He says, " I have no pleasure in the death of him that dieth." Jesus loves you, and grieves to see your folly. He wept over wicked Jerusalem, saying, "I would have gathered thee, but thou wouldst not be gathered." Surely if lost, your blood will be upon your own heads. "Awake,

and arise from the dead, and Christ shall give you light."
(Ezek. xviii. 32; Matt. xxiii. 37; Eph. v. 14.)

Believe me, believe me, true repentance is that one step
that no man ever repented. Thousands have said at their
latter end, they had "served God too little:" no child of
Adam ever said, as he left this world, that he had cared
for his soul too much. The way of life is a narrow path,
but the footsteps in it are all in one direction: not one
child of Adam has ever come back and said it was a delusion. The way of the world is a broad way, but millions
on millions have forsaken it, and borne their testimony
that it was a way of sorrow and disappointment.

3. Let me, in the third place, speak to those who are
living.

Are you indeed alive unto God? Can you say with
truth, "I was dead, and am alive again. I was blind, but
now I see"? Then suffer the word of exhortation, and
incline your hearts unto wisdom.

Are you alive? Then see that you *prove* it *by your
actions*. Be a consistent witness. Let your words, and
works, and ways, and tempers all tell the same story. Let
not your life be a poor torpid life, like that of a tortoise or
a sloth;—let it rather be an energetic stirring life, like
that of a deer or bird. Let your graces shine forth from all
the windows of your conversation, that those who live near
you may see that the Spirit is abiding in your hearts. Let
your light not be a dim, flickering, uncertain flame; let it
burn steadily, like the eternal fire on the altar, and never
become low. Let the savour of your religion, like Mary's
precious ointment, fill all the houses where you dwell.—
Be an epistle of Christ so clearly written, penned in such
large bold characters, that he who runs may read it. Let
your Christianity be so unmistakeable, your eye so single,
your heart so whole, your walk so straightforward that
all who see you may have no doubt whose you are, and
whom you serve. If we are quickened by the Spirit, no

one ought to be able to doubt it. Our conversation should
declare plainly that we " seek a country." (Heb xi 14.)
It ought not to be necessary to tell people, as in the case
of a badly painted picture, " This is a Christian." We
ought not to be so sluggish and still, that men shall be
obliged to come close and look hard, and say, " Is he dead
or alive ? "

Are you alive ? Then see that you *prove* it *by your
growth.* Let the great change within become every year
more evident. Let your light be an increasing light,—not
like Joshua's sun in the valley of Ajalon, standing still,—
nor like Hezekiah's sun, going back,—but ever shining
more and more to the very end of your days. Let the
image of your Lord, wherein you are renewed, grow clearer
and sharper every month. Let it not be like the image
and superscription on a coin, more indistinct and defaced the
longer it is used. Let it rather become more plain the older
it is, and let the likeness of your King stand out more fully
and sharply. I have no confidence in a standing-still
religion. I do not think a Christian was meant to be like
an animal, to grow to a certain age, and then stop growing.
I believe rather he was meant to be like a tree, and to increase more and more in strength and vigour all his days.
Remember the words of the Apostle Peter : " Add to your
faith virtue, and to virtue knowledge, and to knowledge
temperance, and to temperance brotherly kindness, and
to brotherly kindness charity." (2 Peter i. 5, 6, 7.) This
is the way to be a useful Christian. Men will believe you
are in earnest when they see constant improvement, and
perhaps be drawn to go with you.*—This is one way to
obtain comfortable assurance. "So an entrance shall be
ministered unto you abundantly." (2 Peter i. 11.) Oh,
as ever you would be useful and happy in your religion,

---

* "Men who are prejudiced observe actions a great deal more than
words."—*Leighton.*

let your motto be, "Forward, forward!" to your very last day.

I entreat all believing readers to remember that I speak to myself as well as to them. I say the spiritual life there is in Christians ought to be more evident. Our lamps want trimming,—they ought not to burn so dim. Our separation from the world should be more distinct,—our walk with God more decided. Too many of us are like Lot,—lingerers; or like Reuben, Gad, and Manasseh, --borderers; or like the Jews in Ezra's time,—so mixed up with strangers, that our spiritual pedigree cannot be made out. It ought not so to be. Let us be up and doing. If we live in the Spirit, let us also walk in the Spirit. If we really have life, let us make it known.

The state of the world demands it. The latter days have fallen upon us. The kingdoms of the earth are shaking, falling, crashing, and crumbling away. (Isaiah xxiv. 1, etc.) The glorious kingdom that will never be removed is drawing nigh. The King Himself is close at hand. The children of this world are looking round to see what the saints are doing. God, in His wonderful providences, is calling to us,—"Who is on my side? Who?"—Surely we ought to be, like Abraham, very ready with our answer: "Here am I!" (Gen. xxii. 1.)

"Ah!" you may say,—"These are ancient things: these are brave words. We know it all. But we are weak, we have no power to think a good thought, we can do nothing, we must sit still."—Hearken, my believing reader. What is the cause of your weakness? Is it not because the fountain of life is little used? Is it not because you are resting on old experiences, and not daily gathering new manna,—daily drawing new strength from Christ? He has left you the promise of the Comforter. "He giveth more grace,"—grace upon grace to all who ask it.—He came "that you might have life, and have it more abundantly."—"Open your mouths wide," He says this day, "and they shall be filled." (James iv. 6; John x. 10; Ps. lxxxi. 10.)

I say to all believers who read this paper, if you want your spiritual life to be more healthy and vigorous, you must just come more boldly to the throne of grace. You must give up this hanging-back spirit,—this hesitation about taking the Lord at His own word. Doubtless you are poor sinners, and nothing at all. The Lord knows it, and has provided a store of strength for you. But you do not draw upon the store He has provided: you have not, because you ask not. The secret of your weakness is your little faith, and little prayer. The fountain is unsealed, but you only sip a few drops. The bread of life is before you, yet you only eat a few crumbs. The treasury of heaven is open, but you only take a few pence. "O ye of little faith, wherefore do ye doubt?" (Matt. xiv. 31.)

Awake to know your privileges;—awake, and sleep no longer. Tell me not of spiritual hunger, and thirst, and poverty, so long as the throne of grace is before you. Say rather, that you are proud, and will not come to it as poor sinners. Say rather, you are slothful, and will not take pains to get more.

Cast aside the grave-clothes of pride, which still hang around you. Throw off that Egyptian garment of indolence, which ought not to have been brought through the Red Sea. Away with that unbelief, which ties and paralyzes your tongue. You are not straitened in God, but in yourselves. "Come boldly to the throne of grace," where the Father is ever waiting to give, and Jesus ever sits by Him to intercede. (Heb. iv. 16.) Come boldly, for you may, all sinful as you are, if you come in the name of the Great High Priest. Come boldly, and ask largely, and you shall have abundant answers,—mercy like a river, and grace and strength like a mighty stream. Come boldly, and you shall have supplies exceeding all you can

ask or think. "Hitherto you have asked nothing. Ask
and receive, that your joy may be full." (John xvi. 24.)

If we really are *alive and not dead,* let us strive so to
carry ourselves that men may know whose we are. While
we live, may we live unto the Lord. When we die, may
we die the death of the righteous. And when the Lord
Jesus comes, may we be found ready, and " not be ashamed
before Him at His coming." (1 John ii. 28.).

But, after all, are we alive or dead ? That is the great
question.

VI.

OUR SINS!

" Make me to know my trangression and my sin."—JOB xiii. 23.

" Our sins testify against us."—ISA. lix. 12.

" Cleanse me from my sin."—PSALM li. 2.

" The blood of Jesus Christ His Son cleanseth us from all sin."
—1 JOHN i. 7.

THE two words which head this page ought to stir up
within us great searchings of heart. They concern every
man and woman born into the world. To know "our
sins" is the first letter in the alphabet of saving religion.
To understand our position in the sight of God is one step
towards heaven. The true secret of peace of conscience is
to feel "our sins" put away. If we love life we ought
never to rest till we can give a satisfactory answer to the
question,—"WHERE ARE MY SINS?"

I ask my readers this day to look this simple question in
the face. A time draws nigh when the question *must*
be answered. The hour cometh when all other questions
will seem like a drop of water in comparison with this.
We shall not say, "Where is my money?"—or, "Where
are my lands?"—or, "Where is my property?" Our
only thought will be, "My sins! my sins!—Where are my
sins?"

I am going to offer a few remarks which may help to
throw light on the mighty subject which is before our

eyes. My heart's desire and prayer to God is this,—that this paper may be useful to the souls of all who read this volume. I entreat you to give it a fair reading. Read it: read it! Read it to the end! Who can tell but the Holy Ghost may employ this paper for the saving of your soul?

I. My first remark is this. *You have many sins.*

I say this boldly, and without the least hesitation. I know not who you are, or how the time past of your life has been spent. But I know, from the Word of God, that every son and daughter of Adam is a great sinner in the sight of God. There is no exception: it is the common disease of the whole family of mankind in every quarter of the globe. From the king on his throne, to the beggar by the roadside,—from the landlord in his hall, to the labourer in his cottage,—from the fine lady in her drawing-room, to the humblest maid-servant in the kitchen,—from the clergyman in the pulpit, to the little child in the Sunday-school,—we are all by nature guilty, guilty, guilty in the sight of God. "In many things we offend all."—"There is none righteous: no, not one."—"All have sinned."—"If we say that we have no sin, we deceive ourselves, and the truth is not in us." (James iii. 2; Rom. iii. 10; v. 12; 1 John i. 8.) It is useless to deny it. We have all sinned many sins!

Does any one doubt the truth of these words? Then go and examine *the law of God,* as expounded by the Son of God Himself. Read with attention the fifth chapter of St. Matthew's Gospel. See how the commandments of God apply to our words as well as to our actions, and to our thoughts and motives, as well as to our words. Know that "the Lord seeth not as man seeth: man looketh at the outward appearance, but the Lord looketh at the heart." In His sight the very "thought of foolishness is sin." (1 Sam. xvi. 7; Prov. xxiv. 9.)

And now turn to the history of *your own life*, and try it by the standard of this holy law. Think of the days of your childhood, and all your waywardness, and selfishness, and evil tempers, and perversity, and backwardness to that which is good.—Remember the days of your youth,— your self-will, your pride, your worldly inclinations, your impatience of control, your longing after forbidden things. —Call to mind your conduct since you came to man's estate, and the many departures from the right way, of which you have been guilty every year.—Surely, in the face of your life's history, you will not stand up and say, "I have not sinned!"

And then turn to the history of *your own heart*. Consider how many evil things have gone through it, of which the world knows nothing at all.—Remember the thousands of sinful imaginations, and corrupt ideas, which your heart has entertained, even while your outward conduct has been correct, moral, and respectable.—Think of the vile thoughts, and deceitful intentions, and false motives, and malicious, envious, spiteful feelings, which have walked up and down in your inward man, while those nearest to you never dreamed or guessed what was going on.—Surely, in the face of your heart's history, you will not stand up and say, "I have not sinned!"

Once more I ask every reader of this paper, Do you doubt what I am saying? Do you doubt whether you have sinned many sins?—Then go and examine the twenty-fifth chapter of St. Matthew's Gospel. Read the concluding portion of that chapter, which describes the proceedings of the *judgment day*. Note carefully the grounds on which the wicked, at the left hand, are condemned to everlasting fire. No mention is made of great open acts of wickedness which they have committed. They are not charged with having murdered, or stolen, or borne false witness, or committed adultery. They are condemned for *sins of omission!* The mere fact that they have left undone things which they ought to have done, is sufficient to ruin their souls for ever. In short, a man's sins of omission alone are enough to sink him into hell!

And now look at yourself by the light of this wonderful passage of Scripture. Try to remember the countless things you have left undone, which you might have done, and have left unsaid, that you might have said. The acts of self-denying kindness, which you might have performed, but have neglected,—how many they are! The good you might have done, and the happiness you might have caused, at very little trouble to yourself,—how vast is the amount of it! Surely, in the face of our Lord's teaching about sins of omission, you will not stand up and say, " I have not sinned!"

Once more I ask, Do you doubt the truth of what I am saying? I think it quite possible that you do. As a minister of Christ for more than a quarter of a century, I know something of man's exceeding blindness to his own natural state. Listen to me once more, whilst I ply your conscience with another argument. Oh, that God may open your eyes, and show you what you are!

Sit down, and take pen and paper, and count up the sins that you have probably sinned since you first knew good from evil. Sit down, I say, and *make a sum.* Grant for a moment that there have been on an average, fifteen hours in every twenty-four during which you have been awake, and an active and accountable being. Grant for a moment that in each one of these fifteen hours you have sinned only two sins. Surely you will not say that this is an unfair supposition. Remember we may sin against God in thought, word, or deed. I repeat, it cannot be thought an extreme thing to suppose that in each waking hour of your life you have, in thought, or word, or deed, sinned two sins. And now add up the sins of your life, and see to what sum they will amount.

At the rate of fifteen waking hours in a day, you have

sinned every day thirty sins !—At the rate of seven days in a week, you have sinned two hundred and ten sins every week !—At the rate of four weeks in every month, you have sinned eight hundred and forty sins every month ! —At the rate of twelve months in every year, you have sinned ten thousand and eighty sins every year !—And, in short, not to go further with the calculation, every ten years of you life you have sinned, at the lowest computation, more than ONE HUNDRED THOUSAND SINS !

I invite you to look calmly at this sum. I defy you to disprove its correctness. I ask you, on the contrary, whether I have not entirely understated your case ? I appeal to you, as an honest person, whether it be not true, that many an hour, and many a day in your life, you have sinned incessantly ? I ask you confidently, whether the sum would not be far more correct if the total number of your sins was multiplied ten-fold ?—Oh, cease from your self-righteousness ! Lay aside this proud affectation or "not being so very bad," in which you are trying to wrap yourself up. Be bold enough to confess the truth. Listen not to that old liar, the devil. Surely in the face of that damning sum which I have just cast up, you will not dare to deny that " you have many sins."

I leave this part of my subject here, and pass on. I sadly fear that many a reader will run his eye over what I have been saying, and remain unconvinced and unmoved. I have learned by mournful experience that the last thing a man finds out and understands, is his own state in the sight of God. Well saith the Holy Ghost, that we are all by nature " blind," and " deaf," and " dumb," and " asleep," and " beside ourselves," and " dead ! " Nothing, nothing will ever convince man of sin but the power of the Holy Ghost. Show him hell, and he will not flee from it ; show him heaven, and he will not seek it ; silence him with warnings, and yet he will not stir ; prick his conscience, and yet he will remain hard. Power from on high must

come down and do the work. To show man what he
really is, is the special work of the Holy Spirit of God.

He that has any feeling of his own sinfulness, ought
to thank God for it. That very sense of weakness,
wickedness, and corruption, which perhaps makes you
uncomfortable, is in reality a token for good, and a cause
for praise. The first step towards being really good, is to
feel *bad*. The first preparation for heaven, is to know that
we deserve nothing but *hell*. Before we can be counted
righteous we must know ourselves to be miserable *sinners*.
Before we can have inward happiness and peace with
God, we must learn to be ashamed and confounded
because of our manifold transgressions. Before we can
rejoice in a well-grounded hope, we must be taught to
say, " Unclean : unclean ! God, be merciful to me a
sinner ! "

He that really loves his own soul must beware of
checking and stifling this inward feeling of sinfulness. I
beseech you, by the mercies of God, do not trample on it,
do not crush it, do not take it by the throat and refuse to
give it your attention. Beware of taking the advice of
worldly men about it. Treat it not as a case of low-
spirits, disordered health, or anything of the kind. Beware of listening to the devil's counsel about it. Do not
try to drown it in drink and revelling ; do not try to drive
over it with horses, and dogs, and carriages, and field-
sports ; do not try to purge it away by a course of card-
parties, and balls, and concerts. Oh, if you love your
soul, do not, do not treat the first sense of sin in this
miserable fashion ! Do not commit spiritual suicide,—
do not murder your soul !

Go rather and pray God to show you what this feeling
of sin means. Ask Him to send the Holy Spirit to teach
you what you are, and what He would have you to do.
Go and read your Bible, and see whether there is not just
cause for your being uncomfortable, and whether this

sense of being "wicked and bad" is not just what you have a right to expect. Who can tell but it is a seed from heaven, which is one day to bear fruit in Paradise in your complete salvation? Who can tell but it is a spark from heaven, which God means to blow up into a steady and shining fire? Who can tell but it is a little stone from above, before which the devil's kingdom in your heart is to go down, and a stone which shall prove the first foundation of a glorious temple of the Holy Ghost?—Happy indeed is that man or woman who can go along with my first remark, and say, "IT IS TRUE: I HAVE MANY SINS."

II. My second remark is this. *It is of the utmost importance to have our sins taken off us and put away.*

I say this boldly and confidently. I am aware of the multitude of things which are thought "important" in the world, and receive the first and best of men's attentions. But I know well what I am saying. I am bold to say that my Master's business deserves to be placed before all other business; and I learn from my Master's book that there is nothing of such importance to a man as to have his sins forgiven and cleansed away.

Let us remember *there is a God above us.* We see Him not in the city. Hurry and bustle, trade and commerce, appear to swallow up men's minds. We see Him not in the country. Farming and labouring go on in regular course, and seed time and harvest never fail. But all this time there is an eternal Eye looking down from heaven and seeing all that men do: an eye that never slumbers, and never sleeps. Yes! there is not only a Queen, and a government, and a landlord, and a master, and an employer, to be remembered. There is One higher, far higher than all these, who expects His dues to be paid. That One is the most high God.

This God is a God of infinite *holiness.* He is of "purer eyes than to behold evil, and canst not look on iniquity." (Habak. i. 13.) He sees defects and infirmities where we see none. In His sight the very "heavens are not clean." (Job. xv. 15.) He is a God of infinite *knowledge*. He knows every thought, and word, and action of every one of Adam's children : there are no secrets hid from Him. All that we think, and say, and do, is noted down and recorded in the book of His remembrance.—He is a God of infinite *power*. He made all things at the beginning. He orders all things according to His will. He casts down the Kings of this world in a moment. None can stand against Him when He is angry.—Above all, He is a God in whose hands are our lives and all our concerns. He first gave us being. He has kept us alive since we were born. He will remove us when He sees fit, and reckon with us according to our ways. Such is the God with whom we have to do.

Let us think of these things. Surely, as Job says, " when you consider you will be afraid." (Job xxiii. 15.) Surely you will see it is of the utmost importance to have your sins cleansed away. Surely you will inquire, " How do matters stand between me and God ? "

Let us remember, furthermore, that *death is before us*. We cannot live always. There must be an end, one day, of all our scheming and planning, and buying and selling, and working and toiling. A visitor will come to our house who will take no denial. The king of terrors will demand admission, and serve us with notice to quit. Where are the rulers and kings who governed millions a hundred years ago ? Where are the rich men who made fortunes and founded houses ? Where are the landlords who received rents and added field to field ? Where are the labourers who ploughed the land and reaped the corn ? Where are the clergymen who read services and preached sermons ? Where are the children who played in the sunshine as if they would never be old ? Where are the old men who leaned on their sticks and gossiped about "the days when they were young"? There is but one answer. They are all dead, dead, dead! Strong, and beautiful, and active as they once were, they are all dust and ashes now. Mighty and important as they all thought their business, it all came to an end. And we are travelling in the same way! A few more years and we also shall be lying in our graves!

Let us think of these things. Surely when you consider your latter end you will not think the cleansing away of sin a light matter. Surely you will see something in the question, "Where are your sins?" Surely you will consider, "How am I going to die?"

Let us remember, furthermore, that *resurrection and judgment await us.* All is not over when the last breath is drawn and our bodies become a lump of cold clay. No: all is not over! The realities of existence then begin. The shadows will have passed away for ever. The trumpet shall one day sound, and call us forth from our narrow bed. The graves shall be rent asunder, and their tenants shall be summoned forth to meet God. The ears that would not obey the church-going bell shall be obliged to obey another summons; the proud wills that would not submit to listen to sermons shall be compelled to listen to the judgment of God. The great white throne shall be set: the books shall be opened. Every man, woman, and child, shall be arraigned at that great assize. Every one shall be judged according to his works. The sins of every one shall be answered for. And every one shall receive his eternal portion either in heaven or in hell!

Let us think of these things. Surely in remembrance of that day you must allow that the subject I am upon deserves attention. Surely you must confess that it is of the utmost importance to have your sins cleansed away. Surely you will consider, "How am I going to be judged?"

I must speak out what is upon my mind. I feel great sorrow and trouble of heart about many men and women in the world. I fear for many who live in this so-called Christian land; I fear for many who profess and call themselves Christians; I fear for many who go to church or chapel every Sunday and have a decent form of religion; I fear that they do not see the immense importance of having their sins cleansed away. I can see plainly that there are many other things which they think far more *important*. Money, and land, and farms, and horses, and carriages, and dogs, and meat, and drink, and clothes, and houses, and marriages, and families, and business, and pleasure,—these, these are the sort of things which many evidently think the "first things." And as for the forgiveness and cleansing away of their sins, it is a matter which has only the second place in their thoughts.

See the man of business, as he pores over his ledger and account books, and runs his eye over the columns of figures. See the man of pleasure, as he tears over the country with his horses and dogs, or rushes after excitement at the races, the theatre, the card party, or the ball. See the poor thoughtless labourer, as he carries off his hard-earned wages to the public house, and wastes them in ruining both body and soul. See them all, how thoroughly they are in earnest! See them all, how they throw their hearts into what they are doing!—And then mark them all at church next Sunday: listless, careless, yawning, sleepy, and indifferent, as if there were no God, and no devil, and no Christ, and no heaven, and no hell! Mark how evident it is that they have left their hearts outside the church! Mark how plain it is that they have no real interest in religion! And then say whether it be not true that many know nothing of the importance of having their sins cleansed away. O, take heed lest this be the case with you!

Does any reader of these pages feel anything of the importance of being forgiven? Then, in the name of God, I call upon you to encourage that feeling more and more.

This is the point to which we desire to bring all people's souls. We want you to understand that religion does not consist in professing certain opinions, and performing certain outward duties, and going through certain outward forms. It consists in being reconciled to God, and enjoying peace with Him. It consists in having our sins cleansed away, and knowing that they are cleansed. It consists in being brought back into friendship with the King of kings, and living in the sunshine of that friendship.—Listen not to those who would fain persuade you that if you only "go to church" regularly you will of course go to heaven. Settle it rather in your mind, that true saving religion, such as the Bible teaches, is another kind of thing altogether. The very foundation of real Christianity is to know that you have many sins, and deserve hell,—and to feel the importance of having these sins cleansed away, in order that you may go to heaven.

Happy, says the world, are they who have plenty of property and fine houses! Happy are they who have carriages, and horses, and servants, and large balances at their bankers, and great troops of friends! Happy are they who are clothed in purple and fine linen, and fare sumptuously every day, who have nothing to do but to spend their money and enjoy themselves!—Yet what is the real value of such happiness? It gives no solid, real satisfaction, even at the time of enjoyment. It endures but for a few years. It only lasts till death comes in, like the hand at Belshazzar's feast, and breaks up all. And then, in too many cases, this so-called happiness is exchanged for ETERNAL MISERY IN HELL.

"Blessed," says the Word of God, "are those whose iniquities are forgiven, and whose sins are covered! Blessed is the man unto whom the Lord imputeth not iniquity!—Blessed are the poor in spirit, for theirs is the kingdom of heaven! Blessed are they that mourn, for they shall be comforted! Blessed are they that hunger and thirst after righteousness, for they shall be filled!' (Psalm xxxii. 1, 2; Matt, v. 2, etc.)—Their blessedness shall never come to an end: their happiness is no summer-dried fountain, just failing when need is the sorest; their friends are no summer swallows, forsaking them, like Adonijah's guests, the first moment that the trumpet sounds. Their sun shall never go down. Their joy shall bud in time, and bloom in eternity. Theirs, in a word, is true happiness, for it is *for evermore.*

Do you believe what I am saying? It is all Scriptural and true. You will see one day whose words shall stand, the words of man or the Word of God. Be wise in time. Settle it in your heart this very hour, that the most important thing that man can attend to is the cleansing and forgiveness of his sins.

III. My third remark is this. *We cannot cleanse away our own sins.*

I make this statement boldly and confidently. Startling as it sounds to the natural heart, I lay it down as a piece of undeniable Scriptural truth. In spite of all the Pharisees, and Roman Catholics, and Socinians, and Deists, and idolaters of human reason and human power, I unhesitatingly repeat my assertion.—Man's sins are many and great. It is of the utmost importance that these sins should be cleansed away. Man's guilt in the sight of God, is enormous. Man's danger of hell, after he dies, is imminent and tremendous. And yet man cannot cleanse away his own sins! It is written, and it is true, "By the deeds of the law shall no flesh be justified." (Rom. iii. 20.)

(*a*) It will not cleanse away your sins *to be sorry for them.* You may mourn over your past wickedness, and humble yourself in sackcloth and ashes. You may shed floods of tears, and acknowledge your own guilt and danger. You may —you must,—you ought to do this. But you will not by so doing wipe out your transgressions from the book of God. SORROW CANNOT MAKE ATONEMENT FOR SIN.

The convicted criminal in a court of justice is often sorry for his offences. He sees the misery and ruin they have brought upon him. He mourns over his folly in not listening to advice and in giving way to temptation. But the judge does not let him off because he is sorry. The deed has been done; the law has been broken; the penalty has been incurred. The punishment must be inflicted, notwithstanding the criminal's tears.—This is precisely your position in the sight of God. Your sorrow is right, and good, and proper. But your sorrow has no power whatever to cleanse away your sins. It needs something more than penitence to take the burden off your heart.

(b) It will not cleanse away your sins *to mend your life.* You may reform your conduct, and turn over a new leaf you may break off many evil habits, and take up many good ones; you may become, in short, an altered man in all your outward behaviour. You may,—you must,—you ought to do so. Without such change no soul ever was saved. But you will not, by so doing, wipe away one particle of your guilt in God's sight. REFORMATION MAKES NO ATONEMENT FOR SIN.

The bankrupt tradesman, who owes ten thousand pounds and has not ten shillings to pay, may resolve to become a reformed character. After wasting his whole substance in riotous living, he may become steady, temperate, and respectable. It is all right and proper that he should be so: but this will not satisfy the claims of those to whom he owes money. Once more I say, this is precisely your case by nature in the sight of God. You owe Him ten thousand talents, and have "nothing to pay." To-day's amendments are all very well, but they do not wipe away yesterday's debts. — It requires something more than amendment and reformation to give you a light heart and to set your conscience free.

(c) It will not cleanse away your sins to become *diligent in the use of the forms and ordinances of religion.* You may alter your habits about Sunday, and attend services from morning to night; you may take pains to hear preaching on week-days, as well as on Sundays; you may receive the Lord's Supper on every possible occasion, and give alms, and keep fasts. It is all very well as far as it goes. It is a right and proper thing to attend to your religious duties. But all the means of grace in the world will never do you any good so long as you trust in them as saviours. They will not bind up the wounds of your heart, and give you inward peace. FORMALITY CANNOT MAKE ATONEMENT FOR SIN.

A lantern on a dark night is a very useful thing. It can help the traveller to find his way home; it can preserve him from losing his path, and keep him from falling into danger. But the lantern itself is not the traveller's fireside. The man who is content to sit down in the road by the side of his lantern, must never be surprised if he dies of cold. If you try to satisfy your conscience with a formal attendance on means of grace, you are no wiser than this traveller. It needs something more than religious formality to take the burden from your conscience and to give you peace with God.

(d) It will not cleanse away your sins *to look to man for help.* It is not in the power of any child of Adam to save another's soul. No bishop, no priest, no ordained man of any Church or denomination has power to forgive sins: no human absolution, however solemnly conferred, can purge that conscience which is not purged by God. It is well to ask the counsel of the ministers of the Gospel when the conscience is perplexed. It is their office to help the labouring and heavy-laden, and to show them the way of peace. But it is not in the power of any minister to deliver any man from his guilt. We can only show the path that must be followed: we can only point out the door at which every one must knock. It requires a hand far stronger than that of man to take the chains off conscience, and set the prisoner free. NO CHILD OF ADAM CAN TAKE AWAY HIS BROTHER'S SINS.

The bankrupt who asks a bankrupt to set him up in business again is only losing time. The pauper who travels off to a neighbour pauper, and begs him to help him out of difficulties, is only troubling himself in vain. The prisoner does not beg his fellow-prisoner to set him free; the shipwrecked sailor does not call on his shipwrecked comrade to place him safe ashore. Help in all these cases must come from some other quarter: relief in all these cases must be sought from some other hand. It is just the same in the matter of cleansing away your sins. So long as you seek it from man, whether man ordained or man not ordained, you seek it where it cannot be found. You must go further: you must look higher. You must turn elsewhere for comfort. It is not in the power of any man on earth or in heaven to take the burden of sin from off another man's soul. "None can by any means redeem his brother, nor give to God a ransom for him." (Psalm xlix. 7.)

Thousands in every age have tried to cleanse themselves from their sins in the ways I have now described, and have tried in vain. Thousands, I doubt not, are trying at this very moment, and find themselves "nothing bettered, but rather worse." (Mark v. 26.) They are climbing up a steep precipice of ice, toiling hard, and yet slipping backwards as fast as they climb.—They are pouring water into a cask full of holes, labouring busily, and yet no nearer the end of their work than when they began.—They are rowing a boat against a rapid stream, plying the oar diligently, and yet in reality losing ground every minute.—They are trying to build up a wall of loose sand, wearing themselves out with fatigue, and yet seeing their work roll down on them as fast as they throw it up.—They are striving to pump dry a sinking ship: the water gains on them and they will soon be drowned.—Such is the experience, in every part of the world, of all who think to cleanse themselves from their sins.

I warn every reader of this paper to beware of quack medicines in religion. Beware of supposing that penitence, and reformation, and formality, and priest-craft, can ever give you peace with God. They cannot do it. It is not in them. The man who says they can must be ignorant of two things. He cannot know the length and breadth of human sinfulness: he cannot understand the height and depth of the holiness of God. There never breathed the man or woman on earth who tried to cleanse himself from his sins, and in so doing obtained relief.

If you have found out this truth by experience, be diligent to impart it to others. Show them as plainly as you can their guilt and danger by nature. Tell them, with no less plainness, the immense importance of having their sins forgiven and cleansed away. But then warn them not to waste time in seeking to be cleansed in unlawful fashions. Warn them against the specious advice of " Mr. Legality " and his companions, so vividly described in " Pilgrim's Progress." Warn them against false remedies and sham medicines for the soul. Send them to the old wicket-gate, described in Scripture, however hard and rough the way may seem. Tell them it is " the old path and the good way," and that, whatever men may say, it is the only way to obtain cleansing of our sins. (Jer. vi. 16.)

IV. The fourth remark I have to make is this. *The blood of Jesus Christ can cleanse away all our sins.*

I enter on this part of my paper with a thankful heart. I bless God that after setting before my readers the deadly nature of their spiritual disease, I am able to set before them an almighty remedy. But I feel it needful to dwell upon this remedy for a few minutes. A thing of such wondrous efficacy as this "blood" ought to be clearly understood: there should be no vagueness or mystery in your ideas about it. When you hear of the "blood of Christ" you ought thoroughly to comprehend what the expression means.

The blood of Christ is that life-blood which the Lord Jesus shed when He died for sinners upon the cross. It is the blood which flowed so freely from His head pierced with thorns, and His hands and feet pierced with nails, and His side pierced with a spear, in the day when He was crucified and slain. The quantity of that blood may very likely have been small; the appearance of that blood was doubtless like that of our own: but never since the day when Adam was first formed out of the dust of the ground, has any blood been shed of such deep importance to the whole family of mankind.

It was blood that had been *long covenanted and promised.* In the day when sin came into the world, God mercifully engaged that "the Seed of the woman should bruise the serpent's head." (Gen. iii. 15.) One born of woman should appear one day, and deliver the children of Adam from Satan's power. That Seed of the woman was our Lord Jesus Christ. In the day that He suffered on the cross, He triumphed over Satan and accomplished redemption for mankind. When Jesus shed His life-blood on the cross, the head of the serpent was bruised, and the ancient promise was fulfilled.

It was blood that had been *long typified and prefigured.* Every sacrifice that was offered up by patriarchs, was a testimony of their faith in a greater sacrifice yet to come. Every shedding of the blood of lambs and goats under the Mosaic law was meant to foreshadow the dying of the true Lamb of God for the sin of the world. When Christ

was crucified, these sacrifices and types received their full
accomplishment. The true sacrifice for sin was at length
offered; the real atoning blood was at length shed. From
that day the offerings of the Mosaic law were no longer
needed. Their work was done. Like old almanacs, they
might be laid aside for ever.

It was blood which was of *infinite merit and value* in
the sight of God. It was not the blood of one who was
nothing more than a singularly holy man, but of one who
was God's own "Fellow," very God of very God. (Zech. xiii.
7.) It was not the blood of one who died involuntarily, as a
martyr for truth, but of one who voluntarily undertook to
be the Substitute and Proxy for mankind, to bear their sins
and carry their iniquities. It made atonement for man's
transgressions; it paid man's enormous debt to God; it
provided a way of righteous reconciliation between sinful
man and his holy Maker; it made a road from heaven to
earth, by which God could come down to man, and show
mercy; it made a road from earth to heaven, by which
man could draw near to God, and yet not feel afraid.
Without it there could have been no remission of sin.
Through it God can be "just and yet the justifier" of the
ungodly. From it a fountain has been formed, wherein
sinners can wash and be clean to all eternity. (Rom. iii. 26.)

This wondrous blood of Christ, applied to your conscience, can cleanse you from all sin. It matters nothing
what your sins may have been, "Though they be as
scarlet they may be made like snow. Though they be
red like crimson they can be made like wool." (Isaiah i.
18.) From sins of youth and sins of age,—from sins of
ignorance and sins of knowledge,—from sins of open
profligacy and sins of secret vice,—from sins against law
and sins against Gospel,—from sins of head, and heart,
and tongue, and thought, and imagination,—from sins
against each and all of the ten commandments,—from all
these the blood of Christ can set us free. To this end

was it appointed; for this cause was it shed; for this purpose it is still a fountain open to all mankind. That thing which you cannot do for yourself can be done in a moment by this precious fountain. YOU CAN HAVE ALL YOUR SINS CLEANSED AWAY.

In this blood all *the dead saints* have been cleansed hitherto, who are now waiting the resurrection of the just. From Abel, the first of whom we read, down to the last who has fallen asleep to-day, they have all "washed their robes, and made them white in the blood of the Lamb." (Rev. vii. 14.)   Not one has entered into rest by his own works and deservings; not one has make himself clean before God by his own goodness and his own strength. They have all "overcome by the blood of the Lamb." (Rev. xii. 11.)   And their testimony in Paradise is clear and distinct : "Thou wast slain, and hast redeemed us to God by Thy blood, out of every kindred, and tongue, and people, and nation."   (Rev. v. 9.)

By this blood all *the living saints* of God have peace and hope now.   By it they have boldness to enter into the holiest; by it they are justified and made nigh to God; by it their consciences are daily purged and filled with holy confidence.   About it all believers are agreed, however much they may differ on other matters.   Episcopalians and Presbyterians, Baptists and Methodists,—all are agreed that the blood of Christ is that only thing that can cleanse the soul.—All are agreed that in ourselves we are "wretched and miserable, and poor, and blind, and naked." (Rev. iii. 17.)   But all are agreed that in the blood of Christ the chief of sinners can be made clean.

Would you like to know what we ministers of the Gospel are ordained to do?   We are not set apart for no other end than to read services, and administer sacraments, and marry people, and bury the dead.   We are not meant to do nothing more than show you the church, or ourselves, or our party.   We are set for the work of showing men the "blood of Christ;" and except we are continually showing it, we are no true ministers of the Gospel.

Would you like to know what is our heart's desire and prayer for the souls to whom we minister? We want to bring them to the "blood of Christ." We are not content to see our churches filled, and our ordinances well attended, our congregations numerous, and our cause outwardly flourishing. We want to see men and women coming to this great Fountain for sin and uncleanness, and washing their souls in it that they may be clean. Here only is rest for the conscience. Here only is peace for the inward man. Here only is a cure for spiritual diseases. Here only is the secret of a light and happy heart. No doubt we have within us a fountain of evil and corruption. But, blessed be God, there is another Fountain of greater power still,—even the precious blood of the Lamb; and, washing daily in that other Fountain, we are clean from all sin.

V. The fifth, and last remark I have to make, is this. *Faith is absolutely necessary, and the only thing necessary, in order to give us an interest in the cleansing blood of Christ.*

I ask the special attention of all my readers to this point. A mistake here is often ruinous to a man's soul. It is a great leak at the bottom of your Christianity if you do not clearly see the true way of union between Christ and the soul.—That way is faith.

Church-membership and reception of the sacraments are no proof that you are washed in Christ's blood. Thousands attend a Christian place of worship, and receive the Lord's Supper from the hands of Christian ministers, and yet show plainly that they are not cleansed from their sins. Beware of despising means of grace, if you have any desire to be saved. But never, never forget that Church-membership is not faith.

Faith is the one thing needful in order to give you the

benefit of Christ's cleansing blood. He is called a "propitiation through faith in His blood."—"He that believeth on Him hath everlasting life."—"By Him all that believe are justified from all things."—"Being justified by faith we have peace with God, through our Lord Jesus Christ." (Rom. iii. 25; John iii. 36; Acts xiii. 39; Rom. v. 1.)— The wisdom of the whole world will never provide a better answer to an anxious inquirer than that which Paul gave to the Philippian jailor: "Believe on the Lord Jesus Christ, and thou shalt be saved." (Acts xvi. 31.)—"Art thou convinced of sin?" says the Gospel. "Dost thou really see that thou hast many sins, and art deserving of hell? Dost thou renounce all hope of cleansing thyself from thy sins by thine own power? Then thou art just the man for whom the Gospel provides comfort. Behold the atoning blood of Christ! Only trust in it, and this day thou shalt be freely pardoned. Only believe, and this very moment thy sins shall be cleansed away."—It is only "Believe and have." It is only "Believe and be clean." Let those who will call such doctrine rant and enthusiasm. I am bold to call it by another name. It is the "glorious Gospel" of the grace of God.

I ask you not to misunderstand my meaning in thus speaking of faith. I do not tell you that faith is the *only* mark of the man whose sins are cleansed away. I do not say that the faith which gives a man an interest in Christ's atoning blood, is ever found *alone*. Saving faith is no barren, solitary grace. It is always accompanied by repentance and personal holiness.—But this I say confidently,—that in the matter of giving the soul an interest in Christ, faith is the only thing required. In the matter of *justification before God*, faith, I repeat emphatically, stands entirely alone. Faith is the hand that lays hold on Christ. Faith begins, faith carries on, faith keeps up the claim which the sinner makes on the Saviour. By faith we are justified. By faith we bathe our souls in the great

Fountain for sin. By faith we go on obtaining fresh supplies of pardoning mercy all through our journey. By faith we live, and by faith we stand.

Nothing whatever beside this faith is required, in order to your complete justification and cleansing from all sin. Let this sink deeply into your mind. Where is the man that desires to enjoy real comfort from the Gospel? Seek, I do entreat you, to have clear and simple views of the nature of saving faith. Beware of those dark, and confused, and muddy notions of faith, by which so many distress their souls. Dismiss from your mind the idea that faith is a mere act of the intellect. It is not assent to doctrines or articles; it is not belief of "Paley's Evidences" or "Pearson on the Creed." It is simply the grasp of a contrite heart on the outstretched hand of an Almighty Saviour,—the repose of a weary head on the bosom of an Almighty Friend.—Cast away all idea of work, or merit, or doing, or performing, or paying, or giving, or buying, or labouring, in the act of believing on Christ. Understand that faith is not giving, but taking,—not paying, but receiving,—not buying, but being enriched. Faith is the eye which looks to the brazen serpent, and looking obtains life and health; it is the mouth which drinks down the reviving medicine, and drinking receives strength and vigour for the whole body; it is the hand of the drowning man which lays hold on the rope thrown to him, and laying hold enables him to be drawn up from the deep water safe and sound. This, and nothing more than this, is the true idea of saving faith. This, and this only, is the faith that is required to give you an interest in the blood of Christ. Believe in this way, and your sins are at once cleansed away!

Nothing whatever except this faith will ever give you an interest in Christ's atoning blood. You may go daily to Christ's church; you may often use Christ's name; you may bow the head at the name of Jesus; you may eat of the bread and wine which Christ commanded to be received. But all this time, without faith, you have neither part nor lot in Christ: without faith, so far as you are concerned, Christ's blood has been shed in vain.

I desire to enter my solemn protest against the modern notions which prevail on this solemn subject. I protest against the opinion which many now maintain, that any are saved by Christ excepting those who *believe.* There is much vague talk in some quarters about the "Fatherhood of God" and the "love of God," as if we who are called "Evangelical" denied these glorious truths. We do not deny them at all: we hold them as strongly as any. We give place to no man in this matter. But we utterly deny that God is the spiritual Father of any excepting those who are His *children by faith* in Christ Jesus. (Gal. iii. 26.) We utterly deny that men have a right to take comfort in God's love, except they *believe* on Him through whom. that love has been manifested, even His dear Son. The atoning blood of the Son of God is the grand exhibition of God's love towards sinners. The sinner who desires to be saved, must have personal dealings with Him who shed that blood. By personal faith he must wash in it; by personal faith he must drink of it; by personal faith he must put in his own claim to all its blessings. Without this faith there can be no salvation.

Would you know one main object which we ministers have in view in our preaching? We preach that you may *believe.* Faith is the thing that we desire to see produced in your souls; faith is the thing that, once produced, we desire to see growing. We rejoice to see you coming regularly to hear the Gospel; we rejoice to see an orderly, well-behaved congregation of worshippers: but faith, faith, faith,—is the grand result which we long to see in your souls. Without faith we cannot feel comfortable about you; without faith you are in imminent danger of hell. According to your faith will be the strength of your

Christianity; according to the degree of your faith will be the increase of your peace and hope, and the closeness of your walk with God. You will not wonder that there is nothing we care for so much as your believing.

I hasten to bring my remarks to a conclusion. I have tried to show you five things, and have endeavoured to set them before you in plain language. (1) I have told you that you have many sins. (2) I have told you that it is of the utmost importance to have these sins cleansed away. (3) I have told you that you cannot cleanse away your own sins. (4) I have told you that the blood of Christ cleanseth from all sin. (5) I have told you that faith only is needful, but absolutely needful, to give you any interest in Christ's blood. I have told you what I am firmly persuaded is God's own truth,—the truth on which I desire myself to live and die. I pray God that the Holy Ghost may apply this truth with mighty power to many souls.

Let me wind up all this subject by three words of parting application. Our years are passing quickly away. The night cometh, when no man can work. Yet a little time, and our place in another world will be settled to all eternity. A few more years, and we shall be either in heaven or in hell. Surely this fact alone ought to set us thinking.

1. My first word of application shall be *a question*. I address it to all into whose hands this paper may fall, without distinction or exception. It is a question which concerns deeply every man, woman, and child in the world, whatever be their rank or station. It is the question which rises naturally out of our subject: "*Where are your sins?*"

Remember, I do not ask you what you call yourself in religion. I do not ask you where you go,—or whom you hear,—or to what party you belong,—or what are your peculiar opinions about Church or Dissent. I leave such matters alone. I am weary to see the enormous waste of time of which multitudes are yearly guilty in respect to these matters. I am for the realities and substance of Christianity; I want to fix your attention on the things which will look important in the hour of death and at the last day. And I say boldly, that one of the first questions which demand your notice, is the question, " *Where are your sins?* "

I am not asking what you intend, or mean, or hope, or resolve to aim at, at some future time; I leave all that to children and fools. To-morrow is the devil's day, but to-day is God's. And here, as in God's sight, this very day, while you are reading my paper, I ask you to find an answer **to** my question: " *Where are your sins?* "

I ask you to mark what I am going to say. I say it calmly, deliberately, advisedly, and with consideration. I tell you that at this moment there are only two places in which your sins can be, and I defy the wisdom of the world to find out a third. Either your sins are UPON YOURSELF, unpardoned, unforgiven, uncleansed, unwashed away,—sinking you daily nearer to hell! Or else your sins are UPON CHRIST, taken away, forgiven, pardoned, blotted out and cleansed away by Christ's precious blood! I am utterly unable to see any third place in which a man's sins can possibly be. I am utterly unable to discover any third alternative. Forgiven or unforgiven,—pardoned or not pardoned,—cleansed away or not cleansed,—this, according to the Bible, is the exact position of every one's sins. How is it with you ? " *Where are your sins?* "

I beseech you to lay this question to heart, and never to rest till you can give it an answer. I do entreat you to examine your own state—to prove your own spiritual condition,—and to find out how matters stand between yourself and God. Let the time past suffice for trifling and indecision about your soul. Give it up,—give it up,—give it up for ever. Let the time past suffice for a mere formal, aimless, meaningless, comfortless religion. Lay it aside,—lay it aside,—lay it aside for ever. Be real; be thorough; be in earnest. Deal with your soul as a reasonable being; deal with it as one who feels that eternal interests are at stake; deal with it as one who has made up his mind, and is determined to live in suspense no longer. Oh, resolve this very day to find an answer to my question : *"Where are your sins?" Are they on yourself? or are they on Christ?*

2. My second word of application shall be *an invitation.* I address it to all who feel unable to give a satisfactory answer to the question of my paper. I address it to all who feel sinful, and lost, and condemned, and unfit to die. It is that invitation which is the glory of the Gospel. I say to you, *"Come to Christ, and be cleansed in His blood without delay."*

I know not what you may have been in your past life : it matters nothing. You may have broken every commandment under heaven; you may have sinned with a high hand against light and knowledge ; you may have despised a father's warnings and a mother's tears; you may have run greedily into every excess of riot, and plunged into every kind of abominable profligacy : you may have turned your back entirely on God, His day, His house, His ministers, His word. I say again it matters nothing.—Do you feel your sins? Are you sick of them? Are you ashamed of them ? Are you weary of them ? Then *come to Christ* just as you are, and Christ's blood shall make you clean.

I see you lingering, and doubting, and fancying the news too good to be true. I hear the devil whispering in your ear, "You are too bad ; you are too wicked to be saved." I charge you, in God's name, not to give way to such doubts. I remind you that Satan always was a liar.

One time he told you it was "too soon" for religion: and now he tells you it is "too late." I tell you confidently, that Jesus Christ is "able to save to the uttermost all who come to God by Him." (Heb. vii. 25.) I tell you confidently, that He has received, cleansed, and pardoned thousands as bad as you. He never changes. Only come to Him, and His blood shall cleanse you from all sin.

I can well fancy that you feel at a loss, and know not what to do. I can well believe that you do not see which way to turn, or what step to take, or in what manner to follow out my counsel. *I bid you go and say so to the Lord Jesus Christ !* I bid you seek some quiet solitary place, and pour out your heart before Him. Tell Him that you are a poor miserable sinner. Tell Him that you know not how to pray, or what to say, or what to do. But tell Him that you have heard something about His blood cleansing a man from all sin, and entreat Him to think on you, and cleanse your soul. Oh, take this advice,—and who can tell but you may say one day, "The blood of Christ does indeed cleanse a man from all sin."

For the last time I offer my invitation. I stand in the life-boat alongside the wreck to which you are clinging, and I entreat you to come in. The day is far spent; the night is coming on; the clouds are gathering; the waves are rising. Yet a little time and the old wreck of this world will go to pieces. Come into the life-boat; come in and be safe. Come to the blood of Christ; wash, and be clean. Come with all your sins to Christ, and cast them on Him. He will bear them away; He will cleanse them; He will pardon them. Only believe and be saved.

3. My last word shall be *an exhortation.* I address it to all who have been taught by the Spirit to feel their sins, and have fled to the hope set before them in the Gospel. I address it to all who have discovered the grand truth that they are guilty sinners, and have washed in the blood of Christ in order to have their sins cleansed away.

That exhortation shall be short and simple. I bid them " cling to Christ."

Cling to Christ, I say : and never forget your debt to Him. Sinners you were, when you were first called by the Holy Ghost, and fled to Jesus. Sinners you have been, even at your best, from the day of your conversion. Sinners you will find yourselves to your dying hour, having nothing to boast of in yourselves. Then cling to Christ.

Cling to Christ, I say : and make use of His atoning blood every day. Go to Him every morning as your morning sacrifice, and confess your need of His salvation. Go to Him every night, after the bustle of the day, and plead for fresh absolution. Wash in the great Fountain every evening, after all the defilement of contact with the world. " He that is washed, needeth not save to wash his feet." But his feet he needs to wash. (John xiii. 10.)

Cling to Christ, I say : and show the world how you love Him. Show it by obedience to His commandments. Show it by conformity to His image. Show it by following His example. Make your Master's cause lovely and beautiful before men, by your own holiness of temper and conversation. Let all the world see that he who is much forgiven is the man who loves much, and that he who loves most is the man who does most for Christ. (Luke vii. 47.)

Cling to Christ, I say : and have high thoughts of the atonement made by His blood upon the cross. Think highly of His incarnation and His example,—think highly of His miracles and His words,—think highly of His resurrection, and intercession, and coming again. But think highest of all of Christ's sacrifice, and the propitiation made by His death. Contend earnestly for the old faith concerning His atonement. See in the old doctrine that He died as a Substitute for sinners, the only solution of a thousand passages in the Old Testament, and a hundred passages in the New. Never, never be ashamed to let men know that you derive all your comfort from the atoning blood of Christ, and from His substitution for you on the cross.

Cling to Christ, I say lastly: and make much of the old foundation truths concerning salvation by His blood. These are the old friends to which our souls will turn at last in the hour of our departure. These are the ancient doctrines on which we shall lean back our aching heads, when life is ebbing away and death is in sight. We shall not ask ourselves then whether we have been Episcopalians or Presbyterians, Churchmen or Dissenters. We shall not find comfort then in new-fangled notions and human inventions,—in baptism and churchmembership,—in sects and parties,—in ceremonies and forms. Nothing will do us good then but the blood of Christ. Nothing will support us then but the witness of the Spirit, that in the blood of Jesus we have washed, and by that blood have been made clean.

I commend these things to the serious attention of all who read this volume. If you never knew these things before, may you soon become acquainted with them! If you have known them in time past, may you know them better for time to come! We can never know too well the right answer to the mighty question,—" *Where are your sins.* "

FORGIVENESS.

" Your sins are forgiven you."—1 JOHN ii. 12.

THERE is a clause near the end of the Belief, or Apostle's Creed, which, I fear, is often repeated without thought or consideration. I refer to the clause which contains these words, "I believe in the Forgiveness of sins." Thousands, I am afraid, never reflect what those words mean. I propose to examine the subject of them in the following paper, and I invite the attention of all who care for their souls, and want to be saved. Do we believe in the "Resurrection of our bodies"? Then let us see to it that we know something by experience of the "Forgiveness of our sins."

I. *Let me show, first of all, our need of forgiveness.*

All men need forgiveness, because all men are sinners. He that does not know this, knows nothing in religion. It is the very A B C of Christianity, that a man should know his right place in the sight of God, and understand his deserts.

We are *all great sinners.* "There is none righteous, no, not one."—"All have sinned, and come short of the glory of God." (Rom. iii. 10, 23.) Sinners we were born, and sinners we have been all our lives. We take to sin naturally from the very first. No child ever needs schooling and education to teach it to do wrong. No devil, or bad companion, ever leads us into such wickedness as our own hearts. And "the wages of sin is death." (Rom. vi. 23.) We must either be forgiven, or lost eternally.

We are *all guilty sinners* in the sight of God. We have broken His holy law. We have transgressed His precepts. We have not done His will. There is not a commandment in all the ten which does not condemn us. If we have not broken it in deed we have in word; if we have not broken it in word, we have in thought and imagination,—and that continually. Tried by the standard of the fifth chapter of St. Matthew, there is not one of us that would be acquitted. All the world is "guilty before God." And "as it is appointed unto men once to die, so after this comes the judgment." We must either be forgiven, or perish everlastingly. (Rom. iii. 19; Heb. ix. 27.)

When I walk through the crowded streets of London, I see hundreds and thousands of whom I know nothing beyond their outward appearance. I see some bent on pleasure, and some on business,—some who look rich, and some who look poor,—some rolling in their carriages, some hurrying along on foot. Each has his own object in view. Each has his own aims and ends, all alike hidden from me. But one thing I know for a certainty, as I look upon them,—they are all sinners. There is not a soul among them all but "deserves God's wrath and condemnation." (See 9th Article.) There breathes not the man or woman in that crowd but must die *forgiven*, or else rise again to be condemned for ever at the last day.

When I look through the length and breadth of Great Britain I must make the same report. From the Land's End to the North Foreland,—from the Isle of Wight to Caithness,—from the Queen on the throne to the pauper in the workhouse,—we are all sinners. We Englishmen have got a name among the empires of the earth. We send our ships into every sea, and our merchandise into every town

in the world. We have bridged the Atlantic with our
steamers. We have made night in our cities like day
with gas. We have changed England into one great
county by railways. We can exchange thought between
London and Edinburgh in a few seconds by the electric
telegraph. But with all our arts and sciences,—with all
our machinery and inventions,—with all our armies and
navies,—with all our lawyers and statesmen, we have not
altered the nature of our people. We are still in the eye
of God an island full of *sinners*.

When I turn to the map of the world I must say the
same thing. It matters not what quarter I examine: I
find men's hearts are everywhere the same, and everywhere
wicked. Sin is the family disease of all the children of
Adam. Never has there been a corner of the earth
discovered where sin and the devil do not reign. Wide as
the difference is between the nations of the earth, they
have always been found to have one great mark in common.
Europe and Asia, Africa and America, Iceland and India,
Paris and Pekin,—all alike have the mark of sin. The
eye of the Lord looks down on this globe of ours, as it
rolls round the sun, and sees it covered with corruption
and wickedness. What He sees in the moon and stars,
in Jupiter and Saturn, I cannot tell,—but on the earth I
know He sees sin. (Psalm xiv. 2, 3.)

I have no doubt such language as this sounds extravagant to some. You think I am going much too far. But
mark well what I am about to say next, and then consider
whether I have not used the words of soberness and truth.

What then, I ask, is *the life of the best Christian*
amongst us all ? What is it but one great career of short-
comings ? What is it but a daily acting out the words of
our Prayer-book,—" leaving undone things we ought to
do, and doing things that we ought not to do " ? Our
faith, how feeble ! Our love, how cold ! Our works, how
few ! Our zeal, how small ! Our patience, how short-

breathed! Our humility, how thread-bare! Our self-denial, how dwarfish! Our knowledge, how dim! Our spirituality, how shallow! Our prayers, how formal! Our desires for more grace, how faint! Never did the wisest of men speak more wisely than when he said, "There is not a just man upon earth, that doeth good, and sinneth not." (Eccles. vii. 20.) "In many things," says the apostle James. "we offend all." (James iii. 2.) And *what is the best action* that is ever done by the very best of Christians? What is it after all but an imperfect work, when tried on its own merits? It is, as Luther says, no better than "a splendid sin." It is always more or less defective. It is either wrong in its motive or incomplete in its performance, —not done from perfect principles, or not executed in a perfect way. The eyes of men may see no fault in it, but weighed in the balances of God it would be found wanting, and viewed in the light of heaven it would prove full of flaws. It is like the drop of water which seems clear to the naked eye, but, placed under a microscope, is discovered to be full of impurity. David's account is literally true: "There is none that doeth good, no, not one." (Psalm xiv. 3.)

And then *what is the Lord God*, whose eyes are on all our ways, and before whom we have one day to give account? "Holy, holy, holy," is the remarkable expression applied to Him by those who are nearest to Him. (Isaiah vi. 3; Rev. iv. 8.) It sounds as if no one word could express the intensity of His holiness. One of His prophets says, "He is of purer eyes than to behold evil, and cannot look on iniquity." (Habak. i. 13.) We think the angels exalted beings, and far above ourselves; but we are told in Scripture, "He charged His angels with folly." (Job iv. 18.) We admire the moon and stars as glorious and splendid bodies; but we read, "Behold even to the moon, and it shineth not, yea the stars are not pure in His sight." (Job xxv. 5.) We talk of the heavens as the noblest and purest part of creation ; but even of them it is written, " The heavens are not clean in His sight." (Job xv. 15.)   What then is any one of us but a miserable sinner in the sight of such a God as this ?

Surely we ought all to cease from proud thoughts about ourselves.   We ought to lay our hands upon our mouths, and say with Abraham, " I am dust and ashes ; " and with Job, " I am vile ; " and with Isaiah, " We are all as an unclean thing ; " and with John, " If we say that we have no sin we deceive ourselves, and the truth is not in us." (Gen. xviii. 27 ; Job xl. 4 ; Isaiah lxiv. 6 ; 1 John i. 8.) Where is the man or woman in the whole catalogue of the Book of Life, that will ever be able to say more than this, —" I obtained mercy " ?   What is the glorious company of the apostles, the goodly fellowship of the prophets, the noble army of martyrs,—what are they all but pardoned sinners ?   Surely there is but one conclusion to be arrived at :—We are all great sinners, and we all need a great forgiveness.

See now what just cause I have to say that to know our need of forgiveness is the first thing in true religion.   Sin is a burden, and must be taken off.   Sin is a defilement, and must be cleansed away.   Sin is a mighty debt, and must be paid.   Sin is a mountain standing between us and heaven, and must be removed.   Happy is that mother's child amongst us that feels all this !   The first step towards heaven is to see clearly that we *deserve hell.*   There are but two alternatives before us,—we must either be forgiven, or be miserable for ever.

See too how little many persons know of the main design of Christianity, though they live in a Christian land.   They fancy they are to go to church to learn their duty, and hear morality enforced, and for no other purpose.   They forget that the heathen philosophers could have told them as much as this.   They forget that such men as Plato and Seneca gave instructions which ought to put to shame the

Christian liar, the Christian drunkard, and the Christian thief. They have yet to learn that the leading mark of Christianity is the *remedy* it provides for sin. This is the glory and excellence of the Gospel. It meets man as he really is. It takes him as it finds him. It goes down to the level to which sin has brought him, and offers to raise him up. It tells him of a remedy equal to his disease,— a great remedy for a great disease,—a great forgiveness for great sinners.

I ask every reader to consider these things well, if he never considered them before. It is no light matter whether you know your soul's necessities or not: it is a matter of life and death. Try, I beseech you, to become acquainted with your own heart. Sit down and think quietly what you are in the sight of God. Bring together the thoughts, and words, and actions of any day in your life, and measure them by the measure of God's Word. Judge yourself honestly, that you may not be condemned at the last day. Oh, that you might find out what you really are! Oh, that you might learn to pray Job's prayer: "Make me to know my transgression and my sin." (Job xiii. 23.) Oh, that you might see this great truth,—that until you are *forgiven* your Christianity has done nothing for you at all!

II. *Let me point out, in the second place, the way of forgiveness.*

I ask particular attention to this point, for none can be more important. Granting for a moment that you want pardon and forgiveness, what ought you to do? Whither will you go? Which way will you turn? Every thing hinges on the answer you give to this question.

Will you turn to *ministers* and put your trust in them? They cannot give you pardon: they can only tell you where it is to be found. They can set before you the bread of life; but you yourself must eat it. They can show you the path of peace; but you yourself must walk in it. The Jewish priest had no power to cleanse the leper, but only to declare him cleansed. The Christian minister has no power to forgive sins;—he can only declare and pronounce who they are that are forgiven.

Will you turn to *sacraments and ordinances*, and trust in them? They cannot supply you with forgiveness, however diligently you may use them. By sacraments "faith is confirmed and grace increased," in all who rightly use them. (See Article 27.) But they cannot justify the sinner. They cannot put away transgression. You may go to the Lord's table every Sunday in your life: but unless you look far beyond the sign to the thing signified, you will after all die in your sins. You may attend a daily service regularly, but if you think to establish a righteousness of your own by it, in the slightest degree, you are only getting further away from God every day.

Will you trust in your own *works* and *endeavours*, your virtues and your good deeds, your prayers and your alms? They will never buy for you an entrance into heaven. They will never pay your debt to God. They are all imperfect in themselves, and only increase your guilt. There is no merit or worthiness in them at the very best. The Lord Jesus Christ says expressly, "When you have done all those things which are commanded you, say, We are unprofitable servants." (Luke xvii. 10.)

Will you trust in your own *repentance and amendment?* You are very sorry for the past. You hope to do better for time to come. You hope God will be merciful. Alas, if you lean on this, you have nothing beneath you but a broken reed! The judge does not pardon the thief because he is sorry for what he did. To-day's sorrow will not wipe off the score of yesterday's sins. It is not an ocean of tears that would ever cleanse an uneasy conscience and give it peace.

Where then must a man go for pardon? Where is forgiveness to be found? There is a way both sure and plain, and into that way I desire to guide every inquirer's feet.

That way is simply to trust in the Lord Jesus Christ as your Saviour. It is to cast your soul, with all its sins, unreservedly on Christ,—to cease completely from any dependence on your own works or doings, either in whole or in part,—and to rest on no other work but Christ's work, no other righteousness but Christ's righteousness, no other merit but Christ's merit, as your ground of hope. Take this course and you are a pardoned soul. "To Christ," says Peter, "give all the prophets witness, that through His name whosoever believeth in Him shall receive remission of sins." (Acts x. 43.) "Through this Man," says Paul at Antioch, "is preached unto you the forgiveness of sins, and by Him all that believe are justified from all things." (Acts xiii. 38.) "In Him," writes Paul to the Colossians, "we have redemption through His blood, even the forgiveness of sins." (Col. i. 14.)

The Lord Jesus Christ, in great love and compassion, has made a full and complete satisfaction for sin, by suffering death in our place upon the cross. There He offered Himself as a sacrifice for us, and allowed the wrath of God, which we deserved, to fall on His own head. For our sins, as our Substitute, He gave Himself, suffered, and died,—the just for the unjust, the innocent for the guilty,—that He might deliver us from the curse of a broken law, and provide a complete pardon for all who are willing to receive it. And by so doing, as Isaiah says,—He has *borne* our sins; as John the Baptist says,—He has *taken away* sin; as Paul says,—He has *purged* our sins, and *put away* sin; and as Daniel says,—He has *made an end of sin,* and *finished* trangression. (Isaiah liii. 11; John i. 29; Heb. i. 3; Heb. ix. 26; Dan. ix. 24.)

And now the Lord Jesus Christ is sealed and appointed by God the Father to be a Prince and a Saviour, to give remission of sins to all who will have it. The keys of death and hell are put in His hand. The government of the gate of heaven is laid on His shoulder. He Himself is the door, and by Him all that enter in shall be saved. (Acts v. 31; Rev. i. 18; John x. 9.)

Christ, in one word, has purchased a full forgiveness, if we are only willing to receive it. He has done all, paid all, suffered all that was needful to reconcile us to God. He has provided a garment of righteousness to clothe us. He has opened a fountain of living waters to cleanse us. He has removed every barrier between us and God the Father, taken every obstacle out of the way, and made a road by which the vilest may return. All things are now ready, and the sinner has only to believe and be saved, to eat and be satisfied, to ask and receive, to wash and be clean.

And faith, simple faith, is the only thing required, in order that you and I may be forgiven. That we will come by faith to Jesus as sinners with our sins,—trust in Him,—rest on Him,—lean on Him,—confide in Him,—commit our souls to Him,—and *forsaking all other hope, cleave only to Him*,—this is all and everything that God asks for. Let a man only do this, and he shall be saved. His iniquities shall be found completely pardoned, and his transgressions entirely taken away. Every man and woman that so trusts is wholly forgiven, and reckoned perfectly righteous. His sins are clean gone, and his soul is justified in God's sight, however bad and guilty he may have been.

Faith is the only thing required, *not knowledge*. A man may be a poor unlearned sinner, and know little of books. But if he sees enough to find the foot of the cross, and trust in Jesus for pardon, I will engage, from the authority of the Bible, that he shall not miss heaven. To know Christ is the corner-stone of all religious knowledge.

Faith, I say, and *not conversion*. A man may have been walking in the broad way up to the very hour he first hears the Gospel. But if in that hearing he is awakened to feel his danger, and wants to be saved, let him come to Christ at once, and wait for nothing. That very coming is the beginning of conversion.

Faith, I repeat, and *not holiness*. A man may feel all full of sin, and unworthy to be saved. But let him not tarry outside the ark till he is better. Let him come to Christ without delay, just as he is. Afterwards he shall be holy.

I call upon every reader of these pages to let nothing move him from this strong ground,—that *faith in Christ is the only thing needed for our justification*. Stand firm here, if you value your soul's peace. I see many walking in darkness and having no light, from confused notions as to what faith is. They hear that saving faith will work by love and produce holiness, and not finding all this at once in themselves, they think they have no faith at all. They forget that these things are the *fruits* of faith, and not faith itself, and that to doubt whether we have faith, because we do not see them at once, is lik doubting whether a tree is alive, because it does not bear fruit the very day we plant it in the ground. I charge you to settle it firmly in your mind, that in the matter of your forgiveness and justification there is but one thing required, and that is, simple faith in Christ.

I know well that the natural heart dislikes this doctrine. It runs counter to man's notions of religion. It leaves him no room to boast. Man's idea is to come to Christ with a price in his hand,—his regularity,—his morality,—his repentance,—his goodness,—and so, as it were, to buy his pardon and justification. The Spirit's teaching is quite different: it is first of all, to believe. Whosoever *believeth shall not perish.* (John iii. 16.)

Some say such doctrine cannot be right, because it makes the way to heaven too easy. I fear that many such persons, if the truth were spoken, find it too hard. I believe in reality it is easier to give a fortune in building a cathedral like York Minster, or to go to the stake and be burned, than thoroughly to receive "justification by faith without the deeds of the law," and to enter heaven as a sinner saved by grace.

Some say this doctrine is foolishness and enthusiasm. I answer, This is just what was said of it 1800 years ago, and it is a vain cavil now, as it was then. So far from the charge being true, a thousand facts can prove this doctrine to be from God. No doctrine certainly has produced sucn mighty effects in the world, as the simple proclamation of free forgiveness through faith in Christ.

This is the glorious doctrine which was the strength of the Apostles when they went forth to the Gentiles to preach a new religion. They began, a few poor fishermen, in a despised corner of the earth. They turned the world upside down. They changed the face of the Roman empire. They emptied the heathen temples of their worshippers, and made the whole system of idolatry crumble away. And what was the weapon by which they did it all ? It was *free forgiveness through faith in Jesus Christ.*

This is the doctrine which brought light into Europe 300 years ago, at the time of the blessed Reformation, and enabled one solitary monk, Martin Luther, to shake the whole Church of Rome. Through his preaching and writing the scales fell from men's eyes, and the chains of their souls were loosed. And what was the lever that gave him his power ? It was *free forgiveness through faith in Jesus Christ.*

This is the doctrine which revived our own Church in the middle of last century, when Whitefield, and the Wesleys, and Berridge, and Venn broke up the wretched "spirit of slumber" which had come over the land, and roused men to think. They began a mighty work, with little seeming likelihood of success. They began, few in number, with small encouragement from the rich and great. But they prospered. And why?—Because they preached *free for-giveness through faith in Christ*.

This is the doctrine which is the true strength of any Church on earth at this day. It is not orders, or endowments, or liturgies, or learning, that will keep a Church alive. Let free forgiveness through Christ be faithfully proclaimed in her pulpits, and the gates of hell shall not prevail against her. Let it be buried, or kept back, and her candlestick will soon be taken away. When the Saracens invaded the lands where Jerome, and Athanasius, and Cyprian, and Augustine once wrote and preached, they found bishops and liturgies, I make no question. But I fear they found no preaching of free forgiveness of sins, and so they swept the Churches of those lands clean away. They were a body without a vital principle, and therefore they fell. Let us never forget the brightest days of a Church are those when " Christ crucified " is most exalted. The dens and caves of the earth, where the early Christians met to hear of the love of Jesus, were more full of glory and beauty in God's sight than ever was St. Peter's at Rome. The meanest barn at this day, where the true way of pardon is offered to sinners, is a far more honourable place than the Cathedral of Cologne or Milan. A Church is only useful so far as she exalts *free forgiveness through Christ*.

This is the doctrine which, of all others, is the mightiest engine for pulling down the kingdom of Satan. The Greenlanders were unmoved so long as the Moravians told them of the creation and the fall of man; but when they heard of redeeming love, their frozen hearts melted like snow in spring. Preach salvation by the sacraments, exalt the Church above Christ, and keep back the doctrine of the Atonement, and the devil cares little,—his goods are at peace. But preach a full Christ, and a free pardon by faith in Him, and then Satan will have great wrath, for he knows he has but a short time. John Berridge said he went on preaching morality and nothing else, till he found there was not a moral man in his parish. But when he changed his plan, and began to preach the love of Christ to sinners, and a free salvation by faith, then there was a stirring of the dry bones, and a mighty turning to God.

This is the only doctrine which will ever bring peace to an uneasy conscience, and rest to a troubled soul. A man may get on pretty well without it so long as he is asleep about his spiritual condition. But once let him awake from his slumber, and nothing will ever calm him but the blood of Atonement, and the peace which comes by faith in Christ. How any one can undertake to be a minister of religion without a firm grasp of this doctrine, I never can understand. For myself, I can only say, I should think my office a most painful one if I had not the message of free forgiveness to convey. It would be miserable work indeed to visit the sick and dying, if I could not say, "Behold the Lamb of God:—believe on the Lord Jesus Christ, and thou shalt be saved." The right hand of a Christian minister is the doctrine of free forgiveness through faith in Christ. Give us this doctrine, and we have power: we will never despair of doing good to men's souls. Take away this doctrine, and we are weak as water. We may read the prayers and go through a round of forms, but we are like Samson with his hair shorn: our strength is gone. Souls will not be benefited by us, and good will not be done.

I commend the things I have been saying to the notice of every reader. I am not ashamed of free pardon through faith in Christ, whatever some may say against the doctrine. I am not ashamed of it, for its fruits speak for themselves. It has done things that no other doctrine can do. It has effected moral changes which laws and punishments have failed to work,—which magistrates and policemen have laboured after in vain,—which mechanics' institutes and secular knowledge have proved utterly powerless to produce. Just as the fiercest lunatics in Bethlehem hospital became suddenly gentle when kindly treated, even so the worst and most hardened sinners have often become as little children, when told of Jesus loving them and willing to forgive. I can well understand Paul ending his Epistle to the erring Galatians with that solemn burst of feeling, " God forbid that I should glory, save in the cross of our Lord Jesus Christ." (Gal. vi. 14.) The crown has indeed fallen from a Christian's head when he leaves the doctrine of justification by faith.

You should ask yourself whether you have really received the truth which I have been dwelling on, and know it by experience. Jesus, and faith in Him, is the only way to the Father. He that thinks to climb into Paradise by some other road, will find himself fearfully mistaken. Other foundation can no man lay for an immortal soul than that of which I have been feebly speaking. He that ventures himself here is safe. He that is off this rock has got no standing ground at all.

You should seriously consider what kind of a ministry you are in the habit of attending, supposing you have a choice. You have reason indeed to be careful. It is not *all the same* where you go, whatever people may say. There are many places of worship, I fear, where you might look long for Christ crucified, and never find Him. He is buried under outward ceremonies,—thrust behind the baptismal font,—lost sight of under the shadow of the Church. " They have taken away my Lord, and I know not where they have laid Him." (John xx. 13.) Take heed where you settle yourself. Try all by this single test, " Is Jesus and free forgiveness proclaimed here ? " There may be comfortable pews,—there may be good singing,—there may be learned sermons. But if Christ's Gospel is not the sun and centre of the whole place, do not pitch your tent there. Say rather with Isaac. " Here,

is the wood and the fire, but where is the lamb?"
(Gen. xxii. 7.) Be very sure this is not the place for your
soul.

III. *Let me, in the third place, encourage all who
wish to be forgiven.*

I dare be sure this paper will be read by some one who
feels he is not yet a forgiven soul. My heart's desire and
prayer is that such an one may seek his pardon at once.
And I would fain help him forward, by showing him the
kind of forgiveness offered to him, and the glorious
privileges within his reach.

Listen to me, then, while I try to exhibit to you the
treasures of Gospel forgiveness. I cannot describe its
fulness as I ought. Its riches are indeed unsearchable.
(Eph. iii. 8.) But if you will turn away from it, you shall
not be able to say in the day of judgment, you did not
at all know what it was.

Consider, then, for one thing, that the forgiveness set
before you is a *great and broad forgiveness.* Hear what
the Prince of Peace Himself declares: "All sins shall be
forgiven unto the sons of men, and blasphemies, where-
withsoever they shall blaspheme." (Mark iii. 28.) "Though
your sins be as scarlet, they shall become white as snow
though they be red like crimson, they shall be as wool."
(Isaiah i. 18.) Yes: though your trespasses be more in
number than the hairs of your head, the stars in heaven,
the leaves of the forest, the blades of grass, the grains of
sand on the sea shore, still they can all be pardoned ! As
the waters of Noah's flood covered over and hid the tops
of the highest hills, so can the blood of Jesus cover over
and hide your mightiest sins. "His blood cleanseth from
all sin." (1 John i. 7.) Though to you they seem written
with the point of a diamond, they can all be effaced
from the book of God's remembrance by that precious
blood. Paul names a long list of abominations which

the Corinthians had committed, and then says, "Such were some of you: but ye are washed." (1 Cor. vi. 11.)

Furthermore, it is a *full and complete forgiveness.* It is not like David's pardon to Absalom,—a permission to return home, but not a full restoration to favour. (2 Sam. xiv. 24.) It is not, as some fancy, a mere letting off, and letting alone. It is a pardon so complete that he who has it is reckoned as righteous as if he had never sinned at all! His iniquities are blotted out. They are removed from him as far as the east from the west. (Psalm ciii. 12.) There remains no condemnation for him. The Father sees him joined to Christ, and is well pleased. The Son beholds him clothed with His own righteousness, and says, "Thou art all fair, there is no spot in thee." (Cant. iv. 7.) Blessed be God that it is so! I verily believe if the best of us all had only one blot left for himself to wipe out, he would miss eternal life. If the holiest child of Adam were in heaven all but his little finger, and to get in depended on himself, I am sure he would never enter the kingdom. If Noah, Daniel, and Job, had had but one day's sins to wash away, they would never have been saved. Praised be God, that in the matter of our pardon there is nothing left for man to do! Jesus does all, and man has only to hold out an empty hand and to receive.

Furthermore, it is a *free and unconditional forgiveness.* It is not burdened with an "if," like Solomon's pardon to Adonijah: "If he will show himself a worthy man." (1 Kings i. 52.) Nor yet are you obliged to carry a price in your hand, or to bring a character with you to prove yourself deserving of mercy. Jesus requires but one character, and that is that you should feel yourself a sinful, bad man. He invites you to "buy wine and milk without money and without price," and declares, "Whosoever will, let him take the water of life freely." (Isaiah lv. 1 ; Rev. xxii. 17.) Like David in the cave of Adullam, He receives every one that feels in distress and a debtor, and rejects none. (1 Sam. xxii. 2.) Are you a sinner? Do you want a Saviour? Then come to Jesus just as you are, and your soul shall live.

Again, it is an *offered forgiveness*. I have read of earthly Kings who knew not how to show mercy; of Henry the Eighth of England who spared neither man nor woman,—of James the Fifth of Scotland, who would never show favour to a Douglas. The King of kings is not like them. He calls on men to come to Him, and be pardoned. "Unto you, O men, I call, and my voice is to the sons of men." (Prov. viii. 4.) "Ho! every one that thirsteth, come ye to the waters." (Isaiah lv. 1.) "If any man thirst, let him come unto Me and drink." (John vii. 37.) "Come unto Me, all ye that labour and are heavy laden, and I will give you rest." (Matt. xi. 28.) It ought to be a great comfort to you and me to hear of any pardon at all; but to hear Jesus Himself inviting us, to see Jesus Himself holding out His hand to us,—the Saviour seeking the sinner before the sinner seeks the Saviour,—this is encouragement, this is strong consolation indeed!

Again, it is a *willing forgiveness*. I have heard of pardons granted in reply to long entreaty, and wrung out by much importunity. King Edward the Third of England would not spare the citizens of Calais till they came to him with halters round their necks, and his own Queen interceded for them on her knees. But Jesus is "good and ready to forgive." (Psalm lxxxvi. 5.) He "delighteth in mercy." (Micah vii. 18.) Judgment is "His strange work." He is not willing that any should perish. (Isai. xxviii. 21, 2 Pet. iii. 9.) He would fain have all men saved, and come to the knowledge of the truth. (1 Tim. ii. 4.) He wept over unbelieving Jerusalem. "As I live," He says, "I have no pleasure in the death of the wicked. Turn ye, turn ye from your evil ways; why will ye die?" (Ezek. xxxiii. 11.) You and I may well come boldly to the throne of grace.

He who sits there is far more willing and ready to give
mercy than we are to receive it. (Heb. iv. 16.)

Besides this, it is a *tried forgiveness.* Thousands and
tens of thousands have sought for pardon at the mercy-
seat of Christ, and not one has ever returned to say that
he sought in vain. Sinners of every name and nation,—
sinners of every sort and description,—have knocked at the
door of the fold, and none have ever been refused admission. Zacchæus the extortioner, Magdalen the harlot, Saul
the persecutor, Peter the denier of his Lord, the Jews who
crucified the Prince of Life, the idolatrous Athenians, the
adulterous Corinthians, the ignorant Africans, the blood-
thirsty New Zealanders,—all have ventured their souls on
Christ's promises of pardon, and none have ever found
them fail. If the way which the Gospel sets before us were
a new and untraveled way, we might well feel faint-hearted.
But it is not so. It is an old path. It is a path worn by
the feet of many pilgrims, and a path in which the footsteps are all one way. The treasury of Christ's mercies
has never been found empty. The well of living waters
has never proved dry.

Besides this, it is a *present forgiveness.* All that believe
in Jesus are at once justified from all things. (Acts xiii.
39.) The very day the younger son returned to his
father's house he was clothed with the best robe, had the
ring put on his hand, and the shoes on his feet. (Luke xv.)
The very day Zacchæus received Jesus he heard those
comfortable words, "This day is salvation come to this
house." (Luke xix. 9.) The very day that David said,
"I have sinned against the Lord," he was told by Nathan,
"The Lord also hath put away thy sin." (2 Sam. xii. 13.)
The very day you first flee to Christ, your sins are all
removed. Your pardon is not a thing far away, to be
obtained only after many years. It is nigh at hand. It
is close to you, within your reach, all ready to be bestowed.
Believe, and that very moment it is your own. "He that

believeth is not condemned." (John iii. 18.) It is not said, "He shall not be," or "will not be," but "*is not.*" From the time of his believing, condemnation is gone. "He that believeth hath everlasting life." (John iii. 36.) It is not said, "He shall have," or "will have," it is "*hath.*" It is his own as surely as if he was in heaven, though not so evidently so to his own eyes. You must not think forgiveness will be nearer to a believer in the day of judgment than it was in the hour he first believed. His complete salvation from the *power* of sin is every year nearer and nearer to him; but as to his forgiveness and justification, and deliverance from the guilt of sin, it is a finished work from the very minute he first commits himself to Christ.

Last, and best of all, it is an *everlasting forgiveness.* It is not like Shimei's pardon,—a pardon that may some time be revoked and taken away. (1 Kings ii. 9.) Once justified, you are justified for ever. Once written down in the book of life, your name shall never be blotted out. The sins of God's children are said to be cast into the depths of the sea,—to be sought for and not found,—to be remembered no more,—to be cast behind God's back. (Mic. vii. 19; Jer. l. 20; xxxi. 34; Isa. xxxviii. 17.) Some people fancy they may be justified one year and condemned another,—children of adoption at one. time, and strangers by and by,—heirs of the kingdom in the beginning of their days, and yet servants of the devil in their end. I cannot find this in the Bible:—as the New Zealander told the Romish priest, "*I do not see it in the Book.*" It seems to me to overturn the good news of the Gospel altogether, and to tear up its comforts by the roots. I believe the salvation Jesus offers is an everlasting salvation, and a pardon once sealed with His blood shall never be reversed.

I have set before you the nature of the forgiveness offered to you. I have told you but a little of it, for my words are weaker than my will. The half of it remains untold. The greatness of it is far more than any report of mine. But I think I have said enough to show you it is worth the seeking, and I can wish you nothing better than that you may strive to make it your own.

Do you call it nothing to look forward to death without fear, and to judgment without doubtings, and to eternity without a sinking heart? Do you call it nothing to feel the world slipping from your grasp, and to see the grave getting ready for you, and the valley of the shadow of death opening before your eyes, and yet to be not afraid? Do you call it nothing to be able to think of the great day of account, the throne, the books, the Judge, the assembled worlds, the revealing of secrets, the final sentence, and yet to feel, "I am safe"? This is the portion, and this the privilege of a forgiven soul.

Such an one is *on a rock.* When the rain of God's wrath descends, and the floods come, and the winds blow, his feet shall not slide, his habitation shall be sure.

Such an one is *in an ark.* When the last fiery deluge is sweeping over all things on the surface of the earth, it shall not come nigh him. He shall be caught up, and borne securely above it all.

Such an one is *in an hiding place.* When God arises to judge terribly the earth, and men are calling to rocks and mountains to fall upon them and cover them, the Everlasting Arms shall be thrown around him, and the storm shall pass over his head. He shall "abide under the shadow of the Almighty." (Psalm xci. 1.)

Such an one is *in a city of refuge.* The accuser of the brethren can lay no charge against him. The law cannot condemn him. There is a wall between him and the avenger of blood. The enemies of his soul cannot hurt him. He is in a secure sanctuary.

Such an one is *rich.* He has treasure in heaven which cannot be affected by worldly changes, compared to which

Peru and California are nothing at all. He need not envy the richest merchants and bankers. He has a portion that will endure when bank-notes and sovereigns are worthless things. He can say, like the Spanish ambassador, when shown the treasury at Venice, "My Master's treasury has no bottom." He has Christ.

Such an one is *insured*. He is ready for anything that may happen. Nothing can harm him. Banks may break, and Governments may be overturned. Famine and pestilence may rage around him. Sickness and sorrow may visit his own fireside. But still he is ready for all, —ready for health, ready for disease,—ready for tears, —ready for joy,—ready for poverty, ready for plenty,— ready for life, ready for death. He has Christ. He is a pardoned soul. "Blessed" indeed "is he whose transgression is forgiven, and whose sin is covered." (Ps. xxxii. 1.)

How will any one escape if he neglects so great salvation? Why should you not lay hold on it at once, and say, Pardon me, even me also, O my Saviour! What would you have, if the way I have set before you does not satisfy you? Come while the door is open. Ask, and you shall receive.

IV. *Let me, in the last place, supply the readers of this paper with some marks of having found forgiveness.*

I dare not leave out this point. Too many persons presume they are forgiven, who have no evidence to show. Not a few cannot think it possible they are forgiven, who are plainly in the way to heaven, though they may not see it themselves. I would fain raise hope in some, and self-inquiry in others; and to do this, let me set down in order the leading marks of a forgiven soul.

(*a*) Forgiven souls *hate* sin. They can enter most fully into the words of our Communion Service: "The remembrance of sin is grievous unto them, and the burden of it is intolerable." It is the serpent which bit them: how should they not shrink from it with horror? It is the poison which brought them to the brink of eternal death how should they not loathe it with a godly disgust? It is the Egyptian enemy which kept them in hard bondage how should not the very memory of it be bitter to their hearts? It is the disease of which they carry the marks and scars about them, and from which they have scarcely recovered: well may they dread it, flee from it, and long to be delivered altogether from its power! Remember how the woman in Simon's house wept over the feet of Jesus. (Luke vii. 38.) Remember how the Ephesians publicly burned their wicked books. (Acts xix. 19.) Remember how Paul mourned over his youthful transgressions: "I am not meet to be called an Apostle, because I persecuted the Church of God." (1 Cor. xv. 9.) If you and sin are friends, you and God are not yet reconciled. You are not meet for heaven; for one main part of heaven's excellence is the absence of all sin.

(b) Forgiven souls *love Christ*. This is that one thing they can say, if they dare say nothing else,—they do love Christ. His person, His offices, His work, His name, His cross, His blood, His words, His example, His day, His ordinances,—all, all are precious to forgiven souls. The ministry which exalts Him most, is that which they enjoy most. The books which are most full of Him, are most pleasant to their minds. The people on earth they feel most drawn to, are those in whom they see something of Christ. His name is as ointment poured forth, and comes with a peculiar sweetness to their ears. (Cant. i. 3.) They would tell you they cannot help feeling as they do. He is their Redeemer, their Shepherd, their Physician, their King, their strong Deliverer, their gracious Guide, their hope, their joy, their All. Were it not for Him they would be of all men most miserable. They would as soon consent that you should take the sun out of the sky, as Christ out of their religion. Those people who talk of "the Lord," and "the Almighty," and "the Deity," and so forth, but have not a word to say about Christ, are in anything but a right state of mind. What saith the Scripture? "He that honoureth not the Son, honoureth not the Father which hath sent Him." (John v. 23.) "If any man love not the Lord Jesus Christ, let him be anathema." (1 Cor. xvi. 22.)

(c) Forgiven souls *are humble.* They cannot forget that they owe all they have and hope for to free grace, and this keeps them lowly. They are brands plucked from the fire,—debtors who could not pay for themselves, —captives who must have remained in prison for ever, but for undeserved mercy,—wandering sheep who were ready to perish when the Shepherd found them; and what right then have they to be proud? I do not deny that there are proud saints. But this I do say,—they are of all God's creatures the most inconsistent, and of all God's children the most likely to stumble and pierce themselves with many sorrows. Forgiveness more often produces the spirit of Jacob: "I am not worthy of the least of all the mercies, and all the truth which Thou hast showed unto Thy servant" (Gen. xxxii. 10); and of Hezekiah:—"I shall go softly all my years" (Isaiah xxxviii. 15); and of the Apostle Paul: "I am less than the least of all saints, —chief of sinners." (Eph. iii. 8; 1 Tim. i. 15.) When you and I have nothing we can call our own but sin and weakness, there is surely no garment that becomes us so well as humility.

(d) Forgiven souls *are holy.* Their chief desire is to please Him who has saved them, to do His will, to glorify Him in body and in Spirit, which are His. "What shall I render unto the Lord for all His benefits?" (Ps. cxvi. 12), is a leading principle in a pardoned heart. It was the remembrance of Jesus showing mercy that made Paul in labours so abundant, and in doing good so unwearied. It was a sense of pardon that made Zaccheus say, "The half of my goods I give to the poor, and if I have taken anything from any man by false accusation, I restore him four-fold." (Luke xix. 8.) If any one points out to me believers who are in a carnal, slothful state of soul, I reply in the words of Peter, "They have forgotten they were purged from their old sins." (2 Pet. i. 9.) But if you show me a man deliberately living an unholy and licentious life, and yet boasting that his sins are forgiven, I answer, "He is under a ruinous delusion, and is not forgiven at all." I would not believe he is forgiven if an angel from heaven affirmed it, and I charge you not to believe it too. Pardon of sin and love of sin are like oil and water,—they will never go together. All that are washed in the blood of Christ are also sanctified by the Spirit of Christ.

(e) Forgiven souls *are forgiving.* They do as they have been done by. They look over the offences of their brethren. They endeavour to "walk in love, as Christ loved them, and gave Himself for them." (Eph. v. 2.) They remember how God for Christ's sake forgave them, and endeavour to do the same towards their fellow-creatures. Has He forgiven them pounds, and shall they not forgive a few pence? Doubtless in this, as in every thing else, they come short;— but this is their desire and their aim. A spiteful quarrelsome Christian is a scandal to his profession. It is very hard to believe that such an one has ever sat at the foot of the cross, and has ever considered how he is praying against himself every time he uses the Lord's Prayer. Is he not saying as it were, "Father, do not forgive me my trespasses at all"? But it is still harder to understand what such a one would do in heaven, if he got there. All ideas of heaven in which forgiveness has not a place, are castles in the air and vain fancies. Forgiveness is the way by which every saved soul enters heaven. Forgiveness is the only title by which he remains in heaven. Forgiveness is the eternal subject of song with all the redeemed who inhabit heaven. Surely an unforgiving soul in heaven would find his heart completely out of tune. Surely we know nothing of Christ's love to us but the name of it, if we do not love our brethren.

I lay these things before every reader of this paper. I know well there are great diversities in the degree of men's attainments in grace, and that saving faith in Christ is consistent with many imperfections. But still I do believe the five marks I have just been naming will generally be found more or less in all forgiven souls.

I cannot conceal from you, these marks should raise in many minds great searchings of heart. I must be plain. I fear there are thousands of persons called Christians, who know nothing of these marks. They are baptized. They attend the services of their Church. They would not on any account be reckoned infidels. But as to true repentance and saving faith, union with Christ and sanctification of the Spirit, they are "names and words" of which they know nothing at all.

Now if this paper is read by such persons, it will probably either alarm them, or make them very angry. If it makes them angry I shall be sorry. If it alarms them I shall be glad. I want to alarm them. I want to awaken them from their present state. I want them to take in the great fact, that they are not yet forgiven, that they have not peace with God, and are on the high road to destruction.

I must say this, for I see no alternative. It seems neither Christian faithfulness, nor Christian charity, to keep it back. I see certain marks of pardoned souls laid down in Scripture. I see an utter want of these marks in many men and women around me. How then can I avoid the conclusion that they are not yet "forgiven"? And how shall I do the work of a faithful watchman if I do not write it down plainly in so many words? Where is the use of crying Peace! Peace! when there is no peace? Where is the honesty of acting the part of a lying physician, and telling people there is no danger, when in reality they are fast drawing near to eternal death ? Surely the blood of souls would be required at my hands if I wrote to you anything less than the truth. " If the trumpet give an uncertain sound, who shall prepare himself to the battle?" (1 Cor. xiv. 8.)

Examine yourself, then, before this subject is forgotten. Consider of what sort your religion is. Try it by the five marks I have just set before you. I have endeavoured to make them as broad and general as I can, for fear of causing any heart to be sad that God has not made sad. If you know anything of them, though it be but a little, I am thankful, and entreat you to go forward. But if you know nothing of them in your own experience, let me say, in all affection, I stand in doubt of you. I tremble for your soul.

1. And now, before I conclude, let me put a *home question* to every one who reads this paper. It shall be short and plain, but it is all important : "Are you forgiven ? "

I have told you all I can about forgiveness. Your need of forgiveness,—the way of forgiveness,—the encouragements to seek forgiveness,—the marks of having found it,—all have been placed before you. Bring the whole subject to bear upon your own heart, and ask yourself, " Am I forgiven ? Either I am, or I am not. Which of the two is it ? "

You believe perhaps, there is forgiveness of sins. You believe that Christ died for sinners, and that He offers a pardon to the most ungodly. But **are** you forgiven *yourself?* Have you yourself laid hold on Christ by faith, and found peace through His blood ? What profit is there to you in forgiveness, except you get the benefit of it ? What does it profit the shipwrecked sailor that the life-boat is alongside, if he sticks by the wreck, and does not jump in and escape ? What does it avail the sick man that the doctor offers him a medicine, if he only looks at it, and does not swallow it down? Except you lay hold for your own soul, you will be as surely lost as if there was no forgiveness at all.

If ever your sins are to be forgiven, it must be now,—now in this life, if ever in the life to come,—now in this world, if they are to be found blotted out when Jesus comes again the second time. There must be actual business between you and Christ. Your sins must be laid on Him by faith: His righteousness must be laid on you. His blood must be applied to your conscience, or else your sins will meet you in the day of judgment, and sink you into hell. Oh, how can you trifle when such things are at stake? How can you be content to leave it uncertain whether you are forgiven? Surely that a man can make his will, insure his life, give directions about his funeral, and yet leave his soul's affairs in uncertainty, is a wonderful thing indeed.

2. Let me next give a *solemn warning* to every one who reads this paper, and knows in his conscience he is not forgiven.

Your soul is in awful danger. You may die this year. And if you die as you are, you are lost for ever. If you die without pardon, without pardon you will rise again at the last day. There is a sword over your head which hangs by a single hair. There is but a step between you and death. Oh, I wonder that you can sleep quietly in your bed!

You are *not yet forgiven*. Then what have you got by your religion? You go to church. You have a Bible, you have a Prayer-book, and perhaps a Hymn-book. You hear sermons. You join in services. It may be you go to the Lord's table. But what have you really got after all? Any hope? Any peace? Any joy? Any comfort? Nothing: literally nothing! You have got nothing but mere temporal things, if you are not a pardoned soul.

You are *not yet forgiven*. But you trust God will be

merciful. Yet why should He be merciful if you will not seek Him in His own appointed way ? Merciful He doubtless is, wonderfully merciful to all who come to Him in the name of Jesus. But if you choose to despise His directions, and make a road to heaven of your own, you will find to your cost there is no mercy for you.

You are *not yet forgiven.* But you hope you will be some day. I cannot away with that expression. It is like thrusting off the hand of conscience, and seizing it by the throat to stop its voice. Why are you more likely to seek forgiveness at a future time ? Why should you not seek it now ? Now is the time for gathering the bread of life. The day of the Lord is fast drawing near, and then no man can work. (Exod. xvi. 26.) The Seventh trumpet will soon sound. The kingdoms of this world will soon become the kingdoms of our Lord and of His Christ. (Rev. xi. 15.) Woe to the house which is found without the scarlet line, and without the mark of blood upon the door ! (Josh. ii 18 ; Exod. xii. 13.)

Well, you may not feel your need of forgiveness now. But a time may come when you will want it. The Lord in mercy grant that it may not then be too late.

3. Let me next give an *earnest invitation* to all who read this paper and desire forgiveness.

I know not who you are, or what you have been in time past, but I say boldly, Come to Christ by faith, and you shall have a pardon. High or low, rich or poor, young men and maidens, old men and children,—you cannot be worse than Manasseh and Paul before conversion,—than David and Peter after conversion : come all of you to Christ, and you shall be freely forgiven.

Think not for a moment that you have some great thing to do before you come to Christ. Such a notion is of the earth, earthy ; the Gospel bids you come just as you are. Man's idea is to make his peace with God by repentance, and then come to Christ at last : the Gospel way is to receive peace from Christ first of all, and begin with Him. Man's idea is to amend, and turn over a new leaf, and so work his way up to reconciliation and friendship with God: the Gospel way is first to be friends with God through Christ, and then to work. Man's idea is to toil up the hill, and find life at the top: the Gospel way is first to live by faith in Christ, and then to do His will.

And judge ye, every one, judge ye, which is true Christianity? Which is the good news? Which is the glad tidings? First the fruits of the Spirit and then peace, or first peace and then the fruits of the Spirit? First sanctification and then pardon, or first pardon and then sanctification? First service and then life, or first life and then service? Your own hearts can well supply the answer.

Come then, willing to receive, and not thinking how much you can bring. Come, willing to take what Christ offers, and not fancying you can give anything in return. Come with your sins, and no other qualification but a hearty desire for pardon, and, as sure as the Bible is true, you shall be saved.

You may tell me you are not worthy, you are not good enough, you are not elect. I answer, You are a sinner, and you want to be saved, and what more do you want? You are one of those whom Jesus came to save. Come to Him and you shall have life. Take with you words, and He will hear you graciously. Tell Him all your soul's necessities, and I know from the Bible He will give heed. Tell Him you have heard He receiveth sinners, and that you are such. Tell Him you have heard He has the keys of life in his hand, and entreat Him to let you in. Tell Him you come in dependence on His own promises, and ask Him to fulfil His word, and "do as He has said." (2 Sam. vii. 25.) Do this in simplicity and sincerity, and, my soul for your's, you shall not ask in vain. Do this and you shall find Him faithful and just to forgive your

sins, and to cleanse you from all unrighteousness. (1 John
i. 9.)

4. Last of all, let me give a *word of exhortation* to
all forgiven souls.

You are forgiven. Then know the full extent of your
privileges, and learn to rejoice in the Lord. You and I
are great sinners, but then we have a great Saviour. You
and I have sinned sins that are past man's knowledge, but
then we have "the love of Christ, which passeth knowledge,"
to rest upon. (Eph. iii. 19.) You and I feel our hearts to be
a bubbling fountain of evil, but then we have another
fountain of greater power in Christ's blood, to which we
may daily resort. You and I have mighty enemies to
contend with, but then the "Captain of our salvation" is
mightier still, and is ever with us. Why should our
hearts be troubled? Why should we be disquieted and
cast down? O men and women of little faith that we
are! Wherefore do we doubt?

Let us strive every year to grow in grace, and in the
knowledge of our Lord Jesus Christ. It is sad to be content with a little religion. It is honourable to covet the
best gifts. We ought not to be satisfied with the same
kind of hearing, and reading, and praying, which satisfied
us in years gone by. We ought to labour every year to
throw more heart and reality into everything we do in our
religion. To love Christ more intensely,—to abhor evil
more thoroughly,—to cleave to what is good more closely,
—to watch even our least ways more narrowly,—to declare
very plainly that we seek a country,—to put on the Lord
Jesus Christ. and be clothed with Him in every place and
company,—to see more,—to feel more,—to know more,—
to do more,—these ought to be our aims and desires every
year we begin. Truly there is room for improvement in
us all.

Let us try to do good to the souls of others, more than
we have done hitherto. Alas, it is poor work indeed to be

swallowed up in our own spiritual concerns, and taken up with our own spiritual ailments, and never to think of others! We forget that there is such a thing as religious selfishness. Let us count it a sorrowful thing to go to heaven alone, and let us seek to draw companions with us. We ought never to forget that every man, woman and child around us, will soon be either in heaven or hell. Let us say to others, as Moses did to Hobab, "Come with us, and we will do thee good." (Num. x. 29.) Oh, it is indeed a true saying, "He that watereth shall be watered himself." (Prov. xi. 25.) The idle, do-little, selfish Christian has little idea what he is missing.

But above all, let us learn to live the life of faith in Jesus more than we have hitherto. Ever to be found by the fountain side,—ever to be eating Christ's body by faith, and drinking Christ's blood by faith,—ever to have before our minds Christ's dying for our sins,—Christ's rising again for our justification,—Christ interceding for us at God's right hand,—Christ soon coming again to gather us to Himself,—this is the mark which we should have continually before our eyes. We may fall short, but let us aim high. Let us walk in the full light of the Sun of righteousness, and then our graces will grow. Let us not be like trees on a cold north wall, weak, half-starved, and unfruitful. Let us rather strive to be like the sun-flower, and follow the great Fountain of Light wherever He goes, and see Him with open face. Oh, for an eye more quick to discern His dealings! Oh, for an ear more ready to hear His voice!

Finally, let us say to everything in the world that interferes between ourselves and Jesus Christ, "Stand aside;" and let us dread *allowing* ourselves in the least evil habits, lest insensibly they rise up like a mist and hide Him from our eyes. "In His light alone shall we see light" and feel warmth, and separate from Him we shall find the world a dark and cold wilderness. (Psalm xxxvi. 9.) We should

call to mind the request of the Athenian philosopher, when
the mightiest Monarch on earth asked him what he desired
most. " I have," said he, " but one request to make ; and
that is that you would stand from between me and the
sun." Let this be the spirit in which you and I are found
continually. Let us think lightly of the world's gifts. Let
us sit calmly under its cares. Let us care for nothing if
we may only ever see the King's face, if we may only
ever abide in Christ.

If our sins are forgiven, our best things are yet to come.

Yet a little time, and we shall " see face to face, and
know as we have been known." We shall " see the King
in His beauty," and " go out no more." (1 Cor. xiii. 12 ;
Isa. xxxiii. 17 ; Rev. iii. 12.) " Blessed then is he whose
transgression is forgiven, and whose sins are covered."
(Psalm xxxii. 1.)

VIII.

JUSTIFICATION!

" Being justified by faith, we have PEACE *with God through our Lord Jesus Christ."*—-ROMANS **v. 1.**

THERE is a word in the text which heads this page which ought to be very precious in the eyes of Englishmen. That word is *"peace."*

Even in "merry England" we have known something of the horrors of war in the last thirty years. The Crimean war, the Indian mutiny, the Chinese, Abyssinian, and Ashantee wars have left deep marks on the history of our country

We have tasted some of the tremendous evils which war, however just and necessary, brings in its train. Battle and disease have done their deadly work among our gallant soldiers and sailors. Gentle and simple blood has been shed like water in far distant lands. Many of the best and bravest of our countrymen are lying cold in untimely graves. Hearts in England have been broken by sudden, stunning, crushing bereavements. Mourning has been put on in many a palace, and many a cottage. The light of hundreds of happy firesides has been quenched. The mirth of thousands of homes is gone. Alas, we have learned by bitter experience what a blessed thing is *peace!*

I desire, however, to call the attention of all who read this paper to the best of all peace,—even peace with God.

I would fain speak to you of a peace which this world can neither give nor take away,—a peace which depends on no earthly governments, and needs no carnal weapons, either to win it or preserve it,—a peace which is freely offered by the King of kings, and is within the reach of all who are willing to receive it.

There is such a thing as "peace with God." It may be felt and known. My heart's desire and prayer is that you may be able to say with the Apostle Paul, "Being justified by faith, I have peace with God through our Lord Jesus Christ." (Rom. v. 1.)

There are four things which I propose to bring before you, in order to throw light on the whole subject.

I. Let me show you the chief privilege of a true Christian:—"*he has peace with God.*"

II. Let me show you the fountain from which that privilege flows:—"*he is justified.*"

III. Let me show you the rock from which that fountain springs:—"*Jesus Christ.*"

IV. Let me show you the hand by which the privilege is made our own:—"*faith.*"

Upon each of these four points I have something to say. May the Holy Ghost make the whole subject peace-giving to some souls!

I. First of all, let me show the chief privilege of a true Christian:—*he has peace with God.*

When the apostle Paul wrote his epistle to the Romans, he used five words which the wisest of the heathen could never have used. Socrates, and Plato, and Aristotle, and Cicero, and Seneca were wise men. On many subjects they saw more clearly than most people in the present day. They were men of mighty minds, and of a vast range of intellect. But not one of them could have said as the apostle did, "I have peace with God." (Rom v. 1.)

When Paul used these words, he spoke not for himself only, but for all true Christians. Some of them no doubt have a greater sense of this privilege than others. All of them find an evil principle within, warring against their spiritual welfare day by day. All of them find their adversary, the devil, waging an endless battle with their souls. All of them find that they must endure the enmity of the world. But all, notwithstanding, to a greater or less extent, "have peace with God."

This peace with God is a calm, intelligent sense of friendship with the Lord of heaven and earth. He that has it, feels as if there was no barrier and separation between himself and his holy Maker. He can think of himself as under the eye of an all-seeing Being, and yet not feel afraid. He can believe that this all-seeing Being beholds him, and yet is not displeased.

Such a man can see *death* waiting for him, and yet not be greatly moved. He can go down into the cold river,— close his eyes on all he has on earth,—launch forth into a world unknown, and take up his abode in the silent grave,— and yet feel peace.

Such a man can look forward to the *resurrection* and the judgment, and yet not be greatly moved. He can see with his mind's eye the great white throne,—the assembled world,—the open books,—the listening angels,—the Judge Himself,—and yet feel peace.

Such a man can think of *eternity*, and yet not be greatly moved. He can imagine a never-ending existence in the presence of God and of the Lamb,—an everlasting Sunday,—a perpetual communion,—and yet feel peace.

I know of no happiness compared to that which this peace affords. A calm sea after a storm,—a blue sky after a black thunder cloud,—health after sickness,—light after darkness,—rest after toil,—all, all are beautiful and pleasant things. But none, none of them all can give more than a feeble idea of the comfort which those enjoy who have been brought into the state of peace with God. It is "a peace which passeth all understanding." (Phil. iv. 7.)

It is *the want* of this very peace which makes many in the world unhappy. Thousands have everything that is thought able to give pleasure, and yet are never satisfied. Their hearts are always aching. There is a constant sense of emptiness within. And what is the secret of all this? They have no peace with God.

It is *the desire* of this very peace which makes many a heathen do much in his idolatrous religion. Hundreds of them have been seen to mortify their bodies, and vex their own flesh in the service of some wretched image which their own hands had made. And why? Because they hungered after peace with God.

It is *the possession* of this very peace on which the value of a man's religion depends. Without it there may be everything to please the eye, and gratify the ear,—forms, ceremonies, services, and sacraments,—and yet no good done to the soul. The grand question that should try all is the state of a man's conscience. Is it peace? *Has he peace with God?*

This is the very peace about which I address every reader of these pages this day. Have you got it? Do you feel it? Is it your own?

If you have it, you are truly *rich*. You have that which will endure for ever. You have treasure which you will not lose when you die and leave the world. You will carry it with you beyond the grave. You will have it and enjoy it to all eternity. Silver and gold you may have none. The praise of man you may never enjoy. But you have that which is far better than either, if you have the peace of God.

If you have it not, you are truly *poor*. You have nothing which will last,—nothing which will wear,—

nothing which you can carry with you when your turn comes to die. Naked you came into this world, and naked in every sense you will go forth. Your body may be carried to the grave with pomp and ceremony. A solemn service may be read over your coffin. A marble monument may be put up in your honour. But after all it will be but a pauper's funeral, if you die without PEACE WITH GOD.

II. Let me show you, in the next place, the fountain from which true peace is drawn. *That fountain is justification.*

The peace of the true Christian is not a vague, dreamy feeling, without reason and without foundation. He can show cause for it. He builds upon solid ground. He has peace with God, because he is justified.

Without justification it is impossible to have real peace. Conscience forbids it. Sin is a mountain between a man and God, and must be taken away. The sense of guilt lies heavy on the heart, and must be removed. Unpardoned sin will murder peace. The true Christian knows all this well. His peace arises from a consciousness of his sins being forgiven, and his guilt being put away. His house is not built on sandy ground. His well is not a broken cistern, which can hold no water. He has peace with God, because he is justified.

He is justified, and his sins are *forgiven.* However many, and however great, they are cleansed away, pardoned, and wiped out. They are blotted out of the book of God's remembrance. They are sunk into the depths of the sea. They are cast behind God's back. They are searched for and not found. They are remembered no more. Though they may have been like scarlet, they are become white as snow; though they may have been red like crimson, they are as wool. And so he has peace.

He is justified and *counted righteous* in God's sight

The Father sees no spot in him, and reckons him innocent.
He is clothed in a robe of perfect righteousness, and may
sit down by the side of angels without feeling ashamed.
The holy law of God, which touches the thoughts and
intents of men's hearts, cannot condemn him.   The devil,
"the accuser of the brethren," can lay nothing to his
charge, to prevent his full acquittal.   And so he has
peace.

Is he not naturally a poor, weak, erring, defective
sinner?   He is.   None knows that better than he does
himself.   But notwithstanding this, he is reckoned complete, perfect, and faultless before God, for he is justified.

Is he not naturally a *debtor?*   He is.   None feels
that more deeply than he does himself.   He owes ten
thousand talents, and has nothing of his own to pay.   But
his debts are all paid, settled, and crossed out for ever, for
he is justified.

Is he not naturally liable to the curse of *a broken law?*
He is.   None would confess that more readily than he
would himself.   But the demands of the law have been
fully satisfied,—the claims of justice have been met to the
last tittle, and he is justified.

Does he not naturally *deserve punishment?*   He does.
None would acknowledge that more fully than he would
himself.   But the punishment has been borne.   The
wrath of God against sin has been made manifest.   Yet
he has escaped, and is justified.

Does any one who is reading this paper know anything of
all this ?   Are you justified ?   Do you feel as if you were
pardoned, forgiven, and accepted before God ?   Can you
draw near to Him with boldness, and say, "Thou art my
Father and my Friend, and I am Thy reconciled child"?
Oh, believe me, you will never taste true peace until you
are *justified !*

Where are your sins ?   Are they removed and taken
away from off your soul ?   Have they been reckoned for,

and accounted for, in God's presence? Oh, be very sure these questions are of the most solemn importance! A peace of conscience not built on justification, is a perilous dream. From such a peace the Lord deliver you!

Go with me in imagination to some of our great London hospitals. Stand with me there by the bedside of some poor creature in the last stage of an incurable disease. He lies quiet perhaps, and makes no struggle. He does not complain of pain perhaps, and does not appear to feel it. He sleeps, and is still. His eyes are closed. His head reclines on his pillow. He smiles faintly, and mutters something. He is dreaming of home, and his mother, and his youth. His thoughts are far away.—But is this health? Oh, no: no! It is only the effect of opiates. Nothing can be done for him. He is dying daily. The only object is to lessen his pain. His quiet is an unnatural quiet. His sleep is an unhealthy sleep. You see in that man's case a vivid likeness of *peace without justification*. It is a hollow, deceptive, unhealthy thing. Its end is death.

Go with me in imagination to some lunatic asylum. Let us visit some case of incurable delusion. We shall probably find some one who fancies that he is rich and noble, or a king. See how he will take the straw from off the ground, twist it round his head, and call it a crown. Mark how he will pick up stones and gravel, and call them diamonds and pearls. Hear how he will laugh, and sing, and appear to be happy in his delusions.—But is this happiness? Oh, no! We know it is only the result of ignorant insanity. You see in that man's case another likeness of *peace built on fancy, and not on justification.* It is a senseless, baseless thing. It has neither root nor life.

Settle it in your mind that there can be no peace with God, unless we feel that we are justified. *We must know what is become of our sins.* We must have a reasonable hope that they are forgiven, and put away. We must

have the witness of our conscience that we are reckoned
not guilty before God. Without this it is vain to talk of
peace. We have nothing but the shadow and imitation
of it. "There is no peace, saith my God, to the wicked."
(Isa. lvii. 21.)

Did you ever hear the sound of the trumpets which are
blown before the judges, as they come into a city to open
the Assizes? Did you ever reflect how different are the
feelings which these trumpets awaken in the minds of
different men? The innocent man, who has no cause to
be tried, hears them unmoved. They proclaim no terrors
to him. He listens and looks on quietly, and is not afraid.
But often there is some poor wretch, waiting his trial in a
silent cell, to whom those trumpets are a knell of despair.
They warn him that the day of trial is at hand. Yet a little
time and he will stand at the bar of justice, and hear
witness after witness telling the story of his misdeeds.
Yet a little time, and all will be over,—the trial, the
verdict, and the sentence,—and there will remain nothing
for him but punishment and disgrace. No wonder the
prisoner's heart beats, when he hears that trumpet's sound!

There is a day fast coming when all who are *not justified*
shall despair in like manner. The voice of the archangel
and the trump of God shall scatter to the winds the false
peace which now buoys up many a soul. The day of
judgment shall convince thousands of self-willed people
too late, that it needs something more than a few beautiful
ideas about "God s love and mercy," to reconcile a man to
his Maker, and to deliver his guilty soul from hell. No
hope shall stand in that awful day but the hope of the
justified man. No peace shall prove solid, substantial,
and unbroken, but the peace which is built on *justification.*

Is this peace your own? Rest not, rest not, if you love
life, till you know and feel that you are a justified man.
Think not that this is a mere matter of names and words.
Flatter not yourself with the idea that justification is an

"abstruse and difficult subject," and that you may get to
heaven well enough without knowing anything about it.
Make up your mind to the great truth that there can be
no heaven without peace with God, and no peace with God
without justification. And then give your soul no rest till
you are a JUSTIFIED MAN.

III. Let me show you, in the third place, the rock from
which justification and peace with God flow. *That rock
is Christ.*

The true Christian is not justified because of any
goodness of his own. His peace is not to be traced up to
any work that he has done. It is not purchased by his
prayers and regularity, his repentance and his amendment,
his morality and his charity. All these are utterly unable
to justify him. In themselves they are defective in many
things and need a large forgiveness. And as to justifying
him, such a thing is not to be named. Tried by the perfect standard of God's law the best of Christians is nothing
better than a justified sinner, a pardoned criminal. As to
merit, worthiness, desert, or claim upon God's mercy, he
has none. Peace built on any such foundations as these is
utterly worthless. The man who rests upon them is
miserably deceived.

Never were truer words words put on paper than those
which Richard Hooker penned on this subject 280 years
ago. Let those who would like to know what English
clergymen thought in olden times, mark well what he
says.—" If God would make us an offer thus large, Search
all the generation of men since the fall of your father
Adam, and find *one man*, that hath done any *one action*,
which hath past from him pure, without any stain or
blemish at all;—and for that one man's one only action,
neither man nor angel shall find the torments which are
prepared for both:—do you think this ransom, to deliver
man and angels, would be found among the sons of men?

The best things we do have somewhat in them to be
pardoned. How then can we do *anything* meritorious and
worthy to be rewarded ? "—To these words I desire entirely
to subscribe. I believe that no man can be justified by his
works before God in the slightest possible degree. Before
man he may be justified: his works may evidence the
reality of his Christianity. Before God he cannot be
justified by anything that he can do: he will be always
defective, always imperfect, always short-coming, always far
below the mark, so long as he lives. It is not by works of
his own that any one ever has peace and is a justified man.

But how then is a true Christian justified ? What is the
secret of that peace and sense of pardon which he enjoys?
How can we understand a Holy God dealing with a sinful
man as with one innocent, and reckoning him righteous
notwithstanding his many sins ?

The answer to all these questions is short and simple.
The true Christian is counted righteous for the sake of Jesus
Christ, the Son of God. He is justified because of the
death and atonement of Christ. He has peace because
" Christ died for his sins according to the Scriptures." This
is the key that unlocks the mighty mystery. Here the
great problem is solved, how God can be just and yet justify
the ungodly. The life and death of the Lord Jesus explain
all. "He is our peace." (1 Cor. xv. 3; Ephes. ii. 14.)

Christ has *stood in the place* of the true Christian. He
has become his Surety and his Substitute. He undertook
to bear all that was to be borne, and to do all that was to
be done, and what He undertook He performed. Hence
the true Christian is a justified man. (Isai. liii. 6.)

Christ has *suffered for sins*, the "just for the unjust."
He has endured our punishment in His own body on the
cross. He has allowed the wrath of God, which we deserved,
to fall on His own head. Hence the true Christian is a
justified man. (1 Pet. iii. 18.)

Christ has *paid the debt* the Christian owed, by His own

blood. He has reckoned for it, and discharged it to the uttermost farthing by His own death. God is a just God, and will not require his debts to be paid twice over. Hence the true Christian is a justified man. (Acts xx. 28; 1 Pet i. 18, 19.)

Christ has *obeyed the law* of God perfectly. The devil, the Prince of this World, could find no fault in Him. By so fulfilling it He brought in an everlasting righteousness, in which all His people are clothed in the sight of God. Hence the true Christian is a justified man. (Dan ix. 24; Rom x. 4.)

Christ, in one word, has lived for the true Christian. Christ has died for him. Christ has gone to the grave for him. Christ has risen again for him. Christ has ascended up on high for him, and gone into heaven to intercede for his soul. Christ has done all, paid all, suffered all that was needful for his redemption. Hence arises the true Christian's justification,—hence his peace. In himself there is nothing, but in Christ he has all things that his soul can require. (Coloss. ii. 3; iii. 11.)

Who can tell the blessedness of the exchange that takes place between the true Christian and the Lord Jesus Christ! Christ's righteousness is placed upon him, and his sins are placed upon Christ. Christ has been reckoned a sinner for his sake, and now he is reckoned innocent for Christ's sake. Christ has been condemned for his sake though there was no fault in Him,—and now he is acquitted for Christ's sake, though he is covered with sins, faults, and short-comings. Here is wisdom indeed! God can now be just and yet pardon the ungodly. Man can feel that he is a sinner, and yet have a good hope of heaven and feel peace within. Who among men could have imagined such a thing? Who ought not to admire it when he hears it? (2 Cor v. 21.)

We read in British history of a Lord Nithsdale who was sentenced to death for a great political crime. He was closely confined in prison after his trial. The day of his execution was fixed. There seemed no chance of escape. And yet before the sentence was carried into effect, he contrived to escape through the skill and affection of his wife. She visited him in prison, and exchanged clothes with him. Dressed in his wife's clothes he walked out of prison and escaped, and neither guards nor keepers detected him, while his wife remained behind in his place. In short, she risked her own life to save the life of her husband. Who would not admire the skill and the love of such a wife as this?

But we read in Gospel history of a display of love, compared to which the love of Lady Nithsdale is nothing. We read of Jesus, the Son of God, coming down to a world of sinners, who neither cared for Him before He came, nor honoured Him when He appeared. We read of Him going down to the prison-house, and submitting to be bound, that we the poor prisoners might be able to go free. We read of Him becoming obedient to death,— and that the death of the cross,—that we the unworthy children of Adam might have a door opened to life ever-lasting. We read of Him being content to bear our sins and carry our trangressions, that we might wear His righteousness, and walk in the light and liberty of the Sons of God. (Phil. ii. 8.)

This may well be called a "love that passeth knowledge!" In no way could free grace ever have shone so brightly as in the way of *justification by Christ.* (Ephes. iii. 19.)

This is *the old way* by which alone the children of Adam, who have been justified from the beginning of the world, have found their peace. From Abel downwards, no man or woman has ever had one drop of mercy excepting through Christ. To Him every altar that was raised before the time of Moses was intended to point. To Him every sacrifice and ordinance of the Jewish law was meant to direct the children of Israel. Of Him all the prophets testified. In a word, if you lose sight of justification by

Christ, a large part of the Old Testament Scripture will become an unmeaning tangled maze.

This, above all, is the way of justification which exactly *meets the wants and requirements of human nature* There is a conscience left in man, although he is a fallen being. There is a dim sense of his own need, which in his better moments will make itself heard, and which nothing but Christ can satisfy. So long as his conscience is not hungry, any religious toy will satisfy a man's soul and keep him quiet. But once let his conscience become hungry, and nothing will quiet him but real spiritual food and no food but Christ.

There is something within a man when his conscience is really awake, which whispers, "*There must be a price paid for my soul, or no peace.*" At once the Gospel meets him with Christ. Christ has already paid a ransom for his redemption. Christ has given Himself for him Christ has redeemed him from the curse of the law, being made a curse for him. (Gal. ii. 20; iii. 13.)

There is something within a man, when his conscience is really awake, which whispers, "*I must have some right-eousness or title to heaven, or no peace.*" At once the Gospel meets him with Christ. He has brought in an everlasting righteousness. He is the end of the law for righteousness. His name is called the Lord our righteous-ness. God has made Him to be sin for us who knew no sin, that we might be made the righteousness of God in Him. (2 Cor. v. 21; Rom. x. 4; Jer. xxiii. 6.)

There is something within a man, when his conscience is really awake, which whispers, "*There must be punishment and suffering because of my sins, or no peace.*" At once the Gospel meets him with Christ. Christ hath suffered for sin, the just for the unjust, to bring him to God. He bore our sins in His own body on the tree. By His stripes we are healed. (1 Peter ii. 24; iii. 18.)

There is something within a man, when his conscience

is really awake, which whispers, "*I must have a priest for my soul, or no peace.*" At once the Gospel meets him with Christ. Christ is sealed and appointed by God the Father to be the Mediator between Himself and man. He is the ordained Advocate for sinners. He is the accredited Counsellor and Physician of sick souls. He is the great High Priest, the Almighty Absolver, the Gracious Confessor of heavy-laden sinners. (1 Tim. ii. 5 ; Heb. viii. 1.)

I know there are thousands of professing Christians who see no peculiar beauty in this doctrine of justification by Christ. Their hearts are buried in the things of the world. Their consciences are palsied, benumbed, and speechless. But whenever a man's conscience begins really to feel and speak, he will see something in Christ's atonement and priestly office which he never saw before. Light does not suit the eye nor music the ear, more perfectly than Christ suits the real wants of a sinful soul. Hundreds can testify that the experience of a converted heathen in the island of Raiatea in the South Pacific Ocean has been exactly their own. " I saw," he said, " an immense mountain, with precipitous sides, up which I endeavoured to climb, but when I had attained a considerable height, I lost my hold and fell to the bottom. Exhausted with perplexity and fatigue, I went to a distance and sat down to weep, and while weeping, I saw a drop of blood fall upon that mountain, and in a moment it was dissolved." He was asked to explain what all this meant. "That mountain," he said, "was my sins, and that drop which fell upon it, was one drop of the precious blood of Jesus, by which the mountain of my guilt was melted away." [*William's South Sea Missions.*]

This is the one true way of peace,—justification by Christ. Beware lest any turn you out of this way and lead you into any of the false doctrines of the Church of Rome. Alas, it is wonderful to see how that unhappy Church has built a house of error hard by the house of truth! Hold fast the truth of God about justification, and be not deceived. Listen not to any thing you may hear about other mediators and helpers to peace. Remember there is no *mediator* but one,—Jesus Christ; no *purgatory* for sinners but one,—the blood of Christ; no *sacrifice* for sin but one,—the sacrifice once made on the cross; no *works* that can merit anything—but the work of Christ; no *priest* that can truly absolve—but Christ. Stand fast here, and be on your guard. Give not the glory due to Christ to another.

What do you know of Christ? I doubt not you have heard of Him by the hearing of the ear, and repeated His name in the Belief. You are acquainted perhaps with the story of His life and death. But what experimental knowledge have you of Him? What practical use do you make of Him? What dealings and transactions have there been between your soul and Him?

Oh, believe me, there is *no peace with God excepting through Christ!* Peace is His peculiar gift. Peace is that legacy which He alone had power to leave behind Him when He left the world. All other peace beside this is a mockery and a delusion. When hunger can be relieved without food, and thirst quenched without drink, and weariness removed without rest, then, and not till then, will men find peace without Christ.

Now, is this peace your own? Bought by Christ with His own blood, offered by Christ freely to all who are willing to receive it,—is this peace your own? Oh, rest not: rest not till you can give a satisfactory answer to my question,—HAVE YOU PEACE?

IV. Let me show you, in the last place, *the hand by which the privilege of peace is received.*

I ask the special attention of all who read these pages to this part of our subject. There is scarcely any point in Christianity so important as the means by which Christ, justification, and peace, become the property of a man's soul. Many, I fear, would go with me so far as I have gone in this paper, but would part company here. Let us endeavour to lay hold firmly on the truth.

The means by which a man obtains an interest in Christ and all His benefits is *simple faith*. There is but one thing needful in order to be justified by His blood, and have peace with God. That one thing is to believe on Him. This is the peculiar mark of a true Christian. He believes on the Lord Jesus for his salvation. "Believe on the Lord Jesus Christ and thou shalt be saved." "Whosoever believeth in Him shall not perish, but have eternal life." (Acts xvi. 31 ; John iii. 16.)

Without this faith it is *impossible to be saved*. A man may be moral, amiable, good-natured, and respectable. But if he does not believe on Christ, he has no pardon, no justification, no title to heaven. "He that believeth not is condemned already." "He that believeth not the Son shall not see life: but the wrath of God abideth on him." "He that believeth not shall be damned." (John iii. 18, 36 ; Mark xvi. 16.)

Beside this faith *nothing whatever is needed for a man's justification*. Beyond doubt, repentance, holiness, love, humility, prayerfulness, will always be seen in the justified man. But they do not in the smallest degree justify him in the sight of God. Nothing joins a man to Christ,—nothing justifies, but simple faith. "To him that worketh not, but believeth on Him that justifieth the ungodly, his faith is counted for righteousness." "We conclude that a man is justified by faith without the deeds of the law." (Rom. iv. 5 ; iii. 28.)

Having this faith, a man *is at once completely justified*. His sins are at once removed. His iniquities are at once put away. The very hour that he believes he is reckoned by God entirely pardoned, forgiven, and a righteous man. His justification is not a future privilege, to be obtained after a long time and great pains. It is an immediate present possession. Jesus says, "He that believeth on Me hath everlasting life." Paul says, "By Him all that believe are justified from all things." (John **vi.** 47; Acts **xiii.** 39.)

I need hardly say that it is of the utmost importance to have clear views about the nature of true saving faith. It is constantly spoken of as the distinguishing characteristic of New Testament Christians. They are called "believers." In the single Gospel of John, "believing" is mentioned eighty or ninety times. There is hardly any subject about which so many mistakes are made. There is none about which mistakes are so injurious to the soul. The darkness of many a sincere inquirer may be traced up to confused views about faith. Let us try to get a distinct idea of its real nature.

True saving faith is *not the possession of everybody.* The opinion that all who are called Christians are, as a matter of course, believers, is a most mischievous delusion. A man may be baptized, like Simon Magus, and yet have "no part or lot" in Christ. The visible Church contains unbelievers as well as believers. "All men have not faith." (2 Thess. iii. 2.)

True saving faith is *not a mere matter of feeling.* A man may have many good feelings and desires in his mind towards Christ, and yet they may all prove as temporary and short-lived as the morning cloud and the early dew. Many are like the stony-ground hearers, and "receive the word with joy." Many will say under momentary excitement, "I will follow Thee whithersoever Thou goest," and yet return to the world. (Matt. viii. 19; xiii. 20.)

True saving faith is *not a bare assent of the intellect* to the fact that Christ died for sinners. This is not a jot better than the faith of devils. They know who Jesus is. "They believe," and they do more, "they tremble." (James ii. 19.)

True saving faith is *an act of the whole inner man.* It is an act of the head, heart, and will, all united and combined. It is an act of the soul, in which,—seeing his own guilt, danger, and hopelessness,—and seeing at the same time Christ offering to save him,—a man ventures on Christ,—flees to Christ,—receives Christ as his only hope,—and becomes a willing dependant on Him for salvation. It is an act which becomes at once the parent of a habit. He that has it may not always be equally sensible of his own faith; but in the main he lives by faith, and walks by faith.

True faith has *nothing whatever of merit* about it, and in the highest sense cannot be called "a work." It is but laying hold of a Saviour's hand, leaning on a husband's arm, and receiving a physician's medicine. It brings with it nothing to Christ but a sinful man's soul. It gives nothing, contributes nothing, pays nothing, performs nothing. It only receives, takes, accepts, grasps, and embraces the glorious gift of justification which Christ bestows, and by renewed daily acts enjoys that gift.

Of all Christian graces, faith is the most important. Of all, it is the simplest in reality. Of all, it is the most difficult to make men understand in practice. The mistakes into which men fall about it are endless. Some who have no faith never doubt for a moment that they are believers. Others, who have real faith, can never be persuaded that they are believers at all. But nearly every mistake about faith may be traced up to the old root of natural pride. Men will persist in sticking to the idea that they are to pay something of their own in order to be saved. As to a faith which consists in receiving only, and paying nothing at all, it seems as if they could not understand it.

Saving faith is the *hand* of the soul. The sinner is like a drowning man at the point of sinking. He sees the Lord Jesus Christ holding out help to him. He *grasps* it and is saved. This is faith. (Heb. vi. 18.)

Saving faith is the *eye* of the soul. The sinner is like the Israelite bitten by the fiery serpent in the wilderness, and at the point of death. The Lord Jesus Christ is offered to him as the brazen serpent, set up for his cure. He *looks* and is healed. This is faith. (John iii. 14, 15.)

Saving faith is the *mouth* of the soul. The sinner is starving for want of food, and sick of a sore disease. The Lord Jesus Christ is set before him as the bread of life, and the universal medicine. He *receives* it, and is made well and strong. This is faith. (John vi. 35.)

Saving faith is the *foot* of the soul. The sinner is pursued by a deadly enemy, and is in fear of being over-taken. The Lord Jesus Christ is put before him as a strong tower, a hiding place, and a refuge. He *runs* into it and is safe. This is faith. (Prov. xviii. 10.)

If you love life cling with a fast hold to the doctrine of justification by faith. If you love inward peace, let your views of faith be very simple. Honour every part of the Christian religion. Contend to the death for the necessity of holiness. Use diligently and reverently every appointed means of grace: but do not give to these things the office of *justifying* your soul in the slightest degree. If you would have peace, and keep peace, remember that faith alone justifies, and that not as a meritorious work, but as the act that joins the soul to Christ. Believe me, the crown and glory of the Gospel is justification by faith without the deeds of the law.

No doctrine can be imagined *so beautifully simple* as justification by faith. It is not a dark mysterious truth, intelligible to none but the great, the rich, and the learned. It places eternal life within the reach of the most unlearned, and the poorest in the land. It must be of God.

No doctrine can be imagined *so glorifying to God*. It honours all His attributes, His justice, mercy, and holiness. It gives the whole credit of the sinner's salvation to the Saviour He has appointed. It honours the Son, and so honours the Father that sent Him. (John v. 23.) It gives man no partnership in his redemption, but makes salvation to be wholly of the Lord. It must be of God.

No doctrine can be imagined *so calculated to put man in his right place.* It shows him his own sinfulness, and weakness, and inability to save his soul by his own works. It leaves him without excuse if he is not saved at last. It offers to him peace and pardon " without money and without price." It must be of God. (Isa. lv. 1.)

No doctrine can be imagined *so comforting to a broken-hearted and penitent sinner.* It brings to such an one glad tidings. It shows him that there is hope even for him. It tells him, though he is a great sinner, there is ready for him a great Saviour; and though he cannot justify himself, God can and will justify him for the sake of Christ. It must be of God.

No doctrine can be imagined *so satisfying to a true Christian.* It supplies him with a solid ground of comfort, —the finished work of Christ. If anything was left for the Christian to do, where would his comfort be? He would never know that he had done enough, and was really safe. But the doctrine that Christ undertakes all, and that we have only to believe and receive peace, meets every fear. It must be of God.

No doctrine can be imagined *so sanctifying.* It draws men by the strongest of all cords, the cord of love. It makes them feel they are debtors, and in gratitude bound to love much, when much has been forgiven. Preaching up works never produces such fruit as preaching them down. Exalting man's goodness and merits never makes men so holy as exalting Christ. The fiercest lunatics at Paris became gentle, mild, and obedient, when Abbé Pinel gave them liberty and hope. The free grace of Christ will produce far greater effects on men's lives than the sternest commands of law. Surely the doctrine must be of God.

No doctrine can be imagined *so strengthening to the*

hands of a minister. It enables him to come to the vilest of men, and say, " There is a door of hope even for you." It enables him to feel, " While life lasts there are no incurable cases among the souls under my charge." Many a minister by the use of this doctrine can say of souls, " I found them in the state of nature. I beheld them pass into the state of grace. I watched them moving into the state of glory." Truly this doctrine must be of God.

No doctrine can be imagined that *wears so well.* It suits men when they first begin, like the Philippian jailer, crying, " What shall I do to be saved ? "—It suits them when they fight in the forefront of the battle. Like the apostle Paul, they say, " The life that I live, I live by the faith of the Son of God." (Gal. ii. 20.)—It suits them when they die, as it did Stephen when he cried, " Lord Jesus, receive my spirit." (Acts vii. 59.)—Yes : many an one has opposed the doctrine fiercely while he lived, and yet on his death-bed has gladly embraced justification by faith, and departed saying that "*he trusted in nothing but Christ.*" It must be of God.

Have you this faith ? Do you know any thing of simple child-like confidence in Jesus ? Do you know what it is to rest your soul's hopes wholly on Christ ? Oh, remember that where there is no faith, there is no interest in Christ ;—where there is no interest in Christ, there is no justification ;—where there is no justification, there can be no peace with God ;—where there is no peace with God, there is no heaven ! And what then ? There remains nothing but hell.

And now, let me commend the solemn matters we have been considering to the serious and prayerful attention of all who read this paper. I invite you to begin by meditating calmly on peace with God,—on justification,—on Christ,—on faith. These are not mere speculative subjects, fit for none but retired students. They lie at the very roots of Christianity. They are bound up with life eternal. Bear with me for a few moments, while I add a few words in order to bring them home more closely to your heart and conscience.

1. Let me, then, for one thing, request every reader of this paper to put *a plain question* to himself.

Have you peace with God? You have heard of it. You have read of it. You know there is such a thing. You know where it is to be found. But do you possess it yourself? Is it yet your own? Oh, deal honestly with yourself, and do not evade my question! *Have you peace with God?*

I do not ask whether you think it an excellent thing, and hope to procure it at some future time before you die. I want to know about your state now. To-day, while it is called to-day, I ask you to deal honestly with my question. *Have you peace with God?*

Do not, I beseech you, allow any public events to make you put off the consideration of your own spiritual welfare. The wars and contentions of nations will never cease. The strife of political parties will never end. But after all, a hundred years hence these very things will seem of little importance to you. The question I am asking will seem a thousand times more important. You may possibly be saying then, too late, "*Oh, that I had thought more about peace with God!*"

May the question ring in your ears, and never leave you till you can give it a satisfactory answer! May the Spirit of God so apply it to your heart that you may be able to say boldly, before you die, "Being justified by faith, I have peace with God through Jesus Christ our Lord!"

2. In the next place, let me offer *a solemn warning* to every reader of this paper who knows that he has not peace with God.

You have not peace! Consider for a moment how fearfully great is your *danger!* You and God are not friends. The wrath of God abideth on you. God is angry with you every day. Your ways, your words, your thoughts, your actions, are a continual offence to Him. They are all unpardoned and unforgiven. They cover you from head to foot. They provoke Him every day to cut you off. The sword that the reveller of old saw hanging over his head by a single hair, is but a faint emblem of the danger of your soul. There is but a step between you and hell.

You have not peace! Consider for a moment how fearfully great is your *folly!* There sits at the right hand of God a mighty Saviour able and willing to give you peace, and you do not seek Him. For ten, twenty, thirty, and perhaps forty years He has called to you, and you have refused His counsel. He has cried, " Come to Me," and you have practically replied, " I will not." He has said, " My ways are ways of pleasantness," and you have constantly said, "I like my own sinful ways far better."

And after all, for what have you refused Christ ? For worldly riches, which cannot heal a broken heart,—for worldly business, which you must one day leave,—for worldly pleasures, which do not really satisfy: for these things, and such as these, you have refused Christ ! Is this wisdom ! is this fairness, is this kindness to your soul ?

I do beseech you to consider your ways. I mourn over your present condition with especial sorrow. I grieve to think how many are within a hair's breadth of some crushing affliction, and yet utterly unprepared to meet it. Fain would I draw near to every one, and cry in his ear, " Seek Christ ! Seek Christ, that you may have peace within and a present help in trouble." Fain would I persuade every anxious parent and wife and child to become acquainted with Him, who is a brother born for adversity, and the Prince of peace,—a friend that never fails nor forsakes, and a husband that never dies

3. Let me, in the next place, offer *an affectionate entreaty* to all who want peace and know not where to find it.

You want peace! Then seek it without delay from Him who alone is able to give it,—Christ Jesus the Lord. Go to Him in humble prayer, and ask Him to fulfil His own promises and look graciously on your soul. Tell Him you have read His compassionate invitation to the "labour-ing and heavy-laden." Tell Him that this is the plight of your soul, and implore Him to give you rest. Do this, and do it without delay.

Seek Christ Himself, and *do not stop short of personal dealings with Him.* Rest not in regular attendance on Christ's ordinances. Be not content with becoming a communicant, and receiving the Lord's supper. Think not to find solid peace in this way. You must see the King's face, and be touched by the golden sceptre. You must speak to the Physician, and open your whole case to Him. You must be closeted with the Advocate, and keep nothing back from Him. Oh, remember this! Many are shipwrecked just outside the harbour. They stop short in means and ordinances, and never go completely to Christ. "Whosoever drinks of this water shall thirst again." (John iv. 13.) Christ Himself can alone satisfy the soul.

Seek Christ, and *wait for nothing.* Wait not till you feel you have repented enough. Wait not till your knowledge is increased. Wait not till you have been sufficiently humbled because of your sins. Wait not till you have no ravelled tangle of doubts and darkness and unbelief all over your heart. Seek Christ just as you are. You will never be better by keeping away from Him. From the bottom of my heart I subscribe to old Traill's opinion, "*It is impossible that people should believe in Christ too soon.*" Alas, it is not humility, but pride and ignorance that make so many anxious souls hang back 'from closing with Jesus. They forget that the more sick a man is, the more need he has of the physician. The more bad a man feels his heart, the more readily and speedily ought he to flee to Christ.

Seek Christ, and *do not fancy you must sit still.* Let not Satan tempt you to suppose that you must wait in a state of passive inaction, and not strive to lay hold upon Jesus. How you can lay hold upon Him I do not pretend to explain. But I am certain that it is better to struggle towards Christ and strive to lay hold, than to sit still with our arms folded in sin and unbelief. Better perish striving to lay hold on Jesus, than perish in indolence and sin. Well says old Traill, of those who tell us·they are anxious but cannot believe in Christ: "This pretence is as inexcusable as if a man wearied with a journey, and not able to go one step further, should argue, '*I am so tired that I am not able to lie down,*' when indeed he can neither stand nor go."

4. Let me, in the next place, offer *some encouragement* to those who have good reason to hope they have peace with God, but are troubled by doubts and fears.

You have doubts and fears ! But what do you expect ? What would you have ? Your soul is married to a body full of weakness, passions, and infirmities. You live in a world that lies in wickedness, a world in which the great majority do not love Christ. You are constantly liable to the temptations of the devil. That busy enemy, if he cannot shut you out of heaven, will try hard to make your journey uncomfortable. Surely'all these things ought to be considered.

I say to every believer, that so far from being surprised that you have doubts and fears, I should suspect the reality of your peace if you had none. I think little of that grace which is accompanied by no inward conflict. There is seldom life in the heart when all is still, quiet, and in one way of thinking. Believe me, a true Christian may be known by his *warfare* as well as by his peace. These very doubts and fears which now distress you are tokens of good. They satisfy me that you have really got something which you are afraid to lose.

Beware that you do not help Satan by becoming an unjust accuser of yourself, and an unbeliever in the reality of God's work of grace. I advise you to pray for more knowledge of your own heart, of the fulness of Jesus, and of the devices of the devil. Let doubts and fears drive you to the throne of grace, stir you up to more prayer, send you more frequently to Christ. But do not let doubts and fears rob you of your peace. Believe me, you must be content to go to heaven as a sinner saved by grace. And you must not be surprised to find daily proof that you really are a sinner so long as you live.

5. Let me, in the last place, offer *some counsel* to all who have peace with God, and desire to keep up a lively sense of it.

It must never be forgotten that a believer's sense of his own justification and acceptance with God admits of many degrees and variations. At one time it may be bright and clear; at another dull and dim. At one time it may be high and full, like the flood tide; at another low, like the ebb. Our justification is a fixed, changeless, immovable thing. But our *sense* of justification is liable to many changes.

What then are the best means of preserving in a believer's heart that lively sense of justification which is so precious to the soul that knows it? I offer a few hints to believers. I lay no claim to infallibility in setting down these hints, for I am only a man. But such as they are I offer them.

(*a*) To keep up a lively sense of peace, there must be constant *looking to Jesus*. As the pilot keeps his eye on the mark by which he steers, so must we keep our eye on Christ.

(*b*) There must be constant *communion with Jesus.* We must use Him daily as our soul's Physician, and High Priest. There must be daily conference, daily confession, and daily absolution.

(*c*) There must be constant *watchfulness* against the enemies of your soul. He that would have peace must be always prepared for war.

(*d*) There must be constant *following after holiness* in every relation of life,—in our tempers, in our tongues, abroad and at home. A small speck on the lens of a telescope is enough to prevent our seeing distant objects clearly A little dust will soon make a watch go incorrectly.

(*e*) There must be a constant *labouring after humility.* Pride goes before a fall. Self-confidence is often the mother of sloth, of hurried Bible-reading, and sleepy prayers. Peter first said he would never forsake his Lord, though all others did;—then he slept when he should have prayed;—then he denied Him three times, and only found wisdom after bitter weeping.

(*f*) There must be constant *boldness in confessing* our Lord before men. Them that honour Christ, Christ will honour with much of His company. When the disciples forsook our Lord they were wretched and miserable. When they confessed Him before the council, they were filled with joy and the Holy Ghost.

(*g*) There must be constant *diligence about means of grace.* Here are the ways in which Jesus loves to walk. No disciple must expect to see much of his Master, who does not delight in public worship, Bible-reading, and private prayer.

(*h*) Lastly, there must be constant *jealousy* over our own souls, and frequent self-examination. We must be careful to distinguish between justification and sanctification. We must beware that we do not make a Christ of holiness.

I lay these hints before all believing readers. I might easily add to them. But I am sure they are among the first things to be attended to by true Christian believers, if they wish to keep up a lively sense of their own justification and acceptance with God.

I conclude all by expressing my heart's desire and prayer that all who read these pages may know what it is to have the peace of God which passeth all understanding in their souls.

If you never had " peace " yet, may it be recorded in the book of God that this year you sought peace in Christ and found it!

If you have tasted " peace " already, may your sense of peace mightily increase!

The following passage from a direction for the Visitation of the Sick, composed by Anselm, Archbishop of Canterbury, about the year 1093, will probably be interesting to many readers.

" Dost thou believe that thou canst not be saved but by the death of Christ? The sick man answereth, Yes. Then let it be said unto him, Go to then, and whilst thy soul abideth in thee, put all thy confidence in this death alone. Place thy trust in no other thing. Commit thyself wholly to this death. Cover thyself wholly with this alone. Cast thyself wholly on this death. Wrap thyself wholly in this death. And if God would judge thee, say, ' Lord, I place the death of our Lord Jesus Christ between me and Thy judgment ; and otherwise I will not contend with Thee.' And if He shall say unto thee that thou art a sinner, say, ' I place the death of our Lord Jesus Christ between me and my sins.' If He shall say unto thee that thou hast deserved damnation, say, ' Lord, I put the death of our Lord Jesus Christ between Thee and all my sins ; and I offer His merits for my own, which I should have, and have not.' If He say that He is angry with thee, say, ' Lord, I place the death of our Lord Jesus Christ between me and Thy anger.' "—*Quoted by Owen in his Treatise on Justification.*—JOHNSTONE'S EDITION OF OWEN'S WORKS. VOL. V., p. 17.

IX

THE CROSS OF CHRIST.

"God forbid that I should glory, save in the cross of our Lord Jesus Christ."—GAL. vi. 14.

WHAT do we think and feel about the cross of Christ? We live in a Christian land. We probably attend the worship of a Christian church. We have, most of us, been baptized in the name of Christ. We profess and call ourselves Christians. All this is well: it is more than can be said of millions in the world. But *what do we think and feel about the cross of Christ?*

I want to examine what one of the greatest Christians that ever lived thought of the cross of Christ. He has written down his opinion: he has given his judgment in words that cannot be mistaken. The man I mean is the Apostle Paul. The place where you will find his opinion, is in the letter which the Holy Ghost inspired him to write to the Galatians. The words in which his judgment is set down, are these,—"God forbid that I should glory, save in the cross of our Lord Jesus Christ."

Now what did Paul mean by saying this? He meant to declare strongly, that he trusted in nothing but "Jesus Christ crucified" for the pardon of his sins and the salvation of his soul. Let others, if they would, look elsewhere for salvation; let others, if they were so disposed, trust in other things for pardon and peace : for his part the apostle was determined to rest on nothing, lean on nothing, build his hope on nothing, place confidence in nothing, glory in nothing, except "the cross of Jesus Christ."

I wish to say something about "the cross" to the readers of this volume. Believe me, the subject is one of the deepest importance. This is no mere question of controversy. It is not one of those points on which men may agree to differ, and feel that differences will not shut them out of heaven. A man must be right on this subject, or he is lost for ever. Heaven or hell, happiness or misery, life or death, blessing or cursing in the last day,—all hinges on the answer to this question : "What do You think about the cross of Christ ? "

I. Let me show you, first of all, *what the Apostle Paul did not glory in.*

There are many things that Paul might have gloried in, if he had thought as some do in this day. If ever there was one on earth who had something to boast of in himself, that man was the great apostle of the Gentiles. Now if he did not dare to glory, who shall ?

He never gloried *in his national privileges.* He was a Jew by birth, and, as he tells us himself,—"An Hebrew of the Hebrews." (Phil. iii. 5.) He might have said, like many of his brethren, "I have Abraham for my forefather I am not a dark unenlightened heathen ; I am one of the favoured people of God : I have been admitted into covenant with God by circumcision. I am a far better man than the ignorant Gentiles." But he never said so. He never gloried in anything of this kind. Never, for one moment!

He never gloried *in his own works.* None ever worked so hard for God as he did. He was "more abundant in labours" than any of the apostles. (2 Cor. xi. 23.) No man ever preached so much, travelled so much, and endured so many hardships for Christ's cause. None was ever made the means of converting so many souls, did so much good to the world, and made himself so useful to mankind. No Father of the early Church, no Reformer, no Puritan, no Missionary, no minister, no layman,—no one man could ever be named, who did so many good works as the Apostle Paul. But did he ever glory in them, as if they were in the least meritorious, and could save his soul? Never! Never for one moment!

He never gloried *in his knowledge.* He was a man of great gifts naturally, and, after he was converted, the Holy Spirit gave him greater gifts still. He was a mighty preacher, and a mighty speaker, and a mighty writer. He was as great with his pen as he was with his tongue. He could reason equally well with Jews and Gentiles. He could argue with infidels at Corinth, or Pharisees at Jerusalem, or self-righteous people in Galatia. He knew many deep things. He had been in the third heaven, and "heard unspeakable words." (2 Cor. xii. 4.) He had received the spirit of prophecy, and could foretell things yet to come. But did he ever glory in his knowledge, as if it could justify him before God? Never: never! Never for one moment!

He never gloried *in his graces.* If ever there was one who abounded in graces, that man was Paul. He was full of love. How tenderly and affectionately he used to write! He could feel for souls like a mother or a nurse feeling for her child.—He was a bold man. He cared not whom he opposed when truth was at stake. He cared not what risks he ran when souls were to be won.—He was a self-denying man,—in hunger and thirst often, in cold and nakedness, in watchings and fastings.—He was a humble man. He thought himself less than the least of all saints, and the chief of sinners.—He was a prayerful man. See how it comes out at the beginning of all his Epistles.—He was a thankful man. His thanksgivings

and his prayers walked side by side. But he never gloried
in all this,—never valued himself on it,—never rested his
soul's hopes on it. Oh, no: never for a moment!

He never gloried *in his Churchmanship.* If ever there
was a good Churchman, that man was Paul. He was
himself a chosen apostle. He was a founder of churches,
and an ordainer of ministers: Timothy and Titus, and
many elders, received their first commission from his
hands. He was the beginner of services and sacraments
in many a dark place. Many an one did he baptize;
many an one did he receive to the Lord's Table; many a
meeting for prayer, and praise, and preaching, did he
begin and carry on. He was the setter up of discipline
in many a young Church. Whatever ordinances, and rules,
and ceremonies were observed in many Churches, were first
recommended by him. But did he ever glory in his office
and Church standing? Does he ever speak as if his
Churchmanship would save him, justify him, put away his
sins, and make him acceptable before God? Oh, no!
Never: never! Never for a moment!

Now if the apostle Paul never gloried in any of these
things, who in all the world, from one end to the other,—
who has any right to glory in them in our day? If Paul
said, " God forbid that I should glory in anything whatever
except the cross," who shall dare to say, " I have something
to glory of: I am a better man than Paul "?

Who is there among the readers of this paper that trusts
in any goodness of his own? Who is there that is resting
on his own amendments,—his own morality,—his own
churchmanship,—his own works and performances of any
kind whatever? Who is there that is leaning the weight
of his soul on anything whatever of his own, in the
smallest possible degree? Learn, I say, that you are very
unlike the apostle Paul. Learn that your religion is not
apostolical religion.

Who is there among the readers of this paper that trusts

in his religious profession for salvation? Who is there that
is valuing himself on his baptism, or his attendance at the
Lord's table,—his church-going on Sundays, or his daily
services during the week,—and saying to himself, "What
lack I yet?" Learn, I say, this day, that you are very
unlike Paul. Your Christianity is *not the Christianity of
the New Testament.* Paul would not glory in anything
but "the cross." Neither ought you.

Oh, let us beware of self-righteousness! Open sin kills
its thousands of souls. Self-righteousness kills its tens of
thousands. Go and study humility with the great apostle
of the Gentiles. Go and sit with Paul at the foot of the
cross. Give up your secret pride. Cast away your vain
ideas of your own goodness. Be thankful if you have
grace, but never glory in it for a moment. Work for God
and Christ, with heart and soul and mind and strength,
but never dream for a second of placing confidence in
any work of your own.

Think, you who take comfort in some fancied ideas of
your own goodness,—think, you who wrap up yourselves
in the notion, "all must be right, if I keep to my Church,"
—think for a moment what a sandy foundation you are
building upon! Think how miserably defective your
hopes and pleas will look in the hour of death, and in the
day of judgment! Whatever men may say of their own
goodness while they are strong and healthy, they will find
but little to say of it when they are sick and dying.
Whatever merit they may see in their own works here in
this world, they will discover none in them when they stand
before the bar of Christ. The light of that great day of
assize will make a wonderful difference in the appearance
of all their doings. It will strip off the tinsel, shrivel up
the complexion, expose the rottenness of many a deed that
is now called good. Their wheat will prove nothing but
chaff: their gold will be found nothing but dross. Millions
of so-called Christian actions will turn out to have been

utterly defective and graceless. They passed current, and were valued among men : they will prove light and worthless in the balance of God. They will be found to have been like the whitened sepulchres of old,—fair and beautiful without, but full of corruption within. Alas, for the man who can look forward to the day of judgment, and lean his soul in the smallest degree on anything of his own now ! *

Once more I say, let us beware of self-righteousness in every possible shape and form. Some people get as much harm from their fancied virtues as others do from their sins. Rest not, rest not till your heart beats in tune with St. Paul's. Rest not till you can say with him, " GOD FORBID THAT I SHOULD GLORY IN ANYTHING BUT THE CROSS."

II. Let me explain, in the second place, *what we are to understand by the cross of Christ.*

The cross is an expression that is used in more than one meaning in the Bible. What did St. Paul mean when he said, "I glory in the cross of Christ," in the Epistle to the Galatians? This is the point I now wish to examine closely and make clear.

The cross sometimes means that wooden cross, on which

---

* "Howsoever men when they sit at ease, do vainly tickle their own hearts with the wanton conceit of I know not what proportionable correspondence between their merits and their rewards, which in the trance of their high speculations, they dream that God hath measured and laid up as it were in bundles for them;—we see notwithstanding by daily experience in a number even of them, that when the hour of death approacheth, when they secretly hear themselves summoned to appear and stand at the bar of that Judge, whose brightness causeth the eyes of angels themselves to dazzle, all those idle imaginations do then begin to hide their faces. To name merits then is to lay their souls upon the rack. The memory of their own deeds is loathsome unto them. They forsake all things wherein they have put any trust and confidence. No staff to lean upon, no rest, no ease, no comfort then, but only in Christ Jesus."— *Richard Hooker.* 1585.

the Lord Jesus Christ was nailed and put to death on Calvary. This is what St. Paul had in his mind's eye, when he told the Philippians that Christ "became obedient unto death, even the death of the cross." (Phil. ii. 8.) This is not the cross in which St. Paul gloried. He would have shrunk with horror from the idea of glorying in a mere piece of wood. I have no doubt he would have denounced the Roman Catholic adoration of the crucifix, as profane, blasphemous, and idolatrous.

The cross sometimes means the afflictions and trials which believers in Christ have to go through, if they follow Christ faithfully, for their religion's sake. This is the sense in which our Lord uses the word when He says, "He that taketh not his cross and followeth after Me, cannot be my disciple." (Matt. x. 38.) This also is not the sense in which Paul uses the word when he writes to the Galatians. He knew that cross well: he carried it patiently. But he is not speaking of it here.

But the cross also means, in some places, the doctrine that Christ died for sinners upon the cross,—the atonement that He made for sinners, by His suffering for them on the cross,—the complete and perfect sacrifice for sin which He offered up, when He gave His own body to be crucified. In short, this one word, "the cross," stands for Christ crucified, the only Saviour. This is the meaning in which Paul uses the expression, when he tells the Corinthians, "the preaching of the cross is to them that perish foolishness." (1 Cor. i. 18.) This is the meaning in which he wrote to the Galatians, "God forbid that I should glory, save in the cross." He simply meant, "I glory in nothing but Christ crucified, as the salvation of my soul" *

---

* "By the cross of Christ the Apostle understandeth the all-sufficient, expiatory, and satisfactory sacrifice of Christ upon the cross, with the whole work of our redemption ; in the saving knowledge of whereof he professeth he will glory and boasts."—*Cudworth on Galatians.* 1613.

Jesus Christ crucified was the joy and delight, the comfort and the peace, the hope and the confidence, the foundation and the resting-place, the ark and the refuge, the food and the medicine of Paul's soul. He did not think of what he had done himself, and suffered himself. He did not meditate on his own goodness, and his own righteousness. He loved to think of what Christ had done, and Christ had suffered,—of the death of Christ, the righteousness of Christ, the atonement of Christ, the blood of Christ, the finished work of Christ. In this he did glory. This was the sun of his soul.

This is the subject he *loved to preach about*. He was a man who went to and fro on the earth, proclaiming to sinners that the Son of God had shed His own heart's blood to save their souls. He walked up and down the world telling people that Jesus Christ had loved them, and died for their sins upon the cross. Mark how he says to the Corinthians, "I delivered unto you first of all that which I also received, how that Christ died for our sins." (1 Cor. xv. 3.) "I determined not to know anything among you save Jesus Christ, and Him crucified." (1 Cor. ii. 2.) He, a blaspheming, persecuting Pharisee, had been washed in Christ's blood. He could not hold his peace about it. He was never weary of telling the story of the cross.

This is the subject he *loved to dwell upon when he wrote* to believers. It is wonderful to observe how full his epistles generally are of the sufferings and death of

---

"Touching these words, I do not find that any expositor, either ancient or modern, Popish, or Protestant, writing on this place, doth expound the cross here mentioned of the sign of the cross, but of the profession of faith in Him that was hanged on the cross."—*Mayer's Commentary.*   1631.

"This is rather to be understood of the cross which Christ suffered for us, than of that we suffer for Him."—*Leigh's Annotations.*   1650.

Christ,—how they run over with "thoughts that breathe and words that burn," about Christ's dying love and power. His heart seems full of the subject. He enlarges on it constantly: he returns to it continually. It is the golden thread that runs through all his doctrinal teaching and practical exhortations. He seems to think that the most advanced Christian can never hear too much about the cross.[*]

This is what he *lived upon* all his life, from the time of his conversion. He tells the Galatians, "The life that I now live in the flesh I live by the faith of the Son of God, who loved me and gave Himself for me." (Galat. ii. 20.) What made him so strong to labour? What made him so willing to work? What made him so unwearied in endeavouring to save some? What made him so persevering and patient? I will tell you the secret of it all. He was always feeding by faith on Christ's body and Christ's blood. Jesus crucified was the meat and drink of his soul.

And we may rest assured that Paul was right. Depend upon it, the cross of Christ,—the death of Christ on the cross to make atonement for sinners,—is the centre truth in the whole Bible. This is the truth we begin with when we open Genesis. The seed of the woman bruising the serpent's head is nothing else but a prophecy of Christ crucified.—This is the truth that shines out, though veiled, all through the law of Moses, and the history of the Jews. The daily sacrifice, the passover lamb, the continual shedding of blood in the tabernacle and temple,—all these were emblems of Christ crucified.—This is the truth that

---

[*] "Christ crucified in the sum of the Gospel, and contains all the riches of it. Paul was so much taken with Christ, that nothing sweeter than Jesus could drop from his pen and lips. It is observed that he hath the word "Jesus" five hundred times in his Epistles."—*Charnock.* 1684.

we see honoured in the vision of heaven before we close the book of Revelation. "In the midst of the throne and of the four beasts," we are told, "and in the midst of the elders, stood a Lamb as it had been slain." (Rev. v. 6.) Even in the midst of heavenly glory we get a view of Christ crucified. Take away the cross of Christ, and the Bible is a dark book. It is like the Egyptian hieroglyphics without the key that interprets their meaning,—curious and wonderful, but of no real use.

Let every reader of this paper mark what I say. You may know a good deal about the Bible. You may know the outlines of the histories it contains, and the dates of the events described, just as a man knows the history of England. You may know the names of the men and women mentioned in it, just as a man knows Cæsar, Alexander the Great, or Napoleon. You may know the several precepts of the Bible, and admire them, just as a man admires Plato, Aristotle, or Seneca. But if you have not yet found out that Christ crucified is the foundation of the whole volume, you have read your Bible hitherto to very little profit. Your religion is a heaven without a sun, an arch without a key-stone, a compass without a needle, a clock without spring or weights, a lamp without oil. It will not comfort you. It will not deliver your soul from hell.

Mark what I say again. You may know a good deal about Christ, by a kind of head knowledge. You may know who He was, and where He was born, and what He did. You may know His miracles, His sayings, His prophecies, and His ordinances. You may know how He lived, and how He suffered, and how He died. But unless you know the power of Christ's cross by experience,—unless you know and feel within that the blood shed on that cross has washed away your own particular sins,—unless you are willing to confess that your salvation depends entirely on the work that Christ did upon the cross,—unless this be the case, Christ will profit you nothing. The mere knowing Christ's name will never save you. You must know His cross, and His blood, or else you will die in your sins.*

As long as you live, *beware of a religion in which there is not much of the cross.* You live in times when the warning is sadly needful. Beware, I say again, of a religion without the cross.

There are hundreds of places of worship, in this day, in which there is everything almost except the cross. There is carved oak, and sculptured stone; there is stained glass, and brilliant painting; there are solemn services, and a constant round of ordinances; but the real cross of Christ is not there. Jesus crucified is not proclaimed in the pulpit. The Lamb of God is not lifted up, and salvation by faith in Him is not freely proclaimed. And hence all is wrong. Beware of such places of worship. They are *not apostolical.* They would not have satisfied St. Paul.†

There are thousands of religious books published in our times, in which there is everything except the cross. They are full of directions about sacraments, and praises of the Church. They abound in exhortations about holy living, and rules for the attainment of perfection. They have plenty of fonts and crosses, both inside and outside. But the real cross of Christ is left out. The Saviour, and His work of atonement and complete salvation, are either

---

* "If our faith stop in Christ's life, and do not fasten upon His blood, it will not be justifying faith. His miracles, which prepared the world for His doctrines; His holiness, which fitted Himself for His sufferings, had been insufficient for us without the addition of the cross. —*Charnock.* 1684.

† "Paul determined to know nothing else but Jesus Christ and Him crucified. But many manage the ministry as if they had taken up a contrary determination,—even to know anything save Jesus Christ and Him crucified."—*Traill.* 1690.

not mentioned, or mentioned in an unscriptural way. And hence they are worse than useless. Beware of such books. They are *not apostolical.* They would never have satisfied St. Paul.

St. Paul gloried in nothing but the cross. Strive to be like him. Set Jesus crucified fully before the eyes of your soul. Listen not to any teaching which would interpose anything between you and Him. Do not fall into the old Galatian error: think not that any one in this day is a better guide than the apostles. Do not be ashamed of the " old paths," in which men walked who were inspired by the Holy Ghost. Let not the vague talk of modern teachers, who speak great swelling words about " catholicity," and " the church," disturb your peace, and make you loose your hands from the cross. Churches, ministers, and sacraments, are all useful in their way, but they are not Christ crucified. Do not give Christ's honour to another. " He that glorieth, let him glory in the Lord." (1 Cor. i. 1.)

III. Let me show, lastly, *why all Christians ought to glory in the cross of Christ.*

I feel that I must say something on this point, because of the ignorance that prevails about it. I suspect that many see no peculiar glory and beauty in the subject of Christ's cross. On the contrary, they think it painful, humbling, and degrading. They do not see much profit in the story of His death and sufferings. They rather turn from it as an unpleasant thing.

Now I believe that such persons are quite wrong. I cannot hold with them. I believe it is an excellent thing for us all to be continually dwelling on the cross of Christ. It is a good thing to be often reminded how Jesus was betrayed into the hands of wicked men,—how they condemned Him with most unjust judgment,—how they spit on Him, scourged Him, beat Him, and crowned Him with thorns,—how they led Him forth as a lamb to the slaughter, without His murmuring or resisting,—how they drove the nails through His hands and feet, and set Him up on Calvary between two thieves,—how they pierced His side with a spear, mocked Him in His sufferings, and let Him hang there naked and bleeding till He died. Of all these things, I say, it is good to be reminded. It is not for nothing that the crucifixion is described four times over in the New Testament. There are very few things that all four writers of the Gospel describe. Generally speaking, if Matthew, Mark, and Luke tell a thing in our Lord's history, John does not tell it. But there is one thing that all the four give us most fully, and that one thing is the story of the cross. This is a telling fact, and not to be overlooked.

People seem to me to forget that all Christ's sufferings on the cross were *fore-ordained*. They did not come on Him by chance or accident: they were all planned, counselled, and determined from all eternity. The cross was foreseen in all the provisions of the everlasting Trinity for the salvation of sinners. In the purposes of God the cross was set up from everlasting. Not one throb of pain did Jesus feel, not one precious drop of blood did Jesus shed, which had not been appointed long ago. Infinite wisdom planned that redemption should be by the cross. Infinite wisdom brought Jesus to the cross in due time. He was crucified " by the determinate counsel and foreknowledge of God." (Acts ii. 23.)

People seem to me to forget that all Christ's sufferings on the cross *were necessary for man's salvation*. He had to bear our sins, if ever they were to be borne at all. With His stripes alone could we be healed. This was the one payment of our debt that God would accept: this was the great sacrifice on which our eternal life depended. If Christ had not gone to the cross and suffered in our stead, the just for the unjust, there would not have been a spark of hope for us. There would have been a mighty gulf between ourselves and God, which no man ever could have passed. *

People seem to me to forget that all Christ's sufferings were endured *voluntarily,* and of His own free will. He was under no compulsion. Of His own choice He laid down His life: of His own choice He went to the cross in order to finish the work He came to do. He might easily have summoned legions of angels with a word, and scattered Pilate and Herod, and all their armies, like chaff before the wind. But He was a willing sufferer. His heart was set on the salvation of sinners. He was resolved to open "a fountain for all sin and uncleanness," by shedding His own blood. (Zech. xiii. 1.)

When I think of all this, I see nothing painful or disagreeable in the subject of Christ's cross. On the contrary, I see in it wisdom and power, peace and hope, joy and gladness, comfort and consolation. The more I keep the cross in my mind's eye, the more fulness I seem to discern in it. The longer I dwell on the cross in my thoughts, the more I am satisfied that there is more to be learned at the foot of the cross than anywhere else in the world.

(a) Would I know the length and breadth of *God the Father's love* towards a sinful world? Where shall I see it most displayed? Shall I look at His glorious sun, shining down daily on the unthankful and evil? Shall I look at seed-time and harvest, returning in regular yearly succession? Oh, no! I can find a stronger proof of love than anything of this sort. I look at the cross of Christ.

---

* "In Christ's humiliation stands our exaltation; in His weakness stands our strength; in His ignominy our glory; in His death our life." —*Cudworth.* 1613.

"The eye of faith regards Christ sitting on the summit of the cross as in a triumphal chariot; the devil bound to the lowest part of the same cross, and trodden under the feet of Christ."—*Bishop Davenant on Colossians.* 1627.

I see in it not the cause of the Father's love, but the effect. There I see that God so loved this wicked world, that He gave His only begotten Son,—gave Him to suffer and die,—that " whosoever believeth in Him should not perish, but have eternal life." (John iii. 16.) I know that the Father loves us, because He did not withhold from us His Son, His only Son. I might sometimes fancy that God the Father is too high and holy to care for such miserable, corrupt creatures as we are ! But I cannot, must not, dare not think it, when I look at the cross of Christ.*

(b) Would I know how exceedingly *sinful and abominable sin is* in the sight of God ? Where shall I see that most fully brought out ? Shall I turn to the history of the flood, and read how sin drowned the world ? Shall I go to the shore of the Dead Sea, and mark what sin brought on Sodom and Gomorrah ? Shall I turn to the wandering Jews, and observe how sin has scattered them over the face of the earth ? No: I can find a clearer proof still ! I look at the cross of Christ. There I see that sin is so black and damnable, that nothing but the blood of God's own Son can wash it away. There I see that sin has so separated me from my holy Maker, that all the angels in heaven could never have made peace between us. Nothing could reconcile us, short of the death of Christ. If I listened to the wretched talk of proud men, I might sometimes fancy sin was not so very sinful ! But I cannot think little of sin, when I look at the cross of Christ.†

---

* " The world we live in had fallen upon our heads, had it not been upheld by the pillar of the cross ; had not Christ stepped in and promised a satisfaction for the sin of man. By this all things consist : not a blessing we enjoy but may put us in mind of it ; they were all forfeited by sin, but merited by His blood. If we study it well we shall be sensible how God hated sin and loved a world."—*Charnock.*

† " If God hateth sin so much that He would allow neither man nor angel for the redemption thereof, but only the death of His only and well-beloved Son, who will not stand in fear thereof ?"—*Church of England Homily for Good Friday.* 1560.

(c) Would I know the *fulness and completeness of the salvation* God has provided for sinners? Where shall I see it most distinctly? Shall I go to the general declarations in the Bible about God's mercy? Shall I rest in the general truth that God is a "God of love"? Oh, no! I will look at the cross of Christ. I find no evidence like that. I find no balm for a sore conscience and a troubled heart, like the sight of Jesus dying for me on the accursed tree. There I see that a full payment has been made for all my enormous debts. The curse of that law which I have broken has come down on One who there suffered in my stead. The demands of that law are all satisfied. Payment has been made for me, even to the uttermost farthing. It will not be required twice over. Ah, I might sometimes imagine I was too bad to be forgiven! My own heart sometimes whispers that I am too wicked to be saved. But I know in my better moments this is all my foolish unbelief. I read an answer to my doubts in the blood shed on Calvary. I feel sure that there is a way to heaven for the very vilest of men, when I look at the cross.

(d) Would I find strong *reasons for being a holy man?* Whither shall I turn for them? Shall I listen to the ten commandments merely? Shall I study the examples given me in the Bible of what grace can do? Shall I meditate on the rewards of heaven, and the punishments of hell? Is there no stronger motive still? Yes: I will look at the cross of Christ! There I see the love of Christ constraining me to "live not unto myself, but unto Him." There I see that I am not my own now: I am "bought with a price." (2 Cor. v. 15; 1 Cor. vi. 20.) I am bound by the most solemn obligations to glorify Jesus with body and spirit, which are His. There I see that Jesus gave Himself for me, not only to redeem me from all iniquity, but also to purify me, and to make me one of a "peculiar people, zealous of good works." (Titus ii. 14.) He bore my sins in His own body on the tree, "that I being dead unto sin

should live unto righteousness." (1 Pet. ii. 24.) There is
nothing so sanctifying as a clear view of the cross of
Christ! It crucifies the world unto us, and us unto the
world. How can we love sin, when we remember that
because of our sins Jesus died? Surely none ought to
be so holy as the disciples of a crucified Lord.

(e) Would I *learn how to be contented and cheerful* under
all the cares and anxieties of life? What school shall I
go to? How shall I attain this state of mind most easily?
Shall I look at the sovereignty of God, the wisdom of God,
the providence of God, the love of God? It is well to do
so. But I have a better argument still. I will look at
the cross of Christ. I feel that "He who spared not His
only-begotten Son, but delivered Him up to die for me,
will surely with Him give me all things" that I really
need. (Rom. viii. 32.) He that endured such agony,
sufferings, and pain for my soul, will surely not withhold
from me anything that is really good. He that has done
the greater things for me, will doubtless do the lesser things
also. He that gave His own blood to procure me a home in
heaven, will unquestionably supply me with all that is really
profitable for me by the way. There is no school for learning
contentment that can be compared with the foot of the cross!

(f) Would I gather *arguments for hoping that I shall
never be cast away?* Where shall I go to find them?
Shall I look at my own graces and gifts? Shall I take
comfort in my own faith, and love, and penitence, and zeal,
and prayer? Shall I turn to my own heart, and say, "this
same heart will never be false and cold"? Oh, no! God
forbid! I will look at the cross of Christ. This is my
grand argument. This is my main stay. I cannot think
that He who went through such sufferings to redeem my
soul, will let that soul perish after all, when it has once
cast itself on Him. Oh, no! what Jesus paid for, Jesus
will surely keep. He paid dearly for it. He will not let
it easily be lost. He called me to Himself when I was a

dark sinner: He will never forsake me after I have
believed.   When Satan tempts us to doubt whether
Christ's people will be kept from falling, we should tell
Satan to look at the cross.*

And now, will you marvel that I said all Christians ought
to glory in the cross? Will you not rather wonder that
any can hear of the cross and remain unmoved? I declare
I know no greater proof of man's depravity, than the fact
that thousands of so-called Christians see nothing in the
cross. Well may our hearts be called stony,—well may the
eyes of our mind be called blind,—well may our whole
nature be called diseased,—well may we all be called dead,
when the cross of Christ is heard of and yet neglected.
Surely we may take up the words of the prophet, and say,
" Hear, O heavens, and be astonished O earth ; a wonderful
and a horrible thing is done,"—Christ was crucified for
sinners, and yet many Christians live as if He was never
crucified at all!

(a) The cross is *the grand peculiarity of the Christian
religion.* Other religions have laws and moral precepts,
forms and ceremonies, rewards and punishments.   But
other religions cannot tell us of a dying Saviour.   They
cannot show us the cross.   This is the crown and glory of
the Gospel.   This is that special comfort which belongs to
it alone.   Miserable indeed is that religious teaching
which calls itself Christian, and yet contains nothing of
the cross.   A man who teaches in this way, might as well
profess to explain the solar system, and yet tell his hearers
nothing about the sun.

(b) The cross is *the strength of a minister.*   I for one

---

* "The believer is so freed from eternal wrath, that if Satan and
conscience say, 'Thou art a sinner, and under the curse of the law,' he
can say, It is true, I am a sinner ; but I was hanged on a tree and died,
and was made a curse in my Head and Lawgiver Christ, and His payment and suffering is my payment and suffering."—*Rutherford's Christ
Dying.*   1647.

would not be without it for all the world. I should feel like
a soldier without arms,—like an artist without his pencil,—
like a pilot without his compass,—like a labourer without
his tools. Let others, if they will, preach the law and
morality; let others hold forth the terrors of hell, and the
joys of heaven; let others drench their congregations with
teachings about the sacraments and the church; give me
the cross of Christ! This is the only lever which has
ever turned the world upside down hitherto, and made
men forsake their sins. And if this will not, nothing will.
A man may begin preaching with a perfect knowledge of
Latin, Greek, and Hebrew; but he will do little or no
good among his hearers unless he knows something of the
cross. Never was there a minister who did much for the
conversion of souls who did not dwell much on Christ
crucified. Luther, Rutherford, Whitefield, M'Cheyne, were
all most eminently preachers of the cross. This is the
preaching that the Holy Ghost delights to bless. He
loves to honour those who honour the cross.

(c) The cross is *the secret of all missionary success.*
Nothing but this has ever moved the hearts of the heathen.
Just according as this has been lifted up missions have
prospered. This is the weapon which has won victories
over hearts of every kind, in every quarter of the globe.
Greenlanders, Africans, South-Sea Islanders, Hindoos,
Chinese, all have alike felt its power. Just as that huge
iron tube which crosses the Menai Straits, is more affected
and bent by half-an-hour's sunshine than by all the dead
weight that can be placed in it, so in like manner the
hearts of savages have melted before the cross, when every
other argument seemed to move them no more than stones.
"Brethren," said a North-American Indian after his conversion, "I have been a heathen. I know how heathens
think. Once a preacher came and began to explain to us
that there was a God; but we told him to return to the
place from whence he came. Another preacher came and

told us not to lie, nor steal, nor drink; but we did not heed him. At last another came into my hut one day and said, 'I am come to you in the name of the Lord of heaven and earth, He sends to let you know that He will make you happy, and deliver you from misery. For this end He became a man, gave His life a ransom, and shed His blood for sinners.' I could not forget his words. I told them to the other Indians, and an awakening began among us. I say, therefore, preach the sufferings and death of Christ, our Saviour, if you wish your words to gain entrance among the heathen." Never indeed did the devil triumph so thoroughly, as when he persuaded the Jesuit missionaries in China to keep back the story of the cross!

(d) The cross is *the foundation of a Church's prosperity.* No Church will ever be honoured in which Christ crucified is not continually lifted up: nothing whatever can make up for the want of the cross. Without it all things may be done decently and in order; without it there may be splendid ceremonies, beautiful music, gorgeous churches, learned ministers, crowded communion tables, huge collections for the poor. But without the cross no good will be done; dark hearts will not be enlightened, proud hearts will not be humbled, mourning hearts will not be comforted, fainting hearts will not be cheered. Sermons about the Catholic Church and an apostolic ministry,—sermons about baptism and the Lord's supper,—sermons about unity and schism,—sermons about fasts and communion,—sermons about fathers and saints, —such sermons will never make up for the absence of sermons about the cross of Christ. They may amuse some: they will feed none. A gorgeous banqueting room, and splendid gold plate on the table, will never make up to a hungry man for the want of food. Christ crucified is God's ordinance for doing good to men. Whenever a Church keeps back Christ crucified, or puts anything whatever in that foremost place which Christ crucified should always have, from that moment a Church ceases to be useful. Without Christ crucified in her pulpits, a church is little better than a cumberer of the ground, a dead carcase, a well without water, a barren fig tree, a sleeping watchman, a silent trumpet, a dumb witness, an ambassador without terms of peace, a messenger without tidings, a lighthouse without fire, a stumbling-block to weak believers, a comfort to infidels, a hot-bed for formalism, a joy to the devil, and an offence to God.

(e) The cross is *the grand centre of union* among true Christians. Our outward differences are many, without doubt. One man is an Episcopalian, another is a Presbyterian,—one is an Independent, another a Baptist,—one is a Calvinist, another an Arminian,—one is a Lutheran, another a Plymouth Brother,—one is a friend to Establishments, another a friend to the voluntary system,—one is a friend to liturgies, another a friend to extempore prayer. But, after all, what shall we hear about most of these differences, in heaven? Nothing, most probably: nothing at all. *Does a man really and sincerely glory in the cross of Christ?* That is the grand question. If he does, he is my brother: we are travelling on the same road; we are journeying towards a home where Christ is all, and everything outward in religion will be forgotten. But if he does not glory in the cross of Christ, I cannot feel comfort about him. Union on outward points only is union only for a time: union about the cross is union for eternity. Error on outward points is only a skin-deep disease: error about the cross is disease at the heart. Union about outward points is a mere man-made union: union about the cross of Christ can only be produced by the Holy Ghost.

I know not what you think of all this. I feel as if I had said nothing compared to what might be said. I feel as if the half of what I desire to tell you about the cross were left untold. But I do hope that I have given you

something to think about. I do trust that I have shown
you that I have reason for the question with which I
began this paper: "What do you think and feel about the
cross of Christ?" Listen to me now for a few moments,
while I say something to apply the whole subject to your
conscience.

(a) *Are you living in any kind of sin?* Are you
following the course of this world, and neglecting your soul?
Hear, I beseech you, what I say to you this day: "Behold
the Cross of Christ." See there how Jesus loved you!
See there what Jesus suffered to prepare for you a way of
salvation. Yes: careless men and women, for you that
blood was shed! For you those hands and feet were
pierced with nails! For you that body hung in agony on
the cross! You are those whom Jesus loved, and for
whom He died! Surely that love ought to melt you.
Surely the thought of the cross should draw you to repentance. Oh, that it might be so this very day! Oh, that
you would come at once to that Saviour who died for you,
and is willing to save! Come, and cry to Him with the
prayer of faith, and I know that He will listen. Come,
and lay hold upon the cross, and I know that He will not
cast you out. Come, and believe on Him who died on
the cross, and this very day you shall have eternal life.
How will you ever escape if you neglect so great salvation? None surely will be so deep in hell as those who
despise the cross!

(b) *Are you inquiring the way toward heaven?* Are
you seeking salvation, but doubtful whether you can find
it? Are you desiring to have an interest in Christ, but
doubting whether Christ will receive you? To you also
I say this day, "Behold the cross of Christ." Here is
encouragement if you really want it. Draw near to the
Lord Jesus with boldness, for nothing need keep you
back. His arms are open to receive you: His heart is full
of love towards you. He has made a way by which you

may approach Him with confidence. Think of the cross. Draw near, and fear not.

(c) *Are you an unlearned man?* Are you desirous to get to heaven, and perplexed and brought to a stand-still by difficulties in the Bible which you cannot explain ? To you also I say this day, " Behold the cross of Christ." Read there the Father's love and the Son's compassion. Surely they are written in great plain letters, which none can well mistake. What though you are now perplexed by the doctrine of election ? What though at present you cannot reconcile your own utter corruption and your own responsibility ? Look, I say, at the cross. Does not that cross tell you that Jesus is a mighty, loving, ready Saviour ? Does it not make one thing plain, and that is that it is all your own fault if you are not saved ? Oh, get hold of that truth, and hold it fast !

(d) *Are you a distressed believer?* Is your heart pressed down with sickness, tried with disappointments, overburdened with cares ? To you also I say this day, " Behold the cross of Christ." Think whose hand it is that chastens you ; think whose hand is measuring to you the cup of bitterness which you are now drinking. It is the hand of Him that was crucified. It is the same hand which in love to your soul was nailed to the accursed tree. Surely that thought should comfort and hearten you. Surely you should say to yourself, " A crucified Saviour will never lay upon me anything that is not for my good. There is a needs be. It must be well."

(e) *Are you a believer that longs to be more holy?* Are you one that finds his heart too ready to love earthly things ? To you also I say, " Behold the cross of Christ." Look at the cross, think of the cross, meditate on the cross, and then go and set your affections on the world if you can. I believe that holiness is nowhere learned so well as on Calvary. I believe you cannot look much at the cross without feeling your will sanctified, and your tastes made

more spiritual. As the sun gazed upon makes everything
else look dark and dim, so does the cross darken the false
splendour of this world. As honey tasted makes all other
things seem to have no taste at all, so does the cross seen
by faith take all the sweetness out of the pleasures of the
world. Keep on every day steadily looking at the cross
of Christ, and you will soon say of the world, as the poet
does,—

> Its pleasures now no longer please,
>   No more content afford ;
> Far from my heart be joys like these,
>   Now I have seen the Lord.
>
> As by the light of opening day
>   The stars are all concealed,
> So earthly pleasures fade away
>   When Jesus is revealed.

(*f*) *Are you a dying believer?* Have you gone to that
bed from which something within tells you you will never
come down alive? Are you drawing near to that solemn
hour, when soul and body must part for a season, and you
must launch into a world unknown? Oh, look steadily at
the cross of Christ by faith, and you shall be kept in
peace! Fix the eyes of your mind firmly, not on a
man-made crucifix, but on Jesus crucified, and He shall
deliver you from all your fears. Though you walk through
dark places, He will be with you. He will never leave
you,—never forsake you. Sit under the shadow of the
cross to the very last, and its fruit shall be sweet to
your taste. "Ah," said a dying missionary, "there is but
one thing needful on a death-bed, and that is to feel one's
arms around the cross!"

I lay these thoughts before your mind. What you
think now about the cross of Christ, I cannot tell. But I
can wish you nothing better than this,—that you may be
able to say with the Apostle Paul, before you die or meet
the Lord, "God forbid that I should glory, save in the
cross of our Lord Jesus Christ.

X.

THE HOLY GHOST.

"If any man have not the Spirit of Christ, he is none of His."—
Rom. viii. 9.

THE subject of this paper is one of the deepest importance to our souls. That subject is the work of God the Holy Ghost. The solemn words of the text which heads this page demand the attention of all who believe the Scriptures to be the living voice of God. "If any man have not the Spirit of Christ, he is NONE OF HIS."

It is probable that most of those into whose hands this paper will fall, have been baptized? And in what name were you baptized? It was "In the name of the Father, and of the Son, and of the Holy Ghost."

It is probable that many readers of this paper are married people. And in what name were you pronounced man and wife together? Again, it was "In the name of the Father, and of the Son, and of the Holy Ghost."

It is not unlikely that many readers of this paper are members of the Church of England. And in what do you declare your belief every Sunday, when you repeat the Creed? You say that you "Believe in God the Father, and in God the Son, and in God the Holy Ghost."

It is likely that many readers of this paper will be

buried one day with the burial service of the Church of England. And what will be the last words pronounced over your coffin, before the mourners go home, and the grave closes over your head ? They will be, "The grace of our Lord Jesus Christ, and the love of God, and the fellowship of the Holy Ghost be with you all." (2 Cor. xiii. 14.)

Now I ask every reader of this paper a plain question : Do you know what you mean by these words, so often repeated,—the Holy Ghost ?—What place has God the Holy Ghost in your religion ?—What do you know of His office, His work, His indwelling, His fellowship, and His power ?—This is the subject to which I ask your attention this day. I want you to consider seriously what you know about the work of God the Holy Ghost.

I believe that the times in which we live demand frequent and distinct testimonies upon this great subject. I believe that few truths of the Christian religion are so often obscured and spoiled by false doctrine as the truth about the Holy Ghost. I believe that there is no subject which an ignorant world is so ready to revile as "cant, fanaticism, and enthusiasm," as the subject of the work of the Holy Ghost. My heart's desire and prayer to God is, that about this subject I may write nothing but the "truth as it is in Jesus," and that I may write that truth in love.

For convenience sake I shall divide my subject into four heads. I shall examine in order :—

I. Firstly,—the *importance* attached to the work of the Holy Ghost in Scripture.

II. Secondly,—the *necessity* of the work of the Holy Ghost to man's salvation.

III. Thirdly,—the *manner* in which the Holy Ghost works in man's heart.

IV. Lastly,—the *marks and evidences* by which the presence of the Holy Ghost in a man's heart may be known.

I. The first point I propose to consider is *the importance attached to the work of the Holy Ghost in Scripture.*

I find it hard to know where to begin and where to leave off, in handling this branch of my subject. It would be easy to fill up all this paper by quoting texts about it. So often is the Holy Ghost mentioned in the New Testament, that my difficulty is not so much the discovery of evidence as the selection. Eighteen times in the eighth chapter of the Epistle to the Romans St. Paul speaks of God the Spirit. In fact the place which the Holy Ghost holds in the minds of most professing Christians bears no proportion to the place which He holds in the Word.*

I shall not spend much time in proving the divinity and personality of the Holy Ghost. They are points which are written in Scripture as with a sun-beam. I am utterly at a loss to understand how any honest-minded reader of the Bible can fail to see them. Above all, I am unable to comprehend how any unprejudiced reader of the Bible can regard the Spirit as nothing more than " an influence or principle." We find it written in the New Testament, that the Holy Ghost was " seen descending in a bodily

---

* "There is a general omission in the saints of God, in their not giving the Holy Ghost that glory that is due to His person, and for His great work of salvation in us; insomuch that we have in our hearts almost lost this Third Person. We give daily in our thoughts, prayers, affections and speeches, an honour to the Father and the Son. But who directs the aims of his praise (more than in that general way of doxology we use to close our prayers with) unto God the Holy Ghost? He is a Person in the Godhead, equal with the Father and the Son. The work He doth for us, in its kind, is as great as those of the Father or the Son. Therefore, by the equity of all law, a proportionable honour is due to Him."—*Thomas Goodwin on the Work of the Holy Ghost.* 1704.

shape." (Luke iii. 22.) He commanded disciples to do acts, and lifted them through the air by His own power. (Acts viii. 29—39.) He sent forth the first preachers to the Gentiles. (Acts xiii. 2.) He spake to the Churches. (Rev. ii. 7.) He maketh intercession. (Rom. viii. 26.) He searcheth all things, teacheth all things, and guideth into all truth. (1 Cor. ii. 10; John xiv. 26; xvi. 13.) He is another Comforter distinct from Christ. (John xiv. 16.) He has personal affections ascribed to Him. (Isaiah lxiii. 10; Ephes. iv. 30; Rom. xv. 30.) He has a mind, will, and power of His own. (Rom. viii. 27; 1 Cor. xii. 11; Rom. xv. 13.) He has baptism administered in His name together with the Father and the Son. (Matt. xxviii. 19.) And whosoever shall blaspheme Him hath never forgiveness, and is in danger of eternal damnation. (Mark iii. 29.)

I make no comment on these passages. They speak for themselves. I only use the words of Ambrose Serle in saying, that "Two and two making four, does not appear more clear and conclusive than that the Holy Spirit is a living divine Agent, working with consciousness, will, and power. If people will not be persuaded by these testimonies, neither would they be persuaded though one rose from the dead." *

I repeat that I will not spend time in dwelling on proofs of the Holy Spirit's divinity and personality. I will rather confine all I have to say on this branch of my subject to two general remarks.

For one thing, I ask my readers to remark carefully that *in every step of the grand work of man's redemption the Bible assigns a prominent place to God the Holy Ghost.*

What do you think of the incarnation of Christ? You know we cannot over-rate its importance. Well! it is written that when our Lord was conceived of the Virgin

---

* Serle's Horæ Solitariæ.

Mary, "the Holy Ghost came upon her, and the power of the Highest overshadowed her." (Luke i. 35.)

What do you think of the earthly ministry of our Lord Jesus Christ? You know that none ever did what He did, lived as He lived, and spake as He spake. Well! it is written that the Spirit "descended from heaven like a dove and abode upon Him,"—that "God anointed Him with the Holy Ghost,"—that "the Father gave not the Spirit by measure unto Him," and that He was "full of the Holy Ghost." (John i. 32; Acts x. 38; John iii. 34; Luke iv. 1.)

What do you think of the vicarious sacrifice of Christ on the cross? Its value is simply unspeakable. No wonder St. Paul says, "God forbid that I should glory, save in the cross." (Gal. vi. 14.) Well! it is written, "Through the eternal Spirit He offered Himself without spot to God." (Heb. ix. 14.)

What do you think of the resurrection of Christ? It was the seal and topstone of all His work. He was "raised again for our justification." (Rom. iv. 25.) Well! it is written that "He was put to death in the flesh, but quickened by the Spirit." (1 Pet. iii. 18.)

What do you think of the departure of Christ from this world, when He ascended up into heaven? It was a tremendous trial to His disciples. They were left like a little orphan family, in the midst of cruel enemies. Well! what was the grand promise wherewith our Saviour cheered them the night before He died? "I will pray the Father and He shall give you another Comforter, even the Spirit of truth." (John xiv. 16, 17.)

What do you think of the mission of the apostles to preach the Gospel? We Gentiles owe to it all our religious light and knowledge. Well! they were obliged to tarry at Jerusalem and "wait for the promise of the Father." They were unfit to go forth till they were "filled with the Holy Ghost," upon the day of Pentecost. (Acts i. 4; ii. 4.)

What do you think of the Scripture, which is written for our learning? You know that our earth without a sun would be but a faint emblem of a world without a Bible. Well! we are informed that in writing that Scripture, "Holy men spake as they were moved by the Holy Ghost." (2 Pet. i. 21.) "The things which we speak," says St. Paul, we speak in the words which the Holy Ghost teacheth." (1 Cor. ii. 13.)

What do you think of the whole dispensation under which we Christians live? You know its privileges as far exceed those of the Jews as twilight is exceeded by noon-day. Well we are especially told that it is the "ministra-tion of the Spirit." (2 Cor. iii. 8.)*

I place these texts before my readers as matter for private meditation. I pass on to the other general remark I promised to make.

I ask you then to remark carefully, that *whatever individual Christians have, are, and enjoy, in contra-distinction to the worldly and unconverted, they owe to the agency of God the Holy Ghost.* By Him they are first called, quickened, and made alive. Of Him they are born again, and made new creatures. By Him they are convinced of sin, guided into all truth and led to Christ. By Him they are sealed unto the day of redemption. He dwells in them as His living temples. He witnesses with their spirits,—gives them the spirit of adoption, makes them to cry Abba Father, and makes intercession for

---

* I would not for a moment have any one suppose that I think Old Testament believers had not the Holy Ghost. On the contrary I hold that there has never been a whit of spiritual life among men, excepting from the Holy Ghost,—and that the Holy Ghost made Abel and Noah what they were no less really than He made St. Paul. All I mean to assert is, that the Holy Ghost is so much more fully revealed and largely poured out under the New Testament than under the Old, that the New Testament dispensation is emphatically and peculiarly called the "ministration of the Spirit." The difference between the two dispensa-tions is only one of degree.

them. By Him they are sanctified. By Him the love of God is shed abroad in their hearts. Through His power they abound in hope. Through Him they wait for the hope of righteousness by faith. Through Him they mortify the deeds of their bodies. After Him they walk. In Him they live. In a word, all that believers have from grace to glory,—all that they are from the first moment they believe to the day they depart to be with Christ,—all, all, all may be traced to the work of God the Holy Ghost. (John vi. 63; iii. 8; xvi. 9, 10; Eph. iv. 30; 1 Cor. vi. 19; Rom. viii. 15, 16, 26; 2 Thess. ii. 13; Rom. v. 5; xv. 13; Gal. v. 5, 25; Rom. viii. 1, 13.)

I may not tarry longer on this branch of my subject. I trust I have said enough to prove that I did not use words without meaning, when I spoke of the importance attached in Scripture to the work of the Spirit of God.

Before I pass on let me entreat all who read this paper to make sure that they hold sound doctrine concerning the work of the Holy Ghost. * Give Him the honour due unto His name. Give Him in your religion the place and the dignity which Scripture assigns to Him. Settle it in your minds that the work of all three Persons in the blessed Trinity, is absolutely and equally needful to the salvation of every saved soul. The election of God the Father, and the atoning blood of God the Son, are the foundation stones of our faith. But from them must never be separated the applicatory work of God the Holy Ghost. The Father chooses. The Son mediates, absolves, justifies, and intercedes. The Holy Ghost applies the whole work to man's soul. Always together in Scripture, never separated in Scripture, let the offices of the three

---

* "To give the Holy Spirit divine worship, if he be not God, is idolatry; and to withhold it, if He is God, is a heinous sin. To be well informed on this point, is of the last importance."—*Hurrion on the Holy Spirit.* 1731.

Persons in the Trinity never be wrenched asunder and disjoined in your Christianity. What God hath so beautifully joined together let no man dare to put asunder.

Accept a brotherly caution against all kinds of Christian teaching, falsely so called, which, either directly or indirectly, dishonour the work of the Holy Ghost. Beware of *the error, on one side*, which practically substitutes church-membership and participation of the sacraments for the Spirit. Let no man make you believe that to be baptized and go to the Lord's Table, is any sure proof that you have the Spirit of Christ.—Beware of *the error, on the other side*, which proudly substitutes the inward light, so called, and the scraps of conscience which remain in every man after the fall, for the saving grace of the Holy Spirit. * Let no man make you believe that as a matter of course, since Christ died, all men and women have within them the Spirit of Christ.—I touch on these points gently. I should be sorry to write one needless word of controversy. But I do say to every one who prizes real Christianity in these days, " Be very jealous about the real work and office of the third Person of the Trinity." Try the spirits whether they be of God. Prove diligently the

---

* "It is not the natural light of conscience, nor that improved by the Word, which converts any man to God, although this is the best spring of most men's practical part of religion. But it is faith, bringing in a new light into conscience, and so conscience lighting its taper at that sun which humbleth for sin in another manner, and drives men to Christ, sanctifieth, changeth, and writes the law in the heart. And this you will find to be the state of difference between Augustine, and the Pelagians, and semi-Pelagians, which the whole stream and current of his writings against them hold forth. They would have had the light of natural conscience, and the seeds of natural virtues in men (as in philosophers), being improved and manured by the revelation of the Word, to be that grace which the Scripture speaks of. He proclaims all their virtues, and their use of natural light to be sins, because deficient of holiness, and requires for us not only the revelation of the objects of faith, which else natural light could not find out, but a new light to see them withal."—*Thomas Goodwin on the Work of the Holy Ghost.* 1704.

many divers and strange doctrines which now infect the
Church. And let the subject brought before you this day
be one of your principal tests. Try every new doctrine
of these latter times by two simple questions. Ask first,
"Where is the Lamb?" And ask secondly, "Where is
the Holy Ghost?"

II. The second point I propose to consider, is the
necessity of the work of the Holy Ghost to man's salvation.

I invite special attention to this part of the subject.
Let it be a settled thing in our minds that the matter we
are considering in this paper is no mere speculative
question in religion, about which it signifies little what we
believe. On the contrary, it lies at the very foundation
of all saving Christianity. Wrong about the Holy Ghost
and His offices, we are wrong to all eternity.

The necessity of the work of the Holy Ghost arises from
the total corruption of human nature. We are all by
nature "dead in sins." (Eph. ii. 1.) However shrewd, and
clever, and wise in the things of this world, we are all dead
towards God. The eyes of our understanding are blinded.
We see nothing aright. Our wills, affections, and inclinations
are alienated from Him who made us. "The carnal mind
is enmity against God." (Rom. viii. 7.) We have naturally
neither faith, nor fear, nor love, nor holiness. In short,
left to ourselves, we should never be saved.

Without the Holy Ghost *no man ever turns to God,
repents, believes, and obeys.*—Intellectual training and
secular education alone make no true Christians. Acquaintance with fine arts and science leads no one to heaven.
Pictures and statues never brought one soul to God. The
" tender strokes of art " never prepared any man or woman
for the judgment day.* They bind up no broken heart;

---

* "To wake the soul by tender strokes of art,"—was the motto which
in large letters caught the eye on entering the Manchester Exhibition of
Fine Arts, at the extreme end of the building.

they heal no wounded conscience. The Greeks had their Zeuxis and Parrhasius, their Phidias and Praxiteles, masters as great in their day as any in modern times; yet the Greeks knew nothing of the way of peace with God. They were sunk in gross idolatry, and bowed down to the works of their own hands.—The most zealous efforts of ministers alone cannot make men Christians. The ablest scriptural reasoning has no effect on the mind; the most fervent pulpit eloquence will not move the heart; the naked truth alone will not lead the will. We who are ministers know this well by painful experience. We can show men the fountain of living waters, but we cannot make them drink. We see many a one sitting under our pulpits year after year, and hearing hundreds of sermons, full of Gospel truth, without the slightest result. We mark him year after year, unaffected and unmoved by every Scriptural argument,—cold as the stones on which he treads as he enters our church,—unmoved as the marble statue which adorns the tomb against the wall,—dead as the old dry oak of which his pew is made,—feelingless as the painted glass in the windows, through which the sun shines on his head. We look at him with wonder and sorrow, and remember Xavier's words as he looked at China: "Oh, rock, rock! when wilt thou open?" And we learn by such cases as these, that nothing will make a Christian but the introduction into the heart of a new nature, a new principle, and a Divine seed from above.

What is it then that man needs?—We need to be "born again:" and this new birth we must receive of the Holy Ghost. The Spirit of life must quicken us. The Spirit must renew us. The Spirit must take away from us the heart of stone. The Spirit must put in us the heart of flesh. A new act of creation must take place. A new being must be called into existence. Without all this we cannot be saved. Here lies the main part of our need of the Holy Ghost. "Except a man be born again he cannot see the kingdom of God." (John iii. 3.) No salvation without a new birth ! *

Let us dismiss from our minds for ever the common idea that natural theology, moral suasion, logical arguments, or even an exhibition of Gospel truth, are sufficient of themselves to turn a sinner from his sins, if once brought to bear upon him. It is a strong delusion. They will not do so. The heart of man is far harder than we fancy : the old Adam is much more strong than we suppose. The ships which run aground at half-ebb, will never stir till the tide flows : the heart of man will never look to Christ, repent, and believe, till the Holy Ghost comes down upon it. Till that takes place, our inner nature is like the earth before the present order of creation began,—" without form and void, and darkness covering the face of the deep." (Gen. i. 2.) The same power which said at the beginning, " Let there be light: and there was light," must work a creating work in us, or we shall never rise to newness of life.

But I have something more to say yet on this branch of my subject. The necessity of the work of the Spirit to man's salvation is a wide field, and I have yet another re-mark to make upon it.

I say then, that without the work of the Holy Ghost *no man could ever be fit to dwell with God in another world.* A fitness of some kind we must have. The mere pardon of our sins would be a worthless gift, unless accom-

---

* "This is that which gives unto the ministry of the Gospel both its glory and its efficacy. Take away the Spirit from the Gospel, and you render it a dead letter, and leave the New Testament of no more use unto Christians than the Old Testament is unto the Jews."—*Owen on the Holy Spirit.*

"In the power of the Holy Ghost resteth all ability to know God and to please Him. It is He that purifieth the mind by His secret working. He enlighteneth the mind to conceive worthy thoughts of Almighty, God."—*Homily for Rogation Week.*

panied by the gift of a new nature, a nature in harmony
and in tune with that of God Himself. We need a meetness for heaven, as well as a title for heaven, and this
meetness we must receive from the Holy Ghost. We must
be made " partakers of the divine nature," by the indwelling
of the Holy Ghost. (2 Pet. i. 4.) The Spirit must sanctify
our carnal natures, and make them love spiritual things.
The Spirit must wean our affections from things below,
and teach us to set them on things above. The Spirit must
bend our stubborn wills, and teach them to be submissive
to the will of God. The Spirit must write again the law
of God on our inward man, and put His fear within us.
The Spirit must transform us by the daily renewing of
our minds, and implant in us the image of Him whose
servants we profess to be. Here lies the other great part
of our need of the Holy Ghost's work. We need sanctification
no less than justification.' " Without holiness no man shall
see the Lord." (Heb. xii. 14.)

Once more I beseech my readers to dismiss from their
minds the common idea, that men and women need nothing
but pardon and absolution, in order to be prepared to meet
God. It is a strong delusion, and one against which I
desire with all my heart to place you on your guard. It is
not enough, as many a poor ignorant Christian supposes
on his death-bed, if God " pardons our sins and takes
us to rest." I say again most emphatically, it is *not
enough.* The love of sin must be taken from us, as
well as the guilt of sin removed; the desire of pleasing
God must be implanted in us, as well as the fear of
God's judgment taken away; a love to holiness must
be engrafted, as well as a dread of punishment removed.
Heaven itself would be no heaven to us if we entered
it without a new heart. An eternal Sabbath and the
society of saints and angels could give us no happiness
in heaven, unless the love of Sabbaths and of holy company had been first shed abroad in our hearts upon earth.

Whether men will hear or forbear, the man who enters heaven must have the sanctification of the Spirit, as well as the sprinkling of the blood of Jesus Christ. To use the words of Owen, "When God designed the great and glorious work of recovering fallen man and saving sinners, He appointed in His infinite wisdom two great means. The one was the giving of His Son for them; and the other was the giving of his Spirit unto them. And hereby was way made for the manifestation of the glory of the whole blessed Trinity." *

I trust I have said enough to show the absolute necessity of the work of the Holy Ghost to the salvation of man's soul. Man's utter inability to turn to God without the Spirit,—man's utter unmeetness for the joys of heaven, without the Spirit,—are two great foundation stones in revealed religion, which ought to be always deeply rooted in a Christian's mind. Rightly understood, they will lead to one conclusion,—"Without the Spirit, no salvation!"

Would you like to know the reason why we who preach the Gospel, preach so often about *conversion?* We do it because of the necessities of men's souls. We do it because we see plainly from the Word of God that nothing short of a thorough change of heart will ever meet the exigencies of your case. Your case is naturally desperate. Your danger is great. You need not only the atonement of Jesus Christ, but the quickening, sanctifying work of the Holy Ghost, to make you a true Christian, and deliver you from hell. Fain would I lead to heaven all who read this volume! My heart's desire and prayer to God is that you may be saved. But I know that none enter

---

* "God the Father had but two grand gifts to bestow; and when once they were given, He had left then nothing that was great (comparatively) to give, for they contained all good in them. These two gifts were His Son, who was His promise in the Old Testament, and the Spirit, the promise of the New."—*Thomas Goodwin on the Work of the Holy Ghost.* 1704.

heaven without a heart to enjoy heaven, and this heart
we must receive from God's Spirit.

Shall I tell you plainly the reason why some receive
these truths so coldly, and are so little affected by them?
You hear us listless and unconcerned. You think us
extreme and extravagant in our statements. And why
is this? It is just because you do not see or know the
disease of your own soul. You are not aware of your
own sinfulness and weakness. Low and inadequate views
of your spiritual disease, are sure to be accompanied by
low and inadequate views of the remedy provided in the
Gospel. What shall I say to you? I can only say, "The
Lord awaken you! The Lord have mercy on your soul!"
The day may come when the scales will fall from your
eyes, when old things will pass away, and all things
become new. And in that day I foretell and forewarn
you confidently that the first truth you will grasp, next
to the work of Christ, will be the absolute necessity of
the work of the Holy Ghost.

III. The third thing I propose to consider, is *the
manner in which the Holy Ghost works on the hearts of
those who are saved.*

I approach this branch of my subject with much
diffidence. I am very sensible that it is surrounded
with difficulties, and involves many of the deepest things
of God. But it is folly for mortal man to turn away from
any truth in Christianity, merely because of difficulties.
Better a thousand times receive with meekness what we
cannot fully explain, and believe that what we know not
now, we shall know hereafter. "Enough for us," says an
old divine, "if we sit in God's court, without pretending to
be of God's counsel."

In speaking of the manner of the Holy Ghost's working, I shall simply state certain great leading facts. They
are facts attested alike by Scripture and experience. They

are facts patent to the eyes of every candid and well-instructed observer. They are facts which I believe it is impossible to gainsay.

(*a*) I say then that the Holy Ghost works on the heart of a man in a *mysterious manner*. Our Lord Jesus Christ Himself tell us that in well-known words;—"The wind bloweth where it listeth, and thou hearest the sound thereof, but canst not tell whence it cometh and whither it goeth; so is every one that is born of the Spirit." (John iii. 8.) We cannot explain how and in what way the Almighty Spirit comes into man, and operates upon him; but neither also can we explain a thousand things which are continually taking place in the natural world. We cannot explain how our wills work daily on our members, and make them walk, or move, or rest, at our discretion; yet no one ever thinks of disputing the fact. So ought it to be with the work of the Spirit. We ought to believe the fact, though we cannot explain the manner.

(*b*) I say furthermore, that the Holy Ghost works on the heart of a man *in a sovereign manner*. He comes to one and does not come to another. He often converts one in a family, while others are left alone. There were two thieves crucified with our Lord Jesus Christ on Calvary. They saw the same Saviour dying, and heard the same words come from His lips. Yet only one repented and went to Paradise, while the other died in his sins.—There were many Pharisees besides Saul, who had a hand in Stephen's murder; but Saul alone became an apostle.—There were many slave captains in John Newton's time; yet none but he became a preacher of the Gospel.—We cannot account for this. But neither can we account for China being a heathen country, and England a Christian land: we only know that so it is.

(*c*) I say furthermore, that the Holy Ghost always works on the heart of a man in *such a manner as to be felt*. I do not for a moment say that the feelings which He produces are always understood by the person in whom they are produced. On the contrary, they are often a cause of anxiety, and conflict, and inward strife. All I maintain is that we have no warrant of Scripture for supposing that there is an indwelling of the Spirit which is not felt at all. Where He is there will always be corresponding feelings.

(*d*) I say furthermore, that the Holy Ghost always works on the heart of a man in *such a manner as to be seen in the man's life*. I do not say that as soon as He comes into a man, that man becomes immediately an established Christian, a Christian in whose life and ways nothing but spirituality can be observed. But this I say,—that the Almighty Spirit is never present in a person's soul without producing some perceptible results in that person's conduct. He never sleeps: He is never idle. We have no warrant of Scripture for talking of " dormant grace." " Whosoever is born of God doth not commit sin ; for his seed remaineth in him." (1 John iii. 9.) Where the Holy Ghost is, there will be something seen.

(*e*) I say furthermore, that the Holy Ghost always works on the heart of a man in *an irresistible manner*. I do not deny for a moment that there are sometimes spiritual strivings and workings of conscience in the minds of uncon- verted men, which finally come to nothing. But I say confidently, that when the Spirit really begins a work of conversion, He always carries that work to perfection. He effects miraculous changes. He turns the character upside down. He causes old things to pass away, and all things to become new. In a word, the Holy Ghost is Almighty. With Him nothing is impossible.

(*f*) I say, finally, under this head, that the Holy Ghost generally works on the heart of man *through the use of means*. The Word of God, preached or read, is generally employed by Him as an instrument in the conversion of a soul. He applies that Word to the conscience : He brings that Word home to the mind. This is His general course of procedure. There are instances, undoubtedly, in which people are converted " without the Word." (1 Pet. iii. 1.) But, as a general rule, God's truth is the sword of the Spirit. By it He teaches, and teaches nothing else but that which is written in the Word.

I commend these six points to the attention of all my readers. A right understanding of them supplies the best antidote to the many false and specious doctrines by which Satan labours to darken the blessed work of the Spirit.

(a) Is there a haughty, highminded person reading this paper, who in his pride of intellect rejects the work of the Holy Ghost, because of its mysteriousness and sovereignty ? I tell you boldly that you must take up other ground than this before you dispute and deny our doctrine. Look to the heaven above you, and the earth beneath you, and deny, if you can, that there are *mysteries* there.—Look to the map of the world you live in, and the marvellous difference between the privileges of one nation and another, and deny if you can, that there is *sovereignty* there.—Go and learn to be consistent. Submit that proud mind of yours to plain undeniable facts. Be clothed with the humility that becomes poor mortal man. Cast off that affectation of reasoning, under which you now try to smother your conscience. Dare to confess that the work of the Spirit may be mysterious and sovereign, and yet for all that is true.

(b) Is there a Romanist, or semi-Romanist reading this paper, who tries to persuade himself that all baptized people, and members of the Church, as a matter of course, have the Spirit ? I tell you plainly that you are deceiving yourself, if you dream that the Spirit is in a man, when His presence cannot be seen. Go and learn this day that the presence of the Holy Ghost is to be tested, not by the name in the register, or the place in the family pew, but by the visible fruits in a man's life.

(c) Is there a worldly man reading this paper, who regards all claims to the indwelling of the Spirit as so much enthusiasm and fanaticism? I warn you also to take heed what you are about. No doubt there is plenty of hypocrisy and false profession in the Churches; no doubt there are thousands whose religious feelings are mere delusion. But bad money is no proof that there is no such thing as good coin: the abuse of a thing does not destroy the use of it. The Bible tells us plainly that there are certain hopes, and joys, and sorrows, and inward feelings, inseparable from the work of the Spirit of God. Go and learn this day that you have not received the Spirit, if His presence within you has not been felt.

(d) Is there an excuse-making indolent person reading this paper, who comforts himself with the thought that decided Christianity is an impossible thing, and that in a world like this he cannot serve Christ? Your excuses will not avail you. The power of the Holy Ghost is offered to you without money and without price. Go and learn this day that there is strength to be had for the asking. Through the Spirit, whom the Lord Jesus offers to give to you, all difficulties may be overcome.

Is there a fanatic reading this paper, who fancies that it matters nothing whether a man stays at home or goes to church, and that if a man is to be saved, he will be saved in spite of himself? I tell you also this day, that you have much to learn. Go and learn that the Holy Ghost ordinarily works through the use of means of grace, and that it is by "hearing" that faith generally comes into the soul." (Rom. x. 17.)

I leave this branch of my subject here, and pass on. I leave it with a sorrowful conviction that nothing in religion so shows the blindness of natural man as his inability to receive the teaching of Scripture on the manner of the Holy Ghost's operations. To quote the saying of our Divine Master,—" The world cannot receive Him." (John

xiv. 17.) To use the words of Ambrose Serle : " This operation of the Spirit hath been, and ever will be, an incomprehensible business to those who have not known it in themselves. Like Nicodemus, and other masters in Israel, they will reason and re-reason, till they puzzle and perplex themselves, by darkening counsel without knowledge ; and when they cannot make out the matter, will give the strongest proof of all that they know nothing of it, by fretting and raving, and calling hard names, and saying, in short, that there is no such thing."

IV. I propose, in the last place, to consider *the marks and evidences by which the presence of the Holy Ghost in a man's heart may be known.*

Last as this point comes in order, it is anything but last in importance. In fact, it is that view of the Holy Ghost which demands the closest attention of every professing Christian. We have seen something of the *place* assigned to the Holy Ghost in the Bible. We have seen something of the absolute *necessity* of the Holy Ghost to a man's salvation. We have seen something of the *manner* of the Holy Ghost's operations. And now comes the mighty question, which ought to interest every reader : " How are we to know whether we are partakers of the Holy Ghost ? By what marks may we find out whether we have the Spirit of Christ ? "

I will begin by taking it for granted that the question I have just asked may be answered. Where is the use of our Bibles, if we cannot find out whether we are in the way to heaven ? Let it be a settled principle in our Christianity, that a man may know whether or not he has the Holy Ghost. Let us dismiss from our minds once and for ever the many unscriptural evidences of the Spirit's presence with which thousands content themselves. Reception of the sacraments and membership of the visible Church are no proofs whatever that we " have the Spirit of Christ." In short, I call it a short cut to the grossest antinomianism to talk of a man having the Holy Ghost so long as he serves sin and the world.

The presence of the Holy Ghost in a man's heart can only be known by the fruits and effects He produces. Mysterious and invisible to mortal eye as His operations are, they always lead to certain visible and tangible results. Just as you know the compass-needle to be magnetized by its turning to the north,—just as you know there is life in a tree by its sap, buds, leaves and fruits,—just as you know there is a steersman on board a ship by its keeping a steady regular course,—just so you may know the Spirit to be in a man's heart by the influence He exercises over his thoughts, affections, opinions, habits, and life. I lay this down broadly and unhesitatingly. I find no safe ground to occupy excepting this. I see no safeguard against the wildest enthusiasm, excepting in this position. And I see it clearly marked out in our Lord Jesus Christ's words: "Every tree is known by his own fruit." (Luke vi. 44.)

But what are the specific fruits by which the presence of the Spirit in the heart may be known? I find no difficulty in answering that question. The Holy Ghost always works after a certain definite pattern. Just as the bee always forms the cells of its comb in one regular hexagonal shape, so does the Spirit of God work on the heart of man with one uniform result. His work is the work of a master. The world may see no beauty in it: it is foolishness to the natural man. But "he that is spiritual discerneth all things." (1 Cor. ii. 15.) A well-instructed Christian knows well the fruits of the Spirit of God. Let me briefly set them before you in order. They are all clear and unmistakable, "plain to him that understandeth, and right to them that find knowledge." (Prov. viii. 9.)

(1) Where the Holy Ghost is, there will always be *deep*

conviction of sin, and true repentance for it. It is His special office to convince of sin. (John xvi. 8.) He shows the exceeding holiness of God. He teaches the exceeding corruption and infirmity of our nature. He strips us of our blind self-righteousness. He opens our eyes to our awful guilt, folly and danger. He fills the heart with sorrow, contrition, and abhorrence for sin, as the abominable thing which God hateth. He that knows nothing of all this, and saunters carelessly through life, thoughtless about sin, and indifferent and unconcerned about his soul, is a dead man before God. He has not the Spirit of Christ.

(2) Where the Holy Ghost is, there will always be *lively faith in Jesus Christ,* as the only Saviour. It is His special office to testify of Christ, to take of the things of Christ and show them to man. (John xvi. 15.) He leads the soul which feels its sin, to Jesus and the atonement made by His blood. He shows the soul that Christ has suffered for sin, the just for the unjust, to bring us to God. He points out to the sin-sick soul that we have only to receive Christ, believe in Christ, commit ourselves to Christ, and pardon, peace, and life eternal, are at once our own. He makes us see a beautiful fitness in Christ's finished work of redemption to meet our spiritual necessities. He makes us willing to disclaim all merit of our own and to venture all on Jesus, looking to nothing, resting on nothing, trusting in nothing but Christ,—Christ,—Christ,—" delivered for our offences, and raised again for our justification." (Rom. iv. 25.) He that knows nothing of all this, and builds on any other foundation, is dead before God. He has not the Spirit of Christ.

(3) Where the Holy Ghost is, there will always be *holiness of life and conversation.* He is the Spirit of holiness. (Rom. i. 4.) He is the sanctifying Spirit. He takes away the hard, carnal, worldly heart of man, and puts in its place a tender, conscientious, spiritual heart, delighting in the law of God. He makes a man turn his

face towards God, and desire above all things to please Him, and turn his back on the fashion of this world, and no longer make that fashion his god. He sows in a man's heart the blessed seeds of "love, joy, meekness, long-suffering, gentleness, goodness, faith, temperance," and causes these seeds to spring up and bear pleasant fruit. (Gal. v. 22.) He that lacketh these things, and knows nothing of daily practical godliness, is dead before God. He has not the Spirit of Christ.

(4) Where the Holy Ghost is, there will always be *the habit of earnest private prayer*. He is the Spirit of grace and supplication. (Zech. xii. 10.) He works in the heart as the Spirit of adoption, whereby we cry Abba, Father. He makes a man feel that he must cry to God, and speak to God,—feebly, falteringly, weakly, it may be,—but cry he must about his soul. He makes it as natural to a man to pray as it is to an infant to breathe; with this one difference,—that the infant breathes without an effort, and the new-born soul prays with much conflict and strife. He that knows nothing of real, living, fervent, private prayer, and is content with some old form, or with no prayer at all, is dead before God. He has not the Spirit of Christ.

(5) Finally, where the Holy Ghost is, there will always be *love and reverence for God's Word*. He makes the new-born soul desire the sincere milk of the Word, just as the infant desires its natural food. He makes it "delight in the law of the Lord." (1 Pet. ii. 2; Psa. i. 2.) He shows man a fulness, and depth, and wisdom, and sufficiency, in the Holy Scripture, which is utterly hid from a natural man's eyes. He draws him to the Word with an irresistible force, as the light and lantern, and manna, and sword, which are essential to a safe journey through this world. If the man cannot read He makes him love to hear: if he cannot hear He makes him love to meditate. But to the Word the Spirit always leads him. He that sees no

special beauty in God's Bible, and takes no pleasure in reading, hearing, and understanding it, is dead before God. He has not the Spirit of Christ.

I place these five grand marks of the Spirit's presence before my readers, and confidently claim attention to them. I believe they will bear inspection. I am not afraid of their being searched, criticized, and cross-examined· Repentance toward God,—faith toward our Lord Jesus Christ,—holiness of heart and life,—habits of real private prayer,—love and reverence toward God's Word,—these are the real proofs of the indwelling of the Holy Ghost in a man's soul. Where He is, these marks will be seen. Where He is not, these marks will be lacking.

I grant freely that the leadings of the Spirit, in some minute details, are not always uniform. The paths over which He conducts souls, are not always precisely one and the same. The experience that true Christians pass through in their beginnings is often somewhat various. This only I maintain,—that the main road into which the Spirit leads people, and the *final results* which He at length produces, are always alike. In all true Christians, the five great marks I have already mentioned will always be found.

I grant freely that the degree and depth of the work of the Spirit in the heart may vary exceedingly. There is weak faith and strong faith,—weak love and strong love,— a bright hope and a dim hope,—a feeble obedience to Christ's will, and a close following of the Lord. This only I maintain,—that the *main outlines* of religious character in all who have the Spirit, perfectly correspond. Life is life, whether strong or feeble. The infant in arms, though weak and dependent, is as real and true a representative of the great family of Adam as the strongest man alive.

Wherever you see these five great marks, you see a true Christian. Let that never be forgotten. I leave it to others to excommunicate and unchurch all who do not belong to their own pale, and do not worship after their own particular fashion. I have no sympathy with such narrowmindedness. Show me a man who repents, and believes in Christ crucified,—who lives a holy life, and delights in his Bible and prayer,—and I desire to regard him as a brother. I see in him a member of the Holy Catholic Church, out of which there is no salvation. I behold in him an heir of that crown of glory which is incorruptible and fadeth not away. If he has the Holy Ghost, he has Christ. If he has Christ, he has God. If he has God the Father, God the Son, and God the Spirit, all things are his. Who am I that I should turn my back on him, because we cannot see all things eye to eye?

Wherever these five great marks of the Spirit are wanting, we have just cause to be afraid about a man's soul. Visible Churches **may** endorse him, sacraments may be administered to him, forms of prayer may be read over him, ministers may charitably speak of him as " a brother," —but all this does not alter the real state of things. The man is in the broad way that leadeth to destruction. Without the Spirit he is without Christ. Without Christ he is without God. Without God the Father, God the Son, and God the Spirit, he is in imminent danger. The Lord have mercy upon his soul!

I hasten on now towards a conclusion. I desire to wind up all I have been saying by a few words of direct personal application.

(1) In the first place, let me *ask a question* of all who read this paper. It is a short and simple one, and grows naturally out of the subject. " Have you, or have you not, the Spirit of Christ?"

I am not afraid to ask this question. I will not be stopped by the commonplace remark that it is absurd, enthusiastic, unreasonable to ask such questions in the present day. I take my stand on a plain declaration or

Scripture. I find an inspired Apostle saying, "If any man have not the Spirit of Christ he is none of His." I want to know what can be more reasonable than to press on your conscience the inquiry, "Have you the Spirit of Christ?"

I will not be stopped by the foolish observation, that no man can tell in this world whether or not he has the Spirit.. No man can tell! Then what was the Bible given to us for? Where is the use of the Scriptures if we cannot discover whether we are going to heaven or hell? The thing I ask can be known. The evidences of the Spirit's presence in the soul are simple, plain, and intelligible. No honest inquirer needs miss the way in this matter. You may find out whether you have the Holy Ghost.

I entreat you not to evade the question I have now asked. I beseech you to allow it to work inwardly in your heart. I charge you, as ever you would be saved, to give it an honest answer. Baptism, Church-membership, respectability, morality, outward correctness, are all excellent things. But do not be content with them. Go deeper: look further. "Have you received the Holy Ghost? Have you the Spirit of Christ?"*

(2) Let me, in the next place, offer a *solemn warning* to all who feel in their own consciences that they have not the Spirit of Christ. That warning is short and simple. If you have not the Spirit, you are not yet Christ's people: you are "none of His."

Think for a moment how much is involved in those few words, "none of His." You are not washed in Christ's blood! You are not clothed in His righteousness! You are not justified! You are not interceded for! Your

---

* "It is a good sign of grace when a man is willing to search and examine himself, whether he be gracious or not. There is a certain instinct in a child of God, whereby he naturally desires to have the title of his legitimation tried; whereas a hypocrite dreads nothing more than to have his rottenness searched into."—*Bishop Hopkins.*

sins are yet upon you! The devil claims you for his own! The pit opens her mouth for you! The torments of hell wait for you!

I have no desire to create needless fear. I only want sensible people to look calmly at things as they are. I only want one plain text of Scripture to be duly weighed. It is written, "If any man have not the Spirit of Christ, he is none of His." And I say in the sight of such a text, if you die without the Spirit, you had better never have been born.

(3) Let me, in the next place, give *an earnest invitation* to all who feel that they have not the Spirit. That invitation is short and simple. Go and cry to God this day in the name of the Lord Jesus Christ, and pray for the Holy Spirit to be poured down on your soul.

There is every possible encouragement to do this. There is warrant of Scripture for doing it. "Turn you at my reproof,—I will pour out my Spirit upon you. I will make known my words unto you."—"If ye, being evil, know how to give good gifts to your children, how much more shall your heavenly Father give the Holy Spirit to them that ask Him." (Prov. i. 23; Luke xi. 13.) There is warrant in the experience of thousands for doing it. Thousands will rise at the last day, and testify that when they prayed they were heard, and when they sought grace, they found it.—Above all, there is warrant in the person and character of our Lord Jesus Christ. He waits to be gracious. He invites sinners to come to Him. He rejects none that come. He gives "power to all who receive Him by faith and come to Him, to become the sons of God." (John i. 12.)

Go then to Jesus, as a needy, wanting, humble, contrite sinner, and you shall not go in vain. Cry to Him mightily about your soul, and you shall not cry to no purpose. Confess to Him your need, and guilt, and fear, and danger, and He will not despise you. Ask, and you shall receive.

Seek, and you shall find. Knock, and it shall be opened to you. I testify to the chief of sinners this day, that there is enough in Christ, and to spare, for your soul. Come, come: come, this very day. Come to Christ!

(4) Let me, in the last place, give a parting *word of exhortation* to all readers of this paper who have received the Spirit of Christ,—to the penitent, the believing, the holy, the praying, the lovers of the Word of God. That exhortation shall consist of three simple things.

(*a*) For one thing, be *thankful* for the Spirit. Who has made you to differ? Whence came all these feelings in your heart, which thousands around you know not, and you yourself knew not at one time? To what do you owe that sense of sin, and that drawing towards Christ, and that hunger and thirst after righteousness, and that taste for the Bible and prayer, which, with all your doubts and infirmities, you find within your soul?

Did these things come of nature? Oh, no!—Did you learn these things in the schools of this world? Oh, no: no!—They are all of grace. Grace sowed them, grace watered them, grace began them, grace has kept them up. Learn to be more thankful. Praise God more every day you live: praise Him more in private, praise Him more in public, praise Him in your own family, praise Him above all in your own heart. This is the way to be in tune for heaven. The anthem there will be, "What hath God wrought?"

(*b*) For another thing, be *filled* with the Spirit. Seek to be more and more under His blessed influence. Strive to have every thought, and word, and action, and habit, brought under obedience to the leadings of the Holy Ghost. Grieve Him not by inconsistencies and conformity to the world. Quench Him not by trifling with little infirmities and small besetting sins. Seek rather to have Him ruling and reigning more completely over you every week that you live. Pray that you may yearly grow in grace, and in the knowledge of Christ. This is the way to do good to the world. An eminent Christian is a North Foreland Light-house, seen far and wide by others, and doing good to myriads, whom he never knows.—This is the way to enjoy much inward comfort in this world, to have bright assurance in death, to leave broad evidences behind us, and at last to receive a great crown.

(c) Finally, *pray* daily for a great outpouring of the Spirit on the Church and on the world. This is the grand want of the day: it is the thing that we need far more than money, machinery, and men. The "company of preachers" in Christendom is far greater than it was in the days of St. Paul; but the actual spiritual work done in the earth, in proportion to tne means used, is undoubtedly far less. We want more of the presence of the Holy Ghost,—more in the pulpit, and more in the congregation,—more in the pastoral visit, and more in the school. Where He is, there will be life, health, growth, and fruitfulness. Where He is not, all will be dead, tame, formal, sleepy, and cold. Then let every one who desires to see an increase of pure and undefiled religion, pray daily for more of the presence of the Holy Ghost in every branch of the visible Church of Christ.

XI.

HAVING THE SPIRIT.

" Having not the Spirit." — JUDE **19.**

I TAKE it for granted that every reader of this paper believes in the Holy Spirit. The number of people in this country who are infidels, deists, or Socinians, and openly deny the doctrine of the Trinity, is happily not very great. Most persons have been baptized in the name of the Father, and of the Son, and of the Holy Ghost. There are few Churchmen, at any rate, who have not often heard the well-known words of our old Catechism, " I believe in God the Holy Ghost, who sanctifieth me and all the elect people of God."

But, notwithstanding all this, it would be well for many if they would consider what they know of the Holy Spirit beyond His name. What experimental acquaintance have you with the Spirit's work? What has He done for you? What benefit have you received from Him? You can say of God the Father, " He made me and all the world ; " you can say of God the Son, "He died for me and all mankind:" but can you say anything about the Holy Ghost? Can you say, with any degree of confidence, " He dwells in me, and sanctifies me"? In one word, *Have you the Spirit?* The text which heads this paper will tell you that there is such a thing as "not having the Spirit." This is the point which I press upon your attention.

I believe the point to be one of vital importance at all seasons. I hold it to be one of special importance in the present day. I consider that clear views about the work of the Holy Spirit are among the best preservatives against the many false doctrines which abound in our times. Suffer me then, to lay before you a few things, which by God's blessing, may throw light on the subject of having the Spirit.

I. Let me *explain the immense importance of* " *Having the Spirit.*"

II. Let me *point out the great general principle by which alone the question can be tried,—" Have you the Spirit?"*

III. Let me *describe the particular effects which the Spirit always produces on the souls in which He dwells.*

I. Let me, in the first place, *explain the immense importance of having the Spirit.*

It is absolutely necessary to make this point clear. Unless you see this I shall appear like one beating the air all through this paper. Once let your mind lay hold on this, and half the work I want to do is already done for your soul.

I can easily fancy some reader saying, " I do not see the use of this question! Supposing I have not the Spirit, where is the mighty harm? I try to do my duty in this world : I attend my church regularly : I receive the Sacrament occasionally: I believe I am as good a Christian as my neighbours. I say my prayers: I trust God will pardon my sins for Christ's sake. I do not see why I should not reach heaven at last, without troubling myself with hard questions about the Spirit."

If these are your thoughts, I entreat you to give me your attention for a few minutes, while I try to supply you with reasons for thinking differently. Believe me, nothing less than your soul's salvation depends on "Having the Spirit." Life or death, heaven or hell, eternal happiness or eternal misery, are bound up with the subject of this paper.

(*a*) Remember, for one thing, if you have not the Spirit, *you have no part in Christ, and no title to heaven.*

The words of St. Paul are express and unmistakable: "If any man have not the Spirit of Christ, he is none of His." (Rom. viii. 9.) The words of St. John are no less clear: "Hereby we know that He abideth in us by the Spirit which He hath given us." (1 John iii. 24.) The indwelling of God the Holy Spirit is the common mark of all true believers in Christ. It is the Shepherd's mark on the flock of the Lord Jesus, distinguishing them from the rest of the world. It is the goldsmith's stamp on the genuine sons of God, which separates them from the dross and mass of false professors. It is the King's own seal on those who are His peculiar people, proving them to be His own property. It is "the earnest" which the Redeemer gives to His believing disciples while they are in the body, as a pledge of the full and complete "redemption" yet to come in the resurrection morning. (Ephes. i. 14.) This is the case of all believers. They all have the Spirit.

Let it be distinctly understood that he who has not the Spirit has not Christ. He who has not Christ has no pardon of his sins,—no peace with God,—no title to heaven, —no well-grounded hope of being saved. His religion is like the house built on the sand. It may look well in fine weather. It may satisfy him in the time of health and prosperity. But when the flood rises, and the wind blows, —when sickness and trouble come up against him, it will fall and bury him under its ruins. He lives without a good hope, and without a good hope he dies. He will rise again only to be miserable. He will stand in the judgment only to be condemned; he will see saints and angels looking on, and remember he might have been among them, but too late; he will see lost myriads around him, and find they cannot comfort him, but too late. This will be the end of the man who thinks to reach heaven without the Spirit.

Settle these things down in your memory, and let them never be forgotten. Are they not worth remembering? No Holy Spirit in you,—no part in Christ! No part in Christ,—no forgiveness of sins! No forgiveness of sins,— no peace with God! No peace with God,—no title to heaven! No title to heaven,—no admission into heaven! No admission into heaven,—and what then? Aye: what then? You may well ask. Whither will you flee? Which way will you turn? To what refuge will you run? There is none at all. There remains nothing but hell. Not admitted into heaven, you must sink at last into hell.

I ask every reader of this paper to mark well what I say. Perhaps it startles you: but may it not be good for you to be startled? Have I told you anything more than simple scriptural truth? Where is the defective link in the chain of reasoning you have heard? Where is the flaw in the argument? I believe in my conscience there is none. From not having the Spirit to being in hell, there is but a long flight of downward steps. Living without the Spirit, you are already on the top; dying without the Spirit, you will find your way to the bottom.

(b) Remember, for another thing, if you have not the Spirit *you have no holiness of heart, and no meetness for heaven.*

Heaven is the place to which all people hope to go after death. It would be well for many if they considered calmly what kind of dwelling-place heaven is. It is the habitation of the King of kings, who is " of purer eyes than to behold iniquity," and it must needs be a holy place. It is a place into which Scripture tells us there shall enter in nothing " that defileth, neither whatsoever worketh abomination." (Rev. xxi. 27.) It is a place where there shall be nothing wicked, sinful, or sensual,—nothing worldly, foolish, frivolous, or profane. *There*, let the covetous man remember, shall be no more money; *there*, let the pleasure-seeker remember, shall be no more races, theatres, novel reading, or balls; *there*, let the drunkard and the gambler remember, shall be no more strong drink, no more dice, no more betting, no more cards. The everlasting presence of God, saints, and angels,—the perpetual doing of God's will,—the complete absence of everything which God does not approve,—these are the chief things which shall make up heaven. It shall be an eternal Sabbath day.

For this heaven we are all by nature utterly unfit. We have no capacity for enjoying its happiness; we have no taste for its blessings; we have no eye to see its beauty; we have no heart to feel its comforts. Instead of freedom, we should find it bondage; instead of glorious liberty, we should find it constant constraint; instead of a splendid palace, we should find it a gloomy prison. A fish on dry land, a sheep in the water, an eagle in a cage, a painted savage in a royal drawing room, would all feel more at ease and in their place than a natural man in heaven. " Without holiness no man shall see the Lord." (Heb. xii. 14.)

For this heaven it is the special office of the Holy Ghost to prepare men's souls. He alone can change the earthly heart, and purify the worldly affections of Adam's children. He alone can can bring their minds into harmony with God, and tune them for the eternal company of saints, and angels, and Christ. He alone can make them love what God loves, and hate what God hates, and delight in God's presence. He alone can set the limbs of human nature, which were broken and dislocated by Adam's fall, and bring about a real unity between man's will and God's. And this He does for every one that is saved. It is written of believers that they are "saved according to God's mercy," but it is "by the washing of regeneration, and renewing of the Holy Ghost." They are chosen unto salvation, but it is "through sanctification of the Spirit," as well as "belief of the truth." (Titus iii. 5 ; 2 Thess. ii. 13.)

Let this also be written down on the tablet of your memory. No entrance into heaven without the Spirit first entering your heart upon earth ! No admission into glory in the next life without previous sanctification in this life ! No Holy Spirit in you in this world,—then no heaven in the world to come ! You would not be fit for it ; you would not be ready for it ; you would not like it ; you would not enjoy it. There is much use made in the present day of the word "holy." Our ears are wearied with "holy church," and "holy baptism," and "holy days," and "holy water," and "holy services," and "holy priests." But one thing is a thousand times more important : and that is, to be made *a really holy man* by the Spirit. We must be made partakers of the Divine nature, while we are alive. We must "sow to the Spirit," if we would ever reap life everlasting. (2 Peter i. 4 ; Gal. vi. 8.)

(*c*) Remember, for another thing, if you have not the Spirit, *you have no right to be considered a true Christian, and no will or power to become one.*

It requires little to make a Christian according to the standard of the world. Only let a man be baptized and attend some place of worship, and the requirements of the world are satisfied. The man's belief may not be so intelligent as that of a Turk : he may be profoundly ignorant of the Bible. The man's practice may be no better than that of a heathen : many a respectable Hindoo might put him to shame.—But what of that ? He is an Englishman ! He has been baptized ! He goes to church or chapel, and behaves decently when there ! What more would you have ? If you do not call him a Christian you are thought very uncharitable !

But it takes a great deal more than this to make a man a real Christian according to the standard of the Bible. It requires the co-operation of all the Three Persons of the Blessed Trinity. The election of God the Father,—the blood and intercession of God the Son,—the sanctification of God the Spirit,—must all meet together on the soul that is to be saved. Father, Son, and Holy Ghost must unite to work the work of making any child of Adam a true Christian.

This is a deep subject, and one that must be handled with reverence. But where the Bible speaks with decision, there we may also speak with decision; and the words of the Bible have no meaning if the work of the Holy Spirit be not just as needful in order to make a man a true Christian, as the work of the Father or the work of the Son. "No man," we are told, "can say that Jesus is the Lord, but by the Holy Ghost." (1 Cor. xii. 3.) True Christians, we are taught in Scripture, are "born of the Spirit." They live in the Spirit; they are led by the Spirit; by the Spirit they mortify the deeds of the body; by one Spirit they have access through Jesus unto the Father. Their graces are all the fruit of the Spirit; they are the temple of the Holy Ghost; they are a habitation of God through the Spirit; they walk after the Spirit; they are strengthened by the Spirit. Through the Spirit they wait for the hope of righteousness by faith. (John iii. 6; Gal. v. 25; Rom. viii. 13, 14; Eph. ii. 18; Gal. v. 22; 1 Cor. vi. 19; Eph. ii. 22; Rom. viii. 4; Eph. iii. 16; Gal. v. 5.) These are plain Scriptural expressions. Who will dare to gainsay them?

The truth is that the deep corruption of human nature would make salvation impossible if it were not for the work of the Spirit. Without Him the Father's love and the Son's redemption are set before us in vain. The Spirit must reveal them, the Spirit must apply them, or else we are lost souls.

Nothing less than the power of Him who moved on the face of the waters in the day of creation can ever raise us from our low estate. He who said, "Let there be light, and there was light," must speak the word before any one of us will ever rise to newness of life. He who came down on the day of Pentecost, must come down on our poor dead souls, before they will ever see the kingdom of God. Mercies and afflictions may move the surface of our hearts, but they alone will never reach the inner man. Sacraments, and services, and sermons may produce outward formality, and clothe us with a skin of religion, but there will be no life. Ministers may make communicants, and fill churches with regular worshippers: the almighty power of the Holy Ghost alone can make true Christians, and fill heaven with glorified saints.

Let this also be written in your memory, and never forgotten. No Holy Spirit,—no true Christianity! You must have the Spirit *in* you, as well as Christ *for* you, if you are ever to be saved. God must be your loving Father, Jesus must be your *known* Redeemer, the Holy Ghost must be your *felt* Sanctifier, or else it will be better for you never to have been born.

I press the subject on the serious consideration of all who read these pages. I trust I have said enough to show you that it is of vital importance to your soul to "have the Spirit." It is no abstruse and mysterious point of divinity; it is no nice question of which the solution matters little one way or another. It is a subject in which is bound up the everlasting peace of your soul.

You may not like the tidings. You may call it enthusiasm, or fanaticism, or extravagance. I take my stand on the plain teaching of the Bible. I say that God must dwell in your heart by the Spirit on earth, or you will never dwell with God in heaven.

"Ah," you may say, "I do not know much about it. I trust Christ will be merciful. I hope I shall go to heaven after all." I answer, No man ever yet tasted of Christ's mercy who did not also receive of His Spirit.—No man was ever justified who was not also sanctified.—No man ever went to heaven who was not led there by the Spirit.

II. Let me, in the second place, point out the *great general rule and principle by which the question may be decided, whether we have the Spirit.*

I can quite understand that the idea of knowing whether we "have the Spirit" is disagreeable to many minds. I am not ignorant of the objections which Satan at once stirs up in the natural heart. "It is impossible to know it," says one person: "it is a deep thing, and beyond our reach."—"It is too mysterious a thing to inquire into," says another: "we must be content to leave the subject in uncertainty."—"It is wrong to pretend to know anything about it," says a third: "we were never meant to look into such questions. It is only fit for enthusiasts and fanatics to talk of having the Spirit."—I hear such objections without being moved by them. I say that it can be known whether a man has the Spirit. It *can* be known,—it *may* be known,—it *ought* to be known. It needs no vision from heaven, no revelation from an angel to discern it; it needs nothing but calm inquiry by the light of God's Word. Let us enter upon that inquiry.

All men have not the Holy Spirit. I regard the doctrine of an inward spiritual light enjoyed by all mankind as an unscriptural delusion. I believe the modern notion of universal inspiration to be a baseless dream. Without controversy, God has not left Himself without a witness in the heart of fallen man. He has left in every mind sufficient knowledge of right and wrong to make all men responsible and accountable. He has given to every child of Adam a *conscience:* but He has not given to every child of Adam the Holy Ghost. A man may have good wishes like Balaam, do many things like Herod, be almost persuaded like Agrippa, and tremble like Felix, and yet be as utterly destitute of the grace of the Spirit as these men were. St. Paul tells us that before conversion men may "know God" in a certain sense, and have "thoughts accusing or excusing one another." But he also tells us that before conversion men are "without God" and "without Christ," have "no hope," and are "darkness" itself. (Rom. i. 21; ii. 15; Eph. ii. 12; v. 8.) The Lord Jesus Himself says of the Spirit, "The world seeth Him not, neither knoweth Him: but ye know Him, for He dwelleth with you, and shall be in you." (John xiv. 17.)

All members of Churches and baptized persons have not the Spirit. I see no ground in Scripture for saying that every man who receives baptism receives the Holy Ghost, and that we ought to regard him as born of the Spirit. I dare not tell baptized people that they all have the Spirit, and that they only need "stir up the gift of God" within them in order to be saved. I see, on the contrary, that Jude speaks of members of the visible Church in his day as "not having the Spirit." Some of them probably had been baptized by the hands of apostles, and admitted into full communion with the professing Church. No matter! they "had not the Spirit." (Jude 19.)

It is vain to attempt to evade the power of this single expression. It teaches plainly that "having the Spirit" is not the lot of every man, and not the portion of every member of the visible Church of Christ. It shows the necessity of finding out some general rule and principle by which the presence of the Spirit in a man may be ascertained. He does not dwell in every one. Baptism and churchmanship are no proofs of His presence. How, then, shall I know whether a man has the Spirit?

The presence of the Spirit in a man's soul can only be known by *the effects* which He produces. *The fruits* He causes to be brought forth in a man's heart and life, are the only evidence which can be depended on. A man's faith, a man's opinions, and a man's practice, are the witnesses we must examine, if we would find out whether a man has the Spirit. This is the rule of the Lord Jesus: " Every tree is known by his own fruit." (Luke vi. 44.)

The effects which the Holy Spirit produces may always be *seen*. The man of the world may not understand them : they may in many cases be feeble and indistinct ; but where the Spirit is, He will not be hid. He is not idle when He enters the heart: He does not lie still ; He does not sleep: He will make His presence known. He will shine out little by little through the windows of a man's daily habits and conversation, and manifest to the world that He is in him. A dormant, torpid, silent indwelling of the Spirit is a notion that pleases the minds of many. It is a notion for which I see no authority in the Word of God. I hold entirely with the Homily for Whit-Sunday : " As the tree is known by his fruit, so is also the Holy Ghost."

In whomsoever I see the effects and fruits of the Spirit, in that man I see one who has the Spirit. I believe it to be not only charitable to think so, but presumption to doubt it. I do not expect to behold the Holy Ghost with my bodily eyes, or to touch Him with my hands. But I need no angel to come down to show me where He dwells ; I need no vision from heaven to tell me where I may find Him. Only show me a man in whom the fruits of the Spirit are to be seen, and I see one who " has the Spirit." I will not doubt the inward presence of the almighty *cause*, when I see the outward fact of an evident *effect*.

Can I see *the wind* on a stormy day ? I cannot : but I can see the effects of its force and power. When I see the clouds driven before it, and the trees bending under it,— when I hear it whistling through doors and windows, or howling round the chimney tops, I do not for a moment doubt its existence. I say, " There is a wind." Just so it is with the presence of the Spirit in the soul.

Can I see the *dew* of heaven as it falls on a summer evening? I cannot. It comes down softly and gently, noiseless and imperceptible. But when I go forth in the morning after a cloudless night, and see every leaf sparkling with moisture, and feel every blade of grass damp and wet, I say at once, " There has been a dew." Just so it is with the presence of the Spirit in the soul.

Can I see the *hand of the sower* when I walk through the corn fields in the month of July? I cannot. I see nothing but millions of ears rich with grain, and bending to the ground with ripeness: but do I suppose that harvest came by chance, and grew of itself? I suppose nothing of the kind. I know when I see those corn fields that the plough and the harrow were at work one day, and that a hand has been there which sowed the seed. Just so it is with the work of the Spirit in the soul.

Can I see the *magnetic fluid* in the compass-needle? I cannot. It acts in a hidden mysterious way: but when I see that little piece of iron always turning to the north, I know at once that it is under the secret influence of magnetic power. Just so it is with the work of the Spirit in the soul.

Can I see the *mainspring of my watch* when I look upon its face? I cannot. But when I see the fingers going round and telling the hours and minutes of the day in regular succession, I do not doubt the mainspring's existence. Just so it is with the work of the Spirit.

Can I see *the steersman* of the homeward-bound ship, when she first comes in sight, and her sails whiten on the horizon? I cannot. But when I stand on the pier-head and see that ship working her course over the sea towards the harbour's mouth, like a thing of life, I know well there is one at the helm who guides her movements. Just so it is with the work of the Spirit.

I charge all my readers to remember this. Establish it as a settled principle in your mind, that if the Holy Ghost really is in a man, it will be *seen* in the effects He produces on his heart and life.

Beware of supposing that a man may have the Spirit when there is no outward evidence of His presence in the soul. It is a dangerous and unscriptural delusion to think so. We must never lose sight of the broad principles laid down for us in Scripture: " If we say that we have fellowship with Him, and walk in darkness, we lie, and do not the truth."—" In this the children of God are manifest and the children of the devil: whosoever doeth not righteousness is not of God." (1 John i. 6; iii. 10.)

You have heard, I doubt not, of a wretched class of Christians called Antinomians. They are persons who boast of having an interest in Christ, and say they are pardoned and forgiven, while at the same time they live in wilful sin and open breach of God's commandments. You have been told, I dare say, that such people are miserably deceived. They are going down to hell with a lie in their right hand. The true believer in Christ is "dead to sin." Every man that has real hope in Christ "purifieth himself even as He is pure." (1 John iii. 3.)

But I will tell you of a delusion quite as dangerous as that of the Antinomians, and far more specious. That delusion is,—to flatter yourself you have the Spirit dwelling in your heart, while there are no fruits of the Spirit to be seen in your life. I firmly believe that this delusion is ruining thousands, as surely as Antinomianism. It is just as perilous to dishonour the Holy Ghost, as it is to dishonour Christ. It is just as offensive to God to pretend to an interest in the work of the Spirit, as it is to pretend to an interest in the work of Christ.

Once for all, I charge my readers to remember that the effects which the Spirit produces are the only trustworthy evidences of His presence. To talk of the Holy

Ghost dwelling in you and yet being unseen in your life,
is wild work indeed. It confounds the first principles of
the Gospel : it confounds light and darkness,—nature and
grace,—conversion and unconversion,—faith and unbelief,
—the children of God and the children of the devil.

There is only one safe position in this matter. There
is only one safe answer to the question, "How shall we
decide who have the Spirit?" We must take our stand
on the old principle laid down by our Lord Jesus Christ:
"By their fruits ye shall know them." (Matt. vii. 20.)
Where the Spirit is there will be fruit: he who has no
fruit of the Spirit has not the Spirit. A work of the
Spirit unfelt, unseen, inoperative, is a positive delusion.
Where the Spirit really is He will be felt, seen, and
known.

III. Let me, in the last place, *describe the particular
effects which the Spirit produces on the souls in which
He dwells.*

I regard this part of the subject as the most important
of all. Hitherto I have spoken generally of the great
leading principles which must guide us in inquiring about
the work of the Holy Ghost. I must now come closer,
and speak of the special marks by which the presence of
the Holy Ghost in any individual heart may be discerned.
Happily, with the Bible for our light, these marks are not
hard to find out.

Some things I wish to premise before entering fully into
the subject. It is needful in order to clear the way.

(a) I grant freely that there are *some deep mysteries*
about the work of the Spirit. I cannot explain the manner
of His coming into the heart. "The wind bloweth where
it listeth, and thou hearest the sound thereof, but canst not
tell whence it cometh and whither it goeth: so is every
one that is born of the Spirit." (John iii. 8.) I cannot
explain why He comes into one heart and not into another.

—why He condescends to dwell in this man and not in that. I only know that so it is. He acts as a sovereign. To use the words of the Church Catechism, He sanctifieth "the elect people of God." But I remember also that I cannot explain why I was born in Christian England, and not in heathen Africa. I am satisfied to believe that all God's work is well done. It is enough for me to be in the King's court, without being of the King's counsel.

(*b*) I grant freely that there are *great diversities* in the operations by which the Spirit carries on His work in men's souls.—There are differences in the *ages* at which He begins to enter the heart. With some He begins young, as with John the Baptist and Timothy: with some he begins old, as with Manasseh and Zacchæus.—There are differences in the *feelings* which He first stirs up in the heart. He leads some by strong terror and alarm, like the jailer at Philippi. He leads some by gently opening their hearts to receive the truth, as Lydia, the purple-seller.— There are differences in *the time occupied* in effecting this complete change of character. With some the change is immediate and sudden, as it was with Saul when he journeyed to Damascus: with others it is gradual and slow, as it was with Nicodemus the Pharisee.—There are differences in *the instruments* He uses in first awakening the soul from its natural death. With some He uses a sermon, with others the Bible, with others a tract, with others a friend's advice, with others a sickness or affliction, with others no one particular thing that can be distinctly traced. All this is most important to understand. To require all persons to be squared down to one kind of experience is a most grievous mistake.

(*c*) I grant freely that the *beginnings of the Spirit's work are often small and imperceptible.* The seed from which the spiritual character is formed is often very minute at first. The fountain-head of the spiritual life, like that of many a mighty river, is frequently at its outset a little trickling stream. The beginnings therefore of the Spirit's work in a soul are generally overlooked by the world,— very frequently not duly valued and encouraged by other Christians,—and almost without exception thoroughly misunderstood by the soul itself which is the subject of them. *Let that never be forgotten.* The man in whom the Spirit begins to work is never hardly aware, till long afterwards, that his state of mind about the time of his conversion arose from the entrance of the Holy Spirit.

But still, after all these concessions and allowances, there are certain great leading effects which the Spirit produces on the soul in which He dwells, which are always one and the same. Those who have the Spirit may be led at first by different *paths*, but they are always brought, sooner or later, into one and the same narrow *way*. Their leading opinions in religion are the same; their leading desires are the same; their general walk is the same. They may differ from one another widely in their natural character, but their spiritual character, in its main features, is always one. The Holy Ghost always produces one general kind of effects. Shades and varieties there are no doubt in the experience of those on whose hearts He works, but the general outline of their faith and life is always the same.

What then are these general effects which the Spirit always produces on those who really have Him? What are the marks of His presence in the soul? This is the question which now remains to be considered. Let us try to set down these marks in order.

1. All who have the Spirit *are quickened by Him, and made spiritually alive.* He is called in Scripture, "The Spirit of life." (Rom. viii. 3.) "It is the Spirit," says our Lord Jesus Christ, "that quickeneth." (John vi. 63.) We are all by nature dead in trespasses and sins. We have neither feeling nor interest about religion; we have neither faith, nor hope, nor fear, nor love: our hearts are

in a state of torpor; they are compared in Scripture to a stone. We may be alive about money, learning, politics, or pleasure, but we are dead towards God.—All this is changed when the Spirit comes into the heart. He raises us from this state of death, and makes us new creatures He awakens the conscience, and inclines the will towards God. He causes old things to pass away, and all things to become new. He gives us a new heart; He makes us put off the old man, and put on the new. He blows the trumpet in the ear of our slumbering faculties, and sends us forth to walk the world as if we were new beings. How unlike was Lazarus shut up in the silent tomb, to Lazarus coming forth at our Lord's command! How unlike was Jairus' daughter lying cold on her bed amidst weeping friends, to Jairus' daughter rising and speaking to her mother as she was wont to do! Just as unlike is the man in whom the Spirit dwells to what he was before the Spirit came into him.

I appeal to every thinking reader. Can he whose heart is manifestly full of everything but God,—hard, cold, and insensible,—can he be said to "have the Spirit"? Judge for yourself.

2. All who have the Spirit are *taught by Him*. He is called in Scripture, "The Spirit of wisdom and revelation." (Eph. i. 17.) It was the promise of the Lord Jesus, "He shall teach you all things;" "He shall guide you into all truth." (John xiv. 26; xvi. 13.) We are all by nature ignorant of spiritual truth. "The natural man receiveth not the things of the Spirit of God: they are foolishness to him." (1 Cor. ii. 14.) Our eyes are blinded. We neither know God, nor Christ, nor ourselves, nor the world, nor sin, nor heaven, nor hell, as we ought. We see everything under false colours.—The Spirit alters entirely this state of things. He opens the eyes of our understandings; He illumines us; He calls us out of darkness into marvellous light; He takes away the veil; He shines into our

hearts, and makes us see things as they really are. No wonder that all true Christians are so remarkably agreed upon the essentials of true religion! The reason is that they have all learned in one school,—the school of the Holy Ghost. No wonder that true Christians can understand each other at once, and find common ground of communion! They have been taught the same language by One whose lessons are never forgotten.

I appeal again to every thinking reader. Can he who is ignorant of the leading doctrines of the Gospel, and blind to his own state,—can he be said to " have the Spirit " ? Judge for yourself.

3. All who have the Spirit *are led by Him to the Scriptures*. This is the instrument by which He specially works on the soul. The Word is called " the sword of the Spirit." Those who are born again are said to be " born by the Word." (Eph. vi. 17; 1 Peter i. 23.) All Scripture was written under His inspiration: He never teaches anything which is not therein written. He causes the man in whom He dwells to " delight in the law of the Lord." (Psalm i. 2.) Just as the infant desires the milk which nature has provided for it, and refuses all other food, so does the soul which has the Spirit desire the sincere milk of the Word. Just as the Israelites fed on the manna in the wilderness, so are the children of God taught by the Holy Ghost to feed on the contents of the Bible.

I appeal again to every thinking reader. Can he who never reads the Bible, or only reads it formally,—can he be said to " have the Spirit " ? Judge for yourself.

4. All who have the Spirit are *convinced by Him of sin*. This is an especial office which the Lord Jesus promised He should fulfil. " When He is come, He shall reprove the world of sin." (John xvi. 8.) He alone can open a man's eyes to the real extent of His guilt and corruption before God. He always does this when He comes into the soul. He puts us in our right place; He shows

us the vileness of our own hearts, and makes us cry with the publican, "God be merciful to me a sinner." He pulls down those proud, self-righteous, self-justifying notions with which we are all born, and makes us feel as we ought to feel,—"I am a bad man, and I deserve to be in hell." Ministers may alarm us for a little season; sickness may break the ice on our hearts; but the ice will soon freeze again if it is not thawed by the breath of the Spirit, and convictions not wrought by Him will pass away like the morning dew.

I appeal again to every thinking reader. Can the man who never feels the burden of his sins, and knows not what it is to be humbled by the thought of them,—can he "have the Spirit"? Judge for yourself.

5. All who have the Spirit *are led by Him to Christ for salvation.* It is one special part of His office to "testify of Christ," to "take of the things of Christ, and to show them to us." (John xv. 26; xvi. 15.) By nature we all think to work our own way to heaven: we fancy in our blindness that we can make our peace with God. From this miserable blindness the Spirit delivers us. He shows us that in ourselves we are lost and hopeless, and that Christ is the only door by which we can enter heaven and be saved. He teaches us that nothing but the blood of Jesus can atone for sin, and that through His mediation alone God can be just and the justifier of the ungodly. He reveals to us the exquisite fitness and suitableness to our souls of Christ's salvation. He unfolds to us the beauty of the glorious doctrine of justification by simple faith. He sheds abroad in our hearts that mighty love of God which is in Christ Jesus. Just as the dove flies to the well-known cleft of the rock, so does the soul of him who has the Spirit flee to Christ and rest on Him. (Rom. v. 5.)

I appeal again to every thinking reader. Can he who knows nothing of faith in Christ, be said to "have the Spirit"? Judge for yourself.

6. All who have the Spirit *are by Him made holy.*
He is "the Spirit of holiness." (Rom. i. 4.) When He
dwells in men, He makes them follow after "love, joy,
peace, long-suffering, gentleness, meekness, faith, patience,
temperance." He makes it *natural* to them, through their
new "Divine nature," to count all God's precepts concerning
all things to be right, and to "hate every false way."
(2 Pet i. 4; Ps. cxix. 128.) Sin is no more pleasant to
them: it is their sorrow when tempted by it; it is their
shame when they are overtaken by it. Their desire is to
be free from it altogether. Their happiest times are when
they are enabled to walk most closely with God: their
saddest times are when they are furthest off from Him.

I appeal again to every thinking reader. Can those
who do not even pretend to live strictly according to God's
will, be said to "have the Spirit"? Judge for yourself.

7. All those who have the Spirit *are spiritually
minded.* To use the words of the Apostle Paul, "They
that are after the Spirit, mind the things of the Spirit."
(Rom. viii. 5.) The general tone, tenor, and bias of their
minds is in favour of spiritual things. They do not serve
God by fits and starts, but habitually. They may be drawn
aside by strong temptations; but the general tendency of
their lives, ways, tastes, thoughts and habits, is spiritual.
You see it in the way they spend their leisure time, the
company they love to keep, and their conduct in their own
homes. And all is the result of the spiritual nature
implanted in them by the Holy Ghost. Just as the cater-
pillar when it becomes a butterfly can no longer be content
to crawl on earth, but will fly upwards and use its wings,
so will the affections of the man who has the Spirit be
ever reaching upwards toward God.

I appeal again to every thinking reader. Can those
whose minds are wholly intent on the things of this world
be said to "have the Spirit"? Judge for yourself.

8. All that have the Spirit *feel a conflict within them.*

between the old nature and the new. The words of St.
Paul are true, more or less, of all the children of God:
"The flesh lusteth against the Spirit, and the Spirit against
the flesh, so that ye cannot do the things that ye would."
(Gal. v. **17.**) They feel a holy principle within their
breasts, which makes them delight in the law of God: but
they feel another principle within, striving hard for the
mastery, and struggling to drag them downwards and
backwards. Some feel this conflict more than others: but
all who have the Spirit are acquainted with it; and it is
a token for good. It is a proof that the strong man armed
no longer reigns within, as he once did, with undisputed
sway. The presence of the Holy Ghost may be known by
inward warfare as well as by inward peace. He that has
been taught to rest and hope in Christ, will always be one
who fights and wars with sin.

I appeal again to every thinking reader. Can he who
knows nothing of inward conflict, and is a servant to sin,
the world, and his own self-will, can he be said to "have
the Spirit"? Judge for yourself.

9. All who have the Spirit *love others who have the
Spirit.* It is written of them by St. John, "We know
that we have passed from death to life, because we love
the brethren." (1 John iii. 14.) The more they see of
the Holy Ghost in any one, the more dear he is to them.
They regard him as a member of the same family, a child
of the same Father, a subject of the same King, and a
fellow-traveller with themselves in a foreign country towards the same father-land. It is the glory of the Spirit
to bring back something of that brotherly love which sin
has so miserably chased out of the world. He makes
men love one another for reasons which to the natural
man are foolishness,—for the sake of a common Saviour,
a common faith, a common service on earth, and the hope
of a common home. He raises up friendships independent
of blood, marriage, interest, business, or any worldly

motive. He unites men by making them feel they are united to one great centre, Jesus Christ.

I appeal again to every thinking reader. Can he who finds no pleasure in the company of spiritually-minded persons, or even sneers at them as saints,—can he be said to "have the Spirit"? Judge for yourself.

10. Finally, all who have the Spirit are *taught by Him to pray*. He is called in Scripture, "The Spirit of grace and supplication." (Zech. xii. 10.) The elect of God are said to "cry to Him night and day." (Luke xviii. 7.) They cannot help it: their prayers may be poor, and weak, and wandering,—but pray they must; something within them tells them they must speak with God and lay their wants before Him. Just as the infant will cry when it feels pain or hunger, because it is its nature, so will the new nature implanted by the Holy Ghost oblige a man to pray. He has the Spirit of adoption, and he must cry, "Abba, Father." (Gal. iv. 6.)

Once more I appeal to every thinking reader. Can the man who never prays at all, or is content with saying a few formal heartless words, can he be said to "have the Spirit"? For the last time I say, Judge for yourself.

Such are the marks and signs by which I believe the presence of the Holy Ghost in a man may be discerned. I have set them down fairly as they appear to me to be laid before us in the Scriptures. I have endeavoured to exaggerate nothing, and to keep back nothing. I believe there are no true Christians in whom these marks may not be found. Some of them, no doubt, stand out more prominently in some, and others in others. My own experience is distinct and decided,—that I never saw a truly godly person, even of the poorest and humblest classes, in whom, on close observation, these marks might not be discovered.

I believe that marks such as these are the only safe

evidence that we are travelling in the way that leads to everlasting life. I charge every one who desires to make his calling and election sure, to see that these marks are his own. There are high-flying professors of religion, I know, who despise the mention of "marks," and call them "legal." I care nothing for their being called legal, so long as I am satisfied they are scriptural. And, with the Bible before me, I give my opinion confidently, that he who is without these marks is without the Spirit of God.

Show me a man who has these marks about him, and I acknowledge him as a child of God. He may be poor and lowly in this world; he may be vile in his own eyes, and often doubt of his own salvation. But he has that within him which only comes from above, and will never be destroyed,—even the work of the Holy Ghost. God is his, Christ is his. His name is already written in the book of life, and before long heaven will be his own.

Show me a man in whom these marks are not to be found, and I dare not acknowledge him to be a true Christian. I dare not as an honest man; I dare not as a lover of his soul; I dare not as a reader of the Bible. He may make a great religious profession; he may be learned, high in the world, and moral in his life. It is all nothing if he has not the Holy Ghost. He is without God, without Christ, without solid hope, and, unless he changes, will at length be without heaven.

And now let me finish this paper by a few practical remarks which arise naturally out of the matter which it contains.

(a) Would you know, first of all, *what is your own immediate duty?* Listen, and I will tell you.

You ought to examine yourself calmly about the subject which I have been trying to set before you. You ought to ask yourself seriously how the doctrine of the Holy Ghost affects your soul. Look away, I beseech you.

for a few minutes, to higher things than the things of earth, and more important things than the things of time. Bear with me, while I ask you a plain question. I ask it solemnly and affectionately, as one who desires your salvation,—Have you the Spirit?

Remember, I do not ask whether you think all I have been saying is true, and right, and good. I ask whether you yourself, who are reading these lines, have within you the Holy Spirit?

Remember, I do not ask whether you believe that the Holy Ghost is given to the Church of Christ, and that all who belong to the Church are within reach of His operations. I ask whether you yourself have the Spirit in your own heart?

Remember, I do not ask whether you sometimes feel strivings of conscience, and good desires flitting about within you. I ask whether you have really experienced the quickening and reviving work of the Spirit upon your heart?

Remember, I do not ask you to tell me the day or month when the Spirit began His work in you. It is enough for me if fruit trees bear fruit, without inquiring the precise time when they were planted. But I do ask, Are you bringing forth any fruits of the Spirit?

Remember, I do not ask whether you are a perfect person, and never feel anything evil within. But I do ask, gravely and seriously, whether you have about your heart and life the marks of the Spirit?

I hope you will not tell me you do not know what the marks of the Spirit are. I have described them plainly. I now repeat them briefly, and press them on your attention. 1. The Spirit quickens men's hearts. 2. The Spirit teaches men's minds. 3. The Spirit leads to the Word. 4. The Spirit convinces of sin. 5. The Spirit draws to Christ. 6. The Spirit sanctifies. 7. The Spirit makes men spiritually-minded. 8. The Spirit produces inward conflict. 9. The

Spirit makes men love the brethren. 10. The Spirit teaches to pray. These are the great marks of the Holy Ghost's presence. Put the question to your conscience like a man,—Has the Spirit done anything of this kind for your soul?

I charge you not to let many days pass away without trying to answer my question. I summon you, as a faithful watchman knocking at the door of your heart, to bring the matter to an issue. We live in an old, worn· out, sin-laden world. Who can tell what "a day may bring forth?" Who shall live to see another year? Have you the Spirit? (Prov. xxvii. 1.)

(b) Would you know, in the next place, what is *the grand defect of the Christianity of our times?* Listen to me, and I will tell you.

The grand defect I speak of is simply this,—that the Christianity of many people is not real Christianity at all. I know that such an opinion sounds hard and shockingly uncharitable. I cannot help that: I am satisfied that it is sadly true. I only want people's Christianity to be that of the Bible; but I doubt exceedingly, in many cases, whether it is so.

There are multitudes of English people, I believe, who go to church or chapel every Sunday merely as a form. Their fathers or mothers went, and so they go; it is the fashion of the country to go, and so they go; it is the custom to attend a religious service and hear a sermon, and so they go. But as to real, vital, saving religion, they neither know nor care anything about it. They can give no account of the distinctive doctrines of the Gospel. Justification, and regeneration, and sanctification, are " words and names" which they cannot explain. They may have a sort of vague idea that they ought to go to the Lord's Table, and may be able to say a few vague words about Christ, but they have no intelligent notion of the way of salvation. As to the Holy Ghost, they can scarcely say more about Him than that they have heard His name, and repeated it in the Belief.

Now, if any reader of this paper is conscious that his religion is such as I have described, I will only warn him affectionately to remember that such religion is utterly *useless.* It will neither save, comfort, satisfy, nor sanctify his soul. And the plain advice I give him is to change it for something better without delay. Remember my words. It will not do at the last.

(c) Would you know, in the next place, *one truth in the Gospel about which we need to be specially jealous in this day.* Listen, and I will tell you.

The truth which I have in view is the truth about the work of the Holy Ghost. All truth no doubt is constantly assailed by Satan. I have no desire for a moment to exaggerate the office of the Spirit, and to exalt Him above the Sun and Centre of the Gospel,—Jesus Christ. But I do believe that, next to the priestly office of Christ, no truth in the present day is so frequently lost sight of, and so cunningly assailed, as the work of the Spirit. Some injure it by ignorant neglect: their talk is all about Christ. They can tell you something about "the Saviour;" but if you ask them about that inward work of the Spirit which all who *really* know the Saviour experience, they have not a word to say.—Some injure the work of the Spirit by taking it all for granted. Membership of the Church, participation of the Sacraments, become their substitutes for conversion and spiritual regeneration.—Some injure the work of the Spirit by confounding it with the action of natural conscience. According to this low view, none but the most hardened and degraded of mankind are destitute of the Holy Ghost.—Against all such departures from the truth let us watch and be on our guard. Let us beware of leaving the proportion of Gospel statements. Let one of our chief watchwords in the present day be,— No salvation without the inward work of the Spirit! No inward work of the Holy Spirit unless it can be seen, felt, and known! No saving work of the Spirit which does not show itself in repentance towards God, and living faith towards Jesus Christ!

(*d*) Would you know, in the next place, *the reason why we, who are ministers of the Gospel, never despair of any one who hears us so long as he lives?* Listen, and I will tell you.

We never despair, because we believe the power of the Holy Ghost. We might well despair when we look at our own performances: we are often sick of ourselves. We might well despair when we look at some who belong to our congregations: they seem as hard and insensible as the nether mill-stone. But we remember the Holy Ghost, and what He has done; we remember the Holy Ghost, and consider that He has not changed. He can come down like fire and melt the hardest hearts; He can convert the worst man or woman among our hearers, and mould their whole character into a new shape. And so we preach on. We hope, because of the Holy Ghost. Oh, that our hearers would understand that the progress of true religion depends "not on might or on power," but on the Lord's Spirit! Oh, that many of them would learn to lean less on ministers, and to pray more for the Holy Spirit! Oh, that all would learn to expect less from schools, and tracts, and ecclesiastical machinery, and, while using all means diligently, would seek more earnestly for the outpouring of the Spirit. (Zech. iv. 6.)

(*e*) Would you know, in the next place, *what you ought to do, if your conscience tells you you have not the Spirit?* Listen, and I will tell you.

If you have not the Spirit, you ought to go at once to the Lord Jesus Christ in prayer, and beseech Him to have mercy on you, and send you the Spirit. I have not the slightest sympathy with those who tell men to pray for the Holy Spirit in the first place, in order that they may go to Christ in the second place. I see no warrant of Scripture for saying so. I only see that if men feel they are needy, perishing sinners, they ought to apply first and foremost, straight and direct, to Jesus Christ. I see that He Himself says, "If any man thirst, let him come unto Me and drink." (John vii. 37.) I know that it is written, "He hath received gifts for men, even for the rebellious, that the Lord God might dwell among them." (Psal. lxviii. 18.) I know it is His special office to baptize with the Holy Ghost, and that "in Him all fulness dwells." I dare not pretend to be more systematic than the Bible. I believe that Christ is the meeting place between God and the soul, and my first advice to any one who wants the Spirit must always be, "*Go to Jesus, and tell your want to Him.*" (Col. i. 19.)

Furthermore I would say, if you have not the Spirit, you must be diligent in attending those means of grace through which the Spirit works. You must regularly hear that Word, which is His sword; you must habitually attend those assemblies where His presence is promised; you must, in short, be found *in the way of the Spirit,* if you want the Spirit to do you good. Blind Bartimeus would never have received sight had he sat lazily at home, and not come forth to sit by the wayside. Zacchæus might never have seen Jesus and become a son of Abraham, if he had not run before and climbed up into the sycamore tree. The Spirit is a loving and good Spirit. *But he who despises means of grace resists the Holy Ghost.*

Remember these two things. I firmly believe that no man ever acted honestly and perseveringly on these two pieces of advice who did not, sooner or later, have the Spirit.

(*f*) Would you know, in the next place, *what you ought to do, if you stand in doubt about your own state, and cannot tell whether you have the Spirit?* Listen, and I will tell you.

If you stand in doubt whether you have the Spirit, you ought to examine calmly whether your doubts are well-founded. There are many true believers, I fear, who are destitute of any firm assurance as to their own state: doubting is their life. I ask such persons to take their Bibles down, and consider quietly the grounds of their anxiety. I ask them to consider whence came their sense of sin, however feeble,—their love to Christ, however faint,—their desire after holiness, however weak,—their pleasure in the company of God's people,—their inclination to prayer and the Word? Whence came these things, I say? Did they come from your own heart? Surely not! Nature bears no such fruit.—Did they come from the devil? Surely not! Satan does not war against Satan. Whence then, I repeat, did these things come? I warn you to beware lest you grieve the Holy Ghost by doubting the truth of His operations. I tell you it is high time for you to reflect whether you have not been expecting an inward perfection which you had no right to expect, and at the same time thanklessly undervaluing a real work which the Holy Ghost has actually wrought in your souls.

A great statesman once said that if a foreigner visited England, for the first time, with his eyes bandaged and his ears open,—hearing everything, but seeing nothing,—he might well suppose that England was on the road to ruin; so many are the murmurings of the English people. And yet if that same foreigner came to England with his ears stopped and his eyes open,—seeing everything and hearing nothing,—he would probably suppose that England was the most wealthy and flourishing country in the world, so many are the signs of prosperity that he would see.

I am often disposed to apply this remark to the case of doubting Christians. If I believed all they say of themselves I should certainly think they were in a bad state. But when I see them living as they do,—hungering and thirsting after righteousness, poor in spirit, desiring holiness, loving the name of Christ, keeping up habits of Bible reading and prayer,—when I see these things I cease to be afraid. I trust my eyes more than my ears. I see manifest marks of the Spirit's presence, and I only grieve that they should refuse to see them themselves. I see the devil robbing them of their peace, by instilling these doubts into their minds, and I mourn that they should injure themselves by believing him. Some professors, without controversy, may well doubt whether they "have the Spirit," for they have no signs of grace about them. But many nurse up a habit of doubt in their minds for which they have no cause, and of which they ought to be ashamed.

(g) Would you know, last of all, *what you ought to do if you really have the Spirit.* Listen to me, and I will tell you.

If you have the Spirit, seek to be "filled with the Spirit." (Ephes. v. 18.) Drink deep of the living waters. Do not be content with a little religion. Pray that the Spirit may fill every corner and chamber of your heart, and that not an inch of room may be left in it for the world and the devil.

If you have the Spirit, "grieve not the Spirit." (Ephes. iv. 30.) It is easy for believers to weaken their sense of His presence, and deprive themselves of His comfort. Little sins not mortified, little bad habits of temper or of tongue not corrected, little compliances with the world,—are all likely to offend the Holy Ghost. Oh, that believers would remember this! There is far more of "heaven on earth" to be enjoyed than many of them attain to: and why do they not attain to it? They do not watch sufficiently over their daily ways,—and so the Spirit's work is damped and hindered. The Spirit must be a thoroughly sanctifying Spirit if He is to be a comforter to your soul.

If you have the Spirit, labour to bring forth *all* " the fruits of the Spirit." (Gal. v. 22.) Read over the list which the Apostle has drawn out, and see that no one of these fruits is neglected. Oh, that believers would seek for more " love," and more " joy!" Then would they do more good to all men; then would they feel happier themselves; then would they make religion more beautiful in the eyes of the world !

I commend the things that I have written to the serious attention of every reader of these pages. Let them not have been written in vain. Join with me in praying that the Spirit may be poured out from on high with more abundant influence than He has ever been yet. Pray that He may be poured out on all believers, at home and abroad, that they may be more united and more holy. Pray that He may be poured out on Jews, Mahometans, and Heathen, that many of them may be converted.

Pray that He may be poured out on Roman Catholics, and especially in Italy and Ireland. Pray that He may be poured out on your own country, and that it may be spared the judgments it deserves. Pray that He may be poured out on all faithful ministers and missionaries, and that their numbers may be increased an hundredfold.

Pray, above all, that He may be poured out, in abundant power, on your own soul, that if you know not the truth, you may be taught to know it,—and that if you know it, you may know it better.

XII

CONVERSION.

"Repent ye therefore, and be converted."—Acts iii. 19.

THE subject which forms the title of this paper is one which touches all mankind. It ought to come home to all ranks and classes, high or low, rich or poor, old or young, gentle or simple. Any one may get to heaven without money, rank, or learning. No one, however wise, wealthy, noble, or beautiful, will ever get to heaven without CONVERSION.

There are six points of view in which I wish to consider the subject of this paper. I will try to show that Conversion is—

I. *A Scriptural thing,*

II. *A real thing,*

III. *A necessary thing,*

IV. *A possible thing,*

V. *A happy thing,*

VI. *A thing that may be seen.*

I. Let me show, in the first place, that conversion is *a Scriptural thing.*

I mean by this, that conversion is a thing plainly

mentioned in the Bible. This is the first point we have to ascertain about anything in religion. It matters nothing who says a thing, and declares it to be religious truth; it matters nothing whether we like or dislike a doctrine. Is it in the Bible? *That* is the only question. If it is, we have no right to refuse it. If we reject a Bible truth because we do not like it, we do so at the peril of our souls, and might as well become infidels at once. This is a principle which ought never to be forgotten.

Let us turn to the Bible. Hear what David says: "The law of the Lord is perfect, converting the soul."—"Sinners shall be converted unto Thee." (Psalm xix. 7; li. 13.) Hear what our Lord Jesus Christ says: "Except ye be converted, and become as little children, ye shall not enter into the kingdom of heaven." (Matt. xviii. 3.) Hear what St. Peter says: "Repent ye, and be converted, that your sins may be blotted out." (Acts iii. 19.) Hear what St. James says: "He which converteth the sinner from the error of his way shall save a soul from death, and shall hide a multitude of sins." (James v. 20.)

I could easily add to this Scriptural evidence. I could quote many passages in which the *idea* of conversion is contained, though the *word* itself is not used. To be renewed,—to be transformed,—to be created anew,—to be raised from the dead,—to be illuminated,—to pass from death to life,—to be born again,—to put off the old man and put on the new man,—all these are Scriptural expressions, which mean the same thing as conversion. They are all the same thing, seen from a different point of view. But enough is as good as a feast, in these matters. There can be no doubt of the truth of my first position,—that conversion is a Scriptural thing. It is not a mere device of man's invention: it is in the Bible.

You may tell me, perhaps, that you do not care for "texts." You may say that you are not accustomed to make single texts decide questions in your religion. If this is your case, I am sorry for you. Our Lord Jesus Christ and His apostles used to quote single texts frequently, and to make everything in their arguments hinge upon them. One plain text with them was sufficient to settle a point. Is it not a serious matter, that while the Lord Jesus and His apostles made such use of single texts, you do not care for them?

I entreat every reader of these pages to beware of ignorant prejudices on religious subjects. I have known people to find fault with doctrines and opinions as enthusiastic, fanatical, and absurd, in perfect ignorance that they were finding fault with Scripture itself! They have given sad proof that they spoke of things which they did not understand, and that they knew nothing, comparatively, of the contents of the Bible. It is recorded that, in Somersetshire, one hundred years ago, a great preacher was summoned before the magistrates for swearing in the pulpit. He had used in his sermon the well-known text, "He that believeth not shall be damned" (Mark xvi. 16); and the constable who laid the information was so ignorant that he did not know the preacher was quoting God's Word!—I myself remember a lady of rank being very indignant, because a speaker at a Missionary meeting described the heathen as "having no hope." And yet the speaker had only used the very expression used by St. Paul, in describing the state of the Ephesians before the Gospel came to them! (Ephes. ii. 12.) Beware of making a like mistake. Take care that you do not expose your own ignorance by talking against conversion. Search the Scriptures. CONVERSION IS A SCRIPTURAL THING.

II. Let me show, in the second place, that *conversion is a real thing*.

I feel it very needful to say something about this point. We live in an age of shams, cheats, deceptions, and impositions. It is an age of white-wash, varnish, lacquer, and veneer. It is an age of plaster, compo, plating, gilding, and electrotyping. It is an age of adulterated food, paste diamonds, false weights and measures, unsound timber, and shoddy clothing. It is an age of wind-bags, and whitened sepulchres, and cymbals in religion. I can hardly wonder that many regard all Christian professors as suspicious characters, if not hypocrites, and deny the reality of any such thing as conversion.

Still, notwithstanding all that such people may say, I assert confidently, that there is such a thing as conversion. There are to be seen among men, every here and there, unmistakable cases of a complete turning round of heart, character, tastes, and life,—cases which deserve no other name than that of *conversion*. I say that when a man turns right round from sin to God,—from worldliness to holiness,—from self-righteousness to self-distrust,—from carelessness about religion to deep repentance,—from unbelief to faith,—from indifference to Christ to strong love to Christ,—from neglect of prayer, the Bible, and the Sabbath, to a diligent use of all means of grace,—I say boldly, that such a man is a *converted* man. When a man's heart is turned upside down in the way I have described, so that he loves what he once hated, and hates what he once loved, I say boldly, that it is a case of *conversion*. To deny it, is mere obstinacy and affectation. Such a change can be described in no other way. By far the most suitable name that can be given to it is the Scriptural name,—conversion.

Of such changes the Bible gives many unmistakable patterns. Let any one read attentively the histories of Manasseh king of Judah, of Matthew the apostle, of the woman of Samaria, of Zacchæus the publican, of Mary Magdalene, of Saul of Tarsus, of the Philippian jailer, of Lydia the purple seller, of the Jews to whom Peter preached on the day of Pentecost, of the Corinthians to whom St. Paul preached. (2 Chron. xxxiii. 1—19. Matt. ix. 9. John iv. 1—29. Luke xix. 1—10; viii. 2. Acts ix. 1—22; xvi. 14—34; ii. 37—41. 1 Cor. vi. 9—11.) In every one of these cases there was a mighty change. What can that change be called but *conversion?*

Of such changes the history of the Church in every age can supply many well-known examples. Let any one study the life of Augustine, of Martin Luther, of Hugh Latimer, of John Bunyan, of Colonel Gardiner, of John Newton, of Thomas Scott. In every one of these lives he will find a description of a mighty turning of heart, opinion, and conduct, towards God. What can that turning be called better than *conversion?*

Of such changes every man's own neighbourhood and circle of acquaintances will furnish many specimens. Let any honest-minded person of observation look around him, and consider what I assert. Let him deny, if he can, that he can put his finger on men and women of his own age and standing, who are now utterly unlike what they once were in the matter of religion. About their own souls, and the importance of being saved,—about sin, and God, and Christ, and repentance, and faith, and holiness,—about Bible-reading, and praying, and Sabbath-keeping—about all these things they are completely changed. I challenge any sensible man to deny that he knows such persons. They are to be met with here and there in every part of the kingdom. Once more I ask, what can such changes be called but *conversions?*

I feel almost ashamed to dwell so long on this point. It seems like spending time in proving that two and two make four, or that the sun rises in the east. But, alas, there are too many people who will allow nothing, and will dispute everything, in religion! They know that they are not yet converted themselves, and they therefore try hard to make out that nobody was ever converted at all! I trust I have given a sufficient answer to all such persons. I have shown you that CONVERSION IS A REAL TRUE THING.

III. Let me show, in the third place, that *conversion is a necessary thing.*

This is a point of great importance. Some worthy people are ready enough to admit that conversion is a Scriptural truth and a reality, but not a thing which needs to be pressed on most English people. The heathen, they grant, need conversion. Even the thieves, and fallen characters, and inmates of jails, they allow, may require conversion. But to talk of conversion being necessary for Church-going people, is to talk of things which they cannot see at all. "Such people may, in some cases, need a little stirring up and amendment. They may not be quite as good as they ought to be: it would be better if they attended more to religion; but you have no right to say they need conversion! It is uncharitable, harsh, narrow-minded, bitter, wrong, to tell them they require conversion!"

This sadly common notion is a complete delusion. It is a pure invention of man's, without a scrap of foundation in God's Word. The Bible teaches expressly that the change of heart, called *conversion*, is a thing absolutely needed by every one. It is needed because of the total corruption of human nature. It is needed because of the condition of every man's natural heart. All people born into the world, of every rank and nation, must have their hearts changed between the cradle and the grave, before they can go to heaven. All, all men, without exception, must be converted.

Without conversion of heart we *cannot serve God on earth.* We have naturally neither faith, nor fear, nor love, toward God and His Son Jesus Christ. We have no delight in His Word. We take no pleasure in prayer or communion with Him. We have no enjoyment in His ordinances, His house, His people, or His day. We may have a form of Christianity, and keep up a round of ceremonies and religious performances. But without conversion we have no more heart in our religion than a brick or a stone. Can a dead corpse serve God? We know it cannot. Well, without conversion we are *dead* toward God.

Look round the congregation with which you worship every Sunday. Mark how little interest the great majority of them take in what is going on. Observe how listless, and apathetic, and indifferent, they evidently are about the whole affair. It is clear their hearts are not there! They are thinking of something else, and not of religion. They are thinking of business, or money, or pleasure, or worldly plans, or bonnets, or gowns, or new dresses, or amusements. Their bodies are there, but not their hearts. —And what is the reason? What is it they all need? They need conversion. Without it they only come to church for fashion and form's sake, and go away from church to serve the world or their sins.

But this is not all. Without conversion of heart *we could not enjoy heaven*, if we got there. Heaven is a place where holiness reigns supreme, and sin and the world have no place at all. The company will all be holy; the employments will all be holy; it will be an eternal Sabbath-day. Surely if we go to heaven, we must have a heart in tune and able to enjoy it, or else we shall not be happy. We must have a nature in harmony with the element we live in, and the place where we dwell. Can a fish be happy out of water? We know it cannot. Well, without conversion of heart we could not be happy in heaven.

Look round the neighbourhood in which you live, and the persons with whom you are acquainted. Think what many of them would do if they were cut off for ever from money, and business, and newspapers, and cards, and balls, and races, and hunting, and shooting, and worldly amusements! Would they like it?—Think what they would feel if they were shut up for ever with Jesus Christ, and saints, and angels! Would they be happy?—Would the eternal company of Moses, and David, and St. Paul, be pleasant to those who never take the trouble to read what those holy men wrote? Would heaven's everlasting praise suit the taste of those who can hardly spare a few minutes in a week for private religion, even for prayer? There is but one answer to be given to all these questions. We must be *converted* before we can enjoy heaven. Heaven would be no heaven to any child of Adam without conversion.

Let no man deceive us. There are two things which are of absolute necessity to the salvation of every man and woman on earth. One of them is the mediatorial work of Christ *for us*,—His atonement, satisfaction, and intercession. The other is the converting work of the Spirit *in us*,—His guiding, renewing, and sanctifying grace.—We must have both a title and a heart for heaven. Sacraments are only *generally* necessary to salvation: a man may be saved without them, like the penitent thief. An interest in Christ and conversion are *absolutely* necessary: without them no one can possibly be saved.—All, all alike, high or low, rich or poor, old or young, gentle or simple, churchmen or dissenters, baptized or unbaptized, all must be converted or perish. There is no salvation without conversion. IT IS A NECESSARY THING.

IV. Let me now show, in the fourth place, that *conversion is a possible thing.*

I think I know the feelings which come across many people's minds, when they read the things which I am writing in this paper. They take refuge in the idea that such a change as conversion is quite impossible, except for a favoured few. "It is all very well," they argue, "for parsons to talk of conversion; but the thing cannot be done; we have work to mind, families to provide for, business to attend to. It is no use expecting miracles now. We cannot be converted." Such thoughts are very common. The devil loves to put them before us, and our own lazy hearts are only too ready to receive them: but they will not stand examination. I am not afraid to lay it down that conversion is a *possible* thing. If it were not so I would not say another word.

In saying this, however, I should be sorry to be mistaken. I do not for a moment mean that any one can convert himself, change his own heart, take away his own corrupt nature, put in himself a new spirit. I mean nothing of the kind. I should as soon expect the dry bones in Ezekiel's vision to give themselves life. (Ezek. xxxvii. 3.) I only mean that there is nothing in Scripture, nothing in God, nothing in man's condition, which warrants any one in saying, " I can never be converted." There lives not the man or woman on earth of whom it could be said, " their conversion is an impossibility."—Any one, however sinful and hardened, any one may be converted.

Why do I speak so confidently ? How is it that I can look round the world, and see the desperate wickedness that is in it, and yet despair of no living man's soul ? How is it that I can say to any one, however hard, fallen, and bad, " Your case is not hopeless: you, even you, may be converted ? "—I can do it because of the things contained in Christ's Gospel. It is the glory of that Gospel that under it nothing is impossible.

Conversion is a possible thing, because of the almighty *power of our Lord Jesus Christ.* In Him is life. In His hand are the keys of death and hell. He has all power in heaven and earth. He quickeneth whom He will. (John i. 4; Rev. i. 18; Matt. xxviii. 18; John v. 21.) It is as easy to Him to create new hearts out of nothing, as it was to create the world out of nothing. It is as easy to Him to breathe spiritual life into a stony, dead heart, as it was to breathe natural life into the clay of which Adam was formed, and make him a living man. There was nothing He could not do on earth. Wind, sea, disease, death, the devil,—all were obedient to His word. There is nothing that He cannot do in heaven at God's right hand. His hand is as strong as ever: His love is as great as ever. The Lord Jesus Christ lives, and therefore conversion is not impossible.

But beside this, conversion is a possible thing, because of the *almighty power of the Holy Ghost,* whom Christ sends into the hearts of all whom He undertakes to save. The same divine Spirit who co-operated with the Father and Son in the work of creation, co-operates specially in the work of conversion. It is He who conveys life from Christ, the great Fountain of Life, into the hearts of sinners. He who moved on the face of the waters before those wonderful words were spoken, "Let there be light," is He who moves over sinners' souls, and takes their natural darkness away. Great indeed is the invisible power of the Holy Ghost! He can soften that which is hard. He can bend that which is stiff and stubborn. He can give eyes to the spiritually blind, ears to the spiritually deaf, tongues to the spiritually dumb, feet to the spiritually lame, warmth to the spiritually cold, knowledge to the spiritually ignorant, and life to the spiritually dead. "None teacheth like Him!" (Job xxxvi. 22.) He has taught thousands of ignorant sinners, and never failed to make them "wise unto salvation." The Holy Ghost lives, and therefore conversion is never impossible.

What can you say to these things? Away with the idea for ever that conversion is not possible. Cast it behind you: it is a temptation of the devil. Look not at yourself, and your own weak heart;—for then you may well despair. Look upward at Christ, and the Holy Ghost, and learn that with them nothing is impossible. Yes! the age of spiritual miracles is not yet past! Dead souls in our congregations can yet be raised; blind eyes can yet be made to see; dumb prayerless tongues can yet be taught to pray. No one ought ever to despair. When Christ has left heaven, and laid down His office as the Saviour of sinners,—when the Holy Ghost has ceased to dwell in hearts, and is no longer God,—then, and not till then, men and women may say, "We cannot be converted." Till then, I say boldly, conversion is a possible thing. If men are not converted, it is because they will not come to Christ for life." (John v. 40.) CONVERSION IS POSSIBLE.

V. Let me show, in the fifth place, that *conversion is a happy thing.*

I shall have written in vain if I leave this point untouched. There are thousands, I firmly believe, who are ready to admit the truth of all I have said hitherto. Scriptural, real, necessary, possible,—all this they willingly allow conversion to be. "Of course," they say, "we know it is all true. People ought to be converted." But will it increase a man's happiness to be converted? Will it add to a man's joys, and lessen his sorrows, to be converted? Here alas, is a point at which many stick fast. They have a secret, lurking fear, that if they are converted they must become melancholy, miserable, and low-spirited. Conversion and a sour face,—conversion and a gloomy brow,—conversion and an ill-natured readiness to snub young people, and put down all mirth, —conversion and a sorrowful countenance,—conversion and sighing and groaning,—all these are things which they seem to think must go together! No wonder that such people shrink from the idea of conversion!

The notion I have just described is very common and very mischievous. I desire to protest against it with all my heart, and soul, and mind, and strength. I assert without hesitation, that the conversion described in

Scripture is a happy thing and not a miserable one, and that if converted persons are not happy, the fault must be in themselves. The happiness of a true Christian, no doubt, is not quite of the same sort as that of a worldly man. It is a calm, solid, deep flowing, substantial joy. It is not made up of excitement, levity, and boisterous spasmodic mirth. It is the sober, quiet joy of one who does not forget death, judgment, eternity, and a world to come, even in his chief mirth. But in the main I am confident the converted man is the happiest man.

What says the Scripture? How does it describe the feelings and experience of persons who have been converted? Does it give any countenance to the idea that conversion is a sorrowful and melancholy thing? Let us hear what Levi felt, when he had left the receipt of custom to follow Christ. We read that "he made a great feast in his own house," as if it was an occasion of gladness. (Luke v. 29.) Let us hear what Zacchæus the publican felt, when Jesus offered to come to his house. We read that "he received Him joyfully." (Luke xix. 6.) Let us hear what the Samaritans felt, when they were converted through Philip's preaching. We read that "there was great joy in that city." (Acts viii. 8.) Let us hear what the Ethiopian eunuch felt in the day of his conversion. We read that "he went on his way rejoicing." (Acts viii. 39.) Let us hear what the Philippian jailer felt in the hour of his conversion. We read that "he rejoiced, believing in God with all his house." (Acts xvi. 34.) In fact the testimony of Scripture on this subject is always one and the same. Conversion is always described as the cause of joy and not of sorrow, of happiness and not of misery.

The plain truth, is that people speak ill of conversion because they know nothing really about it. They run down converted men and women as unhappy, because they judge them by their outward appearance of calmness, gravity, and quietness, and know nothing of their inward peace. They forget that it is not those who boast most of their own performances who do most, and it is not those who talk most of their happiness who are in reality the happiest people.

A converted man is happy, because he has peace with God. His sins are forgiven; his conscience is free from the sense of guilt: he can look forward to death, judgment, and eternity, and not feel afraid. What an immense blessing to feel *forgiven and free !*—He is happy because he finds order in his heart. His passions are controlled, his affections are rightly directed. Everything in his inner man, however weak and feeble, is in its right place, and not in confusion. What an immense blessing *order* is !—He is happy, because he feels independent of circumstances. Come what will, he is provided for: sickness, and losses, and death, can never touch his treasure in heaven, or rob him of Christ. What a blessing to feel *independent !*— He is happy, because he feels ready. Whatever happens he is somewhat prepared: the great business is settled; the great concern of life is arranged. What a blessing to feel *ready !*—These are indeed true springs of happiness. They are springs which are utterly shut up and sealed to an unconverted man.—Without forgiveness of sins, without hope for the world to come, dependent on this world for comfort, unprepared to meet God, he cannot be really happy. Conversion is an essential part of true happiness.

Settle it in your mind to-day that the friend who labours for your conversion to God is the best friend that you have. He is a friend not merely for the life to come, but for the life that now is. He is a friend to your present comfort as well as to your future deliverance from hell. He is a friend for time as well as for eternity. CONVERSION IS A HAPPY THING.

VI. Let me now show you, in the last place, that *conversion is a thing that may be seen.*

This is a part of my subject which ought never to be overlooked. Well would it be for the Church and the world, if in every age it had received more attention. Thousands have turned away in disgust from religion, because of the wickedness of many who profess it. Hundreds have caused the very name of conversion to stink, by the lives they have lived after declaring themselves converted. They have fancied that a few spasmodic sensations and convictions were the true grace of God. They have imagined themselves converted, because their animal feelings were excited. They have called themselves "converts" without the slightest right or title to that honoured name. All this has done immense harm, and it is doing peculiar harm in the present day. The times demand a very clear assertion of the great principle, that true conversion is a thing that can always be seen.

I admit fully that the manner of the Spirit's working is invisible. It is like the wind. It is like the attractive power of the magnet. It is like the influence of the moon upon the tides. There is something about it far beyond the reach of man's eyes or understanding.—But while I admit this decidedly, I maintain no less decidedly that the effects of the Spirit's work in conversion will always be seen. Those effects may be weak and feeble at first: to the natural man they may hardly be visible, and not understood. But effects there always will be: some fruit will always be seen where there is true conversion. Where no effect can be seen, there you may be sure there is no grace. Where no visible fruit can be found, there you may be sure is no conversion.

Does any one ask me what we may expect to see in a true conversion? I reply, There will always be something seen in a converted man's character, and feelings, and conduct, and opinions, and daily life. You will not see in him perfection; but you will see in him something peculiar, distinct, and different from other people. You will see him hating sin, loving Christ, following after holiness, taking pleasure in his Bible, persevering in prayer. You will see him penitent, humble, believing, temperate, charitable, truthful, good-tempered, patient, upright, honourable, kind. These, at any rate, will be his aims : these are the things which he will follow after, however short he may come of perfection. In some converted persons you will see these things more distinctly, in others less. This only I say, wherever there is conversion, something of this kind will be seen.

I care nothing for a conversion which has neither marks nor evidences to show. I shall always say, "Give me some marks if I am to think you are converted. Show me thy conversion without any marks, if thou canst! I do not believe in it. It is worth nothing at all."—You may call such doctrine legal if you please. It is far better to be *called* legal than to *be* an Antinomian. Never, never, will I allow that the blessed Spirit can be in a man's heart, when no fruit of the Spirit can be seen in his life. A conversion which allows a man to live in sin, to lie, and drink, and swear, is not the conversion of the Bible. It is a counterfeit conversion, which can only please the devil, and will lead the man who is satisfied with it, not to heaven, but to hell.

Let this last point sink down into your heart and never be forgotten. Conversion is not only a Scriptural thing, a real thing, a necessary thing, a possible thing, and a happy thing : there remains one more grand characteristic about it,—it is A THING THAT WILL ALWAYS BE SEEN.

And now let me wind up this paper by a few plain appeals to the consciences of all who read it. I have tried to the best of my power to unfold and explain the nature of conversion. I have endeavoured to set it forth in every point of view. Nothing remains but to try to bring it home to the heart of every one into whose hands this book may fall.

(1) First of all, I urge every reader of this paper to *find out whether he is converted.* I am not asking about other people. The heathen no doubt need conversion. The unhappy inmates of jails and reformatories need conversion. There may be people living near your own house who are open sinners and unbelievers, and need conversion. But all this is beside the question. I ask, Are you converted yourself?

Are you converted? It is no reply to tell me that many people are hypocrites and false professors. It is no argument to say that there are many sham revivals, and mock conversions. All this may be very true: but the abuse of a thing does not destroy the use of it. The circulation of bad money is no reason why there should not be good coin. Whatever others may be, Are you converted yourself?

Are you converted? It is no answer to tell me that you go to church or chapel, and have been baptized and admitted to the Table of the Lord. All this proves little: I could say as much for Judas Iscariot, Demas, Simon Magus, Ananias, and Sapphira. The question is still not answered. Is your heart changed? Are you really converted to God?

(2) In the next place, I urge every reader of this book who is not converted, *never to rest till he is.* Make haste: awake to know your danger. Escape for your life: flee from the wrath to come. Time is short: eternity is near. Life is uncertain: judgment is sure. Arise and call upon God. The throne of grace is yet standing: the Lord Jesus Christ is yet waiting to be gracious. The promises of the Gospel are wide, broad, full, and free: lay hold upon them this day. Repent, and believe the Gospel: repent, and be converted. Rest not, rest not, rest not, till you know and feel that you are a converted man.

(3) In the last place, I offer a *word of exhortation* to every reader who has reason to think that he has gone through that blessed change of which I have been speaking in this paper. You can remember the time when you were not what you are now. You can remember a time in your life when old things passed away, and all things became new. To you also I have something to say. Suffer the word of friendly counsel, and lay it to heart.

(*a*) Do you think that you are converted ? Then give all diligence to make your calling and conversion sure. Leave nothing uncertain that concerns your immortal soul. Labour to have the witness of the Spirit with your spirit, that you are a child of God. Assurance is to be had in this world, and assurance is worth the seeking. It is good to have hope : it is far better to feel sure.

(*b*) Do you think that you are converted ? Then do not expect impossibilities in this world. Do not suppose the day will ever come when you will find no weak point in your heart, no wanderings in private prayer, no distraction in Bible-reading, no cold desires in the public worship of God, no flesh to mortify, no devil to tempt, no worldly snares to make you fall. Expect nothing of the kind. Conversion is not perfection ! Conversion is not heaven ! The old man within you is yet alive ; the world around you is yet full of danger ; the devil is not dead. Remember at your best, that a converted sinner is still a poor weak sinner, needing Christ every day. Remember this, and you will not be disappointed.

(*c*) Do you think that you are converted ? Then labour and desire to grow in grace every year that you live. Look not to the things behind ; be not content with old experience, old grace, old attainments in religion. Desire the sincere milk of the Word, that you may grow thereby. (1 Pet. ii. 2.) Entreat the Lord to carry on the work of conversion more and more in your soul, and to deepen spiritual impressions within you. Read your Bible more carefully every year: watch over your prayers more jealously every year. Beware of becoming sleepy and lazy in your religion. There is a vast difference between the lowest and the highest forms in the school of Christ. Strive to get on in knowledge, faith, hope, charity, and patience. Let your yearly motto be, "Onward, Forward, Upward!" to the last hour of your life.

(d) Do you think you are converted? Then show the value you place on conversion by your diligence in trying to do good to others.—Do you really believe it is an awful thing to be an unconverted man? Do you really think that conversion is an unspeakable blessing? Then prove it, prove it, prove it, by constant zealous efforts to promote the conversion of others. Look round the neighbourhood in which you live: have compassion on the multitudes who are yet unconverted. Be not content with getting them to come to your church or chapel; aim at nothing less than their entire conversion to God. Speak to them, read to them, pray for them, stir up others to help them. But never, never, if you are a converted man, never be content to go to heaven alone!

XIII.

THE HEART.

"Give Me thine heart."—Prov. xxiii. 26.
"Thy heart is not right in the sight of God."—Acts viii. 21.

THE heart is the main thing in religion. I make no excuse for asking the special attention of my readers, while I try to say a few things about the heart.

The *head* is not the principal thing. You may know the whole truth as it is in Jesus, and consent that it is good. You may be clear, correct, and sound in your religious opinions. But all this time you may be walking in the broad way which leadeth to destruction. It is your heart which is the main point. "Is thy heart right in the sight of God?"

Your *outward life* may be moral, decent, respectable, in the eyes of men. Your minister, and friends, and neighbours, may see nothing very wrong in your general conduct. But all this time you may be hanging on the brink of everlasting ruin. It is your heart which is the main thing. Is that heart right in the sight of God?

Wishes and desires are not enough to make a Christian. You may have many good feelings about your soul. You may, like Balaam, long to "die the death of the righteous." (Num. xxiii. 10.) You may sometimes tremble at the thought of judgment to come, or be melted to tears by the tidings of Christ's love. But all this time you may be slowly drifting downward into hell. It is your heart which is the main thing. Is that heart right in the sight of God?

There are three things which I propose to do in order to impress the subject of this paper upon your mind.

I. First, I will show you *the immense importance of the heart in religion.*

II. Secondly, I will show you *the heart that is wrong in the sight of God.*

III. Lastly, I will show you *the heart that is right.*

May God bless the whole subject to the soul of every one into whose hands this book may fall! May the Holy Ghost, without whom all preaching and writing can do nothing, apply this paper to many consciences, and make it an arrow to pierce many hearts!

I. In the first place, I will show *the immense importance of the heart in religion.*

How shall I prove this point? From whence shall I fetch my arguments?—I must turn to the Word of God. In questions of this kind it matters nothing what the world thinks right or wrong. There is only one sure test of truth. What saith the Scripture? What is written in the Bible? What is the mind of the Holy Ghost?—If we cannot submit our judgments to this infallible umpire, it is useless to pretend that we have any religion at all.

For one thing, the Bible teaches that the heart is that part of us on which the state of our soul depends. "Out of it are the issues of life." (Prov. iv. 23.) The reason, the understanding, the conscience, the affections, are all second in importance to the heart. *The heart is the man.* It is the seat of all spiritual life, and health, and strength, and growth. It is the hinge and turning-point in the condition of man's soul. If the heart is alive to God and quickened by the Spirit, the man is a living Christian. If the heart is dead and has not the Spirit, the man is dead before God. The heart is the man! Tell me not merely what a man says and professes, and where a man goes on Sunday, and what money he puts in the collecting-plate. Tell me rather what his heart is, and I will tell you what he is. "As a man thinketh in his heart, so is he." (Prov. xxiii. 7.)

For another thing, the Bible teaches that the heart is that part of us at which God especially looks. "Man looketh at the outward appearance, but the Lord looketh on the heart." (1 Sam. xvi. 7.) "Every way of man is right in his own eyes: but the Lord pondereth the heart." (Proverbs xxi. 2.) Man is naturally content with the outward part of religion, with outward morality, outward correctness, outward regular attendance on means of grace. But the eyes of the Lord look much further. He regards our motives. He "weigheth the spirits." (Prov. xvi. 2.) He says Himself, "I the Lord search the heart, I try the reins." (Jer. xvii. 10.)

For another thing, the Bible teaches that the heart is the first and foremost thing which God asks man to give him. "My son," He says, "give Me thine heart." (Prov. xxiii. 26.) We may give God a bowed head and a serious face, our bodily presence in His house, and a loud amen. But until we give God our hearts, we give Him nothing of any value.—The sacrifices of the Jews in Isaiah's time were many and costly. They drew nigh to God with their mouth, and honoured Him with their lips. But they were all wholly useless, because the heart of the worshippers was far from God. (Matt. xv. 8.) The zeal of Jehu against idolatry was very great, and his services in pulling down idols brought him many temporal rewards. But there was one great blot on his character which spoiled all. He did not walk in the law of God "with all his heart." (2

Kings x. 31.) The heart is what the husband desires to have in his wife, the parent in his child, and the master in his servant. And the heart is what God desires to have in professing Christians.

What is the heart in man's *body?* It is the principal and most important organ in the whole frame. A man may live many years in spite of fevers, wounds, and loss of limbs. But a man cannot live if you injure his heart. Just so it is with the heart in religion. It is the fountain of life to the soul.

What is the root to the *tree?* It is the source of all life, and growth, and fruitfulness. You may cut off the branches, and wound the trunk, and the tree may yet survive. But if you hurt the root the tree will die. Just so it is with the heart in religion. It is the root of life to the soul.

What is the mainspring to the *watch?* It is the cause of all its movements, and the secret of all its usefulness. The case may be costly and beautiful. The face and figures may be skilfully made. But if there is anything wrong with the mainspring the works will not go. Just so it is with the heart in religion. It is the mainspring of life to the soul.

What is the fire to the *steam engine?* It is the cause of all its motion and power. The machinery may be properly made. Every screw, and valve, and joint, and crank, and rod may be in its right place. But if the furnace is cold and the water is not turned into steam, the engine will do nothing. Just so is it with the heart in religion. Unless the heart is lighted with fire from on high, the soul will not move.

Would you know the reason why such multitudes around you take no interest in religion? They have no real concern about God, or Christ, or the Bible, or heaven, or hell, or judgment, or eternity. They care for nothing but what they shall eat, or what they shall drink, or what they shall put on, or what money they can get, or what pleasure they can have. *It is their heart which is in fault!* They have not the least appetite for the things of God. They are destitute of any taste or inclination for spiritual things. They need a new mainspring. They want a new heart. "Wherefore is there a price in the hand of a fool to get wisdom, seeing he hath no heart unto it." (Prov. xvii. 16.)

Would you know the reason why so many hear the Gospel year after year, and yet remain unmoved by it? Their minds seem like Bunyan's "slough of despond." Cartloads of good instruction are poured into them without producing any good effect. Their reason is convinced. Their head assents to the truth. Their conscience is sometimes pricked. Their feelings are sometimes roused. Why then do they stick fast? Why do they tarry? *It is their hearts which are in fault!* Some secret idol chains them down to the earth, and keeps them tied hand and foot, so that they cannot move. They want a new heart. Their picture is drawn faithfully by Ezekiel: "They sit before thee as my people, and they hear thy words, but they will not do them: for with their mouth they show much love, but their heart goeth after their covetousness." (Ezek. xxxiii. 31.)

Would you know the reason why thousands of so-called Christians will be lost at last, and perish miserably in hell? They will not be able to say that God did not offer salvation to them. They will not be able to plead that Christ did not send them invitations. Oh no! They will be obliged to confess that "all things were ready" for them, except their own hearts. Their own hearts will prove to have been the cause of their ruin! The life-boat was alongside the wreck, but they would not enter it. Christ "would" have gathered them, but they "would not" be gathered. (Matt. xxiii. 37.) Christ would have saved them, but they would not be saved. "They loved darkness more than light." Their hearts were in fault. "They *would* not come to Christ, that they might have life." (John iii. 19; v. 40.)

I leave this branch of my subject. I trust I have said enough to show you the immense importance of the heart in religion. Surely I have good reason for pressing the subject of this paper on your notice.—Is thy heart right? Is it right in the sight of God?

II. I will now show you, in the second place, *the heart that is wrong in the sight of God.* There are only two sorts of hearts, a right one and a wrong one. What is a wrong heart like?

The wrong heart is the natural heart with which we are all born. There are no hearts which are right by nature. There are no such things as naturally "good hearts," whatever some ignorant people may please to say about "having a good heart at the bottom." Ever since Adam and Eve fell, and sin entered into the world, men and women are born with an inclination to evil. Every natural heart is wrong. If your heart has never been changed by the Holy Ghost since you were born, know this day, that your heart is wrong.

What does the Scripture say about the natural heart? It says many things which are deeply solemn, and painfully true. It says that "the heart is deceitful above all things, and desperately wicked." (Jer. xvii. 9.) It says that "every imagination of the thoughts of the heart is only evil continually." (Gen. vi. 5.) It says that "the heart of the sons of men is full of evil." (Eccles. ix. 3.) It says that "From within, out of the heart of man," as out of a fountain, "proceed evil thoughts, adulteries, fornications, murders, thefts, covetousness, wickedness, deceit, lasciviousness, an evil eye, blasphemy, pride, foolishness. All these evil things come from within." (Mark vii. 21.) Truly this is a humbling picture! The seeds of these things are in the heart of every one born into the world. Surely I may well tell you that the natural heart is wrong.

But is there no one common mark of the wrong heart, which is to be seen in all whom God has not changed? Yes! there is; and to that common mark of the wrong heart I now request your attention. There is a most striking and instructive figure of speech, which the Holy Ghost has thought fit to use, in describing the natural heart. He calls it a "stony heart." (Ezek. **xi.** 19.) I know no emblem in the Bible so full of instruction, and so apt and fitting as this one. A truer word was never written than that which calls the natural heart a heart of stone. Mark well what I am going to say; and may the Lord give you understanding!

(a) A stone is *hard*. All people know that. It is un-yielding, unbending, unimpressible. It may be broken, but it will never bend. The proverb is world-wide, " as hard as a stone." Look at the granite rocks which line the coast of Cornwall. For four thousand years the waves of the Atlantic Ocean have dashed against them in vain. There they stand in their old hardness, unbroken and unmoved. It is just the same with the natural heart. Afflictions, mercies, losses, crosses, sermons, counsels, books, tracts, speaking, writing,—all, all are unable to soften it. Until the day that God comes down to change it, it remains unmoved. Well may the natural heart be called a heart of stone!

(b) A stone is *cold*. There is a chilly, icy feeling about it, which you know the moment you touch it. It is utterly unlike the feeling of flesh, or wood, or even earth. The proverb is in every one's mouth, "As cold as a stone." The old marble statues in many a cathedral church have heard the substance of thousands of sermons. Yet they never show any feeling. Not a muscle of their marble faces ever shrinks or moves. It is just the same with the natural heart. It is utterly destitute of spiritual feeling. It cares less for the story of Christ's death on the cross, than it does for the last new novel, or the last debate in Parliament, or the account of a railway accident, or a shipwreck, or an execution. Until God sends fire from heaven to warm it, the natural heart of man has no feeling about religion. Well may it be called a heart of stone!

(c) A stone is *barren*. You will reap no harvest off rocks of any description. You will never fill your barns with corn from the top of Snowdon or Ben Nevis. You will never reap wheat on granite or slate,—on lime-stone or trap-stone,—on oolite or sandstone,—on flint or on chalk. You may get good crops on Norfolk sands, or Cambridge-shire fens, or Suffolk clay, by patience, labour, money, and good farming. But you will never get a crop worth a farthing off a stone. It is just the same with the natural heart. It is utterly barren of penitence, or faith, or love, or fear, or holiness, or humility. Until God breaks it up, and puts a new principle in it, it bears no fruit to God's praise. Well may the natural heart be called a heart of stone!

(d) A stone is *dead*. It neither sees, nor hears, nor moves, nor grows. Show it the glories of heaven, and it would not be pleased. Tell it of the fires of hell, and it would not be alarmed. Bid it flee from a roaring lion, or an earthquake, and it would not stir. The Bass Rock and Mount Blanc are just what they were 4000 years ago. They have seen kingdoms rise and fall, and they remain utterly unchanged. They are neither higher, nor broader, nor larger than they were when Noah left the ark. It is just the same with the natural heart. It has not a spark of spiritual life about it. Until God plants the Holy Ghost in it, it is dead and motionless about real religion. Well may the natural heart be called a heart of stone!

The wrong heart is now set before you. Look at it. Think about it. Examine yourself by the light of the picture I have drawn. Perhaps your heart has never yet been changed. Perhaps your heart is still just as it was when you were born. If so, remember this day what I tell you. YOUR HEART IS WRONG IN THE SIGHT OF GOD.

Would you know the reason why it is so difficult to do good in the world? Would you know why so few believe the Gospel, and live like true Christians? The reason is, the hardness of man's natural heart. He neither sees nor knows what is for his good. The wonder, to my mind, is not so much that few are converted, as the miraculous fact that any are converted at all. I am not greatly surprised when I see or hear of unbelief. I remember the natural heart is wrong.

Would you know the reason why the state of men is so desperately helpless, if they die in their sins? Would you know why ministers feel so fearful about every one who is cut off unprepared to meet God? The reason is, the hardness of man's natural heart. What would a man do in heaven, if he got there, with his heart unchanged? By which of the saints would he sit down? What pleasure could he take in God's presence and company! Oh no! it is vain to conceal it. There can be no real hope about a man's condition, if he dies with his heart wrong.

I leave this point here. Once more I press the whole subject of my paper upon your conscience. Surely you must allow it is a very serious one.—Is thy heart right? Is it right in the sight of God?

III. I will now show you, in the last place, *the right heart.* It is a heart of which the Bible contains many pictures. I am going to try to place some of those pictures before you. On a question like this, I want you to observe what God says, rather than what is said by man. Come, now, and see the marks and signs of a right heart.

(*a*) The right heart is a "*new heart.*" (Ezek. xxxvi. 26.) It is not the heart with which a man is born, but another

heart put in him by the Holy Ghost. It is a heart which
has new tastes, new joys, new sorrows, new desires, new
hopes, new fears, new likes, new dislikes. It has new
views about the soul, and sin, and God, and Christ, and
salvation, and the Bible, and prayer, and Sunday, and
heaven, and hell, and the world, and holiness. It is like
a farm with a new and good tenant. "Old things are
passed away. Behold all things are become new." (2 Cor.
v. 17.)

(b) The right heart is a "*broken and contrite heart.*"
(Psalm. li. 17.) It is broken off from pride, self-conceit,
and self-righteousness. Its former high thoughts of self
are cracked, shattered, and shivered to atoms. It thinks
itself guilty, unworthy, and corrupt. Its former stubborn-
ness, heaviness, and insensibility have thawed, disappeared,
and passed away. It no longer thinks lightly of offending
God. It is tender, sensitive, and jealously fearful of
running into sin. (2 Kings xxii. 19.) It is humble, lowly,
and self-abased, and sees in itself no good thing.

(c) A right heart is a heart which *believes on Christ*
alone for salvation, and in which Christ dwells by faith.
(Rom. x. 10; Eph. iii. 17.) It rests all its hopes of
pardon and eternal life on Christ's atonement, Christ's
mediation, and Christ's intercession. It is sprinkled in
Christ's blood from an evil conscience. (Heb. x. 22.) It
turns to Christ as the compass-needle turns to the north.
It looks to Christ for daily peace, mercy, and grace, as
the sun-flower looks to the sun. It feeds on Christ for
its daily sustenance, as Israel fed on the manna in the
wilderness. It sees in Christ a special fitness to supply all
its wants and requirements. It leans on Him, hangs on
Him, builds on Him, cleaves to Him, as its physician,
guardian, husband, and friend.

(d) A right heart is a *purified heart.* (Acts xv. 9; Matt.
v. 8.) It loves holiness, and hates sin. It strives daily to
cleanse itself from all filthiness of flesh and spirit. (2 Cor.

vii. 1.) It abhors that which is evil, and cleaves to that which is good. It delights in the law of God, and has that law engraven on it, that it may not forget it. (Psalm cxix. 11.) It longs to keep the law more perfectly, and takes pleasure in those who love the law. It loves God and man. Its affections are set on things above. It never feels so light and happy as when it is most holy; and it looks forward to heaven with joy, as the place where perfect holiness will at length be attained.

(e) A right heart is a *praying heart*. It has within it "the Spirit of adoption whereby we cry, Abba Father." (Rom. viii. 15.) Its daily feeling is, "Thy face, Lord, will I seek." (Psalm xxvii. 8.) It is drawn by an habitual inclination to speak to God about spiritual things,—weakly, feebly, and imperfectly perhaps, but speak it must. It finds it necessary to pour out itself before God, as before a friend, and to spread before Him all its wants and desires. It tells Him all its secrets. It keeps back nothing from Him. You might as well try to persuade a man to live without breathing, as to persuade the possessor of a right heart to live without praying.

(f) A right heart is a heart that *feels within a conflict*. (Gal. v. 17.) It finds within itself two opposing principles contending one with another for the mastery,—the flesh lusting against the spirit, and the spirit against the flesh. It knows by experience what St. Paul means when he says, "I see a law in my members warring against the law of my mind." (Rom. vii. 23.) The wrong heart knows nothing of this strife. The strong man armed keeps the wrong heart as his palace, and his goods are at peace. (Luke xi. 21.) But when the rightful King takes possession of the heart, a struggle begins which never ends till death. The right heart may be known by its warfare, quite as much as by its peace.

(g) Last, but not least, the right heart is *honest*, and *single*, and *true*. (Luke viii. 15; 1 Chron. xii. 33; Heb. x. 22.)

There is nothing about it of falsehood, hypocrisy, or part-acting. It is not double or divided. It really is what it professes to be, feels what it professes to feel, and believes what it professes to believe. Its faith may be feeble. Its obedience may be very imperfect. But one thing will always distinguish the right heart. Its religion will be real, genuine, thorough, and sincere.

A heart such as that which I have now described, has always been the possession of all true Christians of every name, and nation, and people and tongue. They have differed from one another on many subjects, but they have all been of a "right heart." They have some of them fallen, for a season, like David and Peter, but their hearts have never entirely departed from the Lord. They have often proved themselves to be men and women laden with infirmities, but their hearts have been right in the sight of God. They have understood one another on earth. They have found that their experience was everywhere one and the same. They will understand each other even better in the world to come. All that have had "right hearts" upon earth, will find that they have one heart when they enter heaven.

(1) I wish now in conclusion to offer to every reader of this paper, *a question* to promote self inquiry. I ask you plainly this day, "What is your heart? Is your heart right or wrong?"

I know not who you are into whose hands this paper have fallen. But I do know that self-examination cannot do you any harm. If your heart is right, it will be a comfort to know it. "If our heart condemn us not, then have we confidence towards God." (1 John iii. 21.) But if your heart is wrong, it is high time to find it out, and seek a change. The time is short. The night cometh when no man can work. Say to yourself this very day, "Is my heart right or wrong?"

Think not to say within yourself.—"There is no need for such questions as these. There is no need to make such ado about the heart. I go to church or chapel regularly. I live a respectable life. I hope I shall prove right at last."—Beware of such thoughts, I beseech you; —beware of them if you would ever be saved. You may go to the best church on earth, and hear the best of preachers. You may be the best of churchmen, or the soundest member of a chapel. But all this time, if your heart is not right in the sight of God, you are on the high road to destruction. Settle down to quiet consideration of the question before you. Look it manfully in the face, and do not turn aside. Is your heart right or wrong?

Think not to say within yourself, "No one can know what his heart is. We must hope the best. No one can find out with any certainty the state of his own soul." Beware, I say again;—beware of such thoughts. The thing can be known. The thing can be found out. Deal honestly and fairly with yourself. Set up an assize on the state of your inward man. Summon a jury. Let the Bible preside as judge. Bring up the witnesses. Inquire what your tastes are,—where your affections are placed, —where your treasure is,—what you hate most,—what you love most,—what pleases you most,—what grieves you most. Inquire into all those points impartially, and mark what the answers are. "Where your treasure is there will your heart be also." (Matt. vi. 21.) A tree may always be known by its fruit, and a true Christian may always be discovered by his habits, tastes, and affections. Yes! you may soon find out what your heart is, if you are honest, sincere, and impartial. Is it right or wrong?

Think not to say within yourself, "I quite approve of all you say, and hope to examine the state of my heart some day. But I have no time just at present. I cannot find leisure. I wait for a convenient season." Oh, beware of such thoughts;—again I say beware! Life is uncertain,

and yet you talk of "a convenient season." (Acts xxiv. 25.)
Eternity is close at hand, and yet you talk of putting off
preparation to meet God. Alas, that habit of putting
off is the everlasting ruin of millions of souls! Wretched
man that you are! who shall deliver you from this devil
of putting off? Awake to a sense of duty. Throw off
the chains that pride, and laziness, and love of the world
are weaving round you. Arise and stand upon your feet,
and look steadily at the question before you. Churchman
or dissenter, I ask you this day,—Is your heart right or
wrong?

(2) I wish, in the next place, to offer a *solemn warning*
to all who know their hearts are wrong, but have no
desire to change. I do it with every feeling of kindness
and affection. I have no wish to excite needless fears.
But I know not how to exaggerate the danger of your
condition. I warn you that if your heart is wrong in the
sight of God you are hanging over the brink of hell.
There is but a step between you and everlasting death.

Can you really suppose that any man or woman will
ever enter heaven without a right heart? Do you flatter
yourself that any unconverted person will ever be saved?
Away with such a miserable delusion! Cast it from
you at once and for ever. What saith the Scripture?
"Except a man be born again he cannot see the kingdom
of God."—"Except ye be converted and become as little
children, ye shall in no wise see the kingdom of heaven."
—"Without holiness no man shall see the Lord." (John
iii. 3; Matt. xviii. 3; Heb. xii. 14.) It is not enough to
have our sins pardoned, as many seem to suppose. There
is another thing wanted as well as a pardon, and that
thing is a new heart. We must have the Holy Spirit
to renew us, as well as Christ's blood to wash us. Both
renewing and washing are needful before any one can be
saved.

Can you suppose for a moment, that you would be

happy in heaven, if you entered heaven without a right heart? Away with the miserable delusion! Cast it from you at once and for ever! You must have a "meetness for the inheritance of the saints," before you can enjoy it. (Coloss. i. 12.) Your tastes must be tuned and brought into harmony with those of saints and angels, before you can delight in their company. A sheep is not happy when it is thrown into the water. A fish is not happy when it is cast on dry land. And men and women would not be happy in heaven if they entered heaven without right hearts.

My warning is before you. Harden not your heart against it. Believe it. Act upon it. Turn it to account. Awake and arise to newness of life without delay. One thing is very certain. Whether you hear the warning or not, God will not go back from what He has said. "If we believe not, He abideth faithful: He cannot deny Himself." (2 Tim. ii. 13.)

(3) I wish, thirdly, to offer *counsel* to all who know their hearts are wrong, but desire to have them made right. That counsel is short and simple. I advise you to apply at once to the Lord Jesus Christ, and ask for the gift of the Holy Ghost. Entreat Him, as a lost and ruined sinner, to receive you, and supply the wants of your soul. I know well that you cannot make your own heart right. But I know that the Lord Jesus Christ can. And to the Lord Jesus Christ I entreat you to apply without delay.

If any reader of this paper really wants a right heart, I thank God that I can give him good encouragement. I thank God that I can lift up Christ before you, and say boldly, Look at Christ,—Seek Christ,—Go to Christ. For what did that blessed Lord Jesus come into the world? For what did He give His precious body to be crucified? For what did He die and rise again? For what did He ascend up into heaven, and sit down at the right hand of God? For what did Christ do all this, but to provide complete salvation for poor sinners like you and me,—

salvation from the guilt of sin, and salvation from the power of sin, for all who believe? Oh, yes! Christ is no half Saviour. He has "received gifts for men, even for the rebellious." (Psalm lxviii. 18.) He waits to pour out the Spirit on all who will come to Him. Mercy and grace,—pardon and a new heart,—all this Jesus is ready to apply to you by His Spirit, if you will only come to Him. Then come: come without delay to Christ.

What is there that Christ cannot do? He can *create*. By Him were all things made at the beginning. He called the whole world into being by His command.—He can *quicken*. He raised the dead when He was on earth, and gave back life by a word.—He can *change*. He has turned sickness into health, and weakness into strength,— famine into plenty, storm into calm, and sorrow into joy. —He has wrought thousands of miracles on hearts already. He turned Peter the unlearned fisherman into Peter the Apostle,—Matthew the covetous publican into Matthew the Gospel writer,—Saul the self-righteous Pharisee into Paul the Evangelist of the world. What Christ has done once Christ can do again. Christ and the Holy Ghost are always the same. There is nothing in your heart that the Lord Jesus cannot make right. Only come to Christ.

If you had lived in Palestine, in the days when Jesus was upon earth, you would have sought Christ's help if you had been sick. If you had been crushed down by heart-disease in some back lane of Capernaum, or in some cottage by the blue waters of the sea of Galilee, you would surely have gone to Jesus for a cure. You would have sat by the way-side day after day, waiting for His appearing. You would have sought Him, if He did not happen to come near your dwelling, and never rested till you found Him. Oh, why not do the same this very day for the sickness of your soul? Why not apply at once to the Great Physician in heaven, and ask Him to "take away the stony heart and give you a heart of flesh"?

(Ezek. **xi.** 19.) Once more I invite you. If you want a "right heart," do not waste time in trying to make it right by your own strength. It is far beyond your power to do it. Come to the great Physician of souls. Come at once to Jesus Christ.

(4) I wish, lastly, to offer an *exhortation* to all whose hearts have been made right in the sight of God. I offer it as a word in season to all true Christians. Hear me, I say to every believing brother or sister. I speak especially to you.

Is your heart right? Then be *thankful*. Praise the Lord for His distinguishing mercy, in "calling you out of darkness into His marvellous light." (1 Pet. ii. 9.) Think what you were by nature. Think what has been done for you by free undeserved grace. Your heart may not be all that it ought to be, nor yet all that you hope it will be. But at any rate your heart is not the old hard heart with which you were born. Surely the man whose heart is changed ought to be full of praise.

Is your heart right? Then be *humble and watchful*. You are not yet in heaven, but in the world. You are in the body. The devil is near you, and never sleeps. Oh, keep your heart with all diligence! Watch and pray lest you fall into temptation. Ask Christ Himself to keep your heart for you. Ask Him to dwell in it, and reign in it, and garrison it, and to put down every enemy under His feet. Give the keys of the citadel into the King's own hands, and leave them there. It is a weighty saying of Solomon: "He that trusteth in his own heart is a fool." (Prov. xxviii. 26.)

Is your heart right? Then *be hopeful* about the hearts of other people. Who has made you to differ? Why should not any one in the world be changed, when such an one as you has been made a new creature? Work on. Pray on. Speak on. Write on. Labour to do all the good you can to souls. Never despair of any one being saved so long as he is alive. Surely the man who has been changed by grace ought to feel that there are no desperate cases. There are no hearts which it is impossible for Christ to cure.

Is your heart right? Then *do not expect too much* from it. Do not be surprised to find it weak and wayward, faint and unstable, often ready to doubt and fear. Your redemption is not complete until your Lord and Saviour comes again. Your full salvation remains yet to be revealed. (Luke xxi. 28; 1 Pet. i. 5.) You cannot have two heavens,—a heaven here and a heaven hereafter. Changed, renewed, converted, sanctified, as your heart is, you must never forget that it 'is a man's heart after all, and the heart of a man living in the midst of a wicked world.

Finally, let me entreat all right-hearted readers to look onward and forward to the day of Christ's second coming. A time draws near when Satan shall be bound, and Christ's saints shall be changed,—when sin shall no more vex us, and the sight of sinners shall no more sadden our minds,— when believers shall at length attend on God without distraction, and love Him with a perfect heart. For that day let us wait, and watch, and pray. It cannot be very far off. The night is far spent. The day is at hand. Surely if our hearts are right, we ought often to cry, "Come quickly: come Lord Jesus!"

XIV.

CHRIST'S INVITATION.

" Come unto Me, all ye that labour and are heavy laden, and I
will give you rest."—MATTHEW xi. 28.

THE text which heads this paper is one which deserves to
be written in letters of gold. Few verses of Scripture have
done more good to the souls of men than this old familiar
invitation of our Lord Jesus Christ. Let us examine it
carefully, and see what it contains.

There are four points in the text before us, to which I
am going to ask attention. On each of these I have
somewhat to say.

I. First. Who is the Speaker of this invitation?

II. Secondly. To whom is this invitation addressed?

III. Thirdly. What does the Speaker ask us to do?

IV. Lastly. What does the Speaker offer to give?

I. In the first place, *Who is the Speaker of the invita-*
tion which heads this paper? Who is it that invites so
freely, and offers so largely? Who is it that says to your
conscience this day, "Come: come unto Me"?

We have a right to ask these questions. We live in a
lying world. The earth is full of cheats, shams, deceptions,

impositions and falsehoods. The value of a promissory note depends entirely on the name which is signed at the bottom. When we hear of a mighty Promiser, we have a right to say, Who is this? and what is His name?

The Speaker of the invitation before you is the greatest and best friend that man has ever had. It is the Lord Jesus Christ, the eternal Son of God.

He is One who is *almighty.* He is God the Father's fellow and equal. He is very God of very God. by Him were all things made.—In His hand are all the treasures of wisdom and knowledge.—He has all power in heaven and earth.—In Him all fulness dwells.—He has the keys of death and hell.—He is now the appointed Mediator between God and man: He will one day be the Judge and King of all the earth. When such an One as this speaks, you may safely trust Him. What He promises He is able to perform. (Zech. xiii. 7; John i. 3; Col. ii. 3, Matt. xxviii. 18; Col. i. 19; Rev. i. 18.)

He is One who is *most loving.* He loved us so that He left heaven for our sakes, and laid aside for a season the glory that He had with the Father. He loved us so that He was born of a woman for our sakes, and lived thirty-three years in this sinful world. He loved us so that He undertook to pay our mighty debt to God, and died upon the cross to make atonement for our sins. When such an One as this speaks, He deserves a hearing. When He promises a thing, you need not be afraid to trust Him.

He is One who *knows the heart of man* most thoroughly. He took on Him a body like our own, and was made like man in all things, sin only excepted. He knows by experience what man has to go through. He has tasted poverty, and weariness, and hunger, and thirst, and pain, and temptation. He is acquainted with all our condition upon earth. He has "suffered Himself being tempted." When such an One as this makes an offer, He makes it

with perfect wisdom.   He knows exactly what you and I
need.   (Heb. ii. 18.)

He is One who *never breaks His word.*   He always
fulfils His promises: He never fails to do what He undertakes.   He never disappoints the soul that trusts Him.
Mighty as He is, there is one thing which He cannot do:
it is impossible for Him to lie.   (Heb. vi. 18.)   When such
an One as this makes a promise, you need not doubt that
He will stand to it.   You may depend with confidence on
His word.

You have now heard who sends the invitation which is
before you to-day.   It is the Lord Jesus Christ.   Give
Him the credit due to His name.   Grant Him a full and
impartial hearing.   Believe that a promise from His mouth
deserves your best attention.   See that you refuse not Him
that speaketh.   It is written, " If they escaped not who
refused him that spake on earth, much more shall not we
escape if we refuse Him that speaketh from heaven."
(Heb. xii. 25.)

II.   I will now show you, in the second place, *to whom
the invitation before you is addressed.*

The Lord Jesus Christ addresses " all that labour and
are heavy-laden."   The expression is deeply comforting and
instructive.   It is wide, sweeping, and comprehensive.   It
describes the case of millions in every part of the world.

Where are the labouring and heavy-laden ?   They are
everywhere.   They are a multitude that man can scarcely
number; they are to be found in every climate, and in
every country under the sun.   They live in Europe, in
Asia, in Africa, and in America   They dwell by the banks
of the Seine, as well as the banks of the Thames,—by
the banks of the Mississippi as well as the banks of the
Niger.   They abound under republics as well as under
monarchies,—under liberal governments as well as under
despotism.   Everywhere you will find trouble, care, sorrow,

anxiety, murmuring, discontent, and unrest. What does it mean? What does it all come to? Men are "labouring and heavy-laden."

To what class do the labouring and heavy laden belong? They belong to every class: there is no exception. They are to be found among masters as well as among servants, —among rich as well as among poor,—among kings as well as among subjects,—among learned as well as among ignorant people. In every class you will find trouble, care, sorrow, anxiety, murmuring, discontent, and unrest. What does it mean? What does it all come to? Men are "labouring and heavy-laden."

How shall we explain this? What is the cause of the state of things which I have just tried to describe?—Did God create man at the beginning to be unhappy? Most certainly not — Are human governments to blame because men are not happy? At most to a very slight extent. The fault lies far too deep to be reached by human laws. —There is another cause, a cause which many unhappily refuse to see. THAT CAUSE IS SIN.

Sin and departure from God, are the true reasons why men are everywhere labouring and heavy-laden. Sin is the universal disease which infects the whole earth. Sin brought in thorns and thistles at the beginning, and obliged man to earn his bread by the sweat of his brow. Sin is the reason why the "whole creation groaneth and travaileth in pain," and the "foundations of the earth are out of course." (Rom. viii. 22; Psalm lxxxii. 5.) Sin is the cause of all the burdens which now press down mankind. Most men know it not, and weary themselves in vain to explain the state of things around them. But sin is the great root and foundation of all sorrow, whatever proud man may think. How much men ought to hate sin!

Are you one of those who are labouring and heavy-laden? I think it very likely that you are. I am firmly persuaded that there are thousands of men and women in the world who are inwardly uncomfortable, and yet will not confess it. They feel a burden on their hearts, which they would gladly get rid of; and yet they do not know the way. They have a conviction that all is not right in their inward man, which they never tell to any one. Husbands do not tell it to their wives, and wives do not tell it to their husbands; children do not tell it to their parents, and friends do not tell it to their friends. But the inward burden lies heavily on many hearts! There is far more unhappiness than the world sees. Disguise it as some will, there are multitudes uncomfortable because they know they are not prepared to meet God. And you, who are reading this volume, perhaps are one.

If any reader of this paper is "labouring and heavy-laden," you are the very person to whom the Lord Jesus Christ sends an invitation this day. If you have an aching heart, and a sore conscience,—if you want rest for a weary soul, and know not where to find it,—if you want peace for a guilty heart, and are at a loss which way to turn,—you are the man, you are the woman, to whom Jesus speaks to-day. There is hope for you. I bring you good tidings. "Come unto Me," says the Lord Jesus, "and I will give you rest."

You may tell me this invitation cannot be meant for you, because you are not good enough to be invited by Christ. I answer, that Jesus does not speak to the good, but to the "labouring and heavy-laden." Do you know anything of this feeling? Then you are one to whom He speaks.

You may tell me that the invitation cannot be meant for you, because you are a sinner, and know nothing about religion. I answer, that it matters nothing what you are, or what you have been. Do you at this moment feel "labouring and heavy-laden"? Then you are one to whom Jesus speaks.

You may tell me that you cannot think the invitation is meant for you, because you are not yet converted, and have not got a new heart. I answer, that Christ's invitation is not addressed to the converted, but to the "labouring and heavy-laden." Is this what you feel? Is there any burden on your heart? Then you are one of those to whom Christ speaks.

You may tell me that you have no right to accept this invitation, because you do not know that you are one of God's elect. I answer, that you have no right to put words in Christ's mouth, which He has not used. He does not say, "Come unto Me, all ye that are elect." He addresses all the "labouring and heavy-laden ones," without any exception. Are you one of them? Is there weight within on your soul? This is the only question you have to decide. If you are, you are one of those to whom Christ speaks.

If you are one of the "labouring and heavy-laden" ones, once more I entreat you not to refuse the invitation which I bring you to-day. Do not forsake your own mercies. The harbour of refuge is freely before you: do not turn away from it. The best of friends holds out His hand to you: let not pride, or self-righteousness, or fear of man's ridicule, make you reject His proffered love. Take Him at His word. Say to Him, "Lord Jesus Christ, I am one of those whom Thine invitation suits: I am labouring and heavy-laden. Lord, what wilt Thou have me to do?"

III. I will now show you, in the third place, *what the Lord Jesus Christ asks you to do.* Three words make up the sum and substance of the invitation which He sends you to-day. If you are "labouring and heavy-laden," Jesus says, "Come unto Me."

There is a grand simplicity about the three words now before you. Short and plain as the sentence seems, it contains a mine of deep truth and solid comfort. Weigh

it: look at it: consider it: ponder it well. I believe that
it is one half of saving Christianity to understand what
Jesus means, when He says, "Come unto Me."

Mark well, that the Lord Jesus does not bid the
labouring and heavy-laden "go and work." Those words
would carry no comfort to heavy consciences: it would be
like requiring labour from an exhausted man. No: He
bids them "Come!"—He does not say, "Pay Me what
thou owest." That demand would drive a broken heart
into despair: it would be like claiming a debt from a
ruined bankrupt. No: He says, "Come!"—He does not
say, "Stand still and wait." That command would only
be a mockery: it would be like promising to give medicine
at the end of a week to one at the point of death." No:
He says, "Come!" To-day,—at once,—without any
delay, "Come unto Me."

But, after all, what is meant by *coming* to Christ? It
is an expression often used, but often misunderstood.
Beware that you make no mistake at this point. Here
unhappily, thousands turn aside out of the right course,
and miss the truth. Beware that you do not make shipwreck
at the very mouth of the harbour.

(*a*) Take notice, that coming to Christ means something
more than coming to church and chapel. You may fill
your place regularly at a place of worship, and attend all
outward means of grace, and yet not be saved. All this
is not coming to Christ.

(*b*) Take notice, that coming to Christ is something more
than coming to the Lord's table. You may be a regular
member and communicant; you may never be missing in
the lists of those who eat that bread and drink that wine,
which the Lord commanded to be received, and yet you
may never be saved. All this is not coming to Christ.

(*c*) Take notice, that coming to Christ is something more
than coming to ministers. You may be a constant hearer
of some popular preacher, and a zealous partizan of all his

opinions, and yet nevor be saved. All this is not coming
to Christ.

(d) Take notice, once more, that coming to Christ is
something more than coming to the possession of head-
knowledge about Him. You may know the whole system
of evangelical doctrine, and be able to talk, argue, and
dispute on every jot of it, and yet never be saved. All
this is not coming to Christ.

Coming to Christ is coming to Him with the heart by
simple faith. Believing on Christ is coming to Him, and
coming to Christ is believing on Him. It is that act of
the soul which takes place when a man, feeling his own
sins, and despairing of all other hope, commits himself to
Christ for salvation, ventures on Him, trusts Him, and casts
himself wholly on Him. When a man turns to Christ
empty that he may be filled, sick that he may be healed,
hungry that he may be satisfied, thirsty that he may be
refreshed, needy that he may be enriched, dying that he
may have life, lost that he may be saved, guilty that he
may be pardoned, sin-defiled that he may be cleansed,
confessing that Christ alone can supply his need,—then
he comes to Christ. When he uses Christ as the Jews
used the city of refuge, as the starving Egyptians used
Joseph, as the dying Israelites used the brazen serpent,—
then he comes to Christ. It is the empty soul's venture
on a full Saviour. It is the drowning man's grasp on the
hand held out to help him. It is the sick man's reception
of a healing medicine. This, and nothing more than this,
is coming to Christ.

Let every reader of this paper accept at this point a word
of caution. Beware of mistakes as to this matter of
coming to Christ. Do not stop short in any half-way
house. Do not allow the devil and the world to cheat you
out of eternal life. Do not suppose that you will ever get
any good from Christ, unless you go straight, direct,
thoroughly, and entirely to Christ Himself. Trust not in

a little outward formality: content not yourself with a regular use of outward means. A lantern is an excellent help in a dark night, but it is not home. Means of grace are useful aids, but they are not Christ. Oh, no! Press onward, forward, upward, till you have had personal, busi-ness-like dealings with Christ Himself.

Beware of mistakes as to the manner of coming to Christ. Dismiss from your mind for ever all idea of worthiness, merit, and fitness in yourself. Throw away all notions of goodness, righteousness, and deserts. Think not that you can bring anything to recommend you, or to make you deserving of Christ's notice. You must come to Him as a poor, guilty, undeserving sinner, or you might just as well not come at all. "To him that *worketh not* but *believeth* on Him that justifieth the ungodly, his faith is counted for righteousness." (Rom. iv. 5.) It is the peculiar mark of the faith that justifies and saves, that it brings to Christ nothing but an empty hand.

Last, but not least, let there be no mistake in your mind as to the special character of the man who has come to Christ, and is a true Christian. He is not an angel; he is not a half-angelic being, in whom is no weakness, or blemish, or infirmity: he is nothing of the kind. He is nothing more than a sinner who has found out his sinful-ness, and has learned the blessed secret of living by faith in Christ. What was the glorious company of the apostles and prophets? What was the noble army of martyrs? What were Isaiah, Daniel, Peter, James, John, Paul, Poly-carp, Chrysostom, Augustine, Luther, Ridley, Latimer, Bunyan, Baxter, Whitefield, Venn, Chalmers, Bickersteth, M'Cheyne? What were they all, but sinners who knew and felt their sins, and trusted only in Christ? What were they, but men who accepted the invitation I bring you this day, and came to Christ by faith? By this faith they lived: in this faith they died. In themselves and their doings they saw nothing worth mentioning; but in Christ they saw all that their souls required.

The invitation of Christ is now before you. If you never listened to it before, listen to it to-day. Broad, full, free, wide, simple, tender, kind,—that invitation will leave you without excuse if you refuse to accept it. There are some invitations, perhaps, which it is wiser and better to decline. There is one which ought always to be accepted: that one is before you to-day. Jesus Christ is saying, "Come: come unto Me."

IV. I will now show you, in the last place, *what the Lord Jesus Christ promises to give.* He does not ask the "labouring and heavy-laden" to come to Him for nothing. He holds out gracious inducements: He allures them by sweet offers. "Come unto Me," He says, "and I will give you rest."

Rest is a pleasant thing. Few are the men and women in this weary world who do not know the sweetness of it. The man who has been labouring hard with his hands all the week, working in iron, or brass, or stone, or wood, or clay,—digging, lifting, hammering, cutting,—he knows the comfort of going home on Saturday night, and having one day of rest. The man who has been toiling hard with his head all day,—writing, copying, calculating, composing, scheming, planning,—he knows the comfort of laying aside his papers, and having a little rest. Yes! rest is a pleasant thing.

And rest is one of the principal offers which the Gospel makes to man. "Come to me, says the world, "and I will give you riches and pleasure."—"Come with me," says the devil, "and I will give you greatness, power, and wisdom." —"Come unto Me," says the Lord Jesus Christ, "and I will give you rest."

But what is the nature of that rest which the Lord Jesus promises to give? It is no mere repose of body. A man may have that and yet be miserable. You may place him in a palace, and surround him with every possible comfort. You may give him money in abundance, and every thing that money can buy. You may free him from all care about to-morrow's bodily wants, and take away the need of labouring for a single hour. All this you may do to a man, and yet not give him true rest. Thousands know this only too well by bitter experience. Their hearts are starving in the midst of worldly plenty. Their inward man is sick and weary, while their outward man is clothed in purple and fine linen, and fares sumptuously every day! Yes: a man may have houses, and lands, and money, and horses, and carriages, and soft beds, and good fare, and attentive servants, and yet not have true rest.

The rest that Christ gives is an inward and spiritual thing. It is rest of heart, rest of conscience, rest of mind, rest of affection, rest of will. It is rest, from a comfortable sense of sins being all forgiven and guilt all put away. It is rest, from a solid hope of good things to come, laid up beyond the reach of disease, and death, and the grave. It is rest, from the well-grounded feeling, that the great business of life is settled, its great end provided for, that in time all is well done, and in eternity heaven will be our home.

(a) Rest such as this the Lord Jesus gives to those who come to Him, by showing them His own finished work on the cross, by clothing them in His own perfect righteousness, and washing them in His own precious blood. When a man begins to see that the Son of God actually died for his sins, his soul begins to taste something of inward quiet and peace.

(b) Rest such as this the Lord Jesus gives to those who come to Him, by revealing Himself as their everliving High Priest in heaven, and God reconciled to them through Him. When a man begins to see that the Son of God actually lives to intercede for him, he will begin to feel something of inward quiet and peace.

(c) Rest such as this the Lord Jesus gives to those who come to Him, by implanting His Spirit in their hearts, witnessing with their spirits that they are God's children, and that old things are passed away, and all things are become new. When a man begins to feel an inward drawing towards God as a Father, and a sense of being an adopted and forgiven child, his soul begins to feel something of quiet and peace.

(d) Rest such as this the Lord Jesus gives to those who come to Him, by dwelling in their hearts as King, by putting all things within in order, and giving to each faculty its place and work. When a man begins to find order in his heart in place of rebellion and confusion, his soul begins to understand something of quiet and peace. There is no true inward happiness until the true King is on the throne.

(e) Rest such as this is the privilege of all believers in Christ. Some know more of it and some less; some feel it only at distant intervals, and some feel it almost always. Few enjoy the sense of it without many a battle with unbelief, and many a conflict with fear. But all who truly come to Christ, know something of this rest. Ask them, with all their complaints and doubts, whether they would give up Christ and go back to the world. You will get only one answer. Weak as their sense of rest may be, they have got hold of *something* which does them good, and that *something* they cannot let go.

(f) Rest such as this is within reach of all who are willing to seek it and receive it. The poor man is not so poor but he may have it; the ignorant man is not so ignorant but he may know it; the sick man is not so weak and helpless but he may get hold of it. Faith, simple faith, is the one thing needful in order to possess Christ's rest. Faith in Christ is the grand secret of happiness. Neither poverty, nor ignorance, nor tribulation, nor distress can prevent men and women feeling rest of soul, if they will only come to Christ and believe.

(*g*) Rest such as this is the possession which makes men *independent*. Banks may break, and money make itself wings and flee away. War, pestilence, and famine may break in on a land, and the foundations of the earth be out of course. Health and vigour may depart, and the body be crushed down by loathsome disease. Death may cut down wife, and children, and friends, until he who once enjoyed them stands entirely alone. But the man who has come to Christ by faith, will still possess something which can never be taken from him. Like Paul and Silas, he will sing in prison. Like Job, bereaved of children and property, he will bless the name of the Lord. (Acts xvi. 25 ; Job i. 21.) He is the truly independent man who possesses that which nothing can take away.

(*h*) Rest such as this is the possession which makes men truly *rich*. It lasts; it wears; it endures. It lightens the solitary home. It smooths down the dying pillow. It goes with men when they are placed in their coffins. It abides with them when they are laid in their graves. When friends can no longer help us, and money is no longer of use,—when doctors can no longer relieve our pain, and nurses can no longer minister to our wants,—when sense begins to fail, and eye and ear can no longer do their duty, —then, even then, the " rest " which Christ gives will be shed abroad in the heart of the believer. The words "rich" and " poor " will change their meaning entirely one day. He is the only rich man who has come to Christ by faith, and from Christ has received rest.

This is the rest which Christ offers to give to all who are " labouring and heavy-laden." This is the rest for which He invites them to come to Him. This is the rest which I want you to enjoy, and to which I bring you an invitation this day. May God grant that the invitation may not be brought to you in vain !

(1) Does any reader of this paper *feel ignorant* of the " rest " of which I have been speaking ? If so, what have

you got from your religion? You live in a Christian land; you profess and call yourself a Christian. You have probably attended a Christian place of worship many years. You would not like to be called an infidel or a heathen. Yet all this time what benefit have you received from your Christianity? What solid advantage have you obtained from it? For anything one can see, you might just as well have been a Turk or a Jew.

Take advice this day, and resolve to possess the realities of Christianity as well as the name, and the substance as well as the form. Do not be content until you know something of the peace, and hope, and joy, and consolation which Christians enjoyed in former times. Ask yourself what is the reason that you are a stranger to the feelings which men and women experienced in the days of the Apostles. Ask yourself why you do not "joy in the Lord," and feel "peace with God," like the Romans and Philippians, to whom St. Paul wrote. Religious feelings, no doubt, are often deceptive; but surely the religion which produces no feelings at all is not the religion of the New Testament. The religion which gives a man no inward comfort, can never be a religion from God. Take heed to yourself. Never be satisfied until you know something of the "rest that is in Christ."

(2) Does any reader of this paper *desire* rest of soul, and yet knows not where to turn for it? Remember this day, that there is only one place where it can be found. Governments cannot give it; education will not impart it; worldly amusements cannot supply it; money will not purchase it. It can only be found in the hand of Jesus Christ: and to His hand you must turn, if you would find peace within.

There is no royal road to rest of soul. Let that never be forgotten. There is only one way to the Father,—Jesus Christ; one door into heaven,—Jesus Christ; and one path to heart-peace,—Jesus Christ. By that way all "labouring and heavy-laden" ones must go, whatever be their rank or condition. Kings in their palaces and paupers in the workhouse, are all on a level in this matter. All alike must come to Christ, if they feel soul-weary and athirst. All must drink of the same fountain, if they would have their thirst relieved.

You may not believe what I am now writing. Time will show who is right and who is wrong. Go on, if you will, imagining that true happiness is to be found in the good things of this world. Seek it, if you will, in revelling and banqueting, in dancing and merry-making, in races and theatres, in field-sports and cards. Seek it if you will, in reading and scientific pursuits, in music and painting, in politics and business. Seek it: but you will never overtake it, unless you change your plan. Real heart-rest is never to be found except in heart-union with Jesus Christ.

The Princess Elizabeth, daughter of Charles I., lies buried in Newport church, in the Isle of Wight. A marble monument, erected by our gracious Queen Victoria, records in a touching way the manner of her death. She languished in Carisbrook Castle during the unhappy Commonwealth wars, a prisoner, alone, and separate from all the companions of her youth, until death set her free. She was found dead one day with her head leaning on her Bible, and the Bible open at the words, "Come unto Me, all ye that labour and are heavy-laden, and I will give you rest." The monument in Newport church records this fact. It consists of a female figure reclining her head on a marble book, with the text already quoted engraven on the book. Think what a sermon in stone that monument preaches. Think, what a standing memorial it affords of the utter inability of rank and high birth to confer certain happiness! Think what a testimony it bears to the lesson before you this day,—the mighty lesson that there is no true rest for any one excepting in Christ! Happy will it be for your soul if that lesson is never forgotten!

(3) Does any reader of this paper desire to possess the rest that Christ alone can give, and yet *feel afraid* to seek it? I beseech you, as a friend to your soul, to cast this needless fear away. For what did Christ die on the cross, if not to save sinners? For what does He sit at the right hand of God, if not to receive and intercede for sinners? When Christ invites you so plainly, and promises so freely, why should you rob your own soul, and refuse to come to Him?

Who, among all the readers of this paper, desires to be saved by Christ, and yet is not saved at present? Come, I beseech you: come to Christ without delay. Though you have been a great sinner, COME.—Though you have long resisted warnings, counsels, sermons, COME.—Though you have sinned against light and knowledge, against a father's advice and a mother's tears, COME.—Though you have plunged into every excess of wickedness, and lived without a Sabbath and without prayer, yet COME.—The door is not shut, the fountain is not yet closed. Jesus Christ invites you. It is enough that you feel labouring and heavy-laden, and desire to be saved. COME: COME TO CHRIST WITHOUT DELAY!

Come to Him by faith, and pour out your heart before Him in prayer. Tell Him the whole story of your life, and ask Him to receive you. Cry to Him as the penitent thief did, when he He saw Him on the cross. Say to Him, "Lord, save me also! Lord, remember me!" COME: COME TO CHRIST!

If you have never come to this point yet, you must come to it at last, if you mean to be saved. You must apply to Christ as a sinner; you must have personal dealings with the great Physician, and apply to Him for a cure. Why not do it at once? Why not this very day accept the great invitation? Once more, I repeat my exhortation. COME: COME TO CHRIST WITHOUT DELAY!

(4) Has any reader of this paper *found the rest* which Christ gives? Have you tasted true peace by coming to Him and casting your soul on Him? Then go on to the end of your days as you have begun, looking to Jesus and living on Him. Go on drawing daily full supplies of rest, peace, mercy, and grace from the great fountain of rest and peace. Remember that, if you live to the age of Methuselah, you will never be anything but a poor empty sinner, owing all you have and hope for to Christ alone.

Never be ashamed of living the life of faith in Christ. Men may ridicule and mock you, and even silence you in argument; but they can never take from you the feelings which faith in Christ gives. They can never prevent you feeling, " I was weary till I found Christ, but now I have rest of conscience. I was blind, but now I see. I was dead, but I am alive again. I was lost, but I am found."

Invite all around you to come to Christ. Use every lawful effort to bring father, mother, husband, wife, children, brothers, sisters, friends, relatives, companions, fellow-workmen, servants,—to bring all and every one to the knowledge of the Lord Jesus. Spare no pains. Speak to them about Christ: speak to Christ about them. Be instant in season, out of season. Say to them, as Moses did to Hobab, "Come thou with us, and we will do thee good." (Num. x. 29.) The more you work for the souls of others, the more blessing will you get for your own soul.

Last, but not least, look forward with confidence to a better rest in a world to come. Yet a little time, and He that shall come, will come, and will not tarry. He will gather together all who have believed in Him, and take His people to a home where the wicked shall cease from troubling, and the weary shall be at perfect rest. He shall give them a glorious body, in which they shall serve Him without distraction, and praise Him without weariness. He shall wipe away tears from all faces, and make all things new. (Isa. xxv. 8.)

There is a good time coming for all who have come to Christ and committed their souls into His keeping. They shall "remember all the way by which they have been led," and see the wisdom of every step in the way. They shall wonder that they ever doubted the kindness and love of their Shepherd. Above all, they shall wonder that they could live so long without Him, and that when they heard of Him they could hesitate about coming to Him.

There is a pass in Scotland called Glencoe, which supplies a beautiful illustration of what heaven will be to the man who comes to Christ. The road through Glencoe carries the traveller up a long and steep ascent, with many a little winding and many a little turn in its course. But when the top of the pass is reached, a stone is seen by the wayside, with these simple words engraven on it, "Rest, and be thankful." Those words describe the feelings with which every one who comes to Christ will at length enter heaven. The summit of the narrow way will be won. We shall cease from our weary journeying, and sit down in the kingdom of God. We shall look back over all the way of life with thankfulness, and see the perfect wisdom of every little winding and turn in the steep ascent by which we were led. We shall forget the toils of the upward journey in the glorious rest. Here in this world our sense of rest in Christ at best is feeble and partial: but, "when that which is perfect is come, then that which is in part shall be done away." (1 Cor. xiii. 10.) Thanks be unto God, a day is coming when believers shall rest perfectly, and be thankful.

XV.

FAITH!

"*God so loved the world, that He gave His only begotten Son, that whosoever believeth in Him should not perish, but have everlasting life.*"—JOHN iii. 16.

THERE are few texts better known than that which heads this page. Its words are probably familiar to our ears. We have very likely heard them, or read them, or quoted them, a hundred times. But have we ever considered what a vast amount of divinity this text contains? No wonder that Luther called it "the Bible in miniature!"—And have we ever considered the word which forms the turning-point of the text, and the immensely solemn question which arises out of it? The word I refer to is "believeth." The Lord Jesus says, "Whosoever believeth shall not perish." Now, DO WE BELIEVE?

Questions about religion are seldom popular. They frighten people. They oblige them to look within, and to think. The insolvent tradesman does not like his books to be searched. The faithless steward does not like his accounts to be examined. And the unconverted Christian does not like to be asked home-questions about his soul.

But questions about religion are very useful. The Lord Jesus Christ asked many questions during His ministry on earth. The servant of Christ ought not to be ashamed to do likewise. Questions about things necessary to salvation,—questions which probe the conscience, and bring men face to face with God,—such questions often bring life and health to souls. I know few questions more important than the one which arises out of this text :— DO WE BELIEVE ?

The question before us is no easy one to answer. It will not do to thrust it aside by the off-hand answer, " Of course I believe." True belief is no such " matter of course " as many suppose. Myriads of Protestants and Roman Catholics are constantly saying on Sundays, " I believe," who know nothing whatever of believing. They cannot explain what they mean. They neither know what, nor in whom, they believe. They can give no account of their faith. A belief of this kind is utterly useless. It can neither satisfy, nor sanctify, nor save.

In order to see clearly the importance of " believing," we should ponder well the words of Christ which head this paper. It is by the unfolding of these words, that I shall hope to show the weight of the question, " Do you believe ? "

There are four things which I wish to consider, and to impress upon the minds of all who read this volume. These four things are as follows :—

I. God's mind towards the world :—*He " loved " it.*

II. God's gift to the world:—" *He gave His only begotten Son.*"

III. The only way to obtain the benefit of God's gift : —" *Whosoever believeth on Him shall not perish.*"

IV. The marks by which true belief may be known.

I. Let us consider, in the first place, *God's mind towards the world :—He " loved " it.*

The extent of the Father's love towards the world, is a subject on which there is some difference of opinion. It is a subject on which I have long taken my side, and will never hesitate to speak my mind. I believe that the Bible teaches us that God's love extends to all mankind. "His tender mercies are over all His works." (Psalm cxlv. 9.) He did not love the Jews only, but the Gentiles also. He does not love His own elect only. He loves all the world.

But what kind of love is this with which the Father regards all mankind? It cannot be a love of *complacency*, or else He would cease to be a perfect God. He is one who "cannot look upon that which is iniquity." (Hab. i. 13.) Oh, no! The world-wide love of which Jesus speaks, is a love of kindness, pity, and *compassion*. Fallen as man is, and provoking as man's ways are, the heart of God is full of kindness towards him. While as a righteous Judge He hates sin, He is yet able in a certain sense to *love sinners!* The length and breadth of His compassion are not to be measured by our feeble measures. We are not to suppose that He is such an one as ourselves. Righteous, and holy, and pure as God is, it is yet possible for God to love all mankind. "His compassions fail not." (Lam. iii. 22.)

Let us think, for a moment, how wonderful is this extent of God's love. Look at the state of mankind in every part of the earth, and mark the amazing quantity of wickedness and ungodliness by which earth is defiled.—Look at the millions of heathen worshipping stocks and stones, and living in a spiritual darkness "that may be felt."—Look at the millions of Roman Catholics, burying the truth under man-made traditions, and giving the honour due to Christ to the church, the saints, and the priest.—Look at the millions of Protestants who are content with a mere formal Christianity, and know nothing of Christian believing or Christian living, except the name.—Look at the land in which we live at this very day, and mark the sins which abound even in a privileged nation like our own. Think how drunkenness, and Sabbath-breaking, and uncleanness,

and lying, and swearing, and pride, and covetousness, and
infidelity, are crying aloud to God from one end of Great
Britain to the other. And then remember that God *loves*
this world! No wonder that we find it written that He
is "merciful and gracious, long-suffering, and abundant in
goodness and truth." (Exod. xxxiv. 6.) He is "not willing
that any should perish, but that all should come to
repentance."—He "would have all men to be saved, and
to come to the knowledge of the truth."—He "has no
pleasure in the death of him that dieth."—(2 Peter iii. 9;
1 Tim. ii. 4; Ezek. xxxiii. 11.) There lives not the man
or woman on earth whom God regards with absolute
hatred or complete indifference. His mercy is like all His
other attributes. It passes knowledge. God loves the
world.

There are divers and strange doctrines abroad in the
present day about the love of God. It is a precious truth
which Satan labours hard to obscure by misrepresentation
and perversion. Let us grasp it firmly, and stand on our
guard.

Beware of the common idea that God the Father is an
angry Being, whom sinful man can only regard with fear,
and from whom he must flee to Christ for safety. Cast it
aside as a baseless and unscriptural notion. Contend
earnestly for all the attributes of God,—for His holiness
and His justice, as well as for His love. But never allow
for one moment that there is any want of love towards
sinners in any Person in the Blessed Trinity. Oh, no!
Such as the Father is, such is the Son, and such is the
Holy Ghost. The Father loves, and the Son loves, and the
Holy Ghost loves. When Christ came on earth, the
kindness and love of God toward man *appeared*. (Titus
iii. 4.) The cross is the effect of the Father's love, and not
the cause. Redemption is the result of the compassion of
all three Persons in the Trinity. To place the Father and
the Son in opposition one to another, is weak and crude

theology. Christ died, not because God the Father hated, but because He loved the world.

Beware, again, of the common doctrine that God's love is limited and confined to His own elect, and that all the rest of mankind are passed by, neglected, and let alone. This also is a notion that will not bear examination by the light of Scripture. The father of a prodigal son can surely love and pity him, even when he is walking after his own lusts, and refusing to return home. The Maker of all things may surely love the work of His own hands with a love of compassion, even when rebellious against Him.—Let us resist to the death the unscriptural doctrine of universal salvation. It is not true that all mankind will be finally saved. But let us not fly into the extreme of denying God's universal compassion. It is true that God "loves the world."—Let us maintain jealously the privileges of God's elect. It is true that they are loved with a special love, and will be loved to all eternity. But let us not exclude any man or woman from the pale of God's kindness and compassion. We have no right to pare down the meaning of words when Jesus says, "God loved the world." The heart of God is far wider than that of man. There is a sense in which the Father loves all mankind.*

If any reader of these pages never yet took up the service of Christ in real earnest, and has the least desire to begin now, take comfort in the truth before you. Take comfort

---

* If any reader is stumbled by the statements I have made about God's love, I venture to request his attention to the notes on John i. 29, and John iii. 16, in my "Expository Thoughts on St. John's Gospel." I hold firmly the doctrine of election, as set forth in the Seventeenth Article of the Church of England. I glory in that Article, as one of the sheet anchors of my Church. I delight in the blessed truth that God has loved His own elect with an everlasting love, before the foundation of the world. But all this is beside the question before us. That question is, "How does God regard all mankind?" I reply unhesitatingly, that God *loves* them. God loves all the world with a love of compassion.

in the thought that God the Father is a God of infinite love and compassion. Do not hang back and hesitate, under the idea that God is an angry Being, who is unwilling to receive sinners, and slow to pardon. Remember this day that love is the Father's darling attribute. In Him there is perfect justice, perfect purity, perfect wisdom, perfect knowledge, infinite power. But, above all, never forget there is in the Father a perfect love and compassion. Draw near to Him with boldness, because Jesus has made a way for you. But draw nigh to Him also with boldness, because it is written that " He loved the world."

If you have taken up the service of God already, never be ashamed of imitating Him whom you serve. Be full of love and kindness to all men, and full of special love to them that believe. Let there be nothing narrow, limited, contracted, stingy, or sectarian in your love. Do not only love your family and your friends ;—love all mankind. Love your neighbours and your fellow-countrymen. Love strangers and foreigners. Love heathen and Mahometans. Love the worst of men with a love of pity. Love all the world. Lay aside all envy and malice,—all selfishness and unkindness. To keep up such a spirit is to be no better than an infidel. " Let all your things be done with charity."—" Love your enemies, bless them that curse you, do good to them that hate you," and be not weary of doing them good to your life's end. (1 Cor. xvi. 14 ; Matt. v. 44.) The world may sneer at such conduct, and call it mean and low-spirited. But this is the mind of Christ. This is the way to be like God. GOD LOVED THE WORLD.

II. The next thing I want to consider is *God's gift to the world.* " *He gave His only begotten Son.*"

The manner in which the truth before us is stated by our Lord Jesus Christ, demands special attention. It would be well for many who talk big swelling words about

" the love of God " in the present day, if they would mark the way in which the Lord Jesus sets it before us.

The love of God towards the world is not a vague, abstract idea of mercy, which we are obliged to take on trust, without any proof that it is true. It is a love which has been manifested by a mighty gift. It is a love which has been put before us in a plain, unmistakable, tangible form. God the Father was not content to sit in heaven, idly pitying and loving His fallen creatures on earth. He has given the mightiest evidence of His love towards us by a gift of unspeakable value. He has " not spared His own Son, but delivered Him up for us all." (Rom. viii. 32.) He has so loved us that He has given us His only begotten Son, the Lord Jesus Christ! A higher proof of the Father's love could not have been given.

Again, it is not written that God so loved the world that He resolved to save it, but that He so loved it that He gave Christ. His love is not displayed at the expense of His holiness and justice. It flows down from heaven to earth through one particular channel. It is set before men in one special way. It is only through Christ, by Christ, on account of Christ, and in inseparable connection with the work of Christ. Let us glory in God's love by all means. Let us proclaim to all the world that God is love. But let us carefully remember that we know little or nothing of God's love which can give us comfort, excepting in Jesus Christ. It is not written that God so loved the world that He will take all the world to heaven, but that He so loved it, that He has given His only begotten Son. He that ventures on God's love without reference to Christ, is building on a foundation of sand.

Who can estimate the value of God's gift, when He gave to the world His only begotten Son ? It is something unspeakable and incomprehensible. It passes man's understanding. Two things there are which man has no arithmetic to reckon, and no line to measure. One of these things is the extent of that man's loss who loses his own soul. The other is the extent of God's gift when He gave Christ to sinners. He gave no created thing for our redemption, though all the treasures of earth, and all the stars of heaven, were at His disposal. He gave no created being to be our Redeemer, though angels, principalities and powers in heavenly places, were ready to do His will. Oh, no! He gave us One who was nothing less than His own fellow, very God of very God, His only begotten Son. He that thinks lightly of man's need and man's sin, would do well to consider man's Saviour. Sin must indeed be exceeding sinful, when the Father must needs give His only Son to be the sinner's Friend!

Have we ever considered *to what* the Father gave His only begotten Son? Was it to be received with gratitude and thankfulness by a lost and bankrupt world? Was it to reign in royal majesty on a restored earth, and put down every enemy under His feet? Was it to enter the world as a king, and to give laws to a willing and obedient people? No! The Father gave His Son to be "despised and rejected of men," to be born of a poor woman, and live a life of poverty,—to be hated, persecuted, slandered, and blasphemed,—to be counted a malefactor, condemned as a transgressor, and die the death of a felon. Never was there such love as this! Never such condescension! The man among ourselves who cannot stoop much and suffer much in order to do good, knows nothing of the mind of Christ.

For what end and purpose did the Father give His only begotten Son? Was it only to supply an example of self-denial and self-sacrifice? No! It was for a far higher end and purpose than this. He gave Him to be a sacrifice for man's sin, and an atonement for man's transgression. He gave Him to be delivered for our offences, and to die for the ungodly. He gave Him to bear our iniquities, and to suffer for our sins, the just for the unjust. He gave Him to be made a curse for us, that we might be redeemed from the curse of the law. He gave Him to be sin for us who knew no sin, that we might be made the righteousness of God in Him. He gave Him to be a propitiation for our sins, and not for ours only, but for the sins of the whole world. He gave Him to be a ransom for all, and to make satisfaction for our heavy debt to God by His own precious blood. (1 Pet. iii. 18; Gal. iii. 13; 2 Cor. v. 21; 1 John ii. 2; 1 Tim. ii. 6; 1 Pet. i. 18, 19.) He gave Him to be the Almighty Friend of all sinners of mankind,—to be their Surety and Substitute, —to do for them what they never could have done for themselves,—suffer what they could never have suffered,— and pay what they could never have paid. All that Jesus did and suffered on earth was according to the determinate counsel and fore-knowledge of God. The chief end for which He lived and died was to provide eternal redemption for mankind.

Beware of ever losing sight of the great purpose for which Christ was given by God the Father. Let not the false teaching of modern divinity, however plausible it may sound, tempt you to forsake the old paths. Hold fast the faith once delivered to the saints,—that the special object for which Christ was given was to die for sinners, and to make atonement for them by His sacrifice on the cross. Once give up this great doctrine, and there is little worth contending for in Christianity. If Christ did not really "bear our sins on the tree" as our Substitute, there is an end of all solid peace. (1 Pet. ii. 24.)

Beware, again, of holding narrow and confined views of the extent of Christ's redemption. Regard Him as given by God the Father to be the common Saviour for all the world. See in Him the fountain for all sin and unclean-ness, to which every sinner may come boldly, drink and live. See in Him the brazen serpent set up in the midst of the camp, to which every sin-bitten soul may look and be healed. See in Him a medicine of matchless value, sufficient for the wants of all the world, and offered freely to all mankind. The way to heaven is narrow enough already, by reason of man's pride, hardness, sloth, listlessness, and unbelief. But take heed that you do not make that way more narrow than it really is.

I confess, boldly, that I hold the doctrine of particular redemption, in a certain sense, as strongly as any one. I believe that none are *effectually* redeemed but God's elect. They, and they only, are set free from the guilt, and power, and consequences of sin. But I hold no less strongly, that Christ's work of atonement is *sufficient* for all mankind. There is a sense in which He has tasted death for every man, and has taken upon Him the sin of the world. (Heb. ii. 9; John i. 29.) I dare not pare down, and fine away, what appear to me the plain statements of Scripture. I dare not shut a door which God seems, to my eyes, to have left open. I dare not tell any man on earth that Christ has done nothing for him, and that he has no warrant to apply boldly to Christ for salvation. I must abide by the statements of the Bible. Christ is God's gift to the whole world.

Let us observe what a *giving* religion true Christianity is. Gift, love, and free grace are the grand characteristics of the pure gospel. The Father loves the world and gives His only begotten Son. The Son loves us and gives Himself for us. The Father and the Son together give the Holy Spirit to all that ask. All Three Persons in the Blessed Trinity give "grace upon grace" to them that believe. Never let us be ashamed of being *giving* Christians if we profess to have any hope in Christ. Let us give freely, liberally, and self-denyingly, according as we have power and opportunity. Let not our love consist in nothing more than vague expressions of kindness and compassion. Let us make proof of it by actions. Let us help forward the cause of Christ on earth, by money, influence, pains, and prayer. If God so loved us as to give His Son for our souls, we should count it a privilege and not a burden, to give what we can to do good to men.

If God has given us His only begotten Son, let us beware of doubting His kindness and love in any painful providence of our daily life. Let us never allow ourselves to think hard thoughts of God. Let us never suppose that He can give us anything that is not really for our good. Let us remember the words of St. Paul: "He that spared not His own Son, but delivered Him up for us all, how shall He not with Him also freely give us all things." (Rom. viii. 32.) Let us see in every sorrow and trouble of our earthly pilgrimage, the hand of Him who gave Christ to die for our sins. That hand can never smite us except in love. He who gave us His only begotten Son, will never withhold anything from us that is really for our good. Let us lean back on this thought and be content. Let us say to ourselves in the darkest hour of trial, "This also is ordered by Him who gave Christ to die for my sins. It cannot be wrong. It is done in love. It must be well."

III. The third thing I propose to consider, is *the way in which man obtains the benefit of God's love and Christ's salvation.* It is written that " whosoever believeth shall not perish."

The point before us is of the deepest importance. To bring it out clearly before your eyes is one great object of the paper you are now reading. God has loved the world. God has given His Son "to be the Saviour of the world." (1 John iv. 14.) And yet we learn from Scripture that many persons in the world never reach heaven? Here at any rate is limitation. Here the gate is strait and the way narrow. Some and some only out of mankind obtain eternal benefit from Christ. Who then, and what are they?

Christ and His benefits are only available to those who

believe. To believe, in the language of the New Testa‧ment, is simply to trust.   Trusting and believing are the same thing.   This is a doctrine repeatedly laid down in Scripture, in plain and unmistakable language.   Those who will not trust or believe in Him have no part in Him. Without believing there is no salvation.   It is vain to suppose that any will be saved, merely because Christ was incarnate,—or because Christ is in heaven,—or because they belong to Christ's Church,—or because they are baptized,—or because they have received the Lord's supper. All this is entirely useless to any man except he believes. Without faith, or trust, on his part, all these things together will not save his soul.   We must have personal faith in Christ, personal dealings with Christ, personal transactions with Christ, or we are lost for evermore.   It is utterly false and unscriptural to say that Christ is in every man.   Christ no doubt is *for* every one, but Christ is not *in* every one. He dwells only in those hearts which have faith ; and all, unhappily, have not faith.   He that believeth not in the Son of God is yet in his sins, "the wrath of God abideth on him."   "He that believeth not," says our Lord Jesus Christ in words of fearful distinctness,—"he that believeth not shall be damned." *   (Mark xvi. 16 ; John iii. 36.)

But Christ and all His benefits are the property of any one of mankind that believes.   Every one that believes on the Son of God, and trusts his soul to Him, is at once pardoned, forgiven, justified, counted righteous, reckoned innocent, and freed from all liability to condemnation.   His sins, however many, are at once cleansed away by Christ's precious blood.   His soul, however guilty, is at once clothed with Christ's perfect righteousness.   It matters not what he may have been in time past.   His sins may have been of the worst kind.   His former character may be of the

---

* It is perhaps almost needless to say, that I am not speaking of idiots, or those who die in infancy, in this paragraph.

blackest description. But does He believe on the Son of God? This is the one question. If he does believe, he is justified from all things in the sight of God.—It matters not that he can bring to Christ nothing to recommend him, no good works, no long-proved amendments, no unmistakable repentance and change of life. But does he this day believe in Jesus Christ? This is the grand question. If he does he is at once accepted. He is accounted righteous for Christ's sake.

But what is this *believing*, which is of such matchless importance. What is the nature of this faith which gives a man such amazing privileges? This is an important question. I ask attention to the answer. Here is a rock on which many make shipwreck. There is nothing really mysterious and hard to understand about saving belief. But the whole difficulty arises from man's pride and self-righteousness. It is the very simplicity of justifying faith at which thousands stumble. They cannot understand it because they will not stoop.

Believing on Christ is no mere *intellectual assent*, or belief of the head. This is no more than the faith of devils. We may believe that there was a divine Person called Jesus Christ, who lived and died and rose again, eighteen hundred years ago, and yet never believe so as to be saved. Doubtless there must be some knowledge before we can believe. There is no true religion in ignorance. But knowledge alone is not saving faith.

Believing on Christ, again, is not mere *feeling* something about Christ. This is often no more than temporary excitement, which, like the early dew, soon passes away. We may be pricked in conscience, and feel drawings toward the Gospel, like Herod and Felix. We may even tremble and weep, and show much affection for the truth and those that profess it. And yet all this time our hearts and wills may remain utterly unchanged, and secretly chained down to the world. Doubtless there is no saving faith where there is no feeling. But feeling alone is not faith.

True belief in Christ is the unreserved *trust* of a heart convinced of sin, in Christ, as an all-sufficient Saviour. It is the combined act of the whole man's head, conscience, heart, and will. It is often so weak and feeble at first, that he who has it cannot be persuaded that he has it. And yet, like life in the new-born infant, his belief may be real, genuine, saving, and true. The moment that the conscience is convinced of sin, and the head sees Christ to be the only One who can save, and the heart and will lay hold on the hand that Christ holds out, that moment there is saving faith. In that moment a man believes.

True belief in Christ is so immensely important that the Holy Ghost has graciously used many figures in the Bible in describing it. The Lord God knows the slowness of man to comprehend spiritual things. He has therefore multiplied forms of expression, in order to set faith fully before us. The man who cannot understand " believing " in one form of words, will perhaps understand it in another.

(1) Believing is the soul's *coming* to Christ. The Lord Jesus says, " He that cometh to Me shall never hunger." "Come unto Me, all ye that labour and are heavy laden, and I will give you rest." (John vi. 35; Matt. xi. 28.) Christ is that Almighty Friend, Advocate, and Physician, to whom all sinners, needing help, are commanded to apply. The believer comes to Him by faith, and is relieved.

(2) Believing is the soul's *receiving* Christ. St. Paul says, "Ye have received Christ Jesus the Lord." (Col. ii. 6.) Christ offers to come into man's heart with pardon, mercy, and grace, and to dwell there as its Peace-maker and King. He says, "I stand at the door and knock." (Rev. iii. 20.) The believer hears His voice, opens the door, and admits Christ, as his Master, Priest, and King.

(3) Believing is the soul's *building* on Christ. St.

Paul says, ye are "built up in Him."—"Ye are built upon
the foundation of the apostles and prophets." (Eph. ii. 20;
Col. ii. **7**.)   Christ is that sure corner-stone, that strong
foundation, which alone can bear the weight of a sinful
soul.   The believer places his hopes for eternity on Him,
and is safe.   The earth may be shaken and dissolved; but
he is built upon a rock, and will never be confounded.

(4) Believing is the soul's *putting on* Christ.   St.
Paul says, "As many of you as have been baptized into
Christ, have put on Christ." (Galat. iii. 27.)   Christ is
that pure white robe which God has provided for all
sinners who would enter heaven.   The believer puts on
this robe by faith, and is at once perfect and free from
any spot in God's sight.

(5) Believing is the soul's *laying hold on Christ*.
St. Paul says, "We have fled for refuge to lay hold on the
hope set before us." (Heb. vi. 18.)   Christ is that true
city of refuge, to which the man fleeing from the avenger
of blood runs, and in which he is safe.   Christ is that
altar which provided a sanctuary to him who laid hold on
its horns.   Christ is that almighty hand of mercy, which
God holds out from heaven to lost and drowning sinners.
The believer lays hold on this hand by faith, and is
delivered from the pit of hell.

(6) Believing is the soul's *eating* Christ.   The Lord
Jesus says, "My flesh is meat indeed.   He that eateth ot
this bread shall live for ever." (John vi. 55, 58.)   Christ
is that divine food which God has provided for starving
sinners.   He is that divine bread which is at the same
time life, nourishment, and medicine.   The believer feeds
on this bread of life by faith.   His hunger is relieved.
His soul is delivered from death.

(7) Believing is the soul's *drinking* Christ.   The Lord
Jesus says, "My blood is drink indeed." (John vi. 55.)
Christ is that fountain of living water which God has
opened for the use of all thirsty and sin-defiled sinners,

proclaiming, "Whosoever will, let him take the water of life freely." (Rev. xxii. 17.) The believer drinks of this living water, and his thirst is quenched.

(8) Believing is the soul's *committal* of itself to Christ. St. Paul says, "He is able to keep that which I have committed to Him against that day." (2 Tim. i. 12.) Christ is the appointed keeper and guardian of souls. It is His office to preserve from sin, death, hell, and the devil, anything committed to his charge. The believer places his soul in the hands of the Almighty treasure-keeper, and is insured against loss to all eternity. He trusts himself to Him and is safe.

(9) Last, but not least, believing is the soul's *look* to Christ. St. Paul describes the saints as "looking to Jesus." (Heb. xii. 2.) The invitation of the Gospel is, "Look unto Me, and be ye saved." (Isai. xlv. 22.) Christ is that brazen serpent which God has set up in the world, for the healing of all sin-bitten souls who desire to be cured. The believer looks to Him by faith, and has life, health, and spiritual strength.

One common remark applies to all the nine expressions which I have just gone through. They all give us the *simplest* idea of faith, or believing and trusting, that man can desire. Not one of them implies the notion of any-thing mysterious, great, or meritorious in the act of belief. All represent it as something within reach of the weakest and feeblest sinner, and within the comprehension of the most ignorant and unlearned. Grant for a moment that a man says he cannot understand what *faith* in Christ is. Let him look at the nine expressions under which faith is described in Scripture, and tell me, if he can, that he cannot understand them. Surely he must allow that coming to Christ, looking to Christ, committing our souls to Christ, laying hold on Christ, are simple ideas. Then let him remember that coming, looking, and committing our souls to Christ, are, in other words, believing.

And now, if any reader of these pages desires to have
peace of conscience in his religion, I entreat him to grasp
firmly the great doctrine which I have tried to set before
him, and never let it go.   Hold fast the grand truth that
saving faith is nothing but simple trust in Christ, that
faith alone justifies, and that the one thing needful in
order to obtain an interest in Christ is to *believe.*—No doubt
repentance, holiness, and charity are excellent things.
They will always accompany true faith.   But in the matter
of justification, they have nothing to do.   In that matter,
the one thing needful is to believe.—No doubt belief is
not the only grace to be found in the heart of a true
Christian.   But only belief gives him an interest in
Christ.   Prize that doctrine as the peculiar treasure of
Christianity.   Once let it go, or add anything to it, and
there is an end of inward peace.*

Prize the doctrine for its *suitableness* to the wants of
fallen man.   It places salvation within reach of the lowest
and vilest sinner, if he has but heart and will to receive
it.   It asks him not for works, righteousness, merit, goodness, worthiness.   It requires nothing of him.   It strips
him of all excuses.   It deprives him of all pretext for
despair.   His sins may have been as scarlet.   But will he
believe ?   Then there is hope.

Prize the doctrine for its glorious *simplicity.*   It brings
eternal life near to the poor, and ignorant, and unlearned.
It does not ask a man for a long confession of doctrinal
orthodoxy.   It does not require a store of head-knowledge,
and an acquaintance with articles and creeds.   Does the
man, with all his ignorance, come to Christ as a sinner,
and commit himself entirely to Him for salvation ?   Will
he believe ?   If he will, there is hope.

---

* If any reader is startled and stumbled by what I here say about
faith, I recommend him to read attentively the Church of England
Homily about Salvation.   My doctrine at any rate is that of the Church
of England.

Above all, prize the doctrine for the glorious *breadth*
and fulness of its terms. It does not say "the elect" who
believe, or "the rich" who believe, or "the moral" people
who believe, or "the Churchman" who believes, or "the
Dissenter" who believes,—these, and these only shall be
saved. Oh, no! it uses a word of far wider signification :—
It says, "*Whosoever* believeth, shall not perish." Whosoever,—whatever his past life, conduct, or character,—
whatever his name, rank, people, or country,—whatever
his denomination, and whatever place of worship he may
have attended,—"*whosoever* believeth in Christ shall not
perish."

This is the Gospel. I marvel not that St. Paul wrote
those words, "If we or an angel from heaven preach any
other Gospel unto you than that which we have preached,
let him be accursed." (Gal. i. 8.)

IV. The fourth and last thing which I propose to
consider is a point of great practical importance. I wish
to show you *the marks by which true belief in Christ may
be discerned and known.*

The faith or believing of which I have spoken, is a
grace of such importance, that we may naturally expect to
hear of many counterfeits of it. There is a dead faith as
well as a living one,—a faith of devils as well as a faith of
God's elect,—a faith which is vain and useless, as well as a
faith that justifies and saves. How shall a man know
whether he has true faith ? How shall he find out
whether he "believes to the saving of his soul" ? The
thing may be found out. The Ethiopian may be known
by his skin, and the leopard by his spots. True faith may
always be known by certain marks. These marks are laid
down unmistakably in Scripture. Let me endeavour to
set down these marks in order.

(1) He that believeth in Christ has inward *peace and
hope.* It is written, "Being justified by faith, we have

peace with God, through our Lord Jesus Christ." "We which have believed do enter into rest." (Rom. **v.** 1; Heb. iv. 3.) The believer's sins are pardoned, and his iniquities taken away. His conscience is no longer burdened with the load of unpardoned transgressions. He is reconciled to God, and is one of His friends. He can look forward to death, judgment, and eternity without fear. The sting of death is taken away. When the great assize of the last day is held, and the books are opened, there will be nothing laid to his charge. When eternity begins, he is provided for. He has a hope laid up in heaven, and a city which cannot be moved. He may not be fully sensible of all these privileges. His sense and view of them may vary greatly at different times, and be often obscured by doubts and fears. Like a child who is yet under age, though heir to a great fortune, he may not be fully aware of the value of his possessions. But with all his doubts and fears, he has a real, solid, true hope, which will bear examination, and at his best moments he will be able to say, "I feel a hope which makes me not ashamed." (Rom. v. 5.)

(2) He that believes in Christ *has a new heart.* It is written, "If any man be in Christ, he is a new creature : old things are passed away : behold all things are become new."—"To as many as received Christ, He gave power to become sons of God, which were born not of blood, nor of the will of the flesh, nor of the will of man, but of God."— "Whosoever believeth that Jesus is the Christ is born of God." (2 Cor. v. 17; John i. 12, 13; 1 John v. 1.) A believer has no longer the same nature with which he was born. He is changed, renewed, and transformed after the image of his Lord and Saviour. He that minds first the things of the flesh, has no saving faith. True faith and spiritual regeneration are inseparable companions. An unconverted person is not a believer !

(3) He that believes in Christ is *a holy person in heart*

and life. It is written that God "purifies the heart by faith;" and, "Whoso hath this hope in him, purifieth himself." (Acts. xv. 9; 1 John iii. 3.) A believer loves what God loves, and hates what God hates. His heart's desire is to walk in the way of God's commandments, and to abstain from all manner of evil. His wish is to follow after the things which are just, and pure, and honest, and lovely, and of good report, and to cleanse himself from all filthiness of flesh and spirit. He falls far short of his aim in many things. He finds his daily life a constant fight with indwelling corruption. But he fights on, and resolutely refuses to serve sin. Where there is no holiness, we may be sure there is no saving faith. An unholy man is not a believer!

(4) He that believes on Christ *works godly works.* It is written, that "faith worketh by love." (Gal. v. 6.) True belief will never make a man idle, or allow him to sit still, contented with his own religion. It will stir him to do acts of love, kindness, and charity, according as he sees opportunity. It will constrain him to walk in the steps of his Master, who "went about doing good." (Acts x. 38.) In one way or another, it will make him work. The works that he does may attract no notice from the world. They may seem trifling and insignificant to many persons. But they are not forgotten by Him who notices a cup of cold water given for His sake. Where there is no working love, there is no faith. A lazy, selfish Christian, has no right to regard himself as a believer!

(5) He that believes on Christ *overcomes the world.* It is written, that "whatsoever is born of God overcometh the world, and this is the victory that overcometh the world, even our faith." (1 John v. 4.) A true believer is not ruled by the world's standard of right or wrong, of truth or error. He is independent of the world's opinion. He cares little for the world's praise. He is not moved by the world's blame. He does not seek for the world's

pleasures. He is not ambitious of the world's rewards.
He looks at things unseen. He sees an invisible Saviour,
a coming judgment, a crown of glory that fadeth not away.
The sight of these objects makes him think comparatively
little of this world. Where the world reigns in the heart,
there is no faith. A man that is habitually conformed to
the world, has no title to the name of a believer!

(6) He that believes on Christ, has an *inward testimony* of his belief. It is written, that " he that
believeth on the Son of God, hath the witness in
himself." (1 John v. 10.) The mark before us requires
very delicate handling. The witness of the Spirit is
unquestionably a very difficult subject. But I cannot
shrink from declaring my own firm persuasion that a
true believer always has inward feelings peculiar to
himself,—feelings which are inseparably connected with
his faith, and flow from it,—feelings of which unbelievers
know nothing at all. He " has the Spirit of adoption," by
which he regards God as a reconciled Father, and looks
up to Him without fear. (Rom. viii. 15.) He has the
testimony of his conscience, sprinkled with Christ's blood,
that weak as he is, he rests on Christ. He has hopes, joys,
fears, sorrows, consolations, expectations, of which he knew
nothing before he believed. He has pocket evidences
which the world cannot understand, but which are better
to him than all the books of evidence in existence. Feelings are, no doubt, very deceitful. But where there are
no inward religious feelings there is no faith. A man
who knows nothing of an inward, spiritual, experimental
religion, is not yet a believer!

(7) Last, but not least, he that believes on Christ, has a
*special regard in all his religion to the person of Christ
Himself.* It is written, "Unto you that believe Christ is
precious." (1 Pet. ii. 7.) That text deserves especial
notice. It does not say " Christianity " is precious, or the
" Gospel " is precious, or " salvation " is precious, but

Christ Himself. A believer's religion does not consist in mere intellectual assent to a certain set of propositions and doctrines. It is not a mere cold belief of a certain set of truths and facts concerning Christ. It consists in union, communion, and fellowship with an actual living Person, even Jesus the Son of God. It is a life of faith in Jesus, confidence in Jesus, leaning on Jesus, drawing out of the fulness of Jesus, speaking to Jesus, working for Jesus, loving Jesus, and looking for Jesus to come again. St. Paul said, "The life that I live in the flesh I live by the faith of the Son of God."—"To me to live is Christ." (Galat. ii. 20; Phil. i. 21.) Such life may sound like enthusiasm to many. But where there is true faith, Christ will always be known and realized, as an actual living personal Friend. He that knows nothing of Christ as his own Priest, Physician, and Redeemer, knows nothing yet of believing!

I place these seven marks of believing before every one who reads this paper, and I ask him to consider them well. I do not say, that all believers have them equally. I do not say, that no one will be saved who cannot discover all these marks in himself. I concede, freely, that many believers are so weak in faith, that they go doubting all their days, and make others doubt about them too. I simply say that these are the marks to which a man should first direct his attention, if he would know whether he believes.

Where the seven marks, of which I have just been speaking, are utterly wanting, I dare not tell a man that he is a true believer. He may be called a Christian, and attend on Christian ordinances. He may have been baptized with Christian baptism, and be a member of a Christian church. But if he knows nothing of peace with God, conversion of heart, newness of life, and victory over the world, I dare not pronounce him a believer. He is yet dead in trespasses and sins. Except he awakes to newness of life, he will perish everlastingly.

Show me a man who has about him the seven marks which I have described, and I feel a strong confidence about the state of his soul. He may be poor and needy in this world, but he is rich in the sight of God. He may be despised and sneered at by man, but he is honourable in the sight of the King of kings. He is travelling towards heaven. He has a mansion ready for him in the Father's house. He is cared for by Christ, while on earth. He will be owned by Christ before assembled worlds, in the life which is to come.

(1) And now, in drawing this paper to a conclusion, I return to *the question* with which I began. I press that question on the conscience of every one whose eyes are on this page. I ask you, in my Master's name, whether you yet know anything of the subject of it? I ask you to look my inquiry in the face. I ask you, Do you believe?

DO YOU BELIEVE? I think it impossible to over-rate the immense importance of the question before you. Life or death, heaven or hell, blessing or cursing, all hinge and turn upon it. He that believeth on Christ is not condemned. He that believeth not shall be damned. If you believe you are pardoned, justified, accepted in God's sight, and have a title to everlasting life. If you do not believe, you are perishing daily. Your sins are all upon your head, sinking you down to perdition. Every hour you are so much nearer to hell.

DO YOU BELIEVE? It matters nothing what others are doing. The question concerns yourself. The folly of other men is no excuse for yours. The loss of heaven will not be less bitter, because you lose it in company. Look at home. Think of your own soul.

DO YOU BELIEVE? It is no answer to say, that "you sometimes hope Christ died for you." The Scriptures never tell us to spend our time in doubts and hesitation on that point. We never read of a single case of one who stood still on that ground. Salvation is never made to turn on the question, whether Christ died for a man or not. The turning-point which is always set before us is believing.

DO YOU BELIEVE? This is the point to which all must come at last, if they would be saved. It will signify little, when we hang on the brink of the grave, what we have professed, and to what denomination we have belonged. All this will sink into nothing, in comparison with the question of this paper. All will be useless, if we have not believed.

DO YOU BELIEVE? This is the common mark of all saved souls. Episcopalians or Presbyterians, Baptists or Independents, Methodists or Plymouth Brethren, Churchmen or Dissenters, all meet on this common ground, if they are true men. On other matters, they are often hopelessly disagreed. But in living by faith on Jesus Christ, they are all one.

DO YOU BELIEVE? What reason can you give for unbelief, that will bear examination? Life is short and uncertain. Death is sure. Judgment is inevitable. Sin is exceeding sinful. Hell is an awful reality. Christ alone can save you. There is no other name given under heaven, whereby you can be saved. If not saved, the blame will be on your own head. You will not believe! You will not come to Christ, that He may give you life!

Take warning this day. You must either believe on Christ, or perish everlastingly. Rest not till you can give a satisfactory answer to the question before you. Never be satisfied, till you can say, By the grace of God I do believe.

(2) I pass on from questions to *counsel.* I offer it to all who are convinced of sin, and dissatisfied with their own spiritual condition. I entreat you to come to Christ by faith without delay. I invite you this day to believe on Christ to the saving of your soul.

I will not let you put me off by the common objection, "We cannot believe,—we must wait till God gives us faith." I grant most fully that saving faith, like true repentance, is the gift of God. I grant that we have no natural power of our own to believe on Christ, receive Christ, come to Christ, lay hold on Christ, and commit our souls to Christ. But I see faith and repentance laid down clearly in Scripture as *duties* which God requires at any man's hands. He "commandeth all men to repent." "This is His commandment, that we should believe." (Acts xvii. 30; 1 John iii. 23.) And I see it laid down with no less clearness, that unbelief and impenitence are sins for which man will be held accountable, and that he who does not repent and believe destroys his own soul. (Mark xvi. 16; Luke xiii. 3.)

Will any one tell me that it is right for a man to sit still in sin? Will any one say that a sinner on the road to hell ought to wait idly for some power to take him up and put him in the way to heaven? Will any one say that it is right for a man to continue *quietly serving the devil*, in open rebellion against God, and that he is to make no effort, no struggle, no attempt to turn towards Christ?

Let others say these things, if they will. I cannot say them. I can find no warrant for them in Scripture. I will not waste time in trying to explain what cannot be explained, and unravel what cannot be unravelled. I will not attempt to show metaphysically in what way an un-converted man *can* look to Christ, or repent, or believe. But this I know, that it is my plain duty to bid every unbeliever to repent and believe. And this I know, that the man who will not accept the invitation, will find at last that he has ruined his own soul!

Trust Christ, look to Christ, cry to the Lord Jesus Christ, if you never yet believed, about your soul. If you have not the right feelings yet, ask Him to give you right feelings. If you dare not think that you have true faith yet, ask Him to give you faith. But in any case do not sit still. Do not idle away your soul into hell in ignorant unscriptural sloth. Do not live on in senseless inactivity,—waiting for you know not what,—expecting what you cannot explain,—increasing your guilt every day,—offending God by continuing in lazy unbelief,—and hourly digging a grave for your own soul. Arise and call upon Christ! Awake and cry to Jesus about your soul! Whatever difficulties there may be about believing, one thing at least is abundantly clear,—no man ever perished and went to hell from the foot of the cross. If you can do nothing else, lie down at the foot of the cross.

(3) I finish all by a word of *exhortation* to all believers into whose hands this paper may fall. I address them as fellow-pilgrims and companions in tribulation. I exhort them, if they love life, and have found any peace in believing, to pray daily for an increase of faith. Let your prayer be continually, "Lord, increase my faith."

True faith admits of many degrees. The weakest faith is enough to join the soul to Christ, and to secure salvation. A trembling hand may receive a healing medicine. The feeblest infant may be heir to the richest possessions. The least faith gives a sinner a title to heaven as surely as the strongest. But little faith can never give so much sensible comfort as strong faith. According to the degree of our faith will be the degree of our peace, our hope, our strength for duty, and our patience in trial. Surely we should pray continually, "Increase our faith."

Would you have more faith? Do you find believing so pleasant that you would like to believe more? Then take heed that you are diligent in the use of every means of grace,—diligent in your private communion with God,—diligent in your daily watchfulness over time, temper, and tongue,—diligent in your private Bible-reading,—diligent in your own private prayers. It is vain to expect spiritual prosperity, when we are careless about these things. Let those who will, call it over-precise and legal to be particular about them. I only reply, that there never was an eminent saint who neglected them.

Would you have more faith ? Then seek to become more acquainted with Jesus Christ. Study your blessed Saviour more and more, and strive to know more of the length and breadth and height of His love. Study Him in all His offices, as the Priest, the Physician, the Redeemer, the Advocate, the Friend, the Teacher, the Shepherd of His believing people. Study Him as one who not only died for you, but is also living for you at the right hand of God, —as one who not only shed His blood for you, but daily intercedes for you at the right hand of God,—as one who is soon coming again for you, and will stand once more on this earth. The miner who is fully persuaded that the rope which draws him up from the pit will not break, is drawn up without anxiety and alarm. The believer who is thoroughly acquainted with the fulness of Jesus Christ, is the believer who travels from grace to glory with the greatest comfort and peace. Then let your daily prayers always contain these words, " Lord, increase my faith."

XVI.

REPENTANCE.

" Except ye repent, ye shall all likewise perish."—LUKE xiii. 3.

THE text which heads this page, at first sight, looks stern and severe: "Except ye repent, ye shall all perish."—I can fancy some one saying, "Is this the Gospel?" "Are these the glad tidings? Are these the good news of which ministers speak?"—"This is a hard saying, who can hear it?" (John vi. 60.)

But from whose lips did these words come? They came from the lips of One who loves us with a love that passeth knowledge, even Jesus Christ, the Son of God. They were spoken by One who so loved us that He left heaven for our sakes,—came down to earth for our sakes,—lived a poor, humble life, for three and thirty years on earth for our sakes,—went to the cross for us, went to the grave for us, and died for our sins. The words that come from lips like these, must surely be words of love.

And, after all, what greater proof of love can be given than to warn a friend of coming danger? The father who sees his son tottering toward the brink of a precipice, and as he sees him cries out sharply, "Stop, stop!"—does not that father love his son?—The tender mother who sees her infant on the point of eating some poisonous berry, and cries out sharply, "Stop, stop! put it down!"—does not that mother love that child?—It is indifference which lets people alone, and allows them to go on every one in his own way. It is love, tender love, which warns, and raises the cry of alarm. The cry of "Fire: fire!" at midnight, may sometimes startle a man out of his sleep, rudely, harshly, unpleasantly. But who would complain, if that cry was the means of saving his life? The words, "Except ye repent, ye shall all perish," may seem at first sight stern and severe. But they are words of love, and may be the means of delivering precious souls from hell.

There are three things to which I ask attention in considering this text of Scripture.

I. First of all, I will speak of the *nature of repentance:* —*What is it?*

II. Secondly, I will speak of the *necessity of repentance:*—*Why is repentance needful?*

III. Thirdly, I will speak of the *encouragements to repentance:*—*What is there to lead men to repent?*

I. First of all, *what is repentance?*

Let us see that we set down our feet firmly on this point. The importance of the inquiry cannot be overrated. Repentance is one of the foundation-stones of Christianity. Sixty times, at least, we find repentance spoken of in the New Testament. What was the first doctrine our Lord Jesus Christ preached? We are told, that He said, "Repent ye, and believe the Gospel." (Mark i. 15.)—What did the Apostles proclaim when the Lord sent them forth the first time? They "preached that men should repent." (Mark vi. 12.)—What was the charge which Jesus gave His disciples when He left the world? That "repentance and remission of sins should be preached in His name among all nations." (Luke xxiv. 47.)—What was the concluding appeal of the first sermons which Peter preached? "Repent, and be baptized." "Repent ye, and be converted."

(Acts ii. 38; iii. 19.)—What was the summary of doctrine which Paul gave to the Ephesian elders, when he parted from them? He told them that he had taught them publicly, and from house to house, "testifying both to the Jews, and also to the Greeks, repentance toward God, and faith toward our Lord Jesus Christ." (Acts xx. 21.)—What was the description which Paul gave of his own ministry, when he made his defence before Festus and Agrippa? He told them that he had showed all men that they should "repent, and do works meet for repentance." (Acts xxvi. 20.)—What was the account given by the believers at Jerusalem of the conversion of the Gentiles? When they heard of it they said, "Then hath God also to the Gentiles granted repentance unto life." (Acts xi. 18.)—What is one of the first qualifications which the Church of England requires of all persons that would come to the Lord's table? They are to "examine themselves whether they repent them truly of their former sins." No impenitent person, according to the Church of England, ought ever to come to the Lord's table.—Surely we must all agree that these are serious considerations. They ought to show the importance of the inquiry I am now making. A mistake about repentance is a most dangerous mistake. An error about repentance is an error that lies at the very roots of our religion. What, then, is repentance? When can it be said of any man, that he repents?

Repentance is a thorough change of man's natural heart upon the subject of sin. We are all born in sin. We naturally love sin. We take to sin, as soon as we can act and think, as the bird takes to flying, and the fish takes to swimming. There never was a child that required schooling or education in order to learn deceitfulness, sensuality, passion, self-will, gluttony, pride, and foolishness. These things are not picked up from bad companions, or gradually learned by a long course of tedious instruction. They spring up of themselves, even when boys and girls are brought up alone. The seeds of them are evidently the natural product of the heart. The aptitude of all children to these things is an unanswerable proof of the corruption and fall of man. Now when this heart of ours is changed by the Holy Ghost, when this natural love of sin is cast out, then takes place that change which the Word of God calls "repentance." The man in whom the change is wrought is said to "repent." He may be called, in one word, a "penitent" man.

But I dare not leave the subject here. It deserves a closer and more searching investigation. It is not safe to deal in general statements, when doctrines of this kind are handled. I will try to take repentance to pieces, and dissect and analyze it before your eyes. I will show you the parts and portions of which repentance is made up. I will endeavour to set before you something of the experience of every truly penitent man.

(a) True repentance begins with *knowledge of sin*. The eyes of the penitent man are opened. He sees with dismay and confusion the length and breadth of God's holy law, and the extent, the enormous extent, of his own transgressions. He discovers, to his surprise, that in thinking himself a "good sort of man," and a man with a "good heart," he has been under a huge delusion. He finds out that, in reality, he is wicked, and guilty, and corrupt, and bad in God's sight. His pride breaks down. His high thoughts melt away. He sees that he is neither more nor less than a great sinner. This is the first step in true repentance.

(b) True repentance goes on to work *sorrow for sin*. The heart of a penitent man is touched with deep remorse because of his past transgressions. He is cut to the heart to think that he should have lived so madly and so wickedly. He mourns over time wasted, over talents mis-spent, over God dishonoured, over his own soul injured. The remembrance of these things is grievous to him. The burden of these things is sometimes almost intolerable. When a man so sorrows, you have the second step in true repentance.

(c) True repentance proceeds, further, to produce in a man *confession of sin.* The tongue of a penitent man is loosed. He feels he must speak to that God against whom he has sinned. Something within him tells him he must cry to God, and pray to God, and talk with God, about the state of his own soul. He must pour out his heart, and acknowledge his iniquities, at the throne of grace. They are a heavy burden within him, and he can no longer keep silence. He can keep nothing back. He will not hide anything. He goes before God, pleading nothing for himself, and willing to say, " I have sinned against heaven and before Thee: my iniquity is great. God be merciful to me, a sinner!" When a man goes thus to God in confession, you have the third step in true repentance.

(d) True repentance, furthermore, shows itself before the world in a thorough *breaking off from sin.* The life of a penitent man is altered. The course of his daily conduct is entirely changed. A new King reigns within his heart. He puts off the old man. What God commands he now desires to practise ; and what God forbids he now desires to avoid. He strives in all ways to keep clear of sin, to fight with sin, to war with sin, to get the victory over sin. He ceases to do evil. He learns to do well. He breaks off sharply from bad ways and bad companions. He labours, however feebly, to live a new life. When a man does this, you have the fourth step in true repentance.

(e) True repentance, in the last place, shows itself by producing in the heart a settled habit of *deep hatred of all sin.* The mind of a penitent man becomes a mind habitually holy. He abhors that which is evil, and cleaves to that which is good. He delights in the law of God. He comes short of his own desires not unfrequently. He

finds in himself an evil principle warring against the
spirit of God. He finds himself cold when he would be
hot, backward when he would be forward, heavy when he
would be lively in God's service. He is deeply conscious
of his own infirmities. He groans under a sense of indwelling corruption. But still, for all that, the general
bias of his heart is towards God, and away from evil. He
can say with David, "I count all Thy precepts concerning
all things to be right, and I hate every false way."
(Psa. cxix. 128.) When a man can say this, you have the
fifth, or crowning step, of true repentance.

But now, is the picture of repentance complete? Can
I leave the subject here, and go on? I cannot do it.
There remains yet one thing behind which ought never to
be forgotten. Were I not to mention this one thing, I
might make hearts sad that God would not have made
sad, and raise seeming barriers between men's souls and
heaven.

True repentance, such as I have just described, is never
alone in the heart of any man. It always has a companion—a blessed companion. It is always accompanied
by lively faith in our Lord and Saviour Jesus Christ.
Wherever faith is, there is repentance; wherever repentance is, there is always faith. I do not decide which
comes first,—whether repentance comes before faith, or
faith before repentance. But I am bold to say that
the two graces are never found separate, one from the
other. Just as you cannot have the sun without light, or
ice without cold, or fire without heat, or water without
moisture,—so long you will never find true faith without
true repentance, and you will never find true repentance
without lively faith. The two things will always go side
by side.

And now, before I go any further, let us search and try
our own hearts, and see what we know about true repentance. I do not affirm that the experience of all

penitent people tallies exactly, precisely, and minutely. I do not say that any man ever knows sin, or mourns for sin, or confesses sin, or forsakes sin, or hates sin, perfectly, thoroughly, completely, and as he ought. But this I do say, that all true Christians will recognise something which they know and have felt, in the things which I have just been saying. Repentance, such as I have described, will be, in the main, the experience of every true believer. Search, then, and see what you know of it in your own soul.

Beware that you make no mistake about the nature of true repentance. The devil knows too well the value of that precious grace not to dress up spurious imitations of it. Wherever there is good coin there will always be bad money. Wherever there is a valuable grace, the devil will put in circulation counterfeits and shams of that grace, and try to palm them off on men's souls. Make sure that you are not deceived.

(*a*) Take heed that your repentance be a business of *your heart*. It is not a grave face, or a sanctimonious countenance, or a round of self-imposed austerities,—it is not this alone which makes up true repentance towards God. The real grace is something far deeper than a mere affair of face, and clothes, and days, and forms. Ahab could put on sackcloth when it served his turn. But Ahab never repented.

(*b*) Take heed that your repentance be a repentance wherein you *turn to God*. Roman Catholics can run to priests and confessionals, when they are frightened. Felix could tremble, when he heard the Apostle Paul preach. But all this is not true repentance. See that your repentance lead you unto God, and make you flee to Him as your best Friend.

(*c*) Take heed that your repentance be a repentance attended by a thorough *forsaking of sin*. Sentimental people can cry when they hear moving sermons on Sundays, and yet return to the ball, the theatre, and the opera in the week after. Herod liked to hear John the Baptist preach, and heard him gladly, " and did many things." But feelings in religion are worse than worthless, unless they are accompanied by practice. Mere sentimental excitement, without thorough breaking off from sin, is not the repentance which God approves. (Mark vi. 20.)

(d) Take heed, above all things, that your repentance be closely *bound up with faith in the Lord Jesus Christ.* See that your convictions be convictions which never rest except at the foot of the cross whereon Jesus Christ died. Judas Iscariot could say, " I have sinned," but Judas never turned to Jesus. Judas never looked by faith to Jesus, and therefore Judas died in his sins. Give me that conviction of sin which makes a man flee to Christ, and mourn, because by his sins he has pierced the Lord who bought him. Give me that contrition of soul under which a man feels much about Christ, and grieves to think of the despite he has done to so gracious a Saviour. Going to Sinai, hearing about the ten commandments, looking at hell, thinking about the terrors of damnation—all this may make people afraid, and has its use. But no repentance ever lasts in which a man does not look at Calvary more than at Sinai, and see in a bleeding Jesus the strongest motive for contrition. Such repentance comes down from heaven. Such repentance is planted in man's heart by God the Holy Ghost.

II. I pass on now to the second point which I proposed to handle. I will consider the necessity of repentance. *Why is repentance needful?*

The text which stands at the head of this paper shows clearly the necessity of repentance.—The words of our Lord Jesus Christ are distinct, express, and emphatic: " Except ye repent, ye shall all likewise perish." All, all, without exception, need repentance toward God. It is not only necessary for thieves, murderers, drunkards, adulterers, fornicators, and the inmates of prisons and of jails. No: all born of the seed of Adam,—all, without exception, need repentance toward God. The queen upon her throne and the pauper in the workhouse, the rich man in his drawing room, the servant maid in the kitchen, the professor of sciences at the University, the poor ignorant boy who follows the plough,—all by nature need repentance. All are born in sin, and all must repent and be converted, if they would be saved. All must have their hearts changed about sin. All must repent, as well as believe the Gospel. "Except ye be converted, and become as little children, ye shall in no wise enter the kingdom of heaven." "Except ye repent, ye shall all likewise perish." (Matt. xviii. 3; Luke xiii. 3.)

But whence comes the necessity of repentance? Why is such tremendously strong language used about this necessity? What are the reasons, what the causes, why repentance is so needful?

(a) For one thing, without repentance there is *no forgiveness of sins.* In saying this, I must guard myself against misconstruction. I ask you emphatically not to misunderstand me. The tears of repentance wash away no sins. It is bad divinity to say that they do. That is the office, that the work of the blood of Christ alone.—Contrition makes no atonement for transgression. It is wretched theology to say that it does. It can do nothing of the kind. Our best repentance is a poor, imperfect thing, and needs repenting over again. Our best contrition has defects enough about it to sink us into hell.—"We are counted righteous before God only for the sake of our Lord Jesus Christ, by faith, and not for our own works or deservings:" not for our repentance, holiness, almsgiving, sacrament-receiving, or anything of the kind.—All this is perfectly true. But still it is no less true that justified people are always penitent people, and that a forgiven sinner will always be a man who mourns over, and loathes his sins.

God in Christ is willing to receive rebellious man, and grant him peace, if he only come to Him in Christ's name however wicked he may have been. But God requires, and requires justly, that the rebel shall throw down his arms. The Lord Jesus Christ is ready to pity, pardon, relieve, cleanse, wash, sanctify, and fit for heaven. But the Lord Jesus Christ desires to see a man hate the sins that he wishes to be forgiven. Let some men call this "legality" if they will. Let some call it "bondage" if they please. I take my stand on Scripture. The testimony of God's Word is plain and unmistakable. Justified people are always penitent people. Without repentance there is no forgiveness of sins.

(b) For another thing, without repentance there is *no happiness in the life that now is.* There may be high spirits, excitement, laughter and merriment, so long as health is good, and money is in the pocket. But these things are not solid happiness. There is a conscience in all men, and that conscience must be satisfied. So long as conscience feels that sin has not been repented of and forsaken, so long it will not be quiet, and will not let a man feel comfortable within. We all of us have an inner man, unknown to the world,—an inner man, with which our companions and friends have often no acquaintance. That inner man has a burden upon it, so long as sin is not repented of; and until that burden is taken off, that inner man has no real comfort. Can you and I be comfortable, when we are not in a right position? It is impossible. And what is a man's true position? He is never in his right position till he has turned his back upon sin, and turned his face towards God.—A man's house is never comfortable till all things are in order. And when is the house of the inward man in order? Never, till God is king, and the world put down in the second place; never, till God is upon the throne, and sin cast down and put out of doors. You might as well expect the solar system to go on well without the sun, as expect that heart of yours to be comfortable when God is not in His place. The great account with God must be settled. The King must be upon His throne. Then, and not till then, there will be peace within. Without repentance there can be no true happiness. We must repent if we want to be happy.

For another thing, without repentance there can be *no meetness for heaven in the world that is yet to come.* Heaven is a prepared place, and they who go to heaven must be a prepared people. Our hearts must be in tune for the employments of heaven, or else heaven itself would be a miserable abode. Our minds must be in harmony with those of the inhabitants of heaven, or else the society of heaven would soon be intolerable to us. Gladly would I help every one to heaven into whose hands this paper may fall. But I never would have you ignorant that if you went there with an impenitent heart, heaven would be no heaven to your soul. What could you possibly do in heaven, if you got there with a heart loving sin? To which of all the saints would you speak? By whose side would you sit down? Surely the angels of God would make no sweet music to the heart of him who cannot bear *saints* upon earth, and never praised the Lamb for redeeming love! Surely the company of patriarchs, and apostles, and prophets, would be no joy to that man who will not read his Bible now, and does not care to know what apostles and prophets wrote. Oh, no! no! there can be no happiness in heaven, if we get there with an impenitent heart. The fish is not happy when it is out of water. The bird is not happy when it is confined in a cage. And why? They are all out of their proper element and natural position. And man, unconverted man, impenitent man, would not be happy if he got to heaven without a heart changed by the Holy Ghost. He would be a creature out of his proper element. He would have no faculties to enable him to enjoy his holy abode. Without a penitent heart there is no "meetness for the inheritance of the saints in light." We must repent, if we want to go to heaven. (Coloss. i. 12.)

I beseech you by the mercies of God, to lay to heart the things which I have just been saying, and to ponder them well. You live in a world of cheating, imposition, and deception. Let no man deceive you about the necessity of repentance. Oh, that professing Christians would see, and know, and feel, more than they do, the necessity, the absolute necessity, of true repentance towards God! There are many things which are not needful. Riches are not needful. Health is not needful. Fine clothes are not needful. Noble friends are not needful. The favour of the world is not needful. Gifts and learning are not needful. Millions have reached heaven without these things. Thousands are reaching heaven every year without them. But no one ever reached heaven without "repentance toward God, and faith toward our Lord Jesus Christ."

Let no man ever persuade you that any religion deserves to be called the Gospel, in which repentance toward God has not a most prominent place. A Gospel, indeed! That is no Gospel in which repentance is not a principal thing.—A Gospel! It is the Gospel of man, but not of God.—A Gospel! It comes from earth, but not from heaven.—A Gospel! It is not the Gospel at all; it is rank antinomianism, and nothing else. So long as you hug your sins, and cleave to your sins, and will have your sins, so long you may talk as you please about the Gospel, but your sins are not forgiven. You may call that legal, if you like You may say, if you please, you "hope it will be all right at the last;—God is merciful;—God is love;—Christ has died;—I hope I shall go to heaven after all." No! I tell you, it is not all right. It will never be all right, at that rate. You are trampling under foot the blood of atonement. You have as yet no part or lot in Christ. So long as you do not repent of sin, the Gospel of our Lord Jesus Christ is no Gospel to your soul. Christ is a Saviour *from* sin, not a Saviour for man *in* sin. If a man will have his sins, the day will come when that merciful Saviour will say to him, "Depart from Me, thou worker of iniquity! depart into everlasting fire, prepared for the devil and his angels." (Matt. xxv. 41.)

Let no man ever delude you into supposing that you can be happy in this world without repentance. Oh, no! You may laugh and dance, and go upon Sundays in excursion-trains, and crack good jokes, and sing good songs, and say, " Cheer, boys, cheer!" and "There's a good time coming;"—but all this is no proof that you are happy. So long as you do not quarrel with sin, you will never be a truly happy man. Thousands go on for a time in this way, and seem merry before the eyes of men, and yet in their hearts carry about a lurking sorrow. When they are *alone* they are wretched. When they are not in jovial company they are low. Conscience makes cowards of them. They do not like being by themselves. They hate quiet thinking. They must constantly have some new excitement. Every year they must have more. Just as an opium-eater needs a larger dose every year he goes on eating opium, so does the man who seeks happiness in anything except in God need greater excitement every year that he lives, and after all is never happy.

Yes! and worse than all, the longer you go on without repentance, the more unhappy will that heart of your's be. When old age creeps over you, and grey hairs appear upon your head,—when you are unable to go where you once went, and take pleasure where you once took pleasure,— your wretchedness and misery will break in upon you like an armed man. The more impenitent a man is, the more miserable he becomes. Have you ever heard of the great clock of St. Paul's cathedral, in London? At midday, in the roar of business, when carriages, and carts, and waggons, and omnibuses, go rolling through the streets, how many never hear that great clock strike, unless they live very near it. But when the work of the day is over, and the roar of business has passed away,—when men are gone to sleep, and silence reigns in London,—then at twelve, at one, at two, at three, at four, the sound of that clock may be heard for miles round. Twelve!—One!—Two!—Three! —Four!—How that clock is heard by many a sleepless man! That clock is just like the conscience of the impenitent man. While he has health and strength, and goes on in the whirl of business, he will not hear conscience. He drowns and silences its voice by plunging into the world. He will not allow the inner man to speak to him. But the day will come when conscience will be heard, whether he likes it or not. The day will come when its voice will sound in his ears, and pierce him like a sword. The time will come when he must retire from the world, and lie down on the sick bed, and look death in the face. And then the clock of conscience, that solemn clock, will sound in his heart, and if he has not repented, will bring wretchedness and misery to his soul. Oh, no! write it down in the tablets of your heart,— without repentance no peace!

Above all, let no man make you dream that there is a possibility of reaching heaven without repentance toward God. We all want to go to heaven. A man would be justly set down as a madman, if he said that he wanted to go to hell. But never let it be forgotten, that none go to heaven except those whom the Holy Ghost has prepared for it. I make my solemn protest against those modern delusions, " that all men shall go to heaven at last, —that it matters not how you live,—that whether you are holy or unholy it does not signify,—that whether you are godless or God-fearing, it is all the same thing,—that all at length will get to heaven." I cannot find such teaching in the Bible. I find the Bible contradicting it flatly. However speciously this new idea may be propounded, and however plausibly it may be defended, it cannot stand the test of the Word of God. No! let God be true, and every man a liar. Heaven is no such place as some seem to fancy. The inhabitants of heaven are no such mixed multitude as many try to believe. They are all of one heart, and one mind. Heaven is the place to which God's people shall go. But for those who are impenitent and unbelieving, and will not come to Christ, for such the Bible says, plainly and unmistakably, there remains nothing but hell.

It is a solemn thought that an impenitent man is unfit for heaven. He could not be happy in heaven, if he got there. I remember hearing of a clergyman who many years ago was travelling by coach. He sat by the coachman's side upon the box. The coachman was one of those unhappy men who fancy nothing is to be done without swearing. He was cursing, swearing, blaspheming, taking God's name in vain, for many a long mile together. On he drove, now flying into a passion, now beating his horses, now cursing and swearing again. Such were the coachman's ways. At last the clergyman said to him quietly, "Coachman, I am exceedingly afraid about you."—"Sir," said the coachman, "what should you be afraid of? All is going on right, we are not likely to be upset."—"Coachman," said the clergyman again, "I am exceedingly afraid about you; because I cannot think what you would do in heaven, if you got there. There will be no cursing in heaven; there will be no swearing in heaven; there will be no passion in heaven; there will be no horses to beat in heaven." "Coachman," said the minister once more, "I cannot think what you would do in heaven."—"Oh," said the coachman," that is your opinion:" and no more was said.— Years passed away. A day came when a person told this same clergyman that a sick man desired to see him. He was a

stranger. He had come into the parish, he said, because he
wanted to die there. The clergyman went to see him. He
entered a room and found a dying man, whose face he did not
know. "Sir," said the dying man, "you do not remember
me?" "No," said the clergyman, "I do not." "Sir," said the
man, "I remember you. I am that coachman to whom,
many years ago, you said, 'Coachman, I am afraid about
you, because I do not know what you would do if you
got to heaven.' Sir, those words laid hold upon me. I
saw I was not fit to die. Those words worked, and worked,
and worked in my heart, and I never rested till I had
repented of sin, and fled to Christ, and found peace in
Him, and became a new man. And now," said he, "by
the grace of God I trust I am prepared to meet my Maker,
and am meet for the inheritance of the saints in light."

Once more I charge you to remember,—without repentance toward God, there can be no meetness for heaven.
It would give pain to an impenitent man to place him
there. It would be no mercy to him.—He would not be
happy. He could not be happy. There could be no
enjoyment in heaven to a man who got there without a
heart hating sin, and a heart loving God. I expect to see
many wonders at the last day. I expect to see some at
the right hand of the Lord Jesus Christ, whom I once
feared I should see upon the left. I expect to see some
at the left hand whom I supposed to be good Christians,
and expected to see at the right. But there is one thing
I am sure I shall not see.—I shall not see at the right
hand of Jesus Christ one single impenitent man. I shall
see Abraham there, who said, "I am dust and ashes."—I
shall see Jacob there, who said, "I am not worthy of the
least of all Thy mercies."—I shall see Job there, who said,
"I am vile."—I shall see David there, who said, "I was
shapen in iniquity: in sin did my mother conceive me."—
I shall see Isaiah there, who said, "I am a man of unclean
lips."—I shall see Paul there, who said, "I am the chief

of sinners." (Gen. xviii. 27; xxxii. 10; Job. xl. 4; Psalm li. 5; Isa. vi. 5; 1 Tim. i. 15.) I shall see the martyr John Bradford there, who often signed himself at the end of his letters, "That wretched sinner, that miserable sinner, John Bradford:" that same John Bradford who said, whenever he saw a man going to be hanged, "There goes John Bradford, but for the grace of God."—I shall see Archbishop Usher there, whose last words were, "Pardon my many sins, especially my sins of omission."—I shall see Grimshaw there, whose last words were, "Here goes an unprofitable servant."—But they will all be of one heart, one mind, one experience. They will all have hated sin. They will all have mourned for sin. They will all have confessed sin. They will all have forsaken sin. They will all have repented as well as believed,—repented toward God as well as believed in Jesus Christ. They will all say with one voice, "What hath God wrought!" They will all say, "By the grace of God I am where I am," as well as "By the grace of God I am what I am."

III. I come now to the third and last thing of which I promised to speak. I will consider *the encouragement there is to repentance.* What is there to lead a man to repent?

I feel it very important to say something on this point. I know that many difficulties arise in the way when the subject of repentance is brought before us. I know how slow man is to give up sin. You might as well tell him to cut off a right hand, or pluck out a right eye, or cut off a right foot, as tell him to part with his darling sins.— I know the strength of old habits and early ways of thinking about religion. At first they are all like cobwebs. At last they are iron chains.—I know the power of pride, and that "fear of man that bringeth a snare."—I know the dislike there is in people to being thought a saint, and supposed to care about religion.—I know that hundreds and thousands would never shrink from storming a Redan, a Malakhoff, and yet cannot bear to be laughed at and thought ridiculous because they care for their souls.—And I know, too, the malice of our great enemy, the devil. Will he part with his "lawful captives" without a conflict? Never. Will he give up his prey without a fight? Never. I once saw a lion, at the Zoological Gardens, being fed. I saw his meal cast down before him. I saw the keeper try to take that meal away.—I remember the lion's roar, his spring, his struggle to retain his food. And I remember the "roaring lion that walketh about, seeking whom he may devour." (1 Pet. v. 8.) Will he give up a man, and let him repent, without a struggle? Never, never, never! Man wants many encouragements to make him repent.

But there are encouragements, great, broad, wide, full and free. There are things in the Word of God which ought to nerve every heart, and arouse every one to repent without delay. I desire to bring these things before the readers of this volume. I would not have one soul lay down this paper and say," The thing cannot be done: it is impossible." I should like all to say, "There is hope: there is hope! There is an open door! It is possible: the thing can be done! By the grace of God a man may repent!"

(a) Hear, for one thing, *what a gracious Saviour the Lord Jesus Christ is.* I place Him first and foremost, as the great argument to encourage a man to repentance. I say to every doubting soul, Look at Christ, think of Christ. He is one "able to save to the uttermost all that come unto God by Him." He is one anointed "a Prince and a Saviour, to give repentance as well as remission of sins." He is one who "came to seek and to save that which was lost." He is one who said, "I came not to call the righteous, but sinners to repentance." He is one who cries, "Come unto Me, all ye that labour and are heavy laden, and I will give you rest." He is one who has pledged His royal word: "Him that cometh unto Me, I will in no wise cast out." And He it is of whom it is written, "As many as received Him, to them gave He power to become the sons of God, even to them that believe on His name." I answer all doubts, and questions, and difficulties, and objections, and fears with this simple argument. I say to every one who wants encouragement, Look at Christ, think of Christ. Consider Jesus Christ the Lord; and then doubt about repentance no more. (Heb. vii. 25; Acts v. 31; Luke xix. 10; Mark ii. 17; Matt. xi. 28; John vi. 37; John i. 12.)

(b) Hear, for another thing, *what glorious promises the Word of God contains.* It is written: "Whosoever confesseth and forsaketh his sins shall find mercy." It is written again: "If we confess our sins, He is faithful and just to forgive us our sins, and to cleanse us from all unrighteousness." It is written again: "Blessed are the poor in spirit, for their's is the kingdom of God. Blessed are they that mourn, for they shall be comforted. Blessed are they that hunger and thirst after righteousness, for they shall be filled." Surely these promises are encouragements. Again I say, *doubt about repentance no more.* (Prov. xxviii. 13; 1 John i. 9; Matt. v. 3, 4, 6.)

(c) Hear, for another thing, *what gracious declarations the Word of God contains:* "When the wicked man turneth away from his wickedness that he hath committed, and doeth that which is lawful and right, he shall save his soul alive."—"The sacrifices of God are a broken spirit: a broken and a contrite heart, O God, Thou wilt not despise."—"God is not willing that any should perish, but that all should come to repentance."—"As I live, saith the Lord, I have no pleasure in the death of the wicked: turn ye, turn ye, why will ye die?"—"There is joy in the presence of the angels of God over one sinner that repenteth."—(Ezek. xviii. 27; Psalm li. 17; 2 Pet. iii. 9; Ezek. xxxiii. 11; Luke xv. 10.) Surely these words are encouraging, if any words can be ! Again I say, *doubt about repentance no more.*

(*d*) Hear, for another thing, *what marvellous parables our Lord Jesus spoke upon this subject.* "Two men went up into the temple to pray ; the one a Pharisee, and the other a publican. The Pharisee stood and prayed thus with himself: God, I thank Thee that I am not as other men are, extortioners, unjust, adulterers, or even as this publican. I fast twice in the week, I give tithes of all that I possess. And the publican, standing afar off, would not lift up so much as his eyes unto heaven, but smote upon his breast,"—as if his heart was so full of sorrow that he could not show it sufficiently,—"he smote upon his breast, saying, God be merciful to me a sinner. I tell you, this man went down to his house justified rather than the other." (Luke xviii. 10—14.) Hear, again, that other marvellous parable,—the parable of the prodigal son. "A certain man had two sons: and the younger of them said to his father, Father, give me the portion of goods that falleth to me. And he divided unto them his living. And not many days after, the younger son gathered all together, and took his journey into a far country, and there wasted his substance with riotous living. And when he had spent all, there arose a mighty famine in that land ; and he began to be in want. And he went and joined himself to a citizen of that country ; and he sent him into his fields to feed swine." And there, feeding swine, in his lowly case "he *came to himself*," and said, "How many hired servants of my father's have bread enough, and to spare, and I perish with hunger ! I will arise, and go to my father, and will say unto him, Father, I have sinned against heaven, and before thee, and am no more worthy to be called thy son : make me as one of thy hired servants. And he arose, and came to his father. But when he was yet a great way off,"—mark that,—"a great way off,—his father saw him, and had compassion, and ran, and fell on his neck, and kissed him. And the son said unto him, Father, I have sinned against heaven, and in thy sight, and am no more worthy to be called thy son. But the father said to his servants, Bring forth the best robe, and put it on him; and put a ring on his hand, and shoes on his feet: and bring hither the fatted calf, and kill it; and let us eat and be merry: for this my son was dead, and is alive again; he was lost, and is found. And they began to be merry." (Luke xv. 11—24.) Surely these are mighty encouragements to repentance. Again I say, *doubt about repentance no more.*

(*e*) Hear, lastly, *what wonderful examples there are in the Word of God, of God's mercy and kindness to penitent men.* Read the story of David. What sin can be greater than David's sin? But when David turned to the Lord, and said, "I have sinned against the Lord," the answer came, "The Lord hath put away thy sin."—Read the story of Manasseh. What wickedness could have been greater than his? He killed his own children. He turned his back upon his father's God. He placed idols in the temple. And yet, when Manasseh was in prison and humbled himself, and prayed to the Lord, the Lord heard his prayer, and brought him out of captivity.—Read the history of Peter. What apostacy could be greater than his? He denied his Master three times over with an oath! And yet, when Peter wept, and mourned for his sin, there was mercy even for Peter, and penitent Peter was restored to his Master's favour.—Read the story of the penitent thief. What case could be more desperate than his? He was a dying man on the brink of hell. Yet when he said to Jesus, "Lord, remember me when Thou comest into Thy kingdom," at once the marvellous answer came, "Verily I say unto thee, To-day shalt thou" (even thou) "be with Me in paradise." (2 Sam. xii. 13; 2 Chron. xxxiii. 1—19; Mark xvi. 7; Luke xxiii. 39—43.)

What greater encouragement to repentance can be

imagined or conceived ?   Why are all these cases recorded
for our learning ?   They are intended to lead men to
repentance.   They are all patterns of God's long-suffering
—patterns of God's mercy—patterns of God's willingness
to receive penitent sinners.   They are proofs of what God's
grace can do.   They are a cloud of witnesses, proving that
it is worth while for man to repent—that there is encouragement for man to turn to God, and that such an
one as goeth on still in his sins is utterly without excuse.
" The goodness of God leadeth him to repentance."
(Rom. ii. 4.)

I remember hearing of a mother whose daughter ran
away from her, and lived a life of sin.   For a long time
no one could tell where she was.—Yet that daughter came
back and was reclaimed.   She became a true penitent.
She was taught to mourn for sin.   She turned to Christ
and believed in Him.   Old things passed away, and all
things became new.   Her mother was asked one day to
tell what she had done to bring her daughter back.—What
means had she used ?—What steps had she taken ?   Her
reply was a very striking one.   She said, " I prayed for
her night and day."   But that was not all.   She went on
to say, " I never went to bed at night without leaving my
front door unlocked, and the door on the latch.   I thought
if my daughter came back some night when I was in bed,
she should never be able to say that she found the door
shut.   She should never be able to say that she came to
her mother's home, but could not get in."   And so it
turned out.   Her daughter came back one night, and tried
the door, and found the door open, and at once came in,
to go out and sin no more.   That open door was the saving
of her soul.—That open door is a beautiful illustration of the
heart of God towards sinners !   The door of mercy is set
wide open.   The door is not yet locked.   The door is always
upon the latch.   God's heart is full of love.   God's heart
is full of compassion.   Whosoever a man may have been,

and whatsoever a man may have been, at midnight, at any time, whenever he returns to God, he will find God willing to receive him, ready to pardon him, and glad to have him at home. All things are ready. Whosoever will may come in.

And, out of all the millions who have turned to God and repented, who ever repented of repentance? I answer boldly, Not one. Thousands every year repent of folly and unbelief. Thousands mourn over time misspent. Thousands regret their drunkenness, and gambling, and fornication, and oaths, and idleness; and neglected opportunities. But no one has ever risen up and declared to the world that he repents of repenting and turning toward God. The steps in the narrow way of life are all in one direction. You will never see in the narrow way the step of one who turned back because the narrow way was not good.

I remember reading of a remarkable event that occurred in a place of worship where a Puritan minister, Mr. Doolittle, was preaching, two hundred years ago. Just as he was about to begin his sermon, he saw a young man, a stranger, coming into his church. He guessed by the young man's manner that he was anxious about his soul, and yet undecided about religion. He took a remarkable course with him. He tried a curious experiment, but God blessed it to the young man's soul. Before Mr. Doolittle gave out his text, he turned to an old Christian whom he saw on one side of his church. He addressed him by name, and said to him, "Brother, do you repent of having served God?" The old Christian stood up manfully before the congregation, and said, "Sir, I have served the Lord from my youth, and He has never done me anything but good."—He turned to the left hand, where he saw another Christian, and addressed him in the same way. "Brother," said he, calling him by his name, "Do you repent of having served Christ?" That man also stood up manfully before the congregation, and said, "Sir, I never was truly happy till I took up the cross, and served the Lord Jesus Christ." Then Mr. Doolittle turned to the young man, and said, "Young man, will you repent? Young man, will you take up the cross? Young man, will you this day begin to serve Christ?" God sent power with these words. The young man stood up before the congregation, and said in a humble tone, "Yes sir, I will." That very day was the beginning of eternal life in the young man's soul. We may depend upon it, the two answers which Mr. Doolittle got that day are the experience of all true Christians. We may be quite sure that no man ever repents of repentance. No man was ever sorry that he served the Lord. No man ever said at the end of his days, "I have read my Bible too much, I have thought of God too much, I have prayed too much, I have been too careful about my soul." Oh, no! The people of God would always say, "Had I my life over again, I would walk far more closely with God than ever I have done. I am sorry that I have not served God better, but I am not sorry that I have served Him. The way of Christ may have its cross. But it is a way of pleasantness, and a path of peace." Surely that fact alone speaks volumes. It is a fact that clinches every argument which I have already advanced. Surely it is worth while for a man to repent. There are encouragements. The impenitent man is without excuse.

And now, I have brought before my readers the three points which I proposed at the outset of this paper to consider. I have shown you the nature of repentance toward God—the necessity of repentance—and the encouragements to repentance. It only remains to conclude this paper by a few words of practical affectionate application to the souls of all who read it.

(1) My first word shall be *a word of warning.* I offer

an affectionate warning to every impenitent soul into whose hands this volume may fall. I cannot for a moment suppose that all who read its pages are truly repentant toward God, and lively believers in Jesus Christ. I dare not think it.—I cannot think it. And my first word shall be a word of warning,—tender, affectionate warning,—to all impenitent and unconverted people who may happen to read this paper.

What stronger warning can I give you than that which my text contains? What words can I use more solemn and more heart-searching than the words of my Lord and Master: "Except ye repent, ye shall all likewise perish"? Yes! you who are reading, and, as you read, know you are not yet at peace with God,—you who are halting, lingering, undecided, in religion,—you are the man to whom the words of the text should come with power: "Except thou repentest, thou," even thou, "shalt perish."

Oh, think what awful words are these! Who can measure out the full amount of what they contain? "Shall perish!" Perish in body,—perish in soul,—perish miserably at last in hell! I dare not attempt to paint the horrors of that thought. The worm that never dies, the fire that is not quenched, the blackness of darkness for ever, the hopeless prison, the bottomless pit, the lake that burns with fire and brimstone,—all, all are but feeble emblems of the reality of hell. And to this hell all impenitent people are daily travelling! Yes: from churches and chapels,—from rich men's drawing rooms and poor men's cottages,—from the midst of knowledge, wealth, and respectability, all who will not repent are certainly travelling towards hell. "Except ye repent, ye shall all perish."

Think how great is *your danger!* Where are your sins, your many sins? You know you are a sinner. You must be aware of it. It is vain to pretend you have committed no sins. And where are your sins, if you have never yet repented, never mourned for sin, never confessed sin, never fled to Christ, and never found pardon through Christ's blood? Oh, take heed to yourself.—The pit opens her mouth for you. The devil is saying of you, "He will be mine." Take heed to yourself. Remember the words of the text: "Except ye repent, ye shall all likewise perish." They are not my words, but Christ's words. It is not my saying, but Christ's saying. Christ says it—Christ, the merciful: Christ, the gracious,—"Except thou repentest, thou wilt certainly perish."

Think again of your guilt.—Yes, I say, deliberately, think of *your guilt*. It is guilt when a man does not repent. We are responsible and accountable to God for repentance. It is vain to say we are not. What does St. Paul say to the Athenians: "God commandeth all men everywhere to repent." (Acts xvii. 30.) What does our Lord say of Chorazin and Bethsaida? Why were they so guilty? Why was their position in hell to be so intolerable? Because they would not repent and believe.—It is the express testimony of the Son of God that the impenitent man who has been called to repentance, and refused to obey the call, is more guilty than the man who has never been urged to repent.

Think again of *the folly* of remaining an impenitent man! Yes, I say the folly. The world you cleave to is melting beneath your feet already. What will bank-notes do for you in the life to come? What will your gold be worth to you a hundred years hence? When your last hour comes, what can all the gold in the globe do for you, if you die an impenitent man? You live for the world, perhaps, now. You strive hard and furiously to be successful in business. You compass sea and land to add acre to acre, or accumulate stock in the funds. You do all you can to get money, to amass riches, to make yourself comfortable, to have pleasure, to leave something for wife and children when you die. But, oh, remember! Remember, if you have not got the grace of God and true repentance, you are a poor man, a pauper in the sight of God.

I shall never forget the effect produced upon my own mind when I read some years ago of that fearful shipwreck, the loss of the Central America, a great steamer which was lost on the voyage from Havannah to New York. That steamer was bringing home from California three or four hundred gold-diggers. They had all got their gold, and were coming home, proposing to spend their latter days in ease in their own country. But man proposes and God disposes.

About four-and-twenty hours after the Central America left Havannah, a mighty storm arose. Three or four heavy seas in succession struck the ship, and seriously damaged her. The engines became disabled and useless, and she fell off into the trough of the sea. She sprung a leak, and in spite of every effort the ship began to fill. And after a while, when all on board had pumped and baled, and baled and pumped, until they were exhausted, it became plain that the Central America, with her three or four hundred passengers and all her crew, was likely to go down into the deep, deep sea, and carry nearly all on board with her. The crew launched the only boats they had. They placed the women passengers in these boats, with just a sufficient complement of sailors to manage them. All honour be to them for their kind feeling to the weak and defenceless at a time like that! The boats put off from the vessel; but there were left behind two or three hundred people, many of them gold-diggers, when the Central America went down. One who left the ship in one of the last boats which took the women, described what he saw in the cabin of the steamer when all hope was gone, and the great ship was about to go down. Men took out their gold. One said, holding his leather bag, containing his long-toiled-for accumulations, "Here: take it who will! Take it who will. It is no more use to me: the ship is going down.

Take it who will." Others took out their gold-dust, and
scattered it broadcast over the cabin. "There," they said,
"take it: take it who will! We are all going down.
There is no more chance for us. The gold will do us no
good." Oh, what a comment that is on the truly valueless
nature of riches when a man draws near to God! "Riches
profit not in the day of wrath, but righteousness delivereth
from death." (Prov. xi. 4.) Think of your folly,—your
folly as well as your danger, your folly as well as your
guilt, if you will cleave to your sins. Think of your folly,
if you will not hear the warning which I give you this day.
In my Master's name, I say to you once more, "Except
thou repentest," thou, even thou who art reading this
paper, "thou shalt likewise perish."

(2) My second word of application shall be *an invitation to all who feel their sins and desire to repent, and
yet know not what to do.* I give it broadly and fully to
all who ask me, "What shall I do, this very day, if I am
to take your advice?" I answer that question without
any hesitation. I say to you, in my Master's name,
Repent, Repent, Repent this very day. Repent without
delay.

I feel no difficulty in saying this. I cannot agree with
those who say that unconverted people should not be told
to repent or pray. I find the Apostle Peter saying to
Simon Magus, "Repent of this thy wickedness." I find
him saying, "Pray God, if perhaps the thought of thy heart
may be forgiven." (Acts viii. 22.) I am content to follow
in the Apostle's wake. I say the same to every one who
is anxious about his soul. I say Repent, Repent, Repent
without delay. The time will soon come when you must
be decided, if you ever mean to be. Why not this very
day? Why not to-night? Sermon-hearing cannot go on
for ever. Going to churches and chapels must have an end.
Liking this minister and liking that minister, belonging to
this church and belonging to that chapel, holding these

views and holding those views, thinking this preacher sound and that preacher unsound, is not enough to save a soul. A man must act at last, as well as think, if he means to go to heaven. A man must break off from his sins, and flee to the Lord Jesus, if he does not intend to be damned. A man must come out from the world, and take up the cross. A man must be decided, and repent, and believe. A man must show his colours, and be on the Lord Jesus Christ's side, if he means to be saved. And why not begin all this to-day? Oh, Repent, Repent, Repent without delay!

Do you ask me again what you ought to do? Go, I tell you, and cry to the Lord Jesus Christ this very day. Go and pour out your heart before Him. Go and tell Him what you are, and tell Him what you desire. Tell Him you are a sinner: He will not be ashamed of you. Tell Him you want to be saved: He will hear you. Tell Him you are a poor weak creature: He will listen to you. Tell Him you do not know what to do or how to repent: He will give you His grace. He will pour out His Spirit upon you. He will hear you. He will grant your prayer. He will save your soul. There is enough in Christ, and to spare, for all the wants of all the world,—for all the wants of every heart that is unconverted, unsanctified, unbelieving, impenitent, and unrenewed. "What is your hope?" said a man to a poor Welsh boy, who could not speak much English, and was found dying in an inn one day.—"What is your hope about your soul?" What was his reply? He turned to the questioner, and said to him, in broken English, "Jesus Christ is plenty for everybody! Jesus Christ is plenty for everybody!" There was a mine of truth in those words. And well said another,—a navigator who died in the Lord at Beckenham: "Tell them all,—tell every man you meet,—Christ is for every man! JESUS CHRIST IS FOR EVERY MAN!" Go to that Saviour this day, and tell Him the wants of your soul.

Go to Him, in the words of that beautiful hymn which
says,—

> "Just as I am : without one plea,
> But that Thy blood was shed for me,
> And that Thou bidst me come to Thee,—
>   O Lamb of God, I come !

> "Just as I am : and waiting not
> To rid my soul of one dark blot,
> To Thee, whose blood can cleanse each spot,—
>   O Lamb of God, I come !"

Go to the Lord Jesus in that spirit, and He will
receive you. He will not refuse you. He will not despise
you. He will grant you pardon, peace, everlasting life,
and give you the grace of the Holy Ghost.

Do you ask me whether there is anything else you
ought to do ? Yes! I reply. Go and resolve to break off
from every known sin. Let those who will call such
advice legal : I trust I may never shrink from giving it. It
never can be right to sit still in wickedness. It never can
be wrong to say with Isaiah, "Cease to do evil." (Isa. i. 16.)
Whatever be your sin, resolve, by God's help, that to-morrow
morning you will rise an altered man, and break off from
that sin.—Whether it be drinking or swearing, or Sabbath-
breaking, or passion, or lying, or cheating, or covetousness,—
whatever your sin and fault,—determine, by God's grace,
that you will break off sharp from it. Give it up without
delay, and turn from it, by God's help, for the rest of your
days. Cast it from you : it is a serpent that will bite you
to death. Throw it from you : it is useless lumber ; it
will sink the ship down to perdition. Cast away your
besetting sin—give it up—turn from it—break it off. By
God's help resolve that in that respect you will sin no
more.

But I think it just possible that some reader of this
volume may be *ashamed* of repentance. I do beseech you
to cast away such shame for ever. Never be ashamed of

repentance toward God. Of sin you might be ashamed. Of lying, swearing, drunkenness, gambling, Sabbath-breaking,—of these a man ought to be ashamed. But of repentance, of prayer, of faith in Christ, of seeking God, of caring for the soul,—never, never, so long as you live, never be ashamed of such things as these. I remember, long ago, a thing that came under my own knowledge, which gave me some idea what the fear of man can do. I was attending a dying man, who had been a sergeant in the 7th Dragoon Guards. He had ruined his health by drinking spirits. He had been a careless, thoughtless man about his soul. He told me upon his death-bed, that when he first began to pray he was so ashamed of his wife knowing it, that when he went upstairs to pray he would take his shoes off and creep up in his stockings, that his wife might not be aware how he was spending his time. Verily, I am afraid there are many like him! Do not you be one of them. Whatever you are ashamed of, never be ashamed of seeking God.

But, I think it just possible that some reader of this volume is *afraid* to repent. You think you are so bad and unworthy that Christ will not have you. I do beseech you once more, to cast away such fear for ever. Never, never be afraid to repent. The Lord Jesus Christ is very gracious. He will not break the bruised reed, nor quench the smoking flax. Fear not to draw near to Him.—There is a confessional ready for you. You need none made by man. The throne of grace is the true confessional.—There is a Confessor ready for you. You need no ordained man, no priest, no bishop, no minister, to stand between you and God. The Lord Jesus is the true High Priest. The Lord Jesus Christ is the real Confessor. None is so wise, and none so loving as He. None but He can give you absolution, and send you away with a light heart and in perfect peace.—Oh, take the invitation I bring you. Fear nothing. Christ is not an " austere man." He " despiseth not any." (Job xxxvi. 5.) Arise this day, and flee to Him. Go to Christ and repent this night without delay.

(3) My last word of application shall be *an exhortation to all who have known what repentance is by experience.* I address it to all who have, by God's grace, felt their sins, sorrowed for their sins, confessed their sins, given up their sins, and found peace in the blood of Jesus Christ. What shall I say to you but this: Keep up your repentance,—*Keep up your repentance.* Let it be a habit of mind you watch over to the last day of your life. Let it be a fire you never allow to burn low or to become dull. Keep up your repentance, if you love life.

I do not want you to make a Christ of repentance, or to turn it into a bondage for your soul. I do not bid you to measure the degree of your justification by your repentance, or to suppose that your sins are not forgiven because your repentance is imperfect. Justification is one thing, and repentance is another. You must not confuse things that differ. It is only faith that justifies. It is only faith that lays hold of Christ. But for all that, keep a jealous watch over your repentance. Keep it up—keep it up, and let not the fire burn low. Whenever you find a slackness coming over your soul,—whenever you feel slow, and dull, and heavy, and cold, and careless about little sins, look to your own heart then, and take heed lest you fall. Say to your soul, "Oh, my soul, what art thou doing? Hast thou forgotten David's fall? Hast thou forgotten Peter's backsliding? Hast thou forgotten David's subsequent misery? Hast thou forgotten Peter's after tears? Awake, O my soul, awake once more. Heap on fuel, make the fire burn bright. Return again to thy God, let thy repentance once more be lively.—Let thy repentance be repented over again."—Alas, how few are the hours in a Christian's best days when he does not "make work for repentance!"

Keep up your repentance till the last day of your life.

There will always be sins to deplore, and infirmities to confess. Take them daily to the Lord Jesus Christ, and obtain from Him daily supplies of mercy and grace. Make confession daily to the great High Priest, and receive from Him daily absolution. Feed daily on the passover Lamb. But never forget that it was to be eaten with bitter herbs. "Sir," said a young man to Philip Henry, "how long should a man go on repenting? How long, Mr. Henry, do you mean to go on repenting yourself?" What did old Philip Henry reply? "Sir, I hope to carry my repentance to the very gates of heaven. Every day I find I am a sinner, and every day I need to repent. I mean to carry my repentance, by God's help, up to the very gates of heaven."

May this be our divinity, your divinity, my divinity; your theology, my theology! May repentance toward God and faith toward our Lord Jesus Christ be Jachin and Boaz,—the two great pillars before the temple of our religion, the corner-stones in our system of Christianity! (2 Chron. iii. 17.) May the two never be disjoined! May we, while we repent, believe; and while we believe, repent! And may repentance and faith, faith and repentance, be ever uppermost, foremost, the chief and principal articles, in the creed of our souls!

XVII.

CHRIST'S POWER TO SAVE.

" He is able also to save them to the uttermost that come unto God by Him, seeing He ever liveth to make intercession for them."
—HEBREWS vii. 25.

THERE is one subject in religion about which we can never know too much. That subject is Jesus Christ the Lord. This is the mighty subject which the text that heads this page unfolds,—Jesus Christ, and Jesus Christ's intercession.

I have heard of a book entitled "The Story without an End." I know no story deserving that title so well as the everlasting Gospel: this is indeed and in truth the story without an end. There is an infinite "fulness" in Christ; there are in Him "unsearchable riches;" there is in Him a "love which passeth knowledge;" He is an "unspeakable gift." (Col. i. 19; Eph. iii. 8; iii. 19; 2 Cor. ix. 15.) There is no end to all the riches which are treasured up in Him,— in His person, in His work, in His offices, in His words, in His deeds, in His life, in His death, in His resurrection. I take up only one branch of the great subject this day. I am going to consider the intercession and priestly office of our Lord Jesus Christ.

There are three points which I purpose to examine in opening the text which heads this paper.

I. You have here *a description of all true Christians:* they are a people who "come to God by Christ"

II. You have *the work that Jesus Christ is ever carrying on on behalf of true Christians:* He "ever lives to make intercession for them."

III. You have *the comfortable conclusion* built by St. Paul upon Christ's work of intercession. He says: "He is able to save to the uttermost them that come unto God by Him, because He ever liveth to make intercession for them."

I. You have, first, *a description of all true Christians.* It is most simple, most beautiful, and most true. Great is the contrast between the description given by the Holy Ghost of a Christian, and the description which is given by man! With man it is often enough to say that such a one "is a Churchman," or that such a one "belongs to this body of Christians, or to that." It is not so when the Holy Ghost draws the picture. The Holy Ghost describes a Christian as a man "who comes unto God by Christ."

True Christians come unto God. They are not as many who turn their backs upon Him:—who "go into a far country," like the prodigal son:—"who go out," like Cain, "from the presence of the Lord:"—who are "alienated, strangers, and enemies in their mind by wicked works." (Coloss. i. 21.) They are reconciled to God and friends of God. They are not as many, who dislike everything that belongs to God,—His word, His day, His ordinances, His people, His house. They love all that belongs to their Master. The very footprints of His steps are dear unto them. "His name is as ointment poured forth." (Cant. i. 3.)—They are not as many, who are content with coming to church, or with coming to chapel, or with coming to the Lord's table. They go further than that. They "come unto God," and in communion with God they live.

But, more than this, true Christians come unto God in a certain peculiar way. They come unto God by Christ,—

pleading no other plea, mentioning no other name, trusting in no other righteousness, resting on no other foundation than this,—that Jesus hath lived, Jesus hath died, Jesus hath risen again for their souls.

> "I the chief of sinners am,
> But Jesus died for me."

This is the way by which the true Christian draws near to God.

The way of which I have been speaking is an *old* way. It is well nigh 6,000 years old. All who have ever been saved have drawn near to God by this way. From Abel, the first saint that entered Paradise, down to the last infant that died this morning, they have all come to God only by Jesus Christ. "No man cometh unto the Father but by Christ." (John xiv. 6.)

It is a *good* way. It is easy for the worldly-wise to sneer at and ridicule it. But all the wit and wisdom of man has never devised a way more perfect, more suitable to our wants, and that will bear more thoroughly all fair and reasonable investigation. It has been to the Jew a stumbling-block ; it has been to the Greek foolishness. But all who have known their hearts, and understood what God demands, have found the way made by Jesus Christ a good way, and a way which stands the fullest examination that can be made as to its wisdom. Therein they find justice and mercy met together, righteousness and peace kissing one another,—God a holy God, yet loving, kind, and merciful, —man knowing himself a poor, weak sinner, yet drawing near to God with boldness, having access with confidence, looking up into His face without fear, and seeing Him in Christ his Father and his Friend.

Not least it is a *tried* way. Thousands and tens of thousands have walked in it, and not one of all that number has ever missed heaven. Apostles, prophets, patriarchs, martyrs, early fathers, reformers, puritans, men of God in every age, and of every people and tongue,—holy men of our own day, men like Simeon, Bickersteth, Havelock,—have all walked in this way. They have had their battles to fight and their enemies to contend with. They have had to carry the cross, and have found lions in their path. They have had to walk through the valley of the shadow of death, and to contend with Apollyon. They have had to cross at last the cold dark river; but they have walked safely through to the other side, and entered with joy into the celestial city. And now they are all waiting for us to walk in their steps, to follow them, and to share in their glory.

This is the way I want every reader of this paper to walk in. I want you to " come unto God by Jesus Christ." Let there be no mistake as to the object which true ministers of the Gospel have in view. We are not set apart merely to perform a certain round of ordinances, —to read prayers, to baptize those that are baptized, to bury those that are buried, to marry those that are married. We are set apart for the grand purpose of proclaiming the one true living way, and inviting you to walk in it. We want to persuade you, by God's blessing, to walk in that way,—the tried way, the good way, the old way,—and to know the " peace which passeth all understanding," which in that way alone is to be found.

II. I pass on now to the second point which I purpose to consider. The text which heads this paper speaks of the *work which the Lord Jesus Christ is ever doing on behalf of true Christians.* I ask special attention to this point. It is one of deep importance to our peace, and to the establishment of our souls in the Christian faith.

There is one great work which the Lord Jesus Christ has done and finished completely. That work is the work of *atonement, sacrifice, and substitution.* It is the work

which He did when He " suffered for sin, the just for the unjust, that He might bring us unto God." (1 Pet. iii. 18.) He
saw us ruined by the fall, a world of poor, lost, shipwrecked
sinners. He saw and He pitied us; and, in compliance with
the everlasting counsels of the Eternal Trinity, He came
down to the world, to suffer in our stead, and to save us.
He did not sit in heaven pitying us from a distance. He
did not stand upon the shore and see the wreck, and
behold poor drowning sinners struggling in vain to get
to shore. He plunged into the waters Himself. He came
off to the wreck, and took part with us in our weakness
and infirmity, becoming a man to save our souls.   As
man, He bore our sins and carried our transgressions.   As
man, He endured all that man can endure, and went
through everything in man's experience, sin only excepted.
As man He lived ; as man He went to the cross ; as man
He died.   As man He shed His blood, in order that He
might save us, poor shipwrecked sinners, and establish a
communication between earth and heaven !   As man He
became a curse for us, in order that He might bridge the
gulf, and make a way by which you and I might draw
near to God with boldness, and have access to God without
fear.   In all this work of Christ, remember, there was
infinite merit, because He who did it was not only man
but God.   Let that never be forgotten !   He who wrought
out our redemption was perfect man ; but He never
ceased for a moment to be perfect God.

But there is another great work which the Lord Jesus
Christ is yet doing.   That work is the work of *intercession*.
—The first work of atonement He did once for all : nothing
can be added to it ; nothing can be taken away from it.   It
was a finished, perfect work, when Christ offered up the
sacrifice upon the cross.   No other sacrifice need be
offered, beside the sacrifice once made by the Lamb of
God, when He shed His own blood at Calvary.   But the
second work He is ever carrying on at the right hand of

God, where He makes intercession for His people.—The first work He did on earth when He died upon the cross: the second work He carries on in heaven, at the right hand of God the Father.—The first work He did for all mankind, and offers the benefit of it to all the world: the second work He carries on and accomplishes solely and entirely on behalf of His own elect, His people, His believing servants, and His children.

How does our Lord Jesus Christ carry on this work? How shall we comprehend and grasp what is the meaning of Christ's intercession? We must not pry rashly into things unseen. We must not "rush in where angels fear to tread." Yet some faint idea we can obtain of the nature of that continual intercession which Christ ever lives to make on behalf of His believing people.

Our Lord Jesus Christ is doing for His people the work which the Jewish high-priest of old did on behalf of the Israelites. He is acting as the manager, the representative, the mediator in all things between His people and God.—He is ever presenting on their behalf His own perfect sacrifice, and His all-sufficient merit, before God the Father.—He is ever obtaining daily supplies of fresh mercy and of fresh grace for His poor, weak servants, who need daily mercy for daily sins, and daily grace for daily necessities.—He ever prays for them. As He prayed for Simon Peter upon earth, so, in a certain mysterious sense, I believe He prays for His people now.— He presents their names before God the Father. He carries their names upon His heart, the place of love, and upon His shoulder, the place of power,—as the high-priest carried the names of all the tribes of Israel, from the least to the greatest, when he wore his robes of office. He presents their prayers before God. They go up before God the Father mingled with Christ's all-prevailing intercession, and so are acceptable in God's sight. He lives, in one word, to be the friend, the advocate, the priest, the all-prevailing agent, of all who are His members here upon earth. As their elder brother He acts for them; and all that their souls require, He, in the court of heaven, is ever carrying on.

Does any reader of this paper need *a friend?* In such a world as this, how many hearts there are which ought to respond to that appeal! How many there are who feel, "I stand alone." How many have found one idol broken after another, one staff failing after another, one fountain dried after another, as they have travelled through the wilderness of this world. If there is one who wants a friend, let that one behold at the right hand of God an unfailing friend, the Lord Jesus Christ. Let that one repose his aching head and weary heart upon the bosom of that unfailing friend, Jesus Christ the Lord. There is one living at God's right hand of matchless tenderness. There is one who never dies. There is one who never fails, never disappoints, never forsakes, never changes His mind, never breaks off friendship. That One, the Lord Jesus, I commend to all who need a friend. No one in a world like this, a fallen world, a world which we find more and more barren, it may be, every year we live,—no one ever need be friendless while the Lord Jesus Christ lives to intercede at the right hand of God.

Does any reader of this paper need *a priest.* There can be no true religion without a priest, and no saving Christianity without a confessional. But who is the true priest? Where is the true confessional? There is only one true priest,—and that is Christ Jesus the Lord. There is only one real confessional,—and that is the throne of grace where the Lord Jesus waits to receive those who come to Him to unburden their hearts in His presence. We can find no better priest than Christ. We need no other Priest. Why need we turn to any priest upon earth, while Jesus is sealed, anointed, appointed, ordained, and commissioned by God the Father, and has an ear ever ready to hear, and a heart ever ready to feel for the poor sinful sons of men? The priesthood is His lawful prerogative. He has deputed that office to none. Woe be to any one upon earth who dares to rob Christ of His prerogative! Woe be to the man who takes upon himself the office which Christ holds in His own hands, and has never transferred to any one born of Adam, upon the face of the globe!

Let us never lose sight of this mighty truth of the Gospel,—the intercession and priestly office of our Lord and Saviour Jesus Christ. I believe that a firm grasp of this truth is one great safeguard against the errors of the Church of Rome. I believe that losing sight of this great truth is one principal reason why so many have fallen away from the faith in some quarters, have forsaken the creed of their Protestant forefathers, and have gone back to the darkness of Rome. Once firmly established upon this mighty truth,—that we *have* a Priest, an altar, and a Confessor,—that we *have* an unfailing, never-dying, ever-living Intercessor, who has deputed His office to none,—and we shall see that we need turn aside nowhere else. We need not hew for ourselves broken cisterns that can hold no water, when we have in the Lord Jesus Christ a fountain of living waters, ever flowing and free to all. We need not seek any human priest upon earth, when we have a divine Priest living for us in heaven.

Let us beware of regarding the Lord Jesus Christ only as one that is dead. Here, I believe, many greatly err. They think much of His atoning death, and it is right that they should do so. But we ought not to stop short there. We ought to remember that He not only died and went to the grave, but that He rose again, and ascended up on high, leading captivity captive. We ought to remember that He is now sitting on the right hand of God, to do a work as real, as true, as important to our souls, as the work which He did when He shed His blood. Christ lives, and is not dead. He lives as truly as any one of ourselves. Christ sees us, hears us, knows us, and is acting as a Priest in heaven on behalf of His believing people. The thought of His life ought to have as great and important a place in our souls, as the thought of His death upon the cross.

III. I will now consider, in the third place, *the comfortable conclusions that the Apostle builds upon the everlasting intercession of the Lord Jesus Christ.* We need much comfort and consolation in a world like this. It is no easy matter for a man to carry the cross and reach heaven. There are many enemies to be encountered and overcome. We have often to stand alone. We have at the best times few with us and many against us. We need cordials and " strong consolation " to sustain and cheer us, and to preserve us from fainting on the way as we travel from Egypt into Canaan. The Apostle appears deeply conscious of all this in the words he uses. He says, " He is able to save to the uttermost,"—to save perfectly, to save completely, to save eternally,—" all that come unto God by Him, because He ever liveth to make intercession for them."

I might say much on the glorious expression which is before us. But I forbear. I will only point out a few of the thoughts which ought to arise in our minds when we hear of Christ's ability to " save to the uttermost." I have not space to dwell on them at length. I rather throw them out as suggestions to supply matter for the private meditation of every one who reads this paper.

(1) Let us think, for one thing, that Christ is able to save to the uttermost, *notwithstanding the old sins* of any believer. Those old sins shall never rise again, nor stand up to condemn the child of God. For what says the Scripture : " Christ hath not entered into the holy place made with hands, but into heaven itself, now to appear in the presence of God for us." (Heb. ix. 24.) Christ, to use a

legal phrase, is ever " putting in an appearance" in the court
of heaven on behalf of them that believe in Him. There
is not a year, nor a month, nor a day, nor an hour, nor a
minute, but there is One living in the presence of God,
to "make an appearance" there on behalf of all the saints.
Christ is ever appearing before God the Father on behalf
of the men and women that believe in Him. His blood
and His sacrifice are ever in God's sight. His work, His
death, His intercession, are always sounding in God the
Father's ears.

I remember reading a story in ancient history which
may help to illustrate the truth on which I am now
dwelling. It is the story of one who was put upon trial
for a capital charge, at Athens, shortly after the great
battle of Marathon. In that famous battle the Athenians
had preserved, by their valour, liberty for their little
State, against the mighty hosts of the Persians. Among
those who had distinguished themselves greatly, the
brother of the prisoner was one, and had been sorely
wounded in the fight. The man was put upon his trial.
The evidence against him was strong and unanswerable :
there seemed no chance of the prisoner escaping condemnation. Suddenly there came forward one who asked
to be heard on his behalf. And who was this ? It was
his own brother. When he was asked what evidence he
had to give, or what reason he had to show why the
prisoner at the bar ought not to be found guilty, he
simply lifted up his mutilated arms—nothing but stumps
—the hands completely cut off, the wounded stumps alone
remaining. He was recognized as a man who, at the
battle of Marathon, had done prodigies of valour, and in
the service of the State had lost his hands. By those
wounds he had helped to win the victory which was still
ringing in Athenian ears. Those wounds were the only
evidence he brought forward. Those wounds were the
only plea he advanced why his brother ought to be let go

free, and sentence ought not to be passed upon him.   And
the story states that for the sake of those wounds—for the
sake of all his brother had suffered,—the prisoner was
acquitted.   The case was dismissed at once, and the
prisoner obtained his liberty.   In like manner the wounds
of the Lord Jesus Christ are ever before God the Father.
The nail-prints in His hands and feet—the marks of the
spear in His side—the thorn marks upon His forehead
—the marks of all that He suffered as a Lamb slain, are,
in a certain sense, ever before God the Father in heaven.
While Christ is in heaven the believer's old sins will
never rise in judgment against him.   Christ lives, and those
old sins will not condemn him.   We have an ever-living,
ever-interceding Priest.   Christ is not dead but alive.

(2) Let us think again, that Christ is able to save to the
uttermost, *notwithstanding all the present weakness* of
His believing people.   How great that weakness is, time
would fail me to show.   There are many of God's children
who know their hearts' bitterness, who bewail with strong
crying and tears their short-comings, their unprofitableness,
and the scanty fruit they bring forth.   But let us take
comfort in the words of St. John : " If any man sin, we
have an advocate with the Father "—ever present with
the Father—" Jesus Christ the righteous : and He is the
propitiation for our sins."   (1 John ii. 1.)   Those weaknesses may well humble us.   Those infirmities may well
make us walk softly before our God.   But while the Lord
Jesus Christ lives those infirmities need not make us
entirely despair.   We have an ever-living, ever-interceding
Priest.   Christ is not dead but alive.

(3) Let us think again, that Jesus Christ is able to save to
the uttermost, *notwithstanding all the trials* that believers
have to go through.   Hear what the Apostle Paul says to
Timothy : " I suffer : nevertheless I am not ashamed, for
I know whom I have believed, and am persuaded that He
is able to keep that which I have committed unto Him

against that day." (2 Tim. i. 12.) So long as Jesus Christ lives, the believer in the Lord Jesus Christ may be assured that no affliction shall be allowed to break off the union between him and his risen Head. He may suffer greatly and be sorely tried. But while Christ lives he shall never be forsaken. Neither poverty, nor sickness, nor bereavements, nor separations, shall ever separate Jesus and His believing people. We have an ever-living, ever-interceding Priest. Christ is not dead but alive.

(4) Let us think again, that Christ is able to save to the uttermost, *notwithstanding all the persecutions* that believers have to go through. See what is said of St. Paul, when he met with much opposition at Corinth. We are told that the Lord stood by him in the night, and said, "Be not afraid, but speak and hold not thy peace; for I am with thee, and no man shall set on thee to hurt thee, for I have much people in this city." (Acts xviii. 10.) Remember what He said to St. Paul at a former time, before his conversion, when He met him on the way to Damascus : " Saul, Saul, why persecutest thou *Me ?* " (Acts ix. 4.) Every injury done to the believer, is an injury done to the living Head in heaven. Every persecution showered down upon the head of the poor child of God here, is known, felt, and, I may add with all reverence, resented, by our Great Elder Brother, who is ever living to make intercession for us. Christ lives, and therefore believers, though persecuted, shall not be destroyed. " In all these things we are more than conquerors through Him that loved us." (Rom. viii. 37.) We have an ever-living, ever-interceding Priest. Christ is not dead but alive.

(5) Let us think again, that Christ is able to save to the uttermost, *notwithstanding all the temptations of the devil.* Remember that famous passage in the Gospel of St. Luke, where our Lord, speaking to St. Peter, says, "Simon, Simon, behold Satan hath desired to have you,

that he may sift you as wheat: but I have prayed for thee, that thy faith fail not." (Luke xxii. 32.) We may surely believe that intercession like that is still carried on. Those words were spoken as an emblem of what the Lord is ever doing on behalf of His believing people. Satan, the prince of this world, is ever "walking about as a roaring lion seeking whom he may devour." (1 Pet. v. 8.) But Christ lives; and, blessed be God, while Christ lives Satan shall not be able to overcome the soul that believes on Him. We have an ever-living, ever-interceding Priest. Christ is not dead but alive.

(6) Let us think again, that Christ is able to save to the uttermost, *notwithstanding the sting of death,* and all that death brings with it. Even David could say, "Though I walk through the valley of the shadow of death, I will fear no evil: for Thou art with me; Thy rod and Thy staff they comfort me." (Ps. xxiii. 4.) Yet David saw through a glass darkly, compared to a believing Christian. The hour may come when friends can do us no more good, when faithful servants can no longer minister to our wants, when all that love, and kindness, and affection can do to alleviate pain, and make the last journey as easy as possible, can no longer render any service to us. But then the thought that Christ lives—Christ interceding, Christ caring for us, Christ at the right hand of God for us— ought to cheer us. The sting of death will be taken away from the man who leans upon a dying and also a living Saviour. Christ never dies. Through faith in that living Saviour we shall have a complete victory. We have an ever-living, ever-interceding Priest. Christ is not dead but alive.

(7) Let us think, again, that Christ is able to save to the uttermost, *notwithstanding the terrors of the judgment day.* Mark how St. Paul rests upon this in the eighth chapter of the Epistle to the Romans,—in that wonderful conclusion to that wonderful chapter,—a chapter unrivalled

in the Word of God for privilege, beginning with "no condemnation," and concluding with "no separation!" Observe
how he dwells upon Christ's intercession in connection
with the judgment of the last day. After saying, "Who
shall lay anything to the charge of God's elect? It is
God that justifieth," he goes on: "Who is he that con-
demneth? It is Christ that died, yea rather, that is risen
again, who is even at the right hand of God, who also
maketh intercession for us." (Rom. viii. 33, 34.) The
thought of Christ's intercession, no less than His dying
and rising again, was one ground of the Apostle Paul's
confidence in looking forward to the great day. His strong
consolation was the recollection of a living Christ. That
consolation is for us as well as for St. Paul. We have an
ever-living, ever-interceding Priest. Christ is not dead
but alive.

(8) Let us think, lastly, and above all, that Christ is able
save to the uttermost *throughout all eternity.* "I am
He," He says, "that liveth, and was dead; and, behold,
I am alive for evermore." (Rev. i. 18.) The root of the
believer never dies, and the branches, therefore, shall never
die. Christ being "raised from the dead, dieth no more;
death hath no more dominion over Him." (Rom. vi. 9.)
He lives, that all who trust in Him may receive honour and
glory to all eternity; and because He lives, His believing
people shall never die. "Because I live," to use His own
words, "ye shall live also." (John xiv. 19.) We have an
ever-living, ever-interceding Priest. Christ is not dead
but alive.

Would you know the secret of the *security* for the perseverance of God's own people? Would you know why it is
that Christ's sheep shall never perish, and none shall ever
pluck them out of His hand? It is a miraculous thing.
When you look at the believer's heart, listen to the
believer's prayers, mark the believer's confessions,—when
you see how a just man may fall, sometimes seven times –

when you see, with all this, the believer's perseverance, it is a marvel indeed. To carry a candle upon a stormy night, when winds and gusty blasts are blowing from every quarter,—to carry it still burning, steadily burning, along the street,—this is a wonderful achievement. To go over a stormy sea in a little boat,—to mount billow after billow, and not see the waves breaking over the boat, and overturning it,—this is well-nigh a miracle. To see a little child tottering along the crowded street, a child some three or four years old—to see it tottering on and making its way in safety, from one end of a long street to the other, —this is a mighty marvel. But after all, what is this but the life, and history, and experience of every true Christian? Though he falls, he rises again; though he is cast down, he is not destroyed. He goes on from one position to another, like the moon upon a stormy night, plunging from one cloud into another, yet by-and-by shining out again and walking in brightness. What is the secret of it all? It is the continual intercession of a mighty Friend at the right hand of God,—a Friend who never slumbers and never sleeps,—a Friend who cares for the believer, morning, noon, and night. The intercession of Christ is the secret of the perseverance of the Christian.

We shall do well to study the words of the Apostle in the 5th chapter of Romans: "Much more then," he says, "being now justified by His blood, we shall be saved from wrath through Him. For if, when we were enemies, we were reconciled to God by the death of His Son, much more, being reconciled, we shall be saved by His life." Mark the connection: "Being already justified by His death, we shall be saved,"—and saved by what? "By His life," by His ever living to make intercession for us. (Rom. v. 10.) Wise and beautiful is the comparison made by that master of allegory, John Bunyan, in the "Pilgrim's Progress." He tells us how Christian was taken into the Interpreter's house, and how the Interpreter showed him many things wonderful and instructive. In one place he took him into a room where there was a fire burning, and showed him one ever pouring water upon that fire, and yet the water did not quench the fire. However much water he poured on, still the fire went on burning steadily! Then said the Interpreter, "Knowest thou what this means?" When Christian did not know, he took him behind the fire, and showed him one pouring on oil out of a vessel. This oil fed the fire, and made it burn more fiercely, notwithstanding all the water that was poured upon it. Then the Interpreter told him that this was a picture of Jesus Christ's intercession. That fire was the fire of grace in the believer's heart. He that poured on the water was the enemy of souls, the devil. But He that poured on the oil, standing behind the fire, was the Lord Jesus Christ, who by continual intercession and the supply of His Spirit, secretly and unseen by man, kept alive His own work in the believer's heart, and did not allow Satan and all his agents to get a victory over Him.

Would you know the secret of the believer's *boldness in prayer?* It is a marvel how a man that feels his sin so deeply as the believer does, can speak with the confidence the believer frequently does. How one that acknowledges he is "wretched, miserable, poor, blind, naked," ruined, undone,—who often does what he ought not to do, and leaves undone what he ought to do, and finds no health in him,—how such a one as this can go before God with confidence, pour out his heart before Him freely, ask from Him what he requires day after day and not feel afraid,—this is wonderful indeed. What is the secret of it? It is the intercession of our Lord and Saviour Jesus Christ, whereby the true Christian knows his prayers are made acceptable, and received in the court of heaven. What is the believer's prayer in itself? A poor, weak thing, unfit to rise above the ground. I know nothing it is more like than a bank-note without the signature in the corner. What is the value of that bank-note without the signature? Nothing at all. Once get a few words, a very few letters, traced in ink upon the corner of that bank-note, and that which was a piece of waste paper a few moments before, becomes worth, it may be, many hundred pounds, through the signature being attached to it. So it is with the intercession of Christ. He signs, endorses, and presents the believer's petitions; and through His all-prevailing intercession they are heard on high, and bring down blessings upon the Christian's soul.

Would you know the *secret of daily comfort* in all the toil, and business, and distractions we have to go through? We all know that they who have to do work in any secular calling, find the work oftentimes a sore burden to their souls. Oftentimes in the morning they feel, "How can I get through this day without a defiled conscience, without being sorely troubled and tempted to forget my God?" How shall a man get through the day with comfort, fill his office in the world, do his duty in the position to which God has called him? Let him lay hold upon the intercession of Jesus Christ. Let him grasp the great thought, that Christ not merely died for him, but rose again, and still lives for him.

It is recorded of a Christian soldier, who fell in the unhappy Commonwealth wars, that a common prayer of his before leaving his tent was something of this kind,— "Lord, I am going this day to do the duty whereunto I am called. I may sometimes forget Thee. I cannot have my thoughts at all times as fully fixed upon Thee as I wish. But, Lord, if I this day forget Thee, do not Thou forget me." This is the kind of thought which every believer should lay hold upon who has much to do in the business of this world. Rising from his bed in the morning, going from his room every morning, leaving his house every morning, let him bear in mind, "There is One living in heaven who intercedes for me, while I am following my lawful calling.

Although I may be absorbed in business, and obliged to give up all the powers of my poor weak mind to it, still there lives One who never forgets me." He may say, as the old soldier did, "Lord,—if I this day forget Thee, do not Thou forget me."

Last of all, would you know the *secret of comfort in looking forward* to that heaven whereunto every believer desires to go? I believe there are few children of God who do not sometimes feel anxious, troubled, and cast down, when they think quietly about the eternal habitation towards which they are travelling. The nature of it, the manner of it, the employments of it, their own apparent unfitness and unmeetness for it, will sometimes perplex their minds. These thoughts will sometimes come across the believer's mind, especially in times of sickness, filling him with heaviness, and making his heart sink. Now I know no remedy against these thoughts to be compared to the recollection of the continual intercession of the Lord and Saviour Jesus Christ. Christ is gone into heaven to be the "forerunner" of a people who are to follow after Him. He is gone "to prepare a place for them;"—and the place whereto He goes is the place whereto His people are to go by-and-by. When they go there they will find all things made ready, a place for every one, and a fitting and proper place, too, through the intercession of their Lord and Saviour. There never will be a time when their company will not be liked in heaven. There never will be a time when their old sins,—the sins of their youth and their backslidings, their wickedness before conversion, their profligacy, it may be, before the grace of God came into their hearts,—there never will be a day when all these sins shall come up against them, and make them feel abashed and ashamed in heaven. Christ will be in the midst. Christ will ever intercede for them. Where Christ is, there His people will be. Where He lives, His perfect merit, His spotless righteousness, His intercession, will make them perfect in the sight of God the Father. They will stand in heaven, seen in Christ, clothed in Christ, members of Christ, part of Christ, and so will possess a firm and solid and eternal title to the eternal joys which shall be hereafter.

I will now conclude this paper by a few words of application to all into whose hands it may fall. My heart's desire and prayer to God is that the words I have been writing may yet bear fruit in some souls. In order that they may do so, I offer a few words of faithful and affectionate exhortation.

(1) I would *offer counsel,* first, to all who are anxious and troubled respecting their soul's salvation, and yet know not what to do. If you are such a person, I charge you and intreat you, I beseech you and invite you, to come into the way of which I have been speaking in this paper. I beseech you to come to God by the old and tried way,— the way of faith in Jesus Christ. Draw near to God, pleading the name of Jesus. Begin this very day to cry mightily unto God, in the name of Jesus, on behalf of your soul. Say not you have anything to plead for yourself. You have nothing to plead. Your life, your thoughts, your ways, all alike condemn you. Say nothing about yourself but this,—that you are a sinner, a great sinner, a guilty sinner, a condemned sinner; but because you are a sinner, you turn to God. Come to Him in the name of Jesus, saying, you have heard that through Jesus a sinner may come near Him. Tell Him that you are a sinner, a great sinner, and an unworthy one. But tell Him that you come in the faith of His promises, in the confidence of His own Bible invitation; and in the name of Jesus, and for the sake of Jesus, and on account of Jesus, you ask to be received, heard, pardoned, forgiven, and accepted. Tell Him that you wish to have your name,—even that name of your's connected hitherto with worldliness, thought-

lessness, carelessness, and sin,—added to the list of God's dear children.

Will you say that you are afraid to come to God? Your fear is needless. You shall not be cast out, if you will but come in the way of faith in Christ. Our God is not "an austere man." Our Father in heaven is full of mercy, love, and grace. I yield to none in desire to exalt the love, mercy, and tenderness of God the Father. I will never concede, for one moment, that what is called an evangelical ministry, will not magnify the mercy, love, and compassion of God the Father as much as any ministry on earth. We know that God is holy. We know He is just. We believe that He can be angry with them that go on still in sin. But we also believe that to those who draw near to Him in Christ Jesus, He is most merciful, most loving, most tender, and most compassionate. We tell you that the cross of Jesus Christ was the result and consequence of that love. The cross was not the cause and reason of God's mercy, but the result and consequence of the everlasting love of God the Father, God the Son, and God the Holy Ghost, towards a poor, lost, and bankrupt world. Draw near in faith, by that living way, Christ Jesus, to the Father. Think not for a moment —the unworthy thought shall never prove true—that so drawing near to God the Father by Christ, God the Father will not receive you. He will receive you gladly. As the father did to the prodigal son when he ran to meet him,— fell on his neck and kissed him,—so will God the Father do to that soul that draws near to Him in the name of Christ.

(2) In the next place, I *would cheer* those readers who have walked in the way of God, and yet are afraid of falling. Why should you be afraid? What should make you fear? What should make you suppose that you shall ever be allowed to fall away, while Jesus Christ lives at the right hand of God to make intercession for you? All

the power of the Lord Jesus Christ is pledged upon your behalf. He has undertaken to care for all the flock that God the Father has committed into His hand. He will care for it. He has cared for it. He went to the cross for it. He died for it. He is ever at the right hand of God, and has not ceased to care for it. Every member of that flock—the weakest, the feeblest sheep or lamb,— is equally dear to the Lord and Saviour, and none shall pluck the least of Christ's sheep out of God's hand. Can you stop the tides of the sea, and make them not rise at your command? Can you make the waters stay when the tide begins to fall? Can you prevent the sun in heaven going down in the west, or prevent the same sun from rising to-morrow morning in the east? You cannot do it: these things are impossible. And all the power of devils, all the power of the world, and all the enemies of the Christian, shall not be able to pluck out of the hand of Jesus Christ one single soul who has been brought by the Spirit's teaching to true union with Christ, and for whom Jesus Christ intercedes. The days of Christ's weakness have passed away. He was "crucified through weakness," and was weak on our account when He went to the cross. (2 Cor. xiii. 4.) The days of His weakness are over: the days of His power have begun. Pilate shall no more condemn Him: He shall come to condemn Pilate. All power is His in heaven and earth, and all that power is engaged on behalf of His believing people.

(3) Finally, *let me gladden* all believers who read this paper, by reminding them that Christ is yet to come again. The Great High Priest is yet to come forth from the Holy of Holies, to bless all the people who have believed on Him. *One* part of His work He did when He died upon the cross; *another* part of His work He is still doing,— interceding for us at God's right hand. But the *third* part of the High Priest's office remains yet to be done. He has yet to come forth from the Holy of Holies, as the

high-priest did upon the day of atonement,—to come forth from within the vail to bless the people. That part of Christ's work is yet to come. He is now gone into heaven itself,—He is within the Holy of Holies: He is gone behind the vail. But our Great High Priest—a greater one than Aaron—shall yet come forth one day. He shall come in power and great glory. He shall come as He left the world, when He went up in the clouds of heaven. He shall come to gather from the north and from the south, from the east and from the west, all who have loved His name and confessed Him before men,—all who have heard His voice and followed Him. He shall gather them together into one happy company. There shall be no more weakness, and no more sorrow,—no more parting, and no more separation,—no more sickness, and no more death,—no more disputing, and no more controversy,—no more fighting with the world, the flesh, and devil,—and, best of all, no more sin. That day shall be a happy day indeed, when the High Priest comes forth to do the third, last, and completing part of His work,—to bless His believing people.

"He that testifieth these things saith, Surely I come quickly. Amen. Even so, come, Lord Jesus." (Rev. xxii. 20.)

XVIII.

ELECTION.

"*Knowing, brethren beloved, your election of God.*"—
1 Thess. i. 4.

"*Give diligence to make your calling and election sure.*"—
2 Peter i. 10.

THE texts which head this page contain a word of peculiar interest. It is a word which is often in men's minds, and on men's tongues, from one end of Great Britain to the other. That word is "Election."

There are few Englishmen who do not know something of a general election to Parliament. Many are the evils which come to the surface at such a time. Bad passions are called out. Old quarrels are dug up, and new ones are planted. Promises are made, like pie-crust, only to be broken. False profession, lying, drunkenness, intimidation, oppression, flattery, abound on every side. At no time perhaps does human nature make such a poor exhibition of itself as at a general election!

Yet it is only fair to look at all sides of an election to Parliament. There is nothing new, or peculiarly English, about its evils. In every age, and in every part of the world, the heart of man is pretty much the same. There have never been wanting men ready to persuade others that they are not so well governed as they ought to be, and that they themselves are the fittest rulers that can be found.* A thousand years before Christ was born the following picture was drawn by the unerring hand of the Holy Ghost:—

"Absalom rose up early, and stood beside the way of the gate: and it was so, that when any man that had a controversy came to the king for judgment, then Absalom called unto him, and said, Of what city art thou? And he said, Thy servant is of one of the tribes of Israel.

"And Absalom said unto him, See, thy matters are good and right; but there is no man deputed of the king to hear thee.

"Absalom said moreover, Oh that I were made judge in the land, that every man which hath any suit or cause might come unto me, and I would do him justice!

"And it was so, that when any man came nigh to him to do him obeisance, he put forth his hand, and took him, and kissed him." (2 Sam. xv. 2—5.)

---

* The following weighty passage, from the pen of the judicious Hooker, is commended to the attention of all in the present day. It is the opening passage of the first book of his "Ecclesiastical Polity."

"He that goeth about to persuade a multitude that they are not so well governed as they ought to be, shall never want attentive and favourable hearers, because they know the manifold defects whereunto every kind of regiment or government is subject; but the secret lets and difficulties, which in public proceedings are innumerable and inevitable, they have not ordinarily the judgment to consider. And because such as openly reprove disorders of States are taken for principal friends to the common benefit of all, and for men that carry singular freedom of mind, under this fair and plausible colour whatsoever they utter passeth for good and current. That which is wanting in the weight of their speech is supplied by the aptness of men's minds to accept and believe it. Whereas, on the other side, if we maintain things that are established, we have not only to strive with a number of heavy prejudices, deeply rooted in the breasts of men, who think that herein we serve the times, and speak in favour of the present state, because we either hold or seek preferment; but also to bear such reception as minds so averted beforehand usually take against that which they are loth should be poured into them."

When we read this passage we must learn not to judge our own times too harshly. The evils that we see are neither peculiar nor new.

After all, we must never forget that popular election, with all its evils, is far better than an absolute form of government. To live under the dominion of an absolute tyrant, who allows no one to think, speak, or act for himself, is miserable slavery. For the sake of liberty we must put up with all the evils which accompany the return of members to Parliament. We must each do our duty conscientiously, and learn to expect little from any party. If those we support succeed, we must not think that all they do will be right. If those we oppose succeed, we must not think that all they do will be wrong. To expect little from any earthly ruler is one great secret of contentment. To pray for all who are in authority, and to judge all their actions charitably, is one of the principal duties of a Christian.

But there is another Election, which is of far higher importance than any election to Parliament,—an Election whose consequences will abide, when Queen, Lords, and Commons have passed away,—an Election which concerns all classes, the lowest as well as the highest, the women as well as the men. It is the Election which the Scriptures call "the Election of God."

I ask the readers of this paper to give me their attention for a few minutes, while I try to set before them the subject of this Election. Believe me, it affects your eternal happiness most deeply. Whether you are in Parliament or not, whether you vote or not, whether you are on the winning side or not, all this will matter very little a hundred years hence. But it will matter greatly whether you are in the number of "God's Elect."

In handling the subject of Election, there are only two things which I propose to do.

I. Firstly, I will state the doctrine of Election, and *show what it is.*

II. Secondly, I will fence the subject with cautions, and *guard it against abuse.*

If I can make these two points clear and plain to the mind of all who read these pages, I think I shall have done their souls a great and essential service.

I. I have firstly *to state the doctrine of Election. What is it? What does it mean?* Accurate statements on this point are of great importance. No doctrine of Scripture perhaps has suffered so much damage from the erroneous conceptions of foes, and the incorrect descriptions of friends, as that which is now before us.

The true doctrine of Election I believe to be as follows. God has been pleased from all eternity to choose certain men and women out of mankind, whom by His counsel secret to us, He has decreed to save by Jesus Christ. None are finally saved except those who are thus chosen. Hence the Scripture gives to God's people in several places the names of "God's Elect," and the choice or appoint· ment of them to eternal life is called "God's election."

Those men and women whom God has been pleased to choose from all eternity, He calls in time, by His Spirit working in due season. He convinces them of sin. He leads them to Christ. He works in them repentance 'and faith. He converts, renews, and sanctifies them. He keeps them by His grace from falling away entirely, and finally brings them safe to glory. In short God's eternal Election is the first link in that chain of a sinner's salvation of which heavenly glory is the end. None ever repent, believe, and are born again, except the Elect. The primary and original cause of a saint's being what he is, is eternal God's election.

The doctrine here stated, no doubt, is peculiarly deep,

mysterious, and hard to understand. We have no eyes to see it fully. We have no line to fathom it thoroughly. No part of the Christian religion has been so much disputed, rejected, and reviled as this. None has called forth so much of that enmity against God which is the grand mark of the carnal mind. Thousands of so-called Christians profess to believe the Atonement, salvation by grace, and justification by faith, and yet refuse to look at the doctrine of Election. The very mention of the word to some persons is enough to call forth expressions of anger, ill-temper, and passion.

But, after all, is the doctrine of Election plainly stated in Scripture? This is the whole question which an honest Christian has to do with. If it is not in the Book of God, let it be for ever discarded, refused, and rejected by man, no matter who propounds it. If it is there, let us receive it with reverence, as a part of Divine revelation, and humbly believe, even where we are not able to understand completely or explain fully. What then is written in the Scriptures? "To the law and to the testimony: if they speak not according to this word, it is because there is no light in them." (Isaiah. viii. 20.) Is Election in the Bible, or is it not? Does the Bible speak of certain persons as God's Elect, or not?

Hear what our Lord Jesus Christ says:—"For the Elect's sake the days shall be shortened." (Matt. xxiv. 22.)

"If it were possible they should deceive even the Elect." (Mark xiii. 22.)

"He shall send His angels, and they shall gather together His Elect." (Matt. xxiv. 31.)

"Shall not God avenge His own Elect?" (Luke xviii. 7.)

Hear what St. Paul says:—"Whom He did foreknow, He also did predestinate to be conformed to the image of His Son, that He might be the firstborn among many brethren. Moreover whom He did predestinate, them He also called: and whom He called, them He also justified:

and whom He justified, them He also glorified." (Rom. viii. 29, 30.)

" Who shall lay anything to the charge of God's Elect ? " (Rom. viii. 33.)

" God hath chosen us in Him before the foundation of the world." (Ephes. i. 4.)

" Who hath saved us, and called us with an holy calling, not according to our works, but according to His own purpose and grace, which was given us in Christ Jesus before the world began." (2 Tim. i. 9.)

" God hath from the beginning chosen you to salvation through sanctification of the Spirit and belief of the truth." (2 Thess. ii. 13.)

Hear what St. Peter says:—" Elect according to the foreknowledge of God the Father, through sanctification of the Spirit, unto obedience and sprinkling of the blood of Jesus Christ." (1 Peter i. 2.)

" Give diligence to make your calling and Election sure." (2 Peter i. 10.)

I place these eleven texts before my readers, and I ask them to consider them well. If words have any meaning at all, they appear to me to teach most plainly the doctrine of personal Election. In the face of such texts I dare not refuse to believe that it is a Scriptural doctrine. I dare not, as an honest man, shut my eyes against the plain, obvious sense of Bible language. If I once began to do so, I should have no ground to stand on in pressing the Gospel on an unconverted man. I could not expect him to believe one set of texts to be true, if I did not believe another set. The eleven texts above quoted seem to my mind to prove conclusively that personal Election is a doctrine of Scripture. As such I must receive it, and I must believe it, however difficult it may be. As such I ask my readers this day to look at it calmly, weigh it seriously, and receive it as God's truth.

After all, whatever men may please to say, there is no

denying that the Election of some men and women to salvation is a simple matter of fact. That all professing Christians are not finally saved, but only some,—that those who are saved owe their salvation entirely to the free grace of God and the calling of His Spirit,—that no man can at all explain why some are called unto salvation and others are not called,—all these are things which no Christian who looks around him can pretend for a moment to deny. Yet what does all this come to but the doctrine of Election?

Right views of human nature are certain to lead us to the same conclusion. Once admit that we are all naturally dead in trespasses and sins, and have no power to turn to God,—once admit that all spiritual life in the heart of man must begin with God,—once admit that He who created the world by saying, "Let there be light," must shine into man's heart, and create light within him,—once admit that God does not enlighten all professing Christians in this manner, but only some, and that He acts in this matter entirely as a Sovereign, giving no account of His matters,—once admit all this, and then see where you are. Whether you know it or not, you admit the whole doctrine of Election!

Right views of God's nature and character, as revealed in the Bible, appear to me to bring us to the same position. Do we believe that God knows all things from all eternity, —that He governs all things by His providence, and that not even a sparrow falleth to the ground without Him? Do we believe that He works all His works by a plan, like an architect of perfect knowledge, and that nothing concerning His saints, as His choicest and most excellent work, is left to chance, accident, and luck?—Well, if we believe all this, we believe the whole doctrine which this paper is meant to support. This is the doctrine of Election.

Now what can be said in reply to these things? What

are the principal weapons of argument with which Election is assailed ? Let us see.

Some tell us that there is no such thing in Scripture as an Election of persons and individuals. Such an Election, they say, would be arbitrary, unjust, unfair, partial, and unkind. The only Election they admit is one of nations, churches, communities,—such as Israel in ancient times, and Christian nations, as compared to heathen nations, in our own day. Now is there anything in this objection that will stand ? I believe there is nothing at all.—For one thing, the Election spoken of in Scripture is an Election attended by the sanctifying influence of the Holy Ghost. This certainly is not the Election of nations. For another thing St. Paul himself draws a clear and sharply-cut distinction between Israel itself and the Election. "Israel hath not obtained that which he seeketh for; but the Election hath obtained it." (Rom. xi. 7.)—Last, but not least, the advocates of the theory of national Election gain nothing whatever by it. How can they account for God withholding the knowledge of Christianity from 350 millions of Chinese for 1800 years, and yet spreading it over the continent of Europe ? They cannot, except on the ground of God's sovereign will and His free Election ! So that, in fact, they are driven to take up the very same position which they blame us for defending, and denounce as arbitrary and uncharitable.

Some tell us that at any rate Election is not the doctrine of the Church of England. It may do very well for dissenters and presbyterians, but not for churchmen. "It is a mere piece of Calvinism," they say,—"an extravagant notion which came from Geneva, and deserves no credit among those who love the Prayer-book." Such people would do well to look at the end of their Prayer-books, and to read the Thirty-nine Articles. Let them turn to the 17th Article, and mark the following words: "Predestination to Life is the everlasting purpose of God, whereby (before the foundations of the world were laid) He hath constantly decreed by His counsel secret to us, to deliver from curse and damnation those whom He hath chosen in Christ out of mankind, and to bring them by Christ to everlasting salvation, as vessels made to honour. Wherefore, they which be endued with so excellent a benefit of God be called according to God's purpose by His Spirit working in due season: they through grace obey the calling: they be justified freely: they be made sons of God by adoption: they be made like the image of His only-begotten Son Jesus Christ: they walk religiously in good works, and at length, by God's mercy, they attain to everlasting felicity."

I commend that Article to the special attention of all English Churchmen. It is one of the sheet-anchors of sound doctrine in the present day. It never can be reconciled with *baptismal regeneration !* A wiser statement of the true doctrine of personal Election was never penned by the hand of uninspired man. It is thoroughly well-balanced and judiciously proportioned. In the face of such an Article it is simply ridiculous to say that the Church of England does not hold the doctrine of this paper.

In controverted matters I desire to speak courteously and cautiously. I wish to make allowance for the many varieties of men's temperaments, which insensibly affect our religious opinions, and for the lasting effect of early prejudices. I freely concede that Wesley, Fletcher, and a whole host of excellent Methodists and Arminians, have always denied Election, and that many deny it to this day. I do not say that to hold Election is absolutely necessary to salvation, though to be one of God's Elect undoubtedly is necessary. But I cannot call any man my master in theological matters. My own eyes see the doctrine of personal Election most clearly stated both in Scripture and the 17th Article of the Church of England. I cannot give it up. I believe firmly that it is an important part of God's truth, and one which to godly persons is " full of sweet, pleasant, and unspeakable comfort."

II. The next thing that I wish to do is *to fence the doctrine of Election with cautions, and to guard it against abuse.*

This is a branch of the subject which I hold to be of vast importance. All revealed truth is liable to be wrested and perverted. It is one of Satan's chief devices to make the Gospel odious by tempting men to distort it. Perhaps no part of Christian theology has suffered so much damage in this way as the doctrine of personal Election. Let me proceed to explain what I mean.

" I am not one of God's Elect," says one man. " It is no use for me to do anything at all in religion. It is waste of time for me to keep the Sabbath, attend the public worship of God, read my Bible, say my prayers. If I am to be saved, I shall be saved. If I am to be lost, I shall be lost. In the mean time I sit still and wait." This is a sore disease of soul. But I fear it is a very common one !

" I am one of God's Elect," says another man. " I am sure to be saved and go to heaven at last, no matter how I may live and go on. Exhortations to holiness are legal. Recommendations to watch, and crucify self, are bondage. Though I fall, God sees no sin in me and loves me all the same. Though I often give way to temptation, God will not let me be altogether lost. Where is the use of doubts and fears and anxieties ? I am confident I am one of the Elect, and as such I shall be found in glory." This again, is a sore disease. But I fear it is not altogether uncommon.

Now what shall be said to men who talk in this way ? They need to be told very plainly that they are wresting a truth of the Bible to their own destruction, and turning meat into poison. They need to be reminded that their notion of Election is a miserably unscriptural one. Election according to the Bible is a very different thing from what they suppose it to be. It is most intimately connected with other truths of equal importance with itself, and from these truths it ought never to be separated. Truths which God has joined together no man should ever dare to put asunder.

(a) For one thing, the doctrine of Election was never meant to destroy *man's responsibility* for the state of his own soul. The Bible everywhere addresses men as free-agents, as beings accountable to God, and not as mere logs, and bricks, and stones. It is false to say that it is useless to tell men to cease to do evil, to learn to do well, to repent, to believe, to turn to God, to pray. Everywhere in Scripture it is a leading principle that man can lose his own soul, that if he is lost at last it will be his own fault, and his blood will be on his own head. The same inspired Bible which reveals this doctrine of Election is the Bible which contains the words, " Why will ye die, O house of Israel ? "—" Ye will not come unto Me that ye might have life."—" This is the condemnation, that light is come into the world, and men loved darkness rather than light, because their deeds were evil." (Ezek. xviii. 31 ; John v. 40 ; iii. 19.) The Bible never says that sinners miss heaven because they are not Elect, but because they "neglect the great salvation," and because they will not repent and believe. The last judgment will abundantly prove that it is not the want of God's Election, so much as laziness, the love of sin, unbelief, and unwillingness to come to Christ, which ruins the souls that are lost.

(b) For another thing, the doctrine of Election was never meant to prevent the *fullest, freest offer of salvation* to every sinner. In preaching and trying to do good we are warranted and commanded to set an open door before every man, woman, and child, and to invite every one to come in. We know not who are God's Elect, and whom He means to call and convert. Our duty is to invite all. To every unconverted soul without exception we ought to say, "God loves you, and Christ has died for you." To everyone we ought to say, "Awake,—repent,—believe,—come to Christ,—be converted,—turn,—call upon God,—strive to enter in,—come, for all things are ready." To tell us that none will hear and be saved except God's Elect, is quite needless. We know it very well. But to tell us that on that account it is useless to offer salvation to any at all, is simply absurd. Who are we that we should pretend to know who will be found God's Elect at last? No! indeed. Those who now seem first may prove last, and those who seem last may prove first in the judgment day. We will invite all, in the firm belief that the invitation will do good to some. We will prophesy to the dry bones, if God commands us. We will offer life to all, though many reject the offer. In so doing we believe that we walk in the steps of our Master and His Apostles.

(c) For another thing, Election can only be *known by its fruits*. The Elect of God can only be discerned from those who are not Elect by their faith and life. We cannot climb up into the secret of God's eternal counsels. We cannot read the book of life. The fruits of the Spirit, seen and manifested in a man's conversation, are the only grounds on which we can ascertain that he is one of God's Elect. Where the marks of God's Elect can be seen, there, and there only, have we any warrant for saying "this is one of the Elect."—How do I know that yon distant ship on the horizon of the sea has any pilot or steersman on board? I cannot with the best telescope discern anything but her masts and sails. Yet I see her steadily moving in one direction. That is enough for me. I know by this that there is a guiding hand on board, though I cannot see it. Just so it is with God's Election. The eternal decree we cannot possibly see. But the result of that decree cannot be hid. It was when St. Paul remembered the faith and hope and love of the Thessalonians, that he cried, I " know your Election of God." (1 Thess. i. 4.) For ever let us hold fast this principle in considering the subject before us. To talk of any one being Elect when he is living in sin, is nothing better than blasphemous folly. The Bible knows of no Election except through " sanctification,"—no eternal choosing except that we should be " holy,"—no predestination except to be " conformed to the image of God's Son." When these things are lacking, it is mere waste of time to talk of Election. (1 Pet. i. 2; Ephes. i. 4; Rom. viii. 29.)

(d) Last, but not least, Election was never intended to prevent men making a *diligent use of all means of grace.* On the contrary, the neglect of means is a most suspicious symptom, and should make us very doubtful about the state of a man's soul. Those whom the Holy Ghost draws He always draws to the written Word of God and to prayer. When there is the real grace of God in a heart, there will always be love to the means of grace. What saith the Scripture ? The very Christians at Rome to whom St. Paul wrote about foreknowledge and predestination, are the same to whom he says, " Continue instant in prayer." (Rom. xii. 12.) The very Ephesians who were " chosen before the foundation of the world," are the same to whom it is said, " Put on the whole armour of God—take the sword of the Spirit—pray always with all prayer." (Ephes. vi. 18.) The very Thessalonians whose Election Paul said he " knew," are the Christians to whom he cries in the same Epistle, " Pray without ceasing." (1 Thess. v. 17.) The very Christians whom Peter calls " Elect according to the foreknowledge of God the Father," are the same to whom he says, " Desire the sincere milk of the Word—watch unto prayer." (1 Pet. ii. 2; iv. 7.) The evidence of texts like these is simply unanswerable and overwhelming. I shall not waste time by making any comment on them. An Election to salvation which teaches men to dispense with the use of all means of grace, may please ignorant people, fanatics, and Antinomians. But I take leave to say that it is an Election of which I can find no mention in God's Word.

I know not that I can wind up this part of my subject better than by quoting the latter part of the Seventeenth Article of the Church of England. I commend it to the special attention of all my readers, and particularly the last paragraph.—" As the godly consideration of Predestination, and our Election in Christ, is full of sweet, pleasant, and unspeakable comfort to godly persons, and such as feel in themselves the working of the Spirit of Christ, mortifying the works of the flesh, and their earthly members, and drawing up their mind to high and heavenly things, as well because it doth greatly establish and confirm their faith of eternal Salvation to be enjoyed through Christ, as because it doth fervently kindle their love towards God: so, for curious and carnal persons, lacking the Spirit of Christ, to have continually before their eyes the sentence of God's Predestination, is a most dangerous downfall, whereby the Devil doth thrust them either into desperation, or into wretchedness of most unclean living, no less perilous than desperation.

" Furthermore, we must receive God's promises in such wise, as they be generally set forth to us in holy Scripture : and, in our doings, that will of God is to be followed which we have expressly declared unto us in the Word of God."

These are wise words. This is sound speech that cannot be condemned. For ever let us cling to the principle contained in this statement. Well would it have been for the Church of Christ, if the doctrine of Election had always been handled in this fashion. Well would it be for all Christians who feel puzzled by the heights and depths of this mighty doctrine, if they would remember the words of Scripture,—"The secret things belong unto the Lord our God: but those which are revealed belong unto us and to our children for ever, that we may do all the words of this law." (Deut. xxix. 29.)

I will now conclude the whole subject with a few plain words of personal application.

(1) First of all let me entreat every reader of this paper *not to refuse this doctrine of Election*, merely because it is high, mysterious, and hard to be understood. Is it reverent to do so? Is it treating God's Word with the respect due to revelation? Is it right to reject anything written for our learning, and to give it hard names, merely because some misguided men have misused it, and turned it to a bad purpose? These are serious questions. They deserve serious consideration. If men begin rejecting a truth of Scripture merely because they do not like it, they are on slippery ground. There is no saying how far they may fall.

What after all do men gain by refusing the doctrine of Election? Does the system of those who deny Election save one soul more than that of those who hold it? Certainly not.—Do those who hold Election narrow the way to heaven, and make salvation more difficult than those who deny it? Certainly not.—The opponents of Election maintain that none will be saved except those who repent and believe. Well: the advocates of Election say just the same!—The opponents of Election proclaim loudly that none but holy people go to heaven. Well: the advocates of Election proclaim the same doctrine just as loudly!—What then, I ask once more, is gained by denying the truth of Election? I answer, Nothing whatever. And yet, while nothing is gained, a great deal of comfort seems to be lost. It is cold comfort to be told that God never thought on me before I repented and believed. But to know and feel that God had purposes of mercy toward me before the foundation of the world, and that all the work of grace in my heart is the result of an everlasting covenant and an eternal Election, is a thought full of sweet and unspeakable consolation. A work that was planned before the foundation of the world, by an Architect of almighty power and perfect wisdom, is a work which will never be allowed to fail and be overthrown.

(2) In the next place, let me entreat every reader of this paper *to approach this doctrine of Election from the right end,* and not to confuse his mind by inverting the order of truth. Let him begin with the first elements of Christianity,—with simple repentance toward God, and faith toward our Lord Jesus Christ, and so work his way toward Election. Let him not waste his time by beginning with inquiries about his own Election. Let him rather attend first to the plain marks of an Elect man, and never rest till these marks are his own. Let him break off from all known sin, and flee to Christ for pardon, peace, mercy, and grace. Let him cry mightily to God in prayer, and give the Lord no rest till he feels within him the real witness of the Spirit. He that begins in this fashion will thank God one day for His electing grace, in eternity if not in time. It is an old and quaint saying, but a very true one : " A man must first go to the little Grammar-school of Repentance and Faith, before he enters the great University of Election and Predestination."

The plain truth is, that God's scheme of salvation is like a ladder let down from heaven to earth, to bring together the holy God, and the sinful creature, man. God is at the top of the ladder and man is at the bottom.—The top of the ladder is far above, out of our sight, and we have no eyes to see it. There, at the top of that ladder, are God's eternal purposes,—His everlasting covenant, His Election, His predestination of a people to be saved by Christ. From the top of that ladder comes down that full and rich provision of mercy for sinners which is revealed to us in the Gospel.—The bottom of that ladder is close to sinful man on earth, and consists of the simple steps of repentance and faith. By them he must begin to climb upwards. In the humble use of them he shall mount higher and higher every year, and get clearer glimpses of good things yet to come.—What can be more plain than the duty of using the steps which are close to our hands? What can be more foolish than to say, I will not put my foot on the steps at the bottom, until I clearly understand the steps at the top? Away with such perverse and childish reasonings! Common sense alone might tell us the path of duty, if we would only make use of it. That duty is to use simple truths honestly, and then to believe that higher truths will one **day** be made plain to our eyes. How, and in what manner the love of the eternal God comes down to us, may have much about it which is hard for poor worms like us to understand. But how we poor sinners are to draw near to God is clear and plain as the sun at noon-day. Jesus Christ stands before us, saying, "Come unto Me!" Let us not waste time in doubting, quibbling, and disputing. Let us come to Christ at once, just as we are. Let us lay hold and believe!

(3) In the last place, let me entreat every true Christian who reads this paper to *remember the exhortation of St Peter,*—" Give diligence, to make your calling and Election sure." (2 Pet. i. 10.)

Surer in the sight of God than your Election has been from all eternity, you cannot make it. With Him there is no uncertainty. Nothing that God does for His people is left to chance, or liable to change. But surer and more evident to yourself and to the Church, your Election can be made; and this is the point that I wish to press on your attention. Strive to obtain such well-grounded assurance of hope that, as St. John says, you may "know that you know Christ." (1 John ii. 3.) Strive so to live and walk in this world that all may take knowledge of you as one of God's children, and feel no doubt that you are going to heaven.

Listen not for a moment to those who tell you that in this life we can never be sure of our own spiritual state, and must always be in doubt. The Roman Catholics say so. The ignorant world says so. The devil says so. But the Bible says nothing of the kind. There is such a thing as strong *assurance* of our acceptance in Christ, and a Christian should never rest till he has obtained it. That a man may be saved without this strong assurance I do not deny. But that without it he misses a great privilege, and much comfort, I am quite sure.

Strive, then, with all diligence, "to make your calling and Election sure."—"Lay aside every weight and the sins that most easily beset you." (Heb. xii. 2.) Be ready to cut off the right hand and pluck out the right eye, if need be. Settle it firmly in your mind, that it is the highest privilege on this side the grave to know that you are one of the children of God.

They that contend for place and office in this world are sure to be disappointed. When they have done all and succeeded to the uttermost, their honours are thoroughly unsatisfying, and their rewards are short-lived. Seats in Parliament and places in Cabinets must all be vacated one day. At best they can only be held for a few years. But he that is one of God's Elect has a treasure which can never be taken from him, and a place from which he can never be removed. Blessed is that man who sets his heart on this Election. There is no election like the Election of God!

XIX.

PERSEVERANCE.

" They shall never perish."—JOHN x. 28,

THERE are two points in religion on which the teaching of the Bible is very plain and distinct. One of these points is the fearful danger of the ungodly; the other is the perfect safety of the righteous. One is the happiness of those who are converted; the other is the misery of those who are unconverted. One is the blessedness of being in the way to heaven; the other is the wretchedness of being in the way to hell.

I hold it to be of the utmost importance that these two points should be constantly impressed on the minds of professing Christians. I believe that the exceeding privileges of the children of God, and the deadly peril of the children of the world, should be continually set forth in the clearest colours before the Church of Christ. I believe that the difference between the man in Christ, and the man not in Christ, can never be stated too strongly and too fully. Reserve on this subject is a positive injury to the souls of men. Wherever such reserve is practised, the careless will not be aroused, believers will not be established, and the cause of God will receive much damage.

Many people, I fear, are not aware what a vast store of

comfortable truths the Bible contains for the peculiar benefit of real Christians. There is a spiritual treasure-house in the Word which many never enter, and some eyes have not so much as seen. There you will find many a golden verity besides the old first principles of repentance, faith, and conversion. There you will see in glorious array the everlasting election of the saints in Christ,—the special love wherewith God loved them before the foundation of the world,—their mystical union with their risen Head in heaven, and His consequent sympathy with them,—their interest in the perpetual intercession of Jesus, their High Priest,—their liberty of daily communion with the Father and the Son,—their full assurance of hope,—their perseverance to the end. These are some of the precious things laid up in Scripture for those who love God. These are truths which some neglect from ignorance. Like the Spaniards in the days when they possessed California, they know not the rich mines beneath their feet, the mines from which the Americans have extracted such untold wealth. These are truths which some neglect from false humility. They look at them afar off with fear and trembling, but dare not touch them. But these are truths which God has given for our learning, and which we are bound to study. It is impossible to neglect them without inflicting injury upon ourselves.

It is to one special truth in the list of a believer's privileges that I now desire to direct attention. That truth is *the doctrine of perseverance,*—the doctrine that true Christians shall never perish or be cast away. It is a truth which the natural heart has bitterly opposed in every age. It is a truth which for many reasons deserves particular attention at the present time. Above all, it is a truth with which the happiness of all God's children is most closely connected.

There are four things which I propose to do in considering the subject of perseverance.

I. I will explain *what the doctrine of perseverance means.*

II. I will show *the Scriptural foundations on which the doctrine is built.*

III. I will point out *some reasons why many reject the doctrine.*

IV. I will mention *some reasons why the doctrine is of great practical importance.*

I approach the subject with diffidence, because I know it is one on which holy men do not see alike. But God is my witness, that in writing this paper, I have no desire to promote any cause but that of Scriptural truth. In pleading for perseverance, I can say with a good conscience, that I firmly believe I am pleading for an important part of the Gospel of Christ. May God the Spirit guide both writer and reader into all truth! May that blessed day soon come when all shall know the Lord perfectly, and differences and divisions pass away for ever!

I. I will first explain *what I mean by the doctrine of perseverance.*

It is of the utmost importance to make this point clear. It is the very foundation of the subject. It lies at the threshold of the whole argument. In all discussions of disputed points in theology, it is impossible to be too accurate in defining terms. Half the abuse which has unhappily been poured on perseverance, has arisen from a thorough misunderstanding of the doctrine in question. Its adversaries have fought with phantoms of their own creation, and spent their strength in beating the air.

When I speak of the doctrine of perseverance, I mean this. I say that the Bible teaches that true believers, real genuine Christians, shall persevere in their religion to the end of their lives. They shall never perish. They shall never be lost. They shall never be cast away. Once in Christ, they shall always be in Christ. Once made children of God by adoption and grace, they shall never cease to be His children and become children of the devil. Once endued with the grace of the Spirit, that grace shall never be taken from them. Once pardoned and forgiven, they shall never be deprived of their pardon. Once joined to Christ by living faith, their union shall never be broken off. Once called by God into the narrow way that leads to life, they shall never be allowed to fall into hell. In a word. every man, woman, and child on earth that receives saving grace, shall sooner or later receive eternal glory. Every soul that is once justified and washed in Christ's blood, shall at length be found safe at Christ's right hand in the day of judgment.

Such statements as this sound tremendously strong. I know that well. But I am not going to leave the subject here : I must dwell upon it a little longer. I desire to clear the doctrine I am defending from the cloud of misrepresentation by which many darken it. I want men to see it in its own proper dress,—not as it is pourtrayed by the hand of ignorance and prejudice, but as it is set forth in the Scripture of truth.

(*a*) Perseverance is *a doctrine with which the ungodly and worldly have nothing to do.* It does not belong to that vast multitude who have neither knowledge, nor thought, nor faith, nor fear, nor anything else of Christianity except the name. It is not true of them, that they will "never perish." On the contrary, except they repent, they will come to a miserable end.

(*b*) Perseverance is *a doctrine with which hypocrites and false professors have nothing to do.* It does not belong to those unhappy people whose religion consists in talk, and words, and a form of godliness, while their hearts are destitute of the grace of the Spirit. It is not true of them, that they will "never perish." On the contrary, except they repent, they will be lost for ever.*

(c) Perseverance is *the peculiar privilege of real, true spiritual Christians.* It belongs to the sheep of Christ who hear His voice and follow Him. It belongs to those who are " washed, and justified, and sanctified in the name of the Lord Jesus, and by the Spirit of God." (1 Cor. vi. 11.) It belongs to those who repent, and believe in Christ, and live holy lives. It belongs to those who have been born again, and converted, and made new creatures by the Holy Ghost. It belongs to those who are of a broken and contrite heart, and mind the things of the Spirit, and bring forth the fruits of the Spirit. It belongs to " the elect of God, who cry to Him night and day." (Luke xviii. 7.) It belongs to those who know the Lord Jesus by experience, and have faith, and hope, and charity. It belongs to those who are the fruit-bearing branches of the vine,— the wise virgins,—the light of the world,—the salt of the earth,—the heirs of the kingdom,—the followers of the Lamb. These are they whom the Bible calls " the saints." And it is the saints and the saints alone of whom it is written, that they shall " never perish." †

Does any one suppose that what I am saying applies to none but eminent saints ? Does any one think that people like the apostles, and prophets, and martyrs, may perhaps persevere to the end, but that it cannot be said of the common sort of believers ? Let him know that he is

---

* "We do not hold that all whom the most discerning minister or Christian considers true Christians, will be 'kept by the power of God through faith unto salvation.' God alone can search the heart, and He may see that to be a dead and temporary faith, which we in the judgment of charity think living and permanent."—*Scott's reply to Tomline,* p. 675.

† "It is grossly contrary to the truth of the Scriptures to imagine that they who are thus renewed, can be unborn again."—*Archbishop Leighton.* 1680.

entirely mistaken. Let him know that this privilege of perseverance belongs to the whole family of God,—to the youngest as well as the oldest,—to the weakest as well as the strongest,—to the babes in grace as well as to the oldest pillars of the Church. The least faith shall as certainly continue indestructible as the greatest. The least spark of grace shall prove as unquenchable as the most burning and shining light. Your faith may be very feeble, your grace may be very weak, your strength may be very small, you may feel that in spiritual things you are but a child. You may doubt the reality of your own conversion. Yet fear not, neither be afraid. It is not on the quantity of a man's grace, but on the truth and genuineness of it that the promise turns. A bronze farthing is as truly a current coin of the realm as a golden sovereign, though it is not so valuable. Wherever sin is truly repented of, and Christ is truly trusted, and holiness is truly followed, there is a work which shall never be overthrown. It shall stand when the earth and all the works thereof shall be burned up.

There are yet some things to be said about perseverance, to which I must request special attention. Without them the account of the doctrine would be imperfect and incomplete. The mention of them may clear up some of the difficulties which surround the subject, and throw light on some points of Christian experience, which God's children find hard to understand.

(a) Remember, then, that when I say believers shall persevere to the end, I *do not for a moment say that they shall never fall into sin.* They may fall sadly, foully, and shamefully, to the scandal of true religion, to the injury of their families, to their own deep and bitter sorrow. Noah once fell into drunkenness. Abraham twice said falsely that Sarah was only his sister. Lot took up his abode in Sodom. Jacob deceived his father Isaac. Moses spoke unadvisedly with his lips. David committed horrible adultery. Solomon lost his first love, and was led away by his many wives. Jehoshaphat made affinity with Ahab. Hezekiah forgot God, and boasted of his riches. Peter denied his Lord three times with an oath. The apostles all forsook Christ in the garden. Paul and Barnabas had such a "sharp contention" that they were obliged to part company. All these are cases in point. They are all melancholy proofs that Christians may fall. But believers shall never fall *totally, finally, and completely.* They shall always rise again from their falls by repentance, and renew their walk with God. Though sorely humbled and cast down, they never entirely lose their grace. The *comfort* of it they may lose, but not the *being.* Like the moon under an eclipse, their light is for a season turned into darkness; but they are not rejected and cast away. Like the trees in winter, they may show neither leaves nor fruit for a time; but the life is still in their roots. They may be overtaken by a fault, and carried away by temptation. But they never perish.

(*b*) Remember, for another thing, that when I say believers shall persevere to the end, *I do not mean that they shall have no doubts and fears about their own safety.* So far from this being the case, the holiest men of God are sometimes sorely troubled by anxieties about their own spiritual condition. They see so much weakness in their own hearts, and find their practice come so short of their desires, that they are strongly tempted to doubt the truth of their own grace, and to fancy they are but hypocrites, and shall never reach heaven at all. To *be safe* is one thing: to *feel sure* that we are safe is quite another. There are many true believers who never enjoy the full assurance of hope all their days. Their faith is so weak, and their sense of sin so strong, that they never feel confident of their own interest in Christ. Many a time they could say with David, "I shall one day perish" (1

Sam. xxvii. 1); and with Job, "Where is my hope?"
(Job xvii. 15.) The "joy and peace in believing," which
some feel, and the "witness of the Spirit," which some
experience, are things which some believers, whose faith
it is impossible to deny, never appear to attain. Called
as they evidently are by the grace of God, they never
seem to taste the full comfort of their calling. But still
they are perfectly safe, though they themselves refuse to
know it.

> "More happy, but not more secure,
> The glorified spirits in heaven."

The full assurance of hope is not necessary to salvation.
The absence of it is no argument against a man's perseverance to the end. That mighty master of theology,
John Bunyan, knew well what he wrote, when he told us
that Despondency and Much-afraid got safe to the celestial
city at last, as well as Christiana and Valiant-for-the-truth
It is as true of the most doubting child of God, as it is
of the strongest, that he shall "never perish." He may
never feel it. But it is true. *

(c) Remember, in the last place, that the certain perseverance of believers *does not free them from the necessity
of watching, praying, and using means, or make it
needless to ply them with practical exhortations.* So far
from this being the case, it is just by the use of means
that God enables them to continue in the faith. He draws
them with the "cords of a man." He uses warnings and
conditional promises as part of the machinery by which
He insures their final safety. The very fact that they
despised the helps and ordinances which God has appointed, would be a plain proof that they had no grace
at all and were on the road to destruction. St. Paul
had a special revelation from God before his shipwreck,

"Every believer doth not know that he is a believer, and therefore,
he cannot know all the privileges that belong to believers."—*Traill*, 1690.

that he and all the ship's company should get safe to land. But it is a striking fact that he said to the soldiers, "Except the shipmen abide in the ship ye cannot be saved." (Acts xxvii. 31.) He knew that *the end* was insured, but he believed also that it was an end to be reached by the use of certain *means.* The cautions, and conditional promises, and admonitions to believers, with which Scripture abounds, are all a part of the Divine agency by which their perseverance is effected. An old writer says, "they do not imply that the saints can fall away: but they are preservatives to keep them from falling away." The man that thinks he can do without such cautions, and despises them as *legal,* may well be suspected as an impostor, whose heart has never yet been renewed. The man who has been really taught by the Spirit will generally have a humble sense of his own weakness, and be thankful for anything which can quicken his conscience, and keep him on his guard. They that persevere to the end are not dependent on any means, but still they are not independent of them. Their final salvation does not hang on their obedience to practical exhortations, but it is just in taking heed to such exhortations that they will always continue to the end. It is the diligent, the watchful, the prayerful, and the humble, to whom belongs the promise,—"They shall never perish."

I have now given an account of what I mean when I speak of the doctrine of perseverance. This, and this only, is the doctrine that I am prepared to defend in this paper. I ask men to weigh well what I have said, and to examine the statement I have made on every side. I believe it will stand inspection.

(a) It will not do to tell us that this doctrine of perseverance has any *tendency to encourage careless and ungodly living.* Such a charge is utterly destitute of truth. It cannot justly be brought forward. I have not a word to say in behalf of any one who lives in wilful sin, however high his profession may be. He is deceiving himself. He has a lie in his hand. He has none of the marks of God's elect. The perseverance I plead for is not that of sinners, but of saints. It is not a perseverance in carnal and ungodly ways, but a perseverance in the way of faith and grace. Show me a man who deliberately lives an unholy life, and yet boasts that he is converted and shall never perish, and I say plainly that I see nothing hopeful about him. He may know all mysteries, and speak with the tongue of angels, but, so long as his life is unaltered, he appears to me in the high road to hell.*

(b) It will not do to tell us that this doctrine of perseverance, *is merely a piece of Calvinism.* Nothing is easier than to get up a prejudice against a truth, by giving it a bad name. Men deal with doctrines they do not like, much as Nero did when he persecuted the early Christians. They dress them up in a hideous garment, and then hold them up to scorn and run them down. The perseverance of the saints is often treated in this manner. People stave it off by some sneering remark about Calvinism, or by some apocryphal old wives' fable about Oliver Cromwell's death-bed, and then think they have settled the question.† Surely it would be more becoming to inquire

---

* "Let none encourage themselves to a freedom in sin, and presume upon God's preservation of them without the use of means. No! The electing counsel upon which this victory is founded, chose us to the means as well as to the end. He that makes such a consequence, I doubt whether he ever was a Christian. I may safely say that any person that hath settled, resolved, and wilful remissness, never yet was in the covenant of Grace."—*Charnock on Weak Grace.* 1684.

† "I allude to the common story that Cromwell on his death-bed asked Dr. Thomas Goodwin whether a believer could fall from grace. Goodwin replied that he could not. Cromwell is reported to have said, that "if so he was safe, for he was sure that he had once been in a state of grace."

The truth of this story is exceedingly questionable. It is a remarkable

whether perseverance was not taught in the Bible from the beginning, and long before Calvin was born. The question to be decided is not whether the doctrine is Calvinistic, but whether it is scriptural. The words of the famous Bishop Horsley deserve to be widely known. "Take especial care," he says, "before you aim your shafts at Calvinism, that you know what is Calvinism and what is not;—that in the mass of doctrine which it is of late become the fashion to abuse under the name of Calvinism, you can distinguish with certainty between that part of it which is nothing better than Calvinism, and that which belongs to our common Christianity and the general faith of the reformed Churches,—lest, when you mean only to fall foul of Calvinism you should unwarily attack something more sacred and of a higher origin."

(c) Last, but not least, it will not do to tell us *that perseverance is not the doctrine of the Church of England.* Whatever men may please to say against it, this is an assertion, at any rate, which they will find it hard to prove. Perseverance is taught in the seventeenth Article of the Church of England, clearly, plainly, unmistakably. It was the doctrine of the first five Archbishops of Canterbury, Parker, Grindal, Whitgift, Bancroft, and Abbott. It was the doctrine preached by the judicious Hooker, as any one may see by reading his sermons.* It was the doctrine

---

fact that Cromwell's faithful servant, who published a collection of all the remarkable sayings and doings of his master in his last sickness, does not mention this conversation. It is more than probable that it is one of those false and malicious inventions with which the great Protector's enemies laboured so hard to blacken his memory after his death.

* "As Christ being raised from the dead, dieth no more, death hath no more power over Him ; so the justified man being allied to God in Christ Jesus our Lord, doth as necessarily from that time forward always live, as Christ by whom He hath life liveth always." (Rom. vi. 10; John xiv. 19.)

which all the leading divines of the Church of England maintained till the reign of Charles the First. The denial of the doctrine up to this time was hardly tolerated. More than one minister who called it in question was compelled to read a public recantation before the University of Cambridge. In short, till the time when Archbishop Laud came into power, perseverance was regarded in the Church of England as an acknowledged truth of the Gospel. Together with the Popish leaven which Laud brought with him, there came the unhappy doctrine that true believers may fall away and perish. This is simple matter of history. The perseverance of the saints is the old doctrine of the Church of England. The denial of it is the new.*

It is time to leave this branch of the subject and pass on. I want no clearer and more distinct statement of perseverance than that contained in the Seventeenth Article of my own Church, to which I have already referred. The Article says of God's elect: "They which be endued with so excellent a benefit of God, be called according to God's purpose by His Spirit working in due season: they through grace obey His calling: they be justified freely: they be made sons of God by adoption: they be made like the image of His only begotten Son Jesus Christ: they walk religiously in good works, and at length, by

---

"As long as that abideth in us which animateth, quickeneth, and giveth life, so long we live; and we know that the cause of our faith abideth in us for ever. If Christ the fountain of life may flit, and leave the habitation where once He dwelleth, what shall become of His promise, 'I am with you to the world's end'? If the seed of God which containeth Christ may be first conceived and then cast out, how doth St. Peter term it immortal? (1 Pet. i. 23.) How doth St. John affirm that it abideth? (1 John iii. 9.) "—*Hooker's Discourse of Justification.* 1590.

* Those readers who wish to know more on this subject, are referred to a note which they will find at the end of this paper.

God's mercy, *they attain to everlasting felicity*." These are precisely the views which I maintain. This is the doctrine which I long ago subscribed. This is the truth which I believe it is my duty, as a clergyman, to defend. This is the truth which I now want my readers to receive and believe.*

II.   I now proceed *to show the Scriptural foundations on which the doctrine of perseverance is built.*

I need hardly say that the Bible is the only test by which the truth of every religious doctrine can be tried. The words of the Sixth Article of the Church of England deserve to be written in letters of gold: "Whatsoever is not read in the Holy Scripture, nor may be proved thereby, is not to be required of any man that it should be believed as an article of the faith." By that rule I am content to abide.   I ask no one to believe the final perseverance of the saints, unless the doctrine can be proved to be that of the Word of God.   One plain verse of Scripture, to my mind, outweighs the most logical conclusions to which human reason can attain.

In bringing forward those texts of Scripture on which this paper is founded, I purposely abstain from quoting from the Old Testament.   I do so, lest any should say that the Old Testament promises belong exclusively to the Jewish people as a nation, and are not available in a disputed question affecting individual believers.   I do not admit the soundness of this argument, but I will not give any one the chance of using it.   I find proofs in abundance in the New Testament, and to them I shall confine myself.

---

* "I would entreat any man that hath his eyes set right in his head, to read and consider the words of the Seventeenth Article, the order and soundness of them ; and then let him judge whether perseverance unto the end be not soundly and roundly set down and averred in this Article." —*George Carlton, Bishop of Chichester*, 1626.   *An Examination*, p. 63.

I shall write down the texts which appear to me to prove final perseverance, without note or comment. I will only ask my readers to observe how deep and broad is the foundation on which the doctrine rests. Observe that it is not for any strength or goodness of their own that the saints shall continue to the end, and never fall away. They are in themselves weak, and frail, and liable to fall like others. Their safety is based on the promise of God, which was never yet broken,—on the election of God, which cannot be in vain,—on the power of the great Mediator Christ Jesus, which is Almighty,—on the inward work of the Holy Ghost, which cannot be overthrown. I ask you to read the following texts carefully, and see whether it is not so.

I give unto them eternal life; and they shall *never perish*, neither shall any man pluck them out of my hand.

"My Father which gave them Me, is greater than all; and no man is able to pluck them out of my Father's hand." (John x. 28, 29.)

"Who shall *separate us* from the love of Christ? Shall tribulation, or distress, or persecution, or famine, or nakedness, or peril, or sword?

"As it is written, For thy sake we are killed all the day long; we are accounted as sheep for the slaughter.

"Nay in all these things we are *more than conquerors* through Him that loved us.

"For I am persuaded, that neither death, nor life, nor angels, nor principalities, nor powers, nor things present, nor things to come,

"Nor height, nor depth, nor any other creature, *shall be able to separate us* from the love of God, which is in Christ Jesus our Lord." (Rom. viii. 35—39.)

"They went out from us, but they were not of us; for if they had been of us, they would no doubt have *continued* with us: but they went out that they might be made manifest that they were not all of us." (1 John ii. 19.)

"Verily, verily, I say unto you, He that heareth my word, and believeth on Him that sent Me, hath everlasting life, and *shall not come into condemnation ;* but is passed from death unto life." (John v. 24.)

"I am the living bread which came down from heaven: if any man eat of this bread, he shall *live for ever.*" (John vi. 51.)

"Because I live, ye *shall live* also." (John xiv. 19.)

"Whosoever liveth and believeth in Me, shall never die." (John xi. 26.)

"By one offering He hath *perfected for ever* them that are sanctified." (Heb. x. 14.)

"He that doeth the will of God *abideth for ever.*" (1 John ii. 17.)

"Sin shall *not have dominion* over you." (Rom. vi. 14.)

"Who shall also *confirm you to the end,* that ye may be blameless in the day of our Lord Jesus Christ." (1 Cor. i. 8.)

"*Kept* by the power of God through faith unto salvation, ready to be revealed in the last time." (1 Peter i. 5.)

"*Preserved* in Jesus Christ, and called." (Jude 1.)

"The Lord shall deliver me from every evil work, and *will preserve* me unto His heavenly kingdom." (2 Tim. iv. 18.)

"I pray God your whole spirit, and soul, and body be preserved blameless unto the coming of our Lord Jesus Christ.

"Faithful is He that calleth you, who also *will do* it." (1 Thess. v. 23, 24.)

"The Lord is faithful, who *shall stablish* you, and keep you from evil." (2 Thess. iii. 3.)

"God is faithful, who will not suffer you to be tempted above that ye are able; but will with the temptation also make a way to escape, that ye may be able to bear it." (1 Cor. x. 13.)

"God, willing more abundantly to show unto the heirs,

of promise the immutability of His counsel, confirmed it by an oath ;

"That by two immutable things, in which it was *impossible for God to lie,* we might have a strong consolation, who have fled for refuge to lay hold upon the hope set before us." (Heb. vi. 17, 18.)

"This is the Father's will which hath sent Me, that of all which He hath given Me I should *lose nothing,* but should raise it up again at the last day." (John vi. 39.)

"The foundation of God *standeth sure,* having this seal, the Lord knoweth them that are His." (2 Tim. ii. 19.)

"Whom He did predestinate, them He also called; and whom He called, them He also justified; and whom He justified, *them He also glorified."* (Rom. viii. 30.)

"God hath not appointed us unto wrath, but to obtain salvation by our Lord Jesus Christ." (1 Thess. v. 9.)

"God hath from the beginning chosen you to salvation through sanctification of the Spirit, and belief of the truth." (2 Thess. ii. 13.)

"The vessels of mercy, which He had afore prepared unto glory." (Rom. ix. 23.)

"The gifts and calling of God are without repentance.' (Rom. xi. 29.)

"If it were possible, they shall deceive the very elect." (Matt. xxiv. 24.)

"He is able to *save to the uttermost* all them that come unto God by Him, seeing He ever liveth to make intercession for them." (Heb. vii. 25.)

"Able to *keep you from falling,* and to present you faultless before the presence of His glory with exceeding joy." (Jude 24.)

"I know whom I have believed, and am persuaded that He is able to keep that which I have committed unto Him against that day." (2 Tim. i. 12.)

"I have prayed for thee, that thy *faith fail not."* (Luke xxii. 32.)

"Holy Father, keep through Thine own name those whom Thou hast given Me." (John xvii. 11.)

"I pray not that Thou shouldest take them out of the world, but that Thou shouldest keep them from the evil." (John xvii. 15.)

"I will that they also whom Thou hast given Me, *be with Me* where I am." (John xvii. 24.)

"If, when we were enemies, we were reconciled to God by the death of His Son; much more, being reconciled, we *shall be saved* by His life." (Rom. v. 10.)

"The Spirit of truth; whom the world cannot receive, because it seeth Him not, neither knoweth Him; but ye know Him, for He dwelleth with you, and *shall be in you.*" (John xiv. 17.)

"Being confident of this very thing, that He which hath begun a good work in you, *will perform it* until the day of Jesus Christ." (Phil. i. 6.)

"The anointing which ye have received of Him abideth in you; and ye need not that any man teach you: but as the same anointing teacheth you of all things, and is truth, and no lie, and even as it hath taught you, ye *shall abide* in Him." (1 John ii. 27.)

"Born again, not of corruptible seed, but of *incorruptible.*" (1 Peter i. 23.)

"He hath said, I will never leave thee nor forsake thee." (Heb. xiii. 5.)

I lay these thirty-nine texts of Scripture before my readers, and ask serious attention to them. I repeat that I will make no comment on them. I had rather leave them to the honest common sense of all who read the Bible. Some of these texts, no doubt, bring out the doctrine of final perseverance more clearly than others. About the interpretation of some of them, men's judgments may differ widely. But there are not a few of the thirty-nine which appear to my mind so plain, that were I to invent words to confirm my views, I should despair of inventing any that would convey my meaning so unmistakably.

I am far from saying that these texts are all the Scriptural evidence that might be brought forward. I am satisfied that the doctrine maintained in this paper might be confirmed by other arguments of great weight and power.

(a) I might point to the *attributes of God's character revealed in the Bible,* and show how His wisdom, unchangeableness, and power, and love, and glory are all involved in the perseverance of the saints. If the elect may finally perish, what becomes of God's counsel about them in eternity, and His doings for them in time ?[*]

(b) I might point to all *the offices which the Lord Jesus fills,* and show what discredit is thrown on His discharge of them, if any of His believing people can finally be lost. What kind of Head would He be, if any of the members of His mystical body could be torn from Him ? What kind of Shepherd would He be, if a single sheep of His flock was left behind in the wilderness ? What kind of Physician would He be, if any patient under His hand were at length found incurable ? What kind of High Priest would He be, if any name once written on His heart were found wanting when He makes up His jewels ? What kind of Husband would He be, if He and any soul once united to Him by faith were ever put asunder ?[†]

---

[*] "Now if Thou shalt kill all this people as one man, then the nations, which have heard the fame of Thee, will speak, saying,

"Because the Lord was not able to bring this people into the land which He sware unto them, therefore He hath slain them in the wilderness."—Numbers xiv. 15, 16.

"What wilt Thou do to Thy great name ?"—Joshua vii. 9.

"If any of the elect perish, God is overcome by man's perverseness : but none of them perish, because God, who is omnipotent, can by no means be overcome."—*Augustine. De Corruptione et Gratia, cap. VII.*

[†] "How well do they consult for Christ's honour that say His sheep may die in a ditch of final apostacy !

(c) Finally, I might point to the great fact that there is *not a single example in all Scripture of any one of God's elect ever finally making shipwreck and going to hell.* We read of false prophets and hypocrites. We read of fruitless branches, stony-ground and thorny-ground hearers. virgins without oil in their vessels, servants who bury their talents. We read of Balaam, and Lot's wife, and Saul. and Judas Iscariot, and Ananias and Sapphira, and Demas. We see their hollow characters. We are told of their end. They had no root. They were rotten at the heart. They endured for a while. They went at last to their own place. But there is not a single instance in the whole Bible of any one falling away who ever showed unquestionable evidences of grace. Men like Abraham, and Moses, and David, and Peter, and Paul always hold on their way. They may slip. They may fall for a season. But they never entirely depart from God. They never perish. Surely if the saints of God can be cast away, it is a curious and striking fact that the Bible should not have given us one single plain example of it.

But time and space would fail me if I were to enter into the field which I have just pointed out. I think it better to rest my case on the texts which I have already given. The mind to which these texts carry no conviction, is not likely to be influenced by other arguments. To myself they appear, when taken altogether, to contain such an immense mass of evidence, that I dare not, as a Christian man, deny perseverance to be true. I dare not, because I feel at this rate I might dispute the truth of any doctrine in the Gospel. I feel that if I could explain away such

---

" Christ and His members make one Christ. Now is it possible a piece of Christ can be found at last burning in hell ? Can Christ be a crippled Christ ? Can this member drop off and that ? How can Christ part with His mystical members and not with His glory ?"—*Gurnall.* 1655.

plain texts as some of those I have quoted, I could explain away almost all the leading truths of Christianity.

I am quite aware that there are some texts and passages of Scripture which appear at first sight to teach a contrary doctrine to that which I maintain in this paper. I know that many attach great weight to these texts, and consider them to prove that the saints of God may perish and fall away. I can only say that I have examined these texts with attention, but have found in them no reason to alter my opinion on the subject of perseverance.* Their number

---

* The following texts, on which the opponents of perseverance principally rely, appear to call for a brief notice.

Ezek. iii. 20 and Ezek xviii. 24. I can see no proof in either of these cases that "the righteous" here spoken of, is anything more than one, whose outward conduct is righteous. There is nothing to show that he is one justified by faith and accounted righteous before God.

1 Cor. ix. 27. I see nothing in this but the godly fear of falling into sin, which is one of the marks of a believer, and distinguishes him from the unconverted, and a simple declaration of the means which Paul used to preserve himself from being a cast-away. It is like 1 John v. 18: "He that is begotten of God *keepeth himself.*"

John xv. 2. This does not prove that true believers shall be taken away from Christ. A branch that "*does not bear fruit*" is not a believer. "A lively faith," says the 12th Article, "may be as evidently known by good works, as a tree is known by the fruit."

1 Thess. v. 19. If "the Spirit" here means the Spirit in ourselves, it means no more than "grieving the Spirit," in Ep. iv. 30. But most good commentators think it is the Spirit's gifts in others, and ought to be taken in connection with verse 20.

Gal. v. 4. The tenor of the whole Epistle seems to show that this "falling" is not from the inward grace of the Spirit, but from the doctrine of grace. The same remarks applies to 2 Cor. vi. 1.

Heb. vi. 4—6. The person here described as "falling away" has no characteristics which may not be discovered in unconverted men, while it is not said that he possesses saving faith, and charity, and is elect.

John viii. 31 ; Col. i. 23. The conditional "if" in both these verses, and several others like them that might be quoted, does not imply an uncertainty as to the salvation of those described. It simply means that the evidence of real grace is "continuance." False grace perishes. True grace lasts. "It is frequent in Scripture," says Charnock, "to put into promises these conditions which in other places are promised to be wrought in us."—*Charnock on Real Grace.* 1684.

is small. Their meaning is unquestionably more open to dispute than that of many of the thirty-nine I have quoted. All of them admit of being interpreted so as not to contradict the doctrine of perseverance. I hold it to be an infallible rule in the exposition of Scripture, that when two texts seem to contradict one another, the less plain must give way to the more plain, and the weak must give way to the strong. That doctrine which reconciles most texts of Scripture is most likely to be right. That doctrine which makes most texts quarrel with one another is most likely to be wrong.

I ask my readers, if not convinced by all I have said hitherto, to put down the texts I have quoted on behalf of perseverance, and the texts commonly quoted against it, in two separate lists. Weigh them one against another. Judge them with fair and honest judgment. Which list contains the greatest number of positive, unmistakable assertions? Which list contains the greatest number of sentences which cannot be explained away? Which list is the strongest? Which list is the weakest? Which list is the most flexible? Which list is the most unbending? If it were possible in a world like this to have this question fairly tried by an unprejudiced, intelligent jury, I have not the least doubt which way the verdict would go. It is my own firm belief and conviction that the final perseverance of the saints is so deeply founded on Scrip-

---

I readily grant that these are not all the texts that the adversaries of final perseverance generally bring forward; but I believe they are the principal ones. The weak point in their case is this: they have no text to prove that saints may fall away, which will at all compare with such an expression as, "*My sheep shall never perish;*" and they have no account to give of such a mighty saying as this promise of our Lord, which is at all satisfactory or even rational. John Goodwin, the famous Arminian, offers the following explanation of this text: "The promise of eternal safety made by Christ to His sheep, doth not relate to their estate in the present world, but to that of the world to come!" A man must be sorely put to straits when he can argue in such a way.

tural foundations, that so long as the Bible is the judge, it cannot be overthrown.

III. The third thing I propose to do, is to *point out the reasons why many reject the doctrine of perseverance.*

It is impossible to deny that multitudes of professing Christians entirely disagree with the views expressed in this paper. I am quite aware that many regard them with abhorrence, as dangerous, enthusiastic, and fanatical, and lose no opportunity of warning people against them. I am also aware that among those who hold that the saints of God may fall away and perish, are to be found many holy, self-denying, spiritually-minded persons,— persons at whose feet I would gladly sit in heaven, though I cannot approve of all their teaching upon earth.

This being the case, it becomes a matter of deep interest to find out, if we can, the reasons why the doctrine of perseverance is so often refused. How is it that a doctrine for which so much Scripture can be alleged, should be stoutly opposed? How is it that a doctrine which for the first hundred years of the Reformed Church of England it was hardly allowable to call in question, should now be so frequently rejected? What new views can have risen up in the last two centuries which make it necessary to discharge this good old servant of Christ? I am confident that such inquiries are of deep importance in the present day. There is far more in this question than appears at first sight. I am satisfied that I am not wasting time in endeavouring to throw a little light on the whole subject.

I desire to clear the way by conceding that many good persons refuse the doctrine of perseverance for no reason whatever excepting that *it is too strong for them.* There are vast numbers of true-hearted Christians just now who never seem able to bear anything strong. Their religious constitution appears so feeble, and their spiritual digestion

so weak, that they must always be "fed with milk and not
with meat." Talk to them strongly about grace, and they
put you down as an Antinomian!—Talk strongly about
holiness, and you are thought legal!—Speak strongly of
election, and you are considered a narrow-minded Calvinist!
—Speak strongly about responsibility and free agency, and
you are regarded as a low Arminian!—In short, *they can
bear nothing strong of any kind or in any direction!*
Of course they cannot receive the doctrine of perseverance.

I leave these people alone. I am sorry for them. There
are sadly too many of them in the Churches of Christ
just now. I can only wish them better spiritual health,
and less narrowness of views, and a quicker growth in
spiritual knowledge. The persons I have in my mind's
eye in this part of my paper are of a different class, and
to them I now address myself.

(1) I believe one reason why many do not hold perseverance is *their general ignorance of the whole system
of Christianity.* They have no clear idea of the nature,
place, and proportion of the various doctrines which compose the Gospel. Its several truths have no definite
position in their minds. Its general outline is not mapped
out in their understandings. They have a vague notion
that it is a right thing to belong to the Church of Christ,
and to believe all the articles of the Christian faith.
They have a floating misty idea that Christ has done
certain things for them, and that they ought to do certain
things for Him, and that if they do them it will be all
right at last. But beyond this they really know nothing!
Of the great systematic statements in the Epistles to the
Romans, Galatians, and Hebrews, they are profoundly
ignorant. As to a clear account of Justification, you might
as well ask them to square the circle, or to write a letter in
Sanscrit. It is a subject they have not even touched with
the tips of their fingers. This is a sore disease, and only
too common in England. Unhappily it is the disease of

thousands who pass muster as excellent Churchmen. It is absurd to expect such people to hold perseverance. When a man does not know what it is to be *justified*, he cannot of course understand what it is to persevere to the end.

(2) I believe another reason why many do not hold perseverance, is *their dislike to any system of religion which draws distinctions between man and man*. There are not a few who entirely disapprove of any Christian teaching which divides congregations into different classes, and speaks of one class of people as being in a better and more favourable state before God than another. Such people cry out, that "all teaching of this kind is *uncharitable*;" that "we ought to hope well of everybody, and suppose everybody will go to heaven."—They think it downright wrong to say that one man has faith and another has not, one is converted and another not, one a child of God and another a child of the world, one a saint and another a sinner. "What right have we to think anything about it?" they say. "We cannot possibly know. Those whom we call good, are very likely no better than others,—hypocrites, impostors and the like.—Those of whom we think badly are very probably quite as much in the way to heaven as the rest of mankind, and have got good hearts at the bottom."—As to any one feeling sure of heaven, or confident of his own salvation, they consider it quite abominable. "No man can be sure. We ought to hope well of all."—There are only too many people of this sort in the present day. Of course the doctrine of perseverance is perfectly intolerable to them. When a man refuses to allow that any one is elect, or has grace, or enjoys any special mark of God's favour more than his neighbours, it stands to reason that he will deny that any one can have the grace of perseverance.

(3) I believe another common reason why many do not hold perseverance, is *an incorrect view of the nature of saving faith*. They regard faith as nothing better than

a feeling or impression. As soon as they see a man somewhat impressed with the preaching of the Gospel, and
manifesting some pleasure in hearing about Christ, they
set him down at once as a believer. By and by the man's
impressions wear away, and his interest about Christ and
salvation ceases altogether. Where is the faith he seemed
to have? It is gone. How can his friends, who had
pronounced him a believer, account for it? They can only
account for it by saying, that "a man may fall away from
faith," and that "there is no such thing as perseverance."
And, in short, this becomes an established principle in
their religion. Now this is a mischievous error, and I am
afraid it is sadly common in many quarters. It may be
traced to ignorance of the true nature of religious affections.
People forget that there may be many religious emotions
in the human mind with which grace has nothing to do.
The "stony-ground" hearers received the word *with joy,*
but it had no root in them. (Matt. xiii. 20.) The history of
all revivals proves that there may often be a great quantity of
seemingly religious impression without any true work of the
Spirit. Saving faith is something far deeper and mightier
than a little sudden feeling. It is not an act of the feelings
only, but of the whole conscience, will, understanding, and
inward man. It is the result of clear knowledge. It springs
from a conscience not grazed merely, but thoroughly
stirred. It shows itself in a deliberate, willing, humble
dependence on Christ. Such faith is the gift of God, and
is never overthrown. Make faith a mere matter of feeling,
and it is of course impossible to maintain perseverance.

(4) I believe another reason why many do not hold
perseverance, is near akin to the one last mentioned. It
is *an incorrect view of the nature of conversion.* Not a
few are ready to pronounce any change for the better in
a man's character, a conversion. They forget that there
may be many blossoms on a tree in spring, and yet no
fruit in autumn, and that a new coat of paint does not

make an old door new. Some, if they see any one weeping under the influence of a sermon, will set it down at once as a case of conversion! Others, if a neighbour suddenly gives up drinking, or swearing, or card-playing, and becomes a communicant and a great professor, at once rush to the conclusion that he is converted! The natural consequence in numerous instances is disappointment. Their supposed case of conversion often turns out nothing more than a case of outward reform, in which the heart was never changed. Their converted neighbour sometimes returns to his old bad habits, as the sow that was washed to her wallowing in the mire. But then, unhappily, the pride of the natural heart, which never likes to allow itself mistaken, induces people to form a wrong conclusion about the case. Instead of telling us that the man never was converted at all, they say that "he was converted, but afterwards lost his grace and fell away." The true remedy for this is a right understanding of conversion. It is no such cheap, and easy, and common thing as many seem to fancy. It is a mighty work on the heart, which none but He who made the world can effect, and a work which will always abide and stand the fire. But once take a low and superficial view of conversion, and you will find it impossible to maintain final perseverance.

(5) I believe another most common reason why many do not hold perseverance, is *an incorrect view of the effect of baptism.* They lay it down, as a cardinal point in their theology, that all who are baptized are born again in baptism, and all receive the grace of the Holy Ghost. Without a single plain text in the Bible to support their opinions, and in the face of the 17th Article, which many of them as Churchmen have subscribed, they still tell us that all baptized persons are necessarily "regenerate." Of course such a view of baptism is utterly destructive of the doctrine that true grace can never be overthrown. It is plain as daylight, that multitudes of baptized persons

never show a spark of grace all their lives, and never give
the slightest evidence of having been born of God. They
live careless and worldly, and careless and worldly they
die, and to all appearance miserably perish. According
to the view to which I am now referring, "they have all
fallen away from grace! They all had it! They were all
made God's children! But they all lost their grace! They
have all become children of the devil!" I will not trust
myself to make a single remark on such doctrine. I leave
those who can to reconcile it with the Bible. All I say is,
that "if baptismal regeneration" be true, there is an end of
final perseverance.*

(6) I believe another reason why many do not hold
perseverance, is *an incorrect view of the nature of the
Church.* They make no distinction between the visible
Church which contains "evil as well as good," and the
invisible Church which is composed of none but God's elect
and true believers. They apply to the one the privileges,
and blessings, and promises which belong to the other.
They call the visible Church, with its crowds of ungodly
members, and baptized infidels, "the mystical body of
Christ, the Bride, the Lamb's wife, the Holy Catholic
Church," and the like! They will not see what Hooker
long ago pointed out, and his admirers would do well to
remember,—that all these glorious titles do not properly
belong to any visible Church, but to the mystical company
of God's elect. The consequence of all this confusion is
certain and plain. Upon this man-made system they are
obliged to allow that thousands of members of Christ's
body have no life, no grace, and no sympathy with their
Head, and end at last by being ruined for ever, and becom-

---

* To those who wish to see a full discussion of this subject, I venture
to recommend a paper of mine called "A Guide to Churchmen about
Baptism and Regeneration." The same paper will be found in my
volume, "Knots Untied."

ing lost members of Christ in hell! Of course at this rate they cannot maintain the doctrine of perseverance. Once embrace the unscriptural notion that all members of the visible Church are, by virtue of their churchmanship members of Christ, and the doctrine of this paper must be thrown aside. Oh, what a wise remark it is of Hooker's, " For want of diligently observing the difference between the Church of God mystical and visible, the oversights are neither few nor light that have been committed."

I commend the things I have just been saying to the sincere and prayerful attention of every reader of these pages. I have gone through them at the risk of seeming wearisome, from a deep conviction of their great importance. I am sure if any part of this paper deserves consideration, it is this.

I entreat you to observe how important it is for Christians to be *sound in the faith,* and to be armed with clear Scriptural knowledge of the whole system of the Gospel. I fear the increasing tendency to regard all doctrinal questions as matters of opinion, and to look on all " earnest-minded " men as right, whatever doctrines they maintain. I warn you that the sure result of giving way to this tendency will be a vague, low, misty theology,—a theology containing no positive hope, no positive motive, and no positive consolation,—a theology which will fail most, just when it is most wanted, in the day of affliction, the hour of sickness, and on the bed of death.

I know well that it is a thankless office to offer such warnings as these. I know well that those who give them must expect to be called bigoted, narrow-minded, and exclusive. But I cannot review the many errors which prevail on the subject of perseverance, without seeing more than ever the immense need there is for urging on all to be careful about doctrine. Oh, learn to know what you mean when you talk of believing the doctrines of

Christianity! Be able to give a reason of your hope. Be able to say what you think true, and what you think false in religion. And never, never forget that the only foundation of soundness in the faith, is a thorough textual knowledge of the Bible.

I entreat you, in the last place, to observe how *one error in religion leads on to another.* There is a close connection between false doctrines. It is almost impossible to take up one alone. Once let a man get wrong about the Church and the sacraments, and there is no saying how far he may go, and where he may land at last. It is a mistake at the fountain-head, and it influences the whole course of his religion. The mistake about baptism is a striking illustration of what I mean. It throws a colour over the whole of a man's divinity. It insensibly affects his views of justification, sanctification, election, and perseverance. It fills his mind with a tangled maze of confusion as to all the leading articles of the faith. He starts with a theory for which no single plain text of Scripture can be alleged, and before this theory he tramples down plain passages of the Bible by the score! They interfere forsooth, with his favourite theory, and therefore cannot mean what common sense tells us they do! We ought to be as jealous about a little false doctrine, as we would be about a little sin! Remember the words of St. Paul about false doctrine,—" a little heaven leaveneth the whole lump." (Gal. v. 9.)

IV. I now proceed, in the last place, to mention *some reasons why the doctrine of final perseverance is of great importance.*

When I speak of the importance of perseverance, I do not for a moment mean that it is necessary to salvation to receive it. I freely grant that thousands and tens of thousands have gone to heaven, who believed all their lives that saints might fall away. But all this does not prove the doctrine maintained in this paper to be a matter of indifference. He that does not believe it, and yet is saved, no doubt does well; but I am persuaded that he that believes it and is saved, does far better. I hold it to be one of the chief privileges of the children of God, and I consider that no privilege contained in the Gospel can be lost sight of without injury to the soul.

(1) Perseverance is a doctrine of great importance because of *the strong colour which it throws on the whole statement of the Gospel.*

The grand characteristic of the Gospel is, that it is glad tidings. It is a message of peace to a rebellious world. It is good news from a far country, alike unexpected and undeserved. It is the glad tidings that there is a hope for us, lost, ruined, and bankrupt as we are by nature,—a hope of pardon, a hope of reconciliation with God, a hope of glory. It is the glad tidings that the foundation of this hope is mighty, deep, and broad,— that it is built on the atoning death and gracious mediation of a Saviour. It is the glad tidings that this Saviour is an actual living person, Jesus the Son of God; able to save to the uttermost all who come to God by Him, and no less merciful, compassionate, and ready to save than able. It is the glad tidings that the way to pardon and peace by this Saviour is the simplest possible. It is not a thing high in heaven, that we cannot reach, or deep in the depths, that we cannot fathom. It is simply to believe, to trust, and to cast ourselves wholly on Jesus for salvation; and then salvation is all our own. It is the glad tidings that all who believe are at once justified and forgiven all things; their sins, however many, are washed away; their souls, however unworthy, are counted righteous before God. They believe on Jesus, and therefore they are saved. This is the good news. This is the glad tidings. This is the truth which is the grand peculiarity of the Gospel. Happy indeed is he that knows and believes it!

But think, for a moment, what a mighty difference it would make in the sound of the Gospel, if I went on to say, that after receiving all these mercies you might by-and-by lose them entirely. What would your feelings be if I told you that you were in daily peril of forfeiting all these privileges, and of having your pardon sealed in Christ's blood taken back again? What would you think if I told you that your safety was yet an uncertain thing, and that you might yet perish, and never reach heaven at all? Oh, "what a falling off" this would seem! Oh, how much of the grace and beauty of the glorious Gospel would disappear and fade away! Yet this is literally and exactly the conclusion to which a denial of perseverance *must* bring us.

Once admit that the saints of God may perish, and you seem to me to tear from the Gospel crown it brightest jewel. We are hanging on the edge of a precipice. We are kept in awful suspense until we are dead. To tell us that there are plenty of gracious promises to encourage us, if we will only persevere, is but mockery. It is like telling the sick man that if he will only get well he will be strong. The poor patient feels no confidence that he will get well, and the poor weak believer feels nothing in him like power to persevere. To-day he may be in Canaan, and to-morrow he may be in Egypt again, and in bondage. This week he may be in the narrow way; but, for anything he knows, next week he may be back in the broad road. This month he may be a justified, pardoned, and forgiven man; but next month his pardon may be all revoked, and he himself in a state of condemnation. This year he may have faith, and be a child of God; next year he may be a child of the devil, and have no part or lot in Christ. Where is the good news in all this? What becomes of the glad tidings? Verily such doctrine seems to me to cut up the joy of the Gospel by the roots. Yet this is the doctrine we *must* hold, if we reject the final perseverance of the saints.*

I bless God that I am able to see another kind of Gospel than this in the Word of God. To my eyes the Bible seems to teach that he who once begins the life of faith in Christ, shall without doubt be preserved from apostasy, and come to a glorious end. Once made alive by the grace of God, he shall live for ever. Once raised from the grave of sin and made a new man, he shall never go back to the grave, and become once more the old man "dead in trespasses and sins." He shall be kept by the power of God. He shall be more than conqueror through Him that loved him. The eternal God is his refuge: underneath him are the Everlasting Arms. The love in which he is interested is eternal. The righteousness in which he is clothed is eternal. The redemption which he enjoys is eternal. The *sense and comfort* of it he may lose by his own carelessness. But *the thing* itself, after once believing, is his for evermore.

Let any thinking man look at the two ways in which the weary and heavy-laden sinner may be addressed, and judge for himself which is most like the Gospel of the grace of God. On the one side stands the doctrine, which says, "Believe on the Lord Jesus Christ and thou shalt be saved. Once believing thou shalt never perish. Thy faith shall never be allowed entirely to fail. Thou shalt be sealed by the Holy Spirit unto the day of redemption."— On the other side stands the doctrine, which says, "Believe on the Lord Jesus Christ and thou shalt be saved. But after thou hast believed take care. Thy faith may fail. Thou mayest fall away. Thou mayest drive the Spirit from thee. Thou mayest at length perish everlastingly."—

---

* "They weaken Christians' comfort that make believers walk with Christ, like dancers upon a rope, every moment in fear of breaking their necks."—*Manton on Jude.* 1658.

Which doctrine of these two contains most good news? Which is most like glad tidings? Is it all the same which way the sinner is addressed? Is it a matter of indifference whether we tell him that believing he is saved, *unless he falls away,* or whether we tell him that believing he is saved *for ever?* I cannot think it. I regard the difference between the two doctrines as very great indeed. It is the difference between January and June. It is the difference between twilight and noonday.

I speak for myself. I cannot answer for the experience of others. To give me solid peace, I must know something about my *future prospects* as well as about my *present position.* It is pleasant to see my pardon to-day : but I cannot help thinking of to-morrow. Tell me that He who leads me to Christ, and gives me repentance and faith in Him, will never leave me nor forsake me, and I feel solid comfort. My feet are on a rock. My soul is in safe hands. I shall get safe home. Tell me, on the other hand, that after being led to Christ I am left to my own vigilance, and that it depends on my watching, and praying, and care, whether the Spirit leaves me or no, and my heart melts within me. I stand on a quicksand. I lean on a broken reed. I shall never get to heaven. It is vain to tell me of the promises; they are only mine if I walk worthy of them. It is vain to talk to me of Christ's mercy; I may lose all my interest in it by indolence and self-will. The absence of the doctrine of perseverance appears to me to give a different colour to the whole Gospel of Christ. You cannot wonder if I regard it as of great importance.

(2) But the doctrine of perseverance is also of importance, because of *the special influence it is calculated to have on all who halt between two opinions in religion.*

There are many persons of this description in the Church of Christ. There are hundreds to be found in every congregation to which the Gospel of Christ is preached, who know well what is right, and yet have not courage to act up to their knowledge. Their consciences are awakened. Their minds are comparatively enlightened. Their feelings are partially aroused to a sense of the value of their souls. They see the path they ought to take. They hope one day to be able to take it. But at present they sit still and *wait*. They will not take up the cross and confess Christ.

And what is it that keeps them back? In a vast proportion of cases they are afraid to begin, lest they should by-and-by fail and fall away. They see innumerable difficulties before them if they serve Christ. They are quite right. It is vain to deny that there are difficulties, both many and great. They stand shivering on the brink of the vast sea on which we would have them embark, and as they mark the rolling, tumbling waves, their hearts faint. They mark many a little boat on the waters of that sea, tossed to and fro, and struggling hard to make its way across, and looking as if it would be engulfed in the angry billows, and never get safe to harbour. "It is of no use," they feel: "it is of no use. We shall certainly fall away. We cannot serve Christ yet. The thing cannot be done."

Now, what is most likely to give courage to these halting souls? What is most likely to hearten them for the voyage? What is most likely to cheer their spirits, nerve their minds, and bring them to the point of boldly launching away?—I answer, without hesitation, The *doctrine of final perseverance.*

I would fain tell them that however great the difficulties of Christ's service, there is grace and strength in store to carry them triumphantly through all. I would tell them that these poor, praying, broken-spirited voyagers whom they watch, and expect to see cast away, are all as safe as if they were already in harbour. They have each a pilot on board, who will carry them safe through every storm. They are each joined to the everlasting God by a tie that can never be broken, and shall all appear at length safe at the right hand of their Lord. Yes: and I would fain tell them that they too shall all make a glorious end if they will only begin. I would have them know that, if they will only commit themselves to Christ, they shall never be cast away. They shall not be plucked away by Satan. They shall never be left to sink and come to shame. Trials they may have, but none that the Spirit will not give them power to endure. Temptations they may have, but none that the Spirit shall not enable them to resist. Only let them begin, and they shall be conquerors. But the great matter is to begin.

I believe firmly that one reason why so many wavering Christians hang back from making a decided profession, is the want of encouragement which the doctrine of perseverance is intended to afford.

(3) The doctrine of perseverance is of importance because of *the special influence it is calculated to have on the minds of true believers.*

The number of true believers is at all times very small. They are a little flock. But even out of that flock there are few who can be called strong in faith, few who know much of uninterrupted joy and peace in believing, few who are not often cast down by doubts, anxieties, and fears.

It is useless to deny that the way to heaven is narrow. There are many things to try the faith of believers. They have trials the world cannot understand. They have *within* a heart weak, deceitful, and not to be trusted, —cold when they would fain be warm,—backward when they would fain be forward,—more ready to sleep than to watch. They have *without* a world that does not love Christ's truth and Christ's people,—a world full of slander, ridicule, and persecution,—a world with which their own dearest relations often join. They have ever *near them* a busy devil, an enemy who has been reading men's hearts for 6,000 years, and knows exactly how to suit and time his temptations,—an enemy who never ceases to lay snares in their way,—who never slumbers and never sleeps. They have the cares of life to attend to, like other people, —the cares of children,—the cares of business,—the cares of servants,—the cares of money,—the cares of earthly plans and arrangements,—the cares of a poor weak body, each daily thrusting itself upon their souls. Who can wonder that believers are sometimes cast down? Who ought not rather to marvel that any believers are saved? Truly I often think that the salvation of each saved person is a greater miracle than the passage of Israel through the Red Sea.*

But what is the best antidote against the believer's fears and anxieties? What is most likely to cheer him as he looks forward to the untried future and remembers the weary past? I answer without hesitation, the *doctrine of the final perseverance of God's elect.* Let him know that God having begun a good work in him will never allow it to be overthrown. Let him know that the footsteps of Christ's little flock are all in one direction. They have erred. They have been vexed. They have been tempted. But not one of them has been lost. Let him know that those whom Jesus loves, He loves unto the end. Let him know that He will not suffer the weakest lamb in His flock to perish in the wilderness, or the tenderest flower in His garden to wither and die. Let him know that Daniel in the den of lions, the three children in the fiery furnace, Paul in the shipwreck, Noah in the Ark, were none of them more cared for and more secure than each believer in Christ is at the present day. Let him know that he is fenced, walled in, protected, guarded by the Almighty power of Father, Son, and Holy Ghost, and cannot perish. Let him know that it is not in the power of things present or things to come,—of men or of devils,

---

* "There are as many miracles wrought as a saint is preserved minutes."—*Jenkyn on Jude.* 1680.

—of cares within or troubles without, to separate one single child of God from the love that is in Christ Jesus.

This is strong consolation ! These are the things which God has laid up in the Gospel, for the establishment and confirmation of His people. Well would it be for His people if these things were more brought forward than they are in the Church of Christ. Verily I believe that one reason of the saints' weakness is their ignorance of the truths which God has revealed in order to make them strong.

I leave the subject of the importance of perseverance here. I trust I have said enough to show my readers that I have not called their attention to it in this paper without good cause. I feel strongly that the hardness of man's heart is such that nothing should be omitted in religious teaching which is likely to do it good. I dare not omit a single grain of truth, however strong, and liable to abuse, it may seem to be. Nothing appears to me of small import- ance which adds to the beauty of the Gospel, or gives encouragement to the halting, or confirms and builds up God's people. I desire to teach that the Gospel not only offers present pardon and peace, but eternal safety and certain continuance to the end. This I believe to be the mind of the Spirit. And what the Spirit reveals I desire to proclaim.

And now I have brought before my readers, to the best of my ability, the whole subject of perseverance. If I have failed to convince you, I am sorry, but I am satisfied the defect is not in the doctrine I defend, but in my manner of stating it. It only remains to conclude this paper by a few words of practical application.

(1) For one thing, let me entreat you to consider well, *whether you have any part at all in the salvation of Christ Jesus.*

It matters nothing what you believe about perseverance, if after all you have no faith in Christ. It matters little whether you hold the doctrine or not, so long as you have no saving faith, and your sins are not forgiven, and your heart not renewed by the Holy Ghost. The clearest head-knowledge will save no man. The most correct and orthodox views will not prevent a man perishing by the side of the most ignorant heathen, if he is not born again. Oh, search and see what is the state of your own soul!

You cannot live for ever. You must one day die. You cannot avoid the judgment after death. You must stand before the bar of Christ. The summons of the Archangel cannot be disobeyed. The last great assembly must be attended. The state of your own soul must one day undergo a thorough investigation. It will be found out one day what you are in God's sight. Your spiritual con-dition will at length be brought to light before the whole world. Oh, find out what it is now! While you have time, while you have health, find out the state of your soul.

Your danger, if you are not converted, is far greater than I can describe. Just in proportion to the thorough safety of the believer is the deadly peril of the unbeliever. There is but a step between the unbeliever and the worm that never dies, and the fire that is not quenched. He is literally hanging over the brink of the bottomless pit. Sudden death to the saint is sudden glory; but sudden death to the unconverted sinner, is sudden hell. Oh, search and see what is the state of your soul!

Remember that you may find out whether you have an interest in the invitations of the Gospel. It is a thing which may be known. It is nonsense to pretend that no man can tell. I never will believe that an honest man, with a Bible in his hand, will fail to discover his own spiritual condition by diligent self-examination. Oh, be an honest man! Search the Scriptures. Look within. Rest not till you find out the state of your soul. To live on and leave the soul's state uncertain, is not to play the part of a wise man but of a fool.

(2) In the next place, *if you know nothing of the privileges of the Gospel, I entreat you this day to repent and be converted, to hear Christ's voice, and follow Him.*

I know no reason, human or divine, why you should not accept this invitation to-day and be saved, if you are really willing. It is not the quantity of your sins that need prevent you. All manner of sin may be forgiven. The blood of Jesus cleanseth away all sin.—It is not the hardness of your heart that need prevent you. A new heart God will give you, and a new spirit will He put in you.— It is not the decrees of God that need prevent you. He willeth not the death of sinners. He is not willing that any should perish, but that all should come to repentance. —It is not any want of willingness in Christ:—He has long cried to the sons of men, " Whosoever will, let him take the water of life freely." "Him that cometh unto Me I will in no wise cast out." Oh, why should not you be saved ? (Rev. xxii. 17 ; John vi. 37.)

A day must come, if you are ever to be God's child, when you will cease to trifle with your soul's interests. An hour must come when at last you will bend your knee in real earnestness, and pour out your heart before God in real prayer. A time must come when the burden of your sins will at last feel intolerable, and when you will feel you must have rest in Christ or perish. All this must come to pass, if you are ever to become a child of God and be saved. And why not to-day? Why not this very night? Why not without delay seek Christ and live ? Answer me, if you can !

(3) In the next place, *let me entreat every reader who holds final perseverance, so to use this precious doctrine as not to abuse it.*

There is an awful readiness in all men to abuse God's mercies. Even the children of God are not free from the sad infection. There is a busy devil near the best of saints, who would fain persuade them to make their privileges a plea for careless living, and to turn their soul's meat into poison. I cannot look round the Church of Christ, and see the end to which many high professors come, without feeling that there is need for a caution. "Let him that thinketh he standeth take heed lest he fall." (1 Cor. x. 12.)

Would we know what it is to abuse the doctrine of perseverance ? It is abused when believers make their safety an excuse for inconsistencies in practice. It is abused when they make their security from final ruin an apology for a low standard of sanctification, and a distant walk with God. Against both these abuses I entreat believers to be on their guard.

Would we know what it is to use the doctrine of perseverance aright ? Let us watch jealously over the daily workings of our own hearts. Let us mortify and nip in the bud the least inclination to spiritual indolence. Let us settle it down in our minds, as a ruling principle of our lives, that the mercies of God are only turned to a good account when they have a *sanctifying effect on our hearts*. Let us root it firmly in our inward man, that the love of Christ is never so really valued as when it constrains us to increased spiritual-mindedness. Let us set before our minds, that the more safe we feel the more holy we ought to be. The more we realize that God has done much for us, the more we ought to do for God. The greater our debt, the greater should be our gratitude. The more we see the riches of grace, the more rich should we be in good works.

Oh, for a heart like that of the Apostle Paul! To realize as he did, our perfect safety in Christ,—to labour as he did for God's glory, as if we could never do too much,—this is the mark,—this is the standard at which we ought to aim.

Let us so use the doctrine of perseverance that our good may never be evil spoken of. Let us so adorn the doctrine by our lives that we may make it beautiful to others, and constrain men to say, "It is a good and holy thing to be persuaded that saints shall never perish."

(4) In the last place, *I entreat all believers who have hitherto been afraid of falling away, to lay firm hold on the doctrine of perseverance, and to realize their own safety in Christ.*

I want you to know the length and breadth of your portion in Christ. I want you to understand the full amount of the treasure to which faith in Jesus entitles you. You have found out that you are a great sinner. Thank God for that.—You have fled to Christ for pardon and peace with God. Thank God for that.—You have committed yourself to Jesus for time and eternity: you have no hope but in Christ's blood, Christ's righteousness Christ's mediation, Christ's daily all-persevering intercession. Thank God for that.—Your heart's desire and prayer is to be holy in all manner of conversation. Thank God for that.—But oh, lay hold upon the glorious truth,— that believing on Jesus you shall never perish, you shall never be cast away, you shall never fall away! It is written for you as well as for the apostles, "My sheep shall never perish."

Yes! Jesus has spoken it, and Jesus meant it to be believed. Jesus has spoken it, who never broke His promises. Jesus has spoken it, who cannot lie. Jesus has spoken it, who has all power in heaven and earth to keep His word. Jesus has spoken it for the least and lowest believers,—"My sheep shall never perish."

Wouldest thou have *perfect peace in life?* Then lay hold on this doctrine of perseverance. Thy trials may be many and great. Thy cross may be very heavy. But the business of thy soul is all conducted according to an "everlasting covenant, ordered in all things and sure." (2 Sam. xxiii. 5.) All things are working together for thy good. Thy sorrows are only purifying thy soul for glory

Thy bereavements are only fashioning thee as a polished stone for the temple above, made without hands. From whatever quarter the storms blow, they only drive thee nearer to heaven. Whatever weather thou mayest go through it is only ripening thee for the garner of God. Thy best things are quite safe. Come what will, thou shalt "never perish."

Wouldest thou have *strong consolation in sickness?* Then lay hold on this doctrine of perseverance. Think, as thou feelest the pins of this earthly tabernacle loosening one by one, "nothing can break my union with Christ." Thy body may become useless; thy members may refuse to perform their office; thou mayest feel like an old useless log,—a weariness to others, and a burden to thyself. But thy soul is safe. Jesus is never tired of caring for thy soul. Thou shalt "never perish."

Wouldest thou have *full assurance of hope in death?* Then lay hold on this doctrine of perseverance. Doctors may have given over their labours; friends may be unable to minister to thy wants; sight may depart; hearing may depart; memory may be almost gone: but the loving-kindness of God shall not depart. Once in Christ thou shalt never be forsaken. Jesus shall stand by thee. Satan shall not harm thee. Death shall not separate thee from the everlasting love of God in Christ. Thou shalt "never perish." *

---

* The death-bed of Bruce, the famous Scotch divine, is a striking illustration of this part of my subject. Old Fleming describes it in the following words. "His sight failed him, whereupon he called for his Bible; but finding his sight gone he said, 'Cast up to me the eighth chapter of Romans and set my finger on these words,—I am persuaded that neither death, nor life, etc., shall be able to separate me from the love of God which is in Christ Jesus our Lord. Now,' said he, 'is my finger upon them?' when they told him it was, he said, 'Now God be with you, my children: I have breakfasted with you, and shall sup with my Lord Jesus Christ this night,' and so gave up the Ghost."—*Fleming's Fulfilment of Prophecy*, 1680.

NOTE REFERRED TO AT PAGE 487.

There are few subjects about which English people are so ignorant as they are about the real doctrines of the Church of England. Many persons know nothing of the theological opinions of the English Reformers, and of all the leading English Divines for nearly a century after the Protestant Reformation. They call opinions old which in reality are new, and they call opinions new which in reality are old.

It would be waste of time to inquire into the causes of this ignorance. Certain it is that it exists. Few people seem to be aware that those doctrines which now are commonly called *evangelical*, were the universally received divinity of English Churchmen throughout the reigns of Queen Elizabeth and James I. They are not, as many ignorantly suppose, new-fangled views of modern invention. They are simply the old paths in which the Reformers and their immediate successors walked. Tractarianism, High Churchism, and Broad Churchism are new systems. Evangelical teaching is neither more nor less than the old school.

The proof of this assertion is to be found in the Church history of the reigns of Elizabeth and James I., and in the writings of the divines of that period. Far be it from me to defend all the sayings and doings of theologians of that date. The student will find in their writings abundant traces of intolerance, illiberality, and bigotry, which I would be the last to defend. But that the vast majority of all Churchmen in that day held the doctrines which are now called Calvinistic and Evangelical, is to my mind as clear as noon-day : and upon no point does the evidence appear to me so clear as upon the doctrine of perseverance.

(1) Is it not a historical fact, that in Queen Elizabeth's reign, in the year 1595, the University of Cambridge compelled Mr. Barret, of Caius College, to read a public recantation and apology in St. Mary's Church, for having denied the doctrines of final perseverance and election ?—*The Church of England's old Antithesis to new Arminianism, by William Prynne, page* 56.

(2) Is it not a historical fact, that the Articles drawn up by the Vice-Chancellor and heads of the University of Cambridge, against the above-mentioned Barret, conclude with the following words ? "This doctrine, being not about inferior points of matters indifferent, but of the substantial ground, and chief comfort and anchor ground of our salvation, hath been to our knowledge continually and generally received, taught, and defended in this University, in lectures, disputations, and sermons, and in other places in sermons, since the beginning of her Majesty's reign, and is so still holden ; and we take it agreeable to the doctrine of the Church of England."—*Edwards' Veritas Redux, page* 534.

(3) Is it not a historical fact, that in the same Queen Elizabeth's reign, in the same year, 1595, the Lambeth Articles were drawn up and approved by Archbishop Whitgift and Bishop Bancroft (afterwards Archbishop of Canterbury) ; and that they contain the following pro-

position: "A true living and justifying faith, and the Spirit of God who justifies, is not extinguished, falleth not away, vanisheth not in the elect, either finally or totally." These articles were not added to our confession of faith ; but Fuller's words nevertheless are perfectly true : "The testimony of these learned divines is an infallible evidence what were the general and received doctrines of England in that age."— *Fuller's Church History. Tegg's edition. Third volume, page* 150.

(4) Is it not a historical fact, that in the year 1604, in James the First's reign, this doctrine of perseverance was considered at the Hampton Court Conference. The Puritan party wished the Lambeth Articles to be added to the Thirty-nine Articles. Their request was not granted : but on what grounds ? *Not because the doctrine of perseverance was objected to, but because King James thought it better "not to stuff the book of Articles with all conclusions theological."* While even Overall, Dean of St. Paul's, whose soundness on this point was most suspected, used these remarkable words : " Those who are justified according to the purpose of God's election, though they might fall into grievous sin, and thereby into the present estate of damnation, yet never totally nor finally from justification, but are in time renewed by God's Spirit unto lively faith and repentance."—*Fuller's Church History, third volume, page* 181.

(5) Is it not a historical fact, that the first exposition of the Thirty-nine Articles, published after the Reformation, contains a full and distinct assertion of the doctrine of perseverance, in the part which treats of the Seventeenth Article ? I allude to the work of Thomas Rogers, Chaplain to Archbishop Bancroft, to whom the book was dedicated, 1607.—*Rogers on the Thirty-nine Articles. Parker Society Edition.*

(6) Is it not a historical fact, that in the year 1612, King James the First published a declaration written by himself, against one Vorstius, an Arminian divine, in which he calls the doctrine that the saints may fall away, "A wicked doctrine, a blasphemous heresy, directly contrary to the doctrine of the Church of England."—*Prynne. Church of England Antithesis, etc., page* 206.

(7) Is it not a historical fact, that the same King James the First, in the same year 1612, wrote a letter to the States of Holland, in consequence of a Dutch divine, named Bertius, having written a book on the Apostacy of the Saints, and sent it to the Archbishop of Canterbury. In this letter, the King speaks of Bertius as "a pestilent heretic," and calls his doctrine "an abominable heresy," and in one place says, "he is not ashamed to lie so grossly as to avow that the heresies contained in the said book are agreeable with the religion and profession of the Church of England."—*Prynne. Church of England's Antithesis to Arminianism, page* 206.

(8) Is it not a historical fact, that the same King James the First, in the year 1616, visited with severe displeasure a clergyman named Sympson, a Fellow of Trinity College, Cambridge, for preaching before

him at Royston, that true believers may totally fall away ?—*Fuller's History of Cambridge, page* 160.

(9) Is it not a historical fact, that in the Synod of Dort, in the year 1619, the doctrine of final perseverance was strongly asserted? Now several English Divines were formally deputed to attend this Synod and take part in its proceedings, and amongst others, Bishop Davenant, and Bishop Carleton. And is it not notorious that however much they differed from the conclusions of the Synod in matters of discipline, they "approved all the points of doctrine ?"—*Fuller's Church History, vol.* 3, *page* 279.

(10) Last, but not least, is it not a historical fact, that all the leading Archbishops and Bishops in the reigns of Elizabeth and James the First, were thorough Calvinists in matters of doctrine ? And is it not a notorious fact that the final perseverance of the saints is one of the leading principles of the system that is called Calvinistic ? Heylin himself is obliged to confess this. He says, "It was safer for any man in those times to have been looked upon as a heathen or publican than an anti-Calvinist."—*Heylin's Life of Laud, page* 52.

I lay these ten facts before my readers and ask their serious attention to them. I am unable to understand how any one can avoid the conclusion which may be drawn from them. To me it appears an established point in history, that the doctrine of the final perseverance of the saints is the old doctrine of the Church of England, and the denial of this doctrine is new.

I could easily add long quotations to strengthen the evidence which I have brought forward. I could turn to marginal notes of the "Bishop's Bible," published under the special superintendence and approval of Archbishop Parker. I could quote passage upon passage from the writings of Archbishops Cranmer, Grindal, Sandys, Whitgift, Abbot, Usher, and Leighton,—of Bishops Ridley, Latimer, Jewell, Pilkington, Babington, Hall, Davenant, Carleton, Prideaux, and Reynolds. In short, the difficulty is to find theological writers in the reigns of Elizabeth and James the First who ever thought of disputing final perseverance. William Prynne gives the names of no less than 130 writers who held that the saints could never perish, and gives the reference to their works. But at the time he wrote (1629) he could only find four writers who had denied the perseverance of the saints, and taught the possibility of their apostacy. I could supply many quotations from the writers he names. But I spare the reader. He has probably heard enough.

I have made this note longer than I intended, but the importance of the facts which it contains must be my apology. The whole subject in the present day is one of the deepest moment.

The evangelical members of the Church of England are constantly taunted by their adversaries with holding new views. They are told that their opinions are not "Church opinions," and that they ought to leave the Church of England and become dissenters without delay. I entreat all readers of these pages never to be moved by such taunts and insinuations. I tell them that those who make them are only exposing their own thorough ignorance of the first principles of their own communion. I tell them not to be ashamed of their own views, for they have no cause. I tell them that the evangelical members of the Church of England are the true representatives of the views of the Reformers and their immediate successors, and that those who oppose them know not what they are saying.

Last, but not least, I would counsel all clergymen who are persecuted for holding evangelical opinions, to arm themselves with a thorough knowledge of old Church of England divinity, and to take comfort in the thought that they have truth on their side. They, at all events, are explaining the Thirty-nine Articles according to the intention of those who composed them. Their opponents are either neglecting the Articles, or attaching to them a new meaning.

How far it is reasonable and fair to persecute godly men for preferring the views of the Reformers to those of Laud, I leave it to others to decide. But those who are persecuted may take comfort in the reflection that if they err, they err in good company. And if they ever suffer loss of character and position for holding final perseverance and denying the inseparable connection of baptism and regeneration, they may boldly tell the world that they suffer because they agree with Latimer, and Hooper, and Jewell, and Whitgift, and Carleton, and Davenant, and Usher, and Leighton, and Hooker, and Hall. He that suffers in company with these good men has no cause to be ashamed !

If I were in a position to offer counsel to my evangelical brethren at this crisis, I would earnestly advise them *to hold fast the doctrine of final perseverance, and never let it go*. There is no doctrine which so entirely overturns the modern view of baptismal regeneration. There is no doctrine in consequence which many dislike so much, and labour so hard to overthrow. It is a barrier in their path. It is a thorn in their side. It is an argument which they cannot answer. The Seventeenth Article of the Church of England is one of the keys of our position. He that gives up the doctrine of perseverance may rest assured that he has sold the pass to his enemy. Once allow that saving grace may be totally lost, and in the day of controversy you will never hold your ground.

Also from Benediction Books ...
Wandering Between Two Worlds: Essays on Faith and Art
Anita Mathias
Benediction Books, 2007
152 pages
ISBN: 0955373700

In these wide-ranging lyrical essays, Anita Mathias writes, in lush, lovely prose, of her naughty Catholic childhood in Jamshedpur, India; her large, eccentric family in Mangalore, a sea-coast town converted by the Portuguese in the sixteenth century; her rebellion and atheism as a teenager in her Himalayan boarding school, run by German missionary nuns, St. Mary's Convent, Nainital; and her abrupt religious conversion after which she entered Mother Teresa's convent in Calcutta as a novice. Later rich, elegant essays explore the dualities of her life as a writer, mother, and Christian in the United States-- Domesticity and Art, Writing and Prayer, and the experience of being "an alien and stranger" as an immigrant in America, sensing the need for roots.

About the Author

Anita Mathias is the author of *Wandering Between Two Worlds: Essays on Faith and Art.* She has a B.A. and M.A. in English from Somerville College, Oxford University, and an M.A. in Creative Writing from the Ohio State University, USA. Anita won a National Endowment of the Arts fellowship in Creative Nonfiction in 1997. She lives in Oxford, England with her husband, Roy, and her daughters, Zoe and Irene.

Visit Anita at http://www.anitamathias.com.

The Church That Had Too Much
Anita Mathias
Benediction Books, 2010
ISBN: 9781849026567

The Church That Had Too Much was very well-intentioned. She wanted to love God, she wanted to love people, but she was both hampered by her muchness and the abundance of her possessions, and beset by ambition, power struggles and snobbery. Read about the surprising way The Church That Had Too Much began to resolve her problems in this deceptively simple and enchanting fable.

The Meek Shall Inherit the Earth
Anita Mathias
Benediction Books, 2013
ISBN: 9781781393956

"Blessed are the meek, for they shall inherit the earth," Jesus says in his most puzzling Beatitude. Puzzling, because, if we are honest, it does not feel true to our experience. So do the meek inherit the earth? Is this true? Or isn't it? In The Meek Shall Inherit the Earth, an extended meditation on the power of gentleness, Anita Mathias grapples with this mystifying Beatitude.

Francesco, Artist of Florence: The Man Who Gave Too Much
Anita Mathias
Benediction Books, 2014
52 pages (full colour)

In this lavishly illustrated book by Anita Mathias, Francesco, artist of Florence, creates magic in pietre dure, inlaying precious stones in marble in life-like "paintings." While he works, placing lapis lazuli birds on clocks, and jade dragonflies on vases, he is purely happy. However, he must sell his art to support his family. Francesco, who is incorrigibly soft-hearted, cannot stand up to his haggling customers. He ends up almost giving away an exquisite jewellery box to Signora Farnese's bambina, who stands, captivated, gazing at a jade parrot nibbling a cherry. Signora Stallardi uses her daughter's wedding to cajole him into discounting his rainbowed marriage chest. His old friend Girolamo bullies him into letting him have the opulent table he hoped to sell to the Medici almost at cost. Carrara is raising the price of marble; the price of gems keeps rising. His wife is in despair. Francesco fears ruin.

* * *

Sitting in the church of Santa Maria Novella at Mass, very worried, Francesco hears the words of Christ. The lilies of the field and the birds of the air do not worry, yet their Heavenly Father looks after them. As He will look after us. He resolves not to worry. And as he repeats the prayer the Saviour taught us, Francesco resolves to forgive the friends and neighbours who repeatedly put their own interests above his. But can he forgive himself for his own weakness, as he waits for the eternal city of gold whose walls are made of jasper, whose gates are made of pearls, and whose foundations are sapphire, emerald, ruby and amethyst? There time and money shall be no more, the lion shall live with the lamb, and we shall dwell trustfully together. Francesco leaves Santa Maria Novella, resolving to trust the One who told him to live like the lilies and the birds, deciding to forgive those who haggled him into bad bargains--while making a little resolution for the future.